# How is your MPA doing?

**A Guidebook of**

**Natural and Social Indicators for Evaluating**

**Marine Protected Area Management Effectiveness**

# How is your MPA doing?

## A Guidebook of Natural and Social Indicators for Evaluating Marine Protected Area Management Effectiveness

Robert S. Pomeroy

John E. Parks

Lani M. Watson

IUCN – The World Conservation Union
2004

This publication has been made possible in part by funding from The David and Lucile Packard Foundation, NOAA National Ocean Service, and WWF.

Published by: IUCN, Gland, Switzerland and Cambridge, UK.

Citation: Pomeroy, R.S., Parks, J.E. and Watson, L.M. (2004). *How is your MPA doing? A Guidebook of Natural and Social Indicators for Evaluating Marine Protected Area Management Effectiveness*. IUCN, Gland, Switzerland and Cambridge, UK. xvi + 216 pp.

ISBN: 2-8317-0735-8

Designed by: Tony Eckersley

Typeset by: The Botanical Information Co. Ltd, UK

Cover photos: Back (clockwise from top): Toni Parras, David Sheppard/IUCN, John Parks; Front (from top): NOAA Photo Library, © WWF-Canon/Mark Edwards, Toni Parras

Produced by: IUCN Publications Services Unit

Printed by: Thanet Press Ltd, Margate, UK

Available from: IUCN Publications Services Unit
219c Huntingdon Road, Cambridge CB3 0DL
United Kingdom
Tel: +44 1223 277894, Fax: +44 1223 277175
E-mail: info@books.iucn.org
www.iucn.org/bookstore

A catalogue of IUCN publications is also available

*The text of this book is printed on Fineblade Smooth 115gsm made from low chlorine pulp.*

# Contents

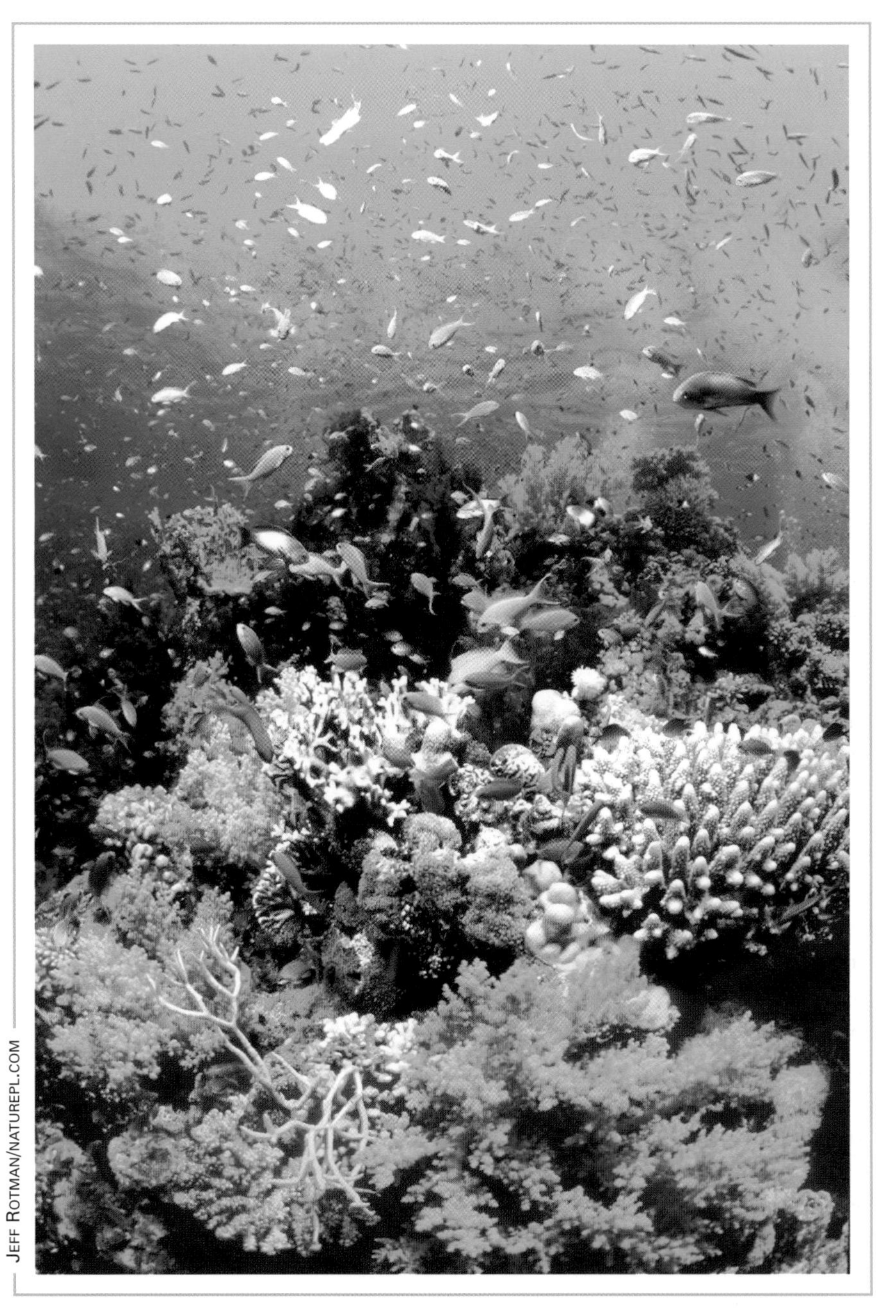

JEFF ROTMAN/NATUREPL.COM

***Most of our planet is a marine system. Human impacts on the seas need to be effectively managed, a process in which Marine Protected Areas (MPAs) are vital.***

# Foreword

Management of the world's ocean resources and habitats is entering a new phase. A key outcome of the 2002 World Summit on Sustainable Development was the commitment to establish "... marine protected areas consistent with international law and based on scientific information, including representative networks, by 2012". This outcome translated a long-standing goal of the IUCN World Commission on Protected Areas under its programme for the marine biome (WCPA Marine) into a political imperative. The challenge of establishing a representative system of marine protected areas (MPAs) is surpassed by the challenge that they are managed effectively over time. There is a long way to go in achieving this goal, with less than 1% of the world's ocean declared under marine protected areas and fewer than 10% of marine protected areas that exist today achieving their management goals and objectives (Kelleher *et al.*, 1995). Ultimately, it is only by assuring their effective management that MPAs can contribute to the ambitious overarching goals of biodiversity conservation, sustainable use of marine resources, and an improved quality of life for coastal communities.

Marine protected areas are established for a wide range of purposes, including protecting marine species and habitats, conserving marine biodiversity, restoring fisheries stocks, managing tourism activities, and minimizing conflicts among diverse resource users. To achieve these goals, specific and measurable objectives must be defined in terms of what outputs and outcomes are being sought. This in turn requires that well-defined management plans be developed, measures of MPA success be identified, impacts of management actions be monitored and evaluated, and that the results of these activities be fed back into the planning process to revise objectives, plans and outcomes. In other words, MPAs need to be adaptively managed. ***It is only by deliberately integrating monitoring and evaluation into the overall MPA management process that such benefits of adaptive management can be fully realized.***

Too often in the past, protected area management has been assessed on the basis of how much money has been spent, how many permits issued, how many enforcement actions have been taken, or how many laws and regulations have been adopted. These 'input' measures may or may not necessarily be indicative of management progress.

Evaluation consists of assessing whether the actions taken have produced the desired results (outcomes and outputs), however they are defined. It is something that many managers already do where the link between actions and consequences can be simply observed.

But the link between action and outcome is often not so obvious. Faced with the daily demands of their jobs, many managers are not able to systematically monitor and review the results of their efforts. In the absence of such reviews, however, money and other resources can be wasted on programmes that do not achieve their objectives. In a climate of ever-greater emphasis on performance and value for money, managers must expect to come under greater pressure to introduce systems for monitoring and evaluation that will:

- Promote and enable an adaptive approach to management where managers learn from their own and others' successes and failures; and

- Keep track of the consequent changes in management objectives and practices so that people can understand how and why management is being undertaken in this way.

Governments, funding agencies and stakeholders who are to benefit from MPAs are increasingly requiring information on management effectiveness that will allow them to assess whether results are commensurate with the effort and resources being expended and are in line with policy and management goals.

Managers are likely to experience greater support and trust when they provide information about what they are doing and what they are achieving. Management is therefore seen to be open and accountable.

Managers can also use the results of management effectiveness evaluations to develop convincing requests for additional resources. Such proposals are more likely to win support when they can be justified on the basis of evaluation results.

In practice, evaluation results are usually used in more than one way. Information used by managers to improve their own performance (adaptive management) can also be used for reporting (accountability), or lessons learned by others can be used to improve future planning.

Regardless of what drives the process, evaluation should be seen primarily as a tool to assist managers in their work, not as a system for punishing managers for inadequate performance.

This initiative to improve the evaluation of management performance in marine protected areas has evolved from the work of a larger IUCN/WCPA collaboration on the management effectiveness of protected areas in all biomes. This guidebook is the result of a close and productive partnership between the programme for the marine biome of the IUCN World Commission on Protected Areas, the World Wide Fund for Nature, and the US National Oceanic and Atmospheric Administration.

*Charles "Bud" N. Ehler*
*Vice-Chair*
*WCPA Marine, and Director*
*NOAA-NOS International*
*Program Office*

*Simon Cripps*
*Director*
*WWF Endangered*
*Seas Program*

*MPA Management Effectiveness Initiative Leads*

# Preface

JOHN PARKS

Greetings. This publication represents over three years of work by dozens of people around the world, many of whom – like you – are MPA managers or practitioners of marine conservation and protection. It is our hope that you will find this guidebook useful in your challenging position as a manager or conservation practitioner.

## *How the guidebook was developed*

This guidebook was developed to help MPA managers and practitioners better achieve the goals and objectives for which their MPA was created. The IUCN World Commission on Protected Areas under its programme for the marine biome (WCPA Marine) and the World Wide Fund for Nature (WWF) both work throughout the world to support MPAs, their managers and constituents. In keeping with their missions, the two organizations jointly formed the *MPA Management Effectiveness Initiative* (MPA MEI) in 2000 with four main objectives: 1. develop a set of *marine-specific* natural and social indicators to evaluate MPA management effectiveness with expert input from around the world; 2. develop a process for conducting an evaluation in the form of an easy-to-use guidebook, incorporating insight and experience from international peer review; 3. field-test and ground-truth a draft of the guidebook process and indicator methods at MPA sites operating in diverse conditions around the world; and 4. encourage and support managers and practitioners to use the revised evaluation methodology and guidebook to adaptively manage their MPAs and increase effectiveness.

To accomplish these objectives a number of activities were conducted between 2001 and 2003 to construct a product that was well grounded in both the marine and social sciences and includes real-world expertise and feedback by those who work closest with MPAs as part of their careers, research or livelihood. These activities included:

- A survey of MPA goals and objectives from around the world, falling into three primary categories: biophysical, socio-economic and governance (April–July 2001).
- Research on over 130 indicators used to measure various aspects of the marine environment and coastal communities, linking indicators to relevant MPA goals and objectives, and peer review of draft sets of goals, objectives and indicators (August–September 2001).
- Holding a workshop of 35 experts from 17 different countries, who reviewed, evaluated and prioritized each of the potential indicators, resulting in a revised set of 52 indicators and information on each indicator (Venezuela, October 2001).
- Refining and making 44 indicators operational by describing definitions, methods of measurement, and guidance on analysis of the results, followed by two rounds of peer review (November 2001–June 2002).
- Identifying and selecting volunteer MPA pilot sites to field-test the guidebook (February–May 2002).
- Preparation of the first draft of the book, and distribution to external experts and pilot sites for peer review (July–August 2002).

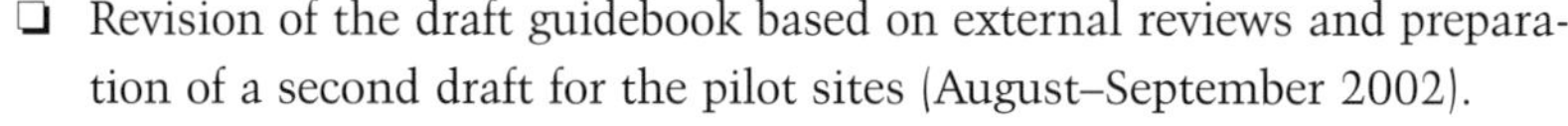

- Revision of the draft guidebook based on external reviews and preparation of a second draft for the pilot sites (August–September 2002).
- Holding of a training workshop with representatives from 20 MPA pilot projects to learn how to use the guidebook and how to test the indicators in the field (Hawaii, September 2002).
- Field-testing of the guidebook at pilot sites (November 2002–April 2003).
- Revising the guidebook into a third draft and distributing this for final peer review (November 2002–March 2003).
- Completion of final revisions to the book based on reports from the MPA pilot projects (April–July 2003).
- Sessions held at the V$^{th}$ World Parks Congress in Durban, South Africa to introduce the guidebook and case studies from field-testing (September 2003).

TONY ECKERSLEY

As you can see with this summary timeline, one of the most important activities in the development of this guidebook was to ground-truth a draft version by field-testing the evaluation process and indicators at different MPA pilot sites around the world (see the Appendix to learn more about these sites). This effort helped to ensure that the draft guidebook was realistic and applicable under real-world MPA conditions, or 'in-the-water' so to speak. Testing and revising the draft guidebook was also a way of involving many of those who work in MPAs everyday and deal with the daily pressures and demands of managing these areas. These colleagues provided the necessary experience and wealth of feedback to make the guidebook practical and as useful as it can be for as many different types of MPAs as possible. In order to highlight some of this knowledge and experience, we have included actual results and examples from the pilot sites.

## *Partners and sponsors*

The **IUCN World Commission on Protected Areas (WCPA)** is one of six Commissions of IUCN – The World Conservation Union and is the world's leading global network of protected area specialists. It has over 1,200 members from 140 countries. It is coordinated by a steering committee and organized into 16 regions, two biomes (including marine), six theme areas (including management effectiveness) and nine task forces. The WCPA work programme is undertaken with the support and partnership of many organizations. WCPA's programme for the marine biome (WCPA Marine) was established in 1986 with the goal of *providing for the protection, restoration, wise use, understanding and enjoyment of the marine heritage of the world in perpetuity through the creation of a global, representative system of marine protected areas and by building the capacity to manage these areas.* The activities of the WCPA Marine programme are conducted at national, regional and global levels to increase the management capacity of institutions and practitioners while building an effective network of globally representative MPAs.

The **World Wide Fund For Nature (WWF)** is one of the world's largest and most experienced independent conservation organizations, with five million supporters and a global network of offices in more than 90 countries worldwide. WWF's mission is to stop, and eventually reverse, the accelerating degradation of our planet's natural environment, and to help build a future in which humans live in harmony with nature. To achieve this ambitious goal, WWF is working to conserve nature and ecological processes by preserving genetic species and ecosystem diversity; to ensure that the use of renewable natural resources is sustainable now and in the longer term, for the benefit of all life on Earth; and to promote actions to reduce to a minimum the pollution and the wasteful exploitation and consumption of resources and energy. WWF-International, based in Gland, Switzerland, leads and coordinates the WWF Network, develops joint policies and standards, fosters global partnerships, and implements part of WWF's international conservation programme.

**National Ocean Service, National Oceanic and Atmospheric Administration (NOS/NOAA).** The National Ocean Service (NOS) is part of the National Oceanic and Atmospheric Administration (NOAA), US Department of Commerce (DOC). NOS views its role as the nation's principal advocate for coastal and ocean stewardship. It works to carry out this role through a combination of scientific research; monitoring, observing and predicting scientific phenomena; preserving and restoring ocean and coastal areas; establishing and enhancing the capacity of state and local governments to manage coastal resources; mapping and charting; and responding to spills of hazardous substances. The NOS International Program Office (IPO) serves as the focal point for NOS-wide international activities and collaboration with national and foreign government agencies, non-governmental organizations (NGOs), academic institutions and others. International activities are focused on integrated coastal management; the management of marine protected areas (MPAs); mitigation of impacts from climate change; safe, efficient and environmentally sound maritime navigation; the reduction of impacts from natural disasters; and capacity-building. In addition to IPO, the NOS Office of Coastal Programs and the NOAA Coral Grants Program sponsored several of the pilot sites that field-tested this guidebook.

Tony Eckersley

**The David and Lucile Packard Foundation** has supported the development of the MPA Management Effectiveness Initiative and has made possible the publication of this guidebook for MPA managers and practitioners around the world.

## *The authors*

**Robert S. Pomeroy** is a marine resource economist and an internationally recognised expert on coastal and marine resource management and collaborative management. He is an Associate Professor in the Department of Agricultural and Resource Economics and a Fisheries Extension Specialist with the Connecticut Sea Grant College Program at the University of Connecticut-Avery Point. He also serves as a Senior Conservation Research Associate with the Community Conservation Network. He has held positions as faculty at the Department of Applied and Agricultural Economics at Clemson University, Senior Scientist at the International Center for Living Aquatic Resources Management, and Senior Coastal and Marine Associate in the Biological Resources Program of the World Resources Institute.

PARKS CANADA

PARKS CANADA

Dr. Pomeroy has led numerous international research projects on fisheries management and aquaculture.

**John E. Parks** is an applied researcher who works through both the biological and behavioural sciences to better understand and improve the practice of marine conservation. He is a Research Associate with the Community Conservation Network in Honolulu, Hawaii and a fellow with the Environmental Leadership Program. Previously, John served as a Research Associate with the Biological Resources Program of the World Resources Institute and as a Senior Program Officer with the Biodiversity Support Program of the World Wildlife Fund. John focuses principally on the adaptive management of marine protected areas, the testing and appropriate use of community-led conservation in the Indo-Pacific, and exploring the role of psychology in addressing conservation questions.

**Lani M. Watson** is a marine ecologist and specializes in the management and protection of the marine environment. She is an International Affairs Specialist with the National Oceanic and Atmospheric Administration National Ocean Service, where she began as a Knauss Sea Grant Fellow in Marine Policy. She works on domestic and international marine policy, management and protected area issues, and advises on applying management effectiveness evaluations and indicators in marine programmes. Lani is the Project Manager for the WCPA-Marine/WWF MPA Management Effectiveness Initiative.

## Acknowledgements

This guidebook reflects an enormous group effort. Each of three drafts were developed through collaboration with dozens of experts and practitioners from numerous organizations working in the fields of the natural and social sciences and the science and management of marine protected areas and marine conservation. The substantial support and contribution made by these colleagues greatly assisted in our writing and revising this guidebook. We would like to acknowledge the contributions of a number of individuals.

This guidebook is a product of the *WCPA Marine/WWF MPA Management Effectiveness Initiative* that is led by Charles "Bud" Ehler, Director of the International Program, NOS/NOAA, and Vice-Chair, WCPA Marine, and Simon Cripps, Director of the Endangered Seas Programme, WWF International. In addition to the authors and leads of the Initiative, a core team of the following NOAA and WWF staff dedicated significant time and skills to assist in all aspects of the Initiative, including the development of this guidebook: Miguel Jorge (WWF) provided guidance in the design and development of the Initiative and coordinated the WWF pilot sites and technical assistance in field-testing this guidebook; Leah Bunce (NOAA) provided expertise and reviewed the draft socio-economic indicators, facilitated an expert group review of them, and assisted in training pilot sites in their use; Gonzalo Cid (NOAA) assisted in the pilot site selection, in the synthesis and analysis of both external peer reviews and reports from pilot sites, and helped in generating the guidebook, including lending his artistic and design talents on draft versions of the guidebook; Steve Morrison (NOAA) and Alison

Hammer (NOAA) developed the internet site for the Initiative (http://effectiveMPA.noaa.gov), which included developing profiles of the pilot sites and ensured that the hyperlinks throughout the guidebook are available online; Lisa Max (NOAA) assisted with the initial research conducted on the biophysical goals, objectives and indicators.

As mentioned previously, field-testing was a critical step in making this guidebook flexible enough for a wide range of MPAs. The people who served as the project leads and represented the MPA pilot sites and management teams devoted their enthusiasm, participation, and technical expertise in applying the process and methods of the draft guidebook at their sites. Their findings, feedback and experiences are reflected in this published version. We would like to express our deep gratitude to the following pilot site representatives for their contributions to this text: Thorne Abbott (Bird Island Marine Sanctuary and Sasanhaya Fish Reserve, CNMI), Antonio Araújo (Banc D'Arguin National Park, Mauritania), Miguel Alamilla (Hol Chan Marine Reserve, Belize), Sylvain Archambault (Saguenay-St. Lawrence Marine Park, Canada), Mohamed Ould Bouceif (Banc D'Arguin National Park, Mauritania), José Campoy (Upper Gulf of California and Colorado River Delta Biosphere Reserve, Mexico), Erica Cochrane (Bird Island Marine Sanctuary and Sasanhaya Fish Reserve, CNMI), Marco Costantini (Miramare Marine Protected Area, Italy), Nancy Dahl-Tacconi (Bunaken National Park and Sebesi Marine Reserve, Indonesia), Marivel Dygico (Tubbataha Reef National Marine Park, Philippines), Simon Ellis (Lenger Island Marine Protected Area, Micronesia), Yimnang Golbuu (Ngemelis and Ngerumekaol, Palau), Pablo Guerrero (Galapagos Islands Marine Reserve, Ecuador), Jay Gutiérrez (Achang Reef Flat Preserve, Piti Bomb Holes Preserve and Tumon Bay Marine Reserve, Guam), Eugene Joseph (Lenger Island Marine Protected Area), Sylvestor Kazimoto (Mafia Island Marine Park, Tanzania), Rosa Maria Loreto (Banco Chinchorro Biosphere Reserve, Mexico), Andrey Malyutin (Far East Marine Preserve, Russia), Jason Rubens (Mafia Island Marine Park, Tanzania), Murray Rudd (Achang Reef Flat Preserve, Piti Bomb Holes Preserve and Tumon Bay Marine Reserve, Guam), Ileana Solares-Leal (Sian Ka'an Biosphere Reserve, Mexico), Jorge Torre (Loreto Bay National Park, Mexico), Mark Tupper (Achang Reef Flat Preserve, Piti Bomb Holes Preserve and Tumon Bay Marine Reserve, Guam), and Anne Walton (Channel Islands National Marine Santuary, USA).

Much appreciation is extended to those who helped support the pilot projects in their training and testing of the draft guidebook: Eileen Alicia, Bernd Cordes, Marcia Cota, Hans Herrman, Will Novy Hildesley, Jonathan Kelsey, Sergio Knaebel, Viveca Solomon May, Lynne Mersfelder-Lewis, William Milhouser, Fatimah Taylor and Tara Wilkinson.

In addition, we have been fortunate to have significant guidance and feedback from a number of international experts. The following individuals substantially contributed by participating in the selection and development of the indicators, attending work-sessions to review draft versions, providing critical thought on each of the three draft versions of this guidebook. We thank these colleagues for their time and constructive feedback: Tundi Agardy, Ernesto Arias-Gonzales, Sylvain Archambault, Antonio Araujo, Charles V. Barber,

JimThorsell/IUCN

Matt Brookhart, Leah Bunce, Georgina Bustamante, Ratana Chuenpagdee, Athline Clark, Tom Culliton, Gary Davis, Gerry Davis, Charlotte de Fontaubert, José Ramon Delgado, Terry Donaldson, Terry Done, Xabier Elguezabal, Leanne Fernández, Carlos Garcia-Saez, Peter Graham, Tim Goodspeed, Marc Hockings, Janice Hodge, Sylvester Kazimoto, Graeme Kelleher, Richard Kenchington, William Kostka, Michael Mascia, Delphine Mallert-King, Richard Margoluis, Tyler McAdam, Patrick McConney, Shiela McKenna, Glenda Medina, Melanie McField, John Munro, John Ogden, Arthur Paterson, John Petterson, Richard Pollnac, Robert Rangely, Cheri Recchia, Carlos Rivero Blanco, Jason Rubens, Enric Sala, Rodney Salm, Leonid Shabad, Linda Shea Flanders, Vassily Spiridonov, Jack Sobel, Ed Tongson, Mark Tupper, Andre Jon Uychiaco, Carlos Valle, Estrella Villamizar, Kuperan Viswanathan, John Waugh, Sue Wells, Alan White, Meriwether Wilson and Doug Yurick. We would like to especially thank Terry Done, Michael Mascia, Shiela McKenna and Richard Pollnac who put in significant hours reviewing the drafts of this guidebook and working with the authors.

The production of this guidebook would not have been possible without the IUCN Publications Services Unit and colleagues, who were a pleasure to work with. Elaine Shaughnessy provided much guidance on the overall production; Katherine Mann and Tiina Rajamets provided the content edit, and we thank Tony Eckersley for the design, which made the guidebook user-friendly. Thanks also to Toni Parras for the use of her beautiful photographs.

The opinions expressed are those of the authors. Any errors or omissions included in the text are the sole responsibility of the authors and should be reported to them accordingly.

## *A few points to keep in mind*

We'd like to ask you to think of this guidebook as a map that is meant to guide you down the general path of evaluating your MPA, but that does not try to predict every step along the way. We recommend that you use this guidebook along with other sources and methodologies that offer alternate routes or short cuts for your particular needs. It is our hope that this guidebook will provide a complementary resource that helps people reach their final destination: a completed evaluation with results that enable them to adaptively manage and improve MPAs.

The aim of this guidebook is to be as practical and applicable as possible, so that it can be used by many different MPA managers and conservation practitioners in varying types of MPAs. Therefore, the methodologies presented in this guidebook have been chosen to reflect more approachable, rather than the most advanced, scientific methods. As such, the data collection and analysis techniques lean towards simplicity, rather than complexity. We did this deliberately so that this guidebook would be a starting point in helping MPA managers and conservation practitioners measure management effectiveness. Our vision is that someday soon, sufficient management capacity will exist globally to develop more advanced sets of measurement and analytical techniques. Until then, we hope that this guidebook strikes a balance for all those who apply it to their particular needs and resources.

One final, but critical, caveat: this guidebook is not intended to be used as a scorecard to compare one MPA site or groups of MPA sites to each other. The evaluation process and indicators are intended for use in a positive way to help managers and practitioners improve the management of MPAs by reaching their MPA goals and objectives more effectively and efficiently. The indicators should highlight successes, as well as challenges, and the information should not be used against an MPA or to negatively impact the support for any given MPA.

In closing, we hope that the process described in this guidebook will be rewarding for all involved. Although conducting an evaluation can seem like a daunting or mundane task, both others and we have learned that the evaluation process can foster much learning and even be fun. The evaluative process can highlight both successes and failures, however the insight and clarity that can be gained are incentives for continuing such important work in marine management and conservation. We wish you a rewarding experience and journey ahead.

*Robert S. Pomeroy* *John E. Parks* *Lani M. Watson*

**Box 1**

### What this Guidebook is

- Flexible so that it can be integrated into what you are already doing
- A basic and generic starting point on how to evaluate your MPA
- A 'toolbox' of indicators to pick and choose from
- Something that should be used with other MPA manuals/texts
- Something you should feel free to adapt, add to and improve on as needed
- Written for MPA managers and conservation practitioners
- To be used with input from scientific professionals and MPA experts
- A short introduction on analysis and interpretation

### What this Guidebook is not

- A summary of all available survey methods
- A source of advanced, state-of-the-art scientific techniques
- One-size-fits-all that should be used by all MPAs everywhere
- A finite set of indicators or prescription of minimum indicators that should be used by MPAs
- Trying to be all things to all MPAs and management levels
- Written for scientific experts and advanced researchers
- Requiring a high level of statistical expertise from the reader
- A complete guide on data analysis

Tony Eckersley

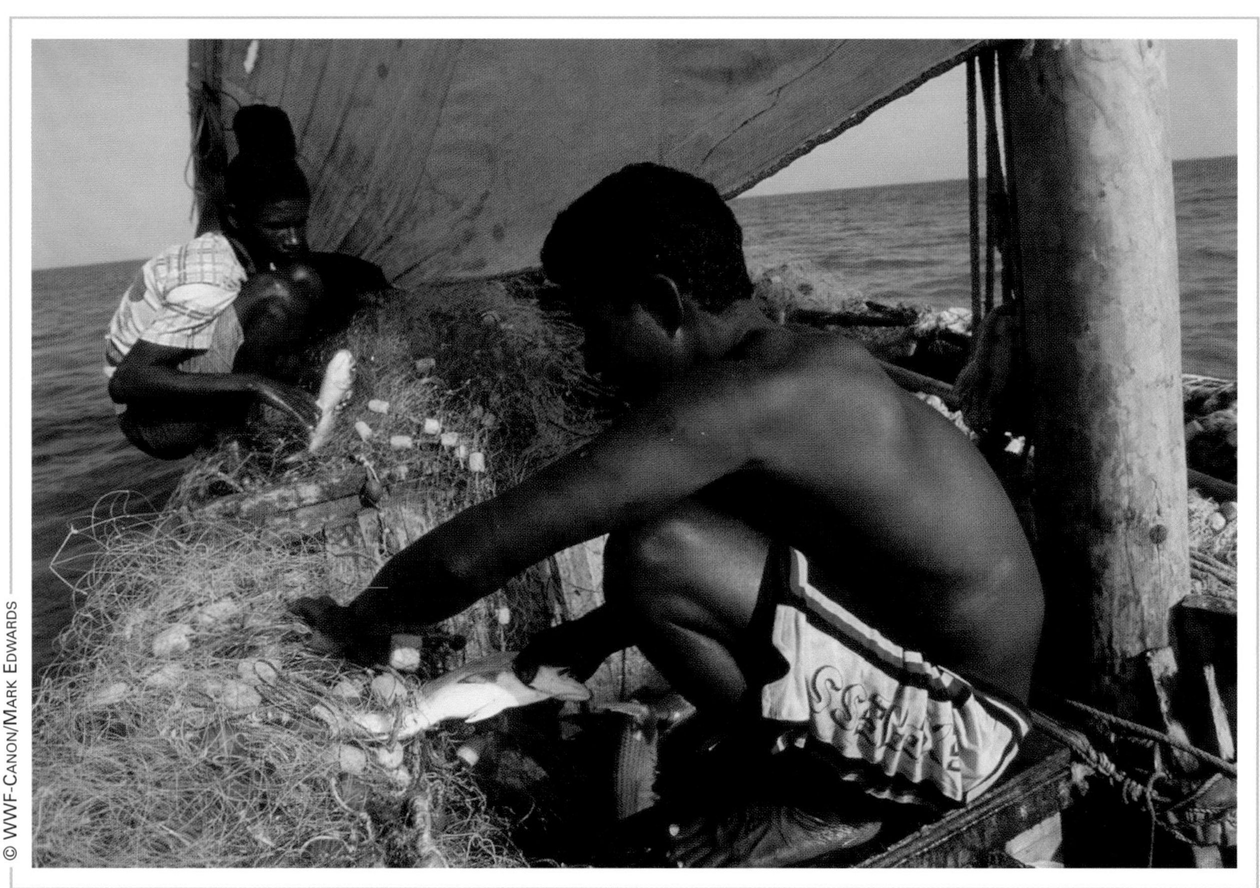



*Artisanal fishing is at the heart of many MPA strategies, in the knowledge that closing areas to fishing can dramatically reverse decline of fish stocks and improve catches in neighbouring areas. Monitoring the effects of such closures can provide evidence of their benefits that helps build the case for conservation.*

# Introduction

## *Purpose of this guidebook*

This guidebook offers managers and other conservation **practitioners**[1] a process and methods to evaluate the effectiveness of **marine protected areas** (MPAs) for the purposes of adaptive management. The evaluation is based on indicators that measure the effectiveness of management actions in attaining **goals** and **objectives** that are specific to MPAs, the marine environment and coastal communities. It presents a flexible approach that can be used in many types of MPAs, such as multiple-use areas or **no-take zones**, where each may have different goals and objectives. It offers a variety of indicators that reflect a diversity of MPA goals and objectives. These can be selected to best match your MPA based on the needs and resources of your site.

*There is strong consensus and a growing volume of scientific evidence that identifies the needs of MPAs and the values that they provide. Guidelines on how best to design and manage MPAs are available (e.g. Salm* et al.*, 2000; Kelleher, 1999; Kelleher and Kenchington, 1992). If you are familiar with this literature and actively managing or working with an MPA – this guidebook is for you. It will help you evaluate whether or not the desired outcomes of your MPA are being achieved.*[2]

There are a number of methods available for monitoring and evaluating protected areas. To date there has not been a comprehensive methodology developed for monitoring and evaluating **management effectiveness** of MPAs. To fill this gap, this guidebook includes indicators that address various aspects of management effectiveness: biophysical, socio-economic, and governance. The majority of these indicators measure **outputs** and **outcomes** of MPA management. Outputs and outcomes represent tangible benefits associated with the MPA. Learning from indicator results can help to improve MPA management and secure resources and support.

*This guidebook is not a 'one-stop-shop' for MPA management or evaluation. This guidebook should be used in conjunction with other materials and literature that are available to practitioners (see References). For example, other works focus on the context, planning, process and inputs into MPAs (Hockings* et al.*, 2000, Mangubhai and Wells, 2004, in draft).*

## *Why evaluate management effectiveness?*

Marine and coastal resource management has evolved into a professional practice. There is recognition of the need for marine and coastal managers to

***"This guidebook offers managers and other conservation practitioners a process and methods to evaluate the effectiveness of marine protected areas (MPAs) for the purposes of adaptive management."***

**Box 2**

### What is a Marine Protected Area?

This guidebook follows the accepted IUCN (1999) definition of an MPA as:

*"Any area of* **intertidal** *or* **subtidal** *terrain, together with its overlying waters and associated flora, fauna, historical and cultural features, which has been reserved by law or other effective means to protect part or all of the enclosed environment."*

In many cases effective MPA management will need to reflect the relationship between the marine and terrestrial environments and human uses. For example, to be an effective coastal MPA, managers will need to work with inland developers and take into consideration broader watershed issues.

---

1 *Terms highlighted in bold in this way are defined in the Glossary (pp. 213–215).*
2 *Points that the authors wish to emphasise are highlighted with a vertical bar.*

### Key principles

The evaluation process in this guidebook is founded on five key principles. It must be:

- ***Useful*** to managers and stakeholders for improving MPA management.
- ***Practical*** in use and cost.
- ***Balanced*** to seek and include scientific input and stakeholder participation.
- ***Flexible*** for use at different sites and in varying conditions.
- ***Holistic*** through a focus on both natural and human perspectives.

be more systematic in using MPAs to improve marine conservation learning and create a set of best management practices. To meet this need, there is general consensus among conservation practitioners that evaluation of management effectiveness will improve MPA practice. It is particularly relevant now given the focus on implementing MPAs and increasing their number.

Effective management of MPAs requires continuous feedback of information to achieve objectives. The management process involves planning, design, implementation, monitoring, evaluation, communication and adaptation. Evaluation consists of reviewing the results of actions taken and assessing whether these actions are producing the desired outcomes. Evaluation is a routine part of the management process and is something that most managers already do. The evaluation of management effectiveness builds on this existing routine.

The link between actions and outcomes is often not so obvious. Faced with the daily demands of their jobs, many managers are not able to regularly and formally step back and reflect on the cumulative results of their efforts. In the absence of such reflection, resources may be wasted and objectives may not be achieved. The evaluation of management effectiveness provides a formal way to learn from successes and failures and help people understand how and why management practices are being adapted.

**Adaptive management** is a fundamental concept underlying this guidebook. Adaptive management is the cyclical process of systematically testing assumptions, generating learning by evaluating the results of such testing, and further revising and improving management practices. The result of adaptive management in a protected area context is improved effectiveness and increased progress towards the achievement of goals and objectives.

Evaluation is often perceived as a difficult, excessive and overly technical activity that requires the involvement of outside 'specialists'. For some, the word 'evaluation' implies supervision, discipline and potential penalties. It is important to clearly communicate the reasons and benefits of doing a management effectiveness evaluation to both internal staff and external stakeholders. This will help you to focus on improving conservation success.

***"Learning from indicator results can help to improve MPA management and secure resources and support."***

*The use of adaptive management in a conservation context is well documented in the literature (see References). An overview of the use of evaluation results for adaptive management of MPAs is included in Chapter 4, Communicating results and adapting management. Materials on adaptive management can be found at http://effectiveMPA.noaa.gov*

**"This guidebook offers a variety of indicators that reflect a diversity of MPA goals and objectives. These can be selected to best match your MPA based on the needs and resources of your site."**

### What is 'management effectiveness'?

This guidebook builds on the IUCN management effectiveness framework (Hockings *et al.*, 2000; see Box 3, The IUCN Management Effectiveness Framework). Management effectiveness is the degree to which management actions are achieving the goals and objectives of a protected area. This allows for the improvement of protected area management through learning, adaptation, and the diagnosis of specific issues influencing whether goals and objectives have been achieved. It also provides a way to show accountability for the management of an MPA.

Evaluating the management effectiveness of protected areas is not an easy task. For example, despite the best management efforts natural disturbances can radically alter ecosystems regardless of how well a protected area is being managed. The evaluation needs to be appropriate and accurate in assessing the degree of achievement directly linked to management actions.

> *In 1997, IUCN's World Commission on Protected Areas (WCPA) created a task force of experts in protected area management from different countries to develop guidelines to measure and evaluate the effectiveness of management and provide tools to better understand and improve the management of protected areas worldwide. Following extensive research, work, and testing, the IUCN Task Force created a framework entitled* "Evaluating Effectiveness: A Framework for Assessing the Management of Protected Areas" *(Hockings* et al., *2000).* See Box 3.

**Fish from Mei Hol Chan, Belize, one of the MPA Management Effectiveness Initiative pilot sites.**

© WWF/Hol Chan Marine Reserve

Box 3

## The IUCN Management Effectiveness Framework

The IUCN management effectiveness framework (Hockings *et al.*, 2000) presents an iterative protected area management cycle of design, management, monitoring, evaluation and adaptation.

Through this process, managers are empowered with the ability to diagnose and adaptively improve their management actions. To begin the evaluation process in this management cycle three sets of simple questions must be answered:

Context: status and threats
Where are we now?
Vision
Where do we want to be?
Planning
How are we going to get there?
Inputs
What do we need?
Management processes
How do we go about it?
Output
What did we do and what products or services were produced?
Outcome
What did we achieve?
Evaluation

| 1. In terms of the design of the protected area: | 2. In terms of how appropriate are the management system and process: | 3. In terms of the achievement of desired objectives: |
|---|---|---|
| What is the *context* in which the protected area is designated? | What *inputs* are required to designate the protected area? | What activities were undertaken and what were the *outputs* (products) of this? |
| What is the desired result and how will *planning* enable its achievement? | What is the *process* used to go about defining it? | What *outcomes* (impacts) were achieved based on the outputs and their application? |

These questions identify six categories of potential indicators for measuring management effectiveness:

- Context indicators
- Planning indicators
- Input indicators
- Process indicators
- Output indicators
- Outcome indicators

Using this general framework allows protected area managers to customize a set of appropriate indicators to be used on relevant scales. It serves as a foundation from which to further investigate a specific category of indicators (e.g. outcomes) or to determine which indicators are most appropriate based on the use of a specific protected area tool. The framework provides a common language and an important structure from which to improve protected area learning, efficacy and achievement. As a tool for designing an evaluation approach – rather than providing a specific set of indicators and methodologies to measure them – it helps to explain variations in the context, available resources, evaluative purpose and specific management objectives across protected areas.

To learn more about how the indicators in this guidebook relate to the IUCN management effectiveness framework, go to http://effectiveMPA.noaa.gov/guidebook/IUCNframework.html

## Things for you to consider when using this guidebook

To conduct a management effectiveness evaluation, it is recommended that your MPA should ideally meet the following minimum requirements:

- ❑ It exists as a formal (legislated) MPA.
- ❑ There is an ongoing management planning process.
- ❑ There is a written management plan including clearly stated goals and objectives (see Box 4, The Goals and Objectives of an MPA).
- ❑ It has been in operation for at least two years.

If your MPA does not meet these minimum requirements, it is still possible to conduct an evaluation if there are stated goals and objectives available.

It is also recommended that you establish an evaluation team made up of individuals with the skills to conduct the type and level of evaluation you want to implement in your MPA. (See Chapter 2, Step 2–3 on forming an evaluation team.)

Finally, it is recommended that your evaluation team should ideally meet the following minimum requirements:

- ❑ Team members have an education or experience that equals a college degree in the natural sciences, social sciences, or related environmental and natural resource management studies.
- ❑ Team members are knowledgeable about the fundamentals and standard methods used in the biological and social sciences.

If you or other MPA staff do not meet these minimum requirements, seek assistance and look through the References.

***"Evaluation is a routine part of the management process and is something that most managers already do. The evaluation of management effectiveness builds on this existing routine."***

Tony Eckersley

DAVID NOTON/NATUREPL.COM

Box 4

## THE GOALS AND OBJECTIVES OF AN MPA

A protected area is one example of a conservation **strategy** that can be used to manage natural resources. When a decision is made to use an MPA strategy, one of the first steps taken is to design an appropriate management plan for the strategy (Salm *et al.*, 2000; Kenchington, 1990). A management plan documents an explicit set of goals, objectives, and activities that will be undertaken over a specified period of time and area, and articulates how the conservation strategy being used is designed to address the **threats** present (Margolius and Salafsky, 1998; for more details). While not all MPAs require a complete management plan to begin operation, eventually a comprehensive plan will be needed to guide the long-term goals and development of the area (Salm *et al.*, 2000).

A **goal** is a broad statement of what the MPA is ultimately trying to achieve. A useful goal is:

- brief and clearly defines the desired long-term vision and/or condition that will result from effective management of the MPA,
- typically phrased as a broad mission statement, and
- simple to understand and communicate.

An **objective** is a more specific measurable statement of what must be accomplished to attain a related goal. Attaining a goal is typically associated with the achievement of two or more corresponding objectives. A useful objective (Margolius and Salafsky, 1998) is one that is:

- specific and easily understood,
- written in terms of what will be accomplished, not how to go about it,
- realistically achievable,
- defined within a limited time period, and
- achieved by being measured and validated.

*For more information on how to develop good objectives go to http://effectiveMPA.noaa.gov/guidebook/MPA goals.html*

Goals and objectives are preferably developed in a participatory manner to reflect a balance of the needs and desires of all stakeholders involved in the management of the MPA and use of marine resources.

Poorly designed and/or articulated goals and objectives can be a serious problem for MPA managers. A set of goals and objectives that have been appropriately developed and are useful for management purposes (as defined by the criteria listed below) will improve the likelihood of the MPA being effectively managed.

To find your goals and objectives and prepare for an evaluation:

- Obtain a list of goals and objectives from the management plan or relevant legislation.
- If there is no such list in the management plan, go through a participatory process to define them.
- Review whether the goals and objectives meet the above criteria that make them useful for doing an evaluation.
- The goals and objectives may need to be clarified or more properly worded for use in conducting an evaluation.

One important application of the results of an evaluation is to improve the quality of goals and objectives that guide management. It is important to examine the goals and objectives regularly to determine if they are appropriate or need to be revised to make them more clearly defined, measurable, and useful for future management purposes.

### *How to use this guidebook*

This guidebook consists of two sections: Section 1 outlines the process for conducting an evaluation, and Section 2 describes the indicators that would be measured in an evaluation.

Section 1 is structured around a set of logical steps that you can follow when you conduct a management effectiveness evaluation. These steps are set out in four chapters that represent the overall evaluation process:

**Chapter 1:** Selecting an appropriate set of indicators to measure.

**Chapter 2:** Planning how to evaluate the indicators selected.

**Chapter 3:** Implementing the evaluation by collecting and analysing data.

**Chapter 4:** Communicating results and using the results for adaptive management.

Each chapter includes:

- ❏ A set of steps to accomplish each stage,
- ❏ A set of tasks or questions to complete each step, and
- ❏ Guidance, supplementary information and references to help you work through the process.

All of this is illustrated in a flowchart (Figure 1) so that you can easily use the guidebook. In addition, there is a worksheet (Worksheet 1) to help you keep track of where you are as you progress through the book. It is recommended that you go through each chapter in advance to become familiar with it and that you follow this step-by-step evaluation process.

Section 2 contains:

- ❏ An introduction to the MPA effectiveness indicators,
- ❏ Summary tables of goals, objectives and indicators, and
- ❏ Outlines of the biophysical, socio-economic and governance indicators.

Finally, this process takes time, people and money. Read carefully through the entire guidebook, become familiar with the process and the indicators, and understand what will be required to follow this approach.

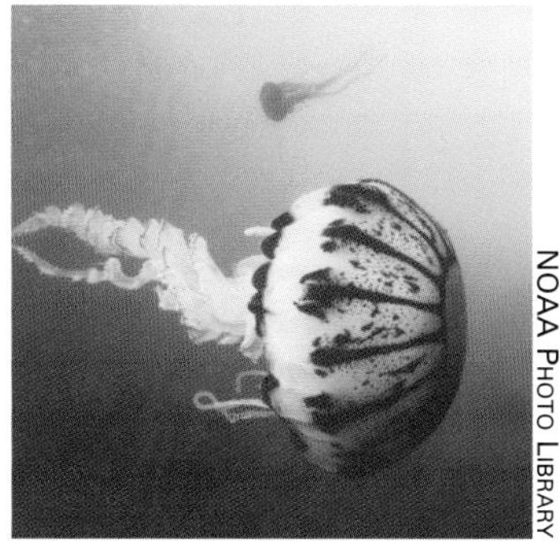
NOAA Photo Library

## Figure 1

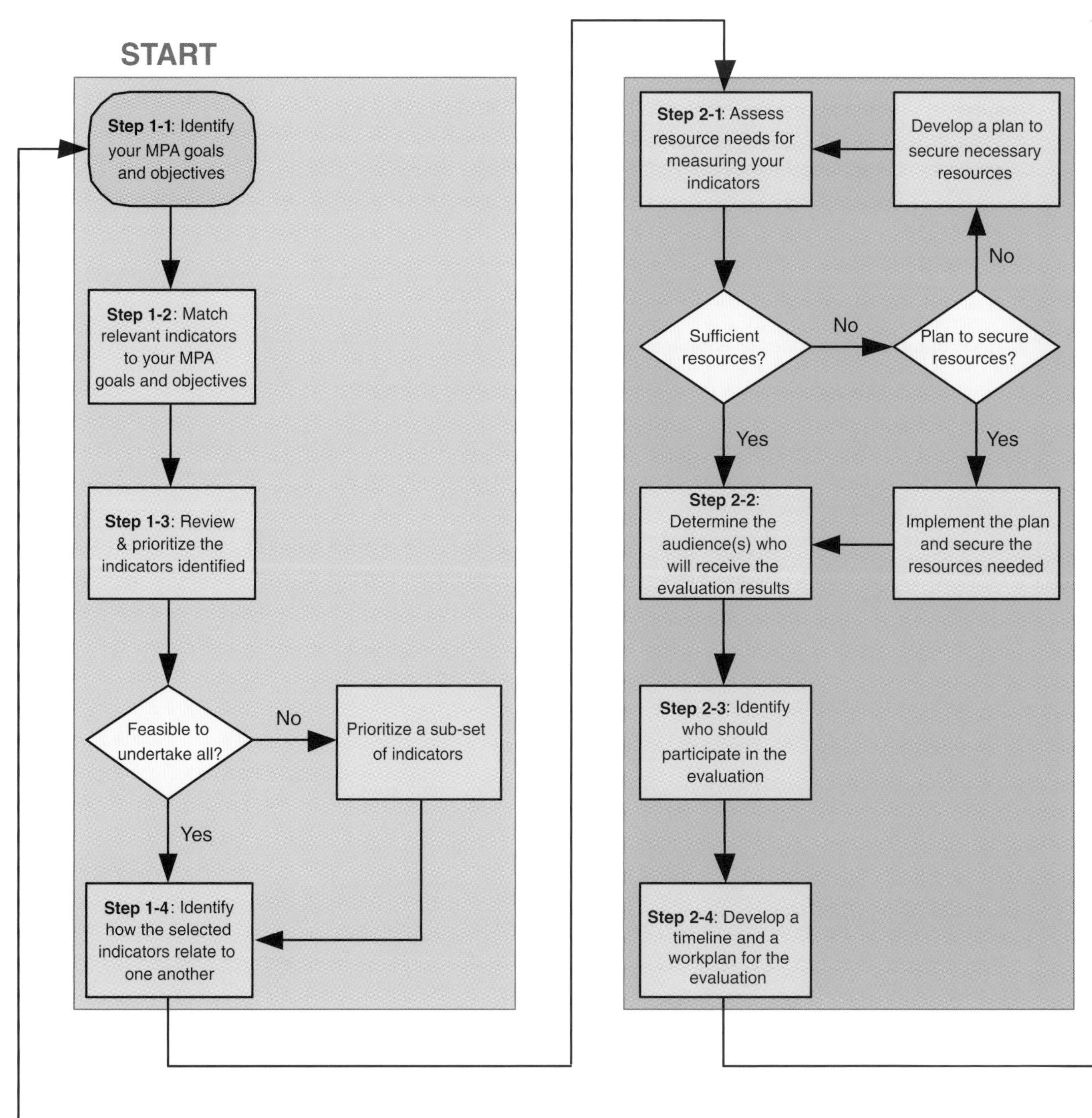

CHAPTER 1
Selecting your indicators
CHAPTER 2
Planning your evaluation
START
Step 1-1: Identify your MPA goals and objectives
Step 1-2: Match relevant indicators to your MPA goals and objectives
Step 1-3: Review & prioritize the indicators identified
Feasible to undertake all?
No
Prioritize a sub-set of indicators
Yes
Step 1-4: Identify how the selected indicators relate to one another
Step 2-1: Assess resource needs for measuring your indicators
Develop a plan to secure necessary resources
No
Sufficient resources?
No
Plan to secure resources?
Yes
Yes
Step 2-2: Determine the audience(s) who will receive the evaluation results
Implement the plan and secure the resources needed
Step 2-3: Identify who should participate in the evaluation
Step 2-4: Develop a timeline and a workplan for the evaluation

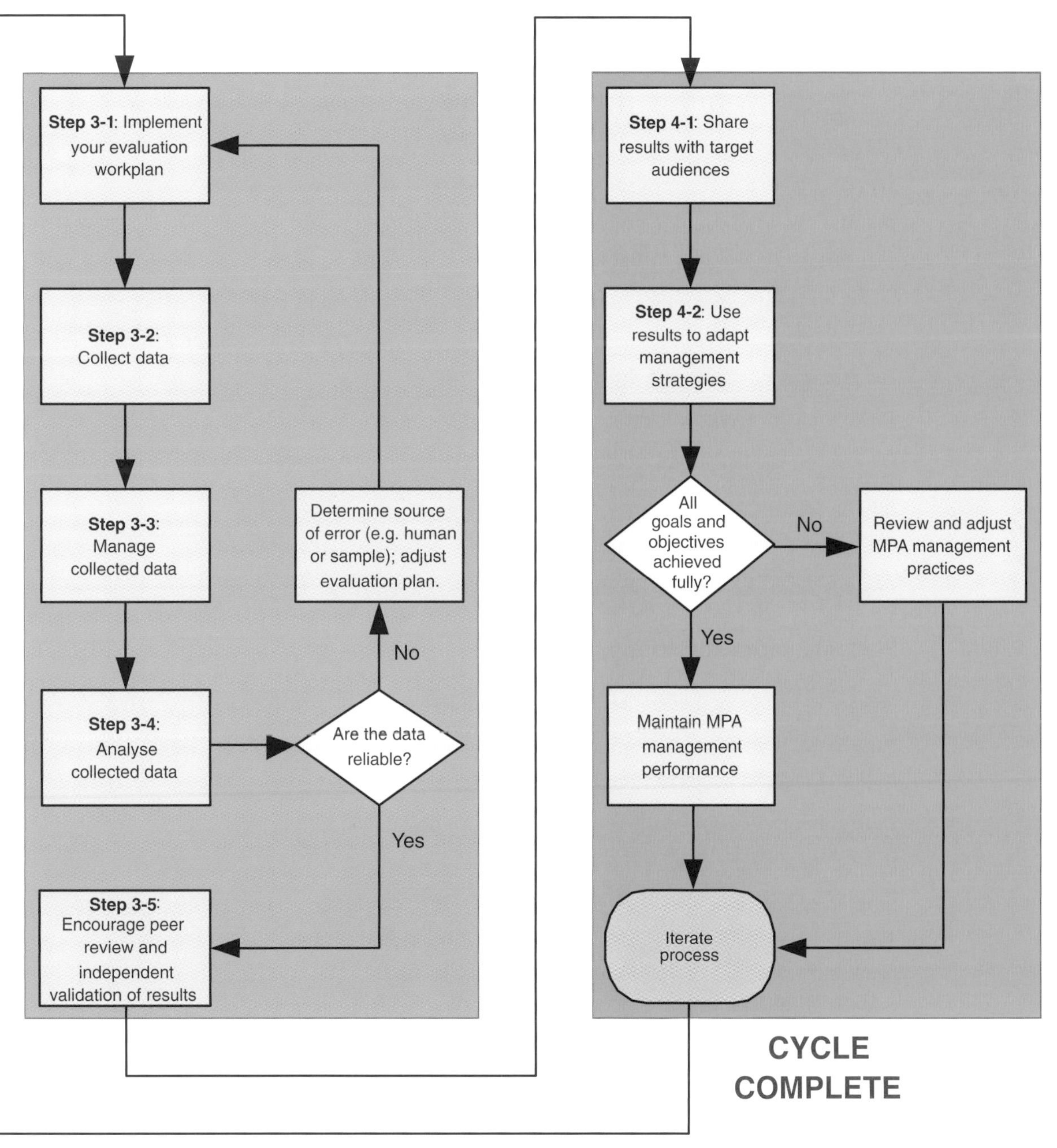

CHAPTER 3
Conducting your evaluation
CHAPTER 4
Communicating results and adapting management
Step 3-1: Implement your evaluation workplan
Step 3-2: Collect data
Step 3-3: Manage collected data
Step 3-4: Analyse collected data
Are the data reliable?
No
Determine source of error (e.g. human or sample); adjust evaluation plan.
Yes
Step 3-5: Encourage peer review and independent validation of results
Step 4-1: Share results with target audiences
Step 4-2: Use results to adapt management strategies
All goals and objectives achieved fully?
No
Review and adjust MPA management practices
Yes
Maintain MPA management performance
Iterate process
CYCLE COMPLETE

# Worksheet 1

| | | |
|---|---|---|
| **PART 1** | **Selecting your indicators** | COMPLETED |
| ***1-1*** | ***Identify your MPA goals and objectives*** | |
| 1-1a | Locate the management plan and other relevant information relating to your MPA | ☐ |
| 1-1b | Review the documents and identify the goals and objectives (see Box 4, The Goals and Objectives of an MPA) | ☐ |
| 1-1c | List the goals and objectives of your MPA on the worksheet provided (Worksheet 2) | ☐ |
| 1-1d | Identify the goals and associated objectives of your MPA that overlap with those listed in the summary tables of goals and objectives (see Figures 2, 3 and 4 in Section 2) | ☐ |
| 1-1e | List the overlapping goals and objectives on the worksheet (using the numbers and names in the summary tables) | ☐ |
| ***1-2*** | ***Match relevant indicators to your MPA goals and objectives*** | |
| 1-2a | Identify the indicators that match your list of goals and objectives (see Figures 2, 3 and 4 in Section 2) | ☐ |
| 1-2b | List the relevant indicators on the worksheet (using the numbers and names in the summary tables) | ☐ |
| ***1-3*** | ***Review and prioritize the indicators identified*** | |
| 1-3a | Review each indicator identified from the description in Appendix 1 | ☐ |
| 1-3b | Determine the feasibility of measuring the indicators identified | ☐ |
| 1-3c | If it is not feasible to measure all indicators, prioritize them | ☐ |
| 1-3d | Complete the list of selected indicators | ☐ |
| ***1-4*** | ***Identify how the selected indicators relate to one another*** | ☐ |
| **PART 2** | **Planning your evaluation** | |
| ***2-1*** | ***Assess resource needs for measuring your indicators*** | |
| 2-1a | Determine the estimated human resources needed to measure and analyse the selected indicators | ☐ |
| 2-1b | Determine the equipment needed to measure and analyse the selected indicators | ☐ |
| 2-1c | Estimate the budget that will be needed for the evaluation | ☐ |
| 2-1d | Assess the available human resources, equipment and budget; if not sufficient, develop a plan to secure funds. Secure additional resources as necessary | ☐ |
| ***2-2*** | ***Determine the audience(s) who will receive the evaluation results*** | |
| 2-2a | Identify the target audience(s) | ☐ |
| 2-2b | Determine and prioritize the primary audience(s) | ☐ |
| ***2-3*** | ***Identify who should participate in the evaluation*** | |
| 2-3a | Determine the level of expertise that is needed to conduct the evaluation | ☐ |

| | | COMPLETED |
|---|---|---|
| 2-3b | Determine which staff or non-staff will conduct the evaluation | ☐ |
| 2-3c | Determine how and when to involve the stakeholders | ☐ |
| 2-3d | Create the evaluation team and determine the people responsible for each task | ☐ |
| ***2-4*** | ***Develop a timeline and a workplan for the evaluation*** | |
| 2-4a | Determine the amount of time needed for each activity | ☐ |
| 2-4b | Determine when the data need to be collected | ☐ |
| 2-4c | Develop an evaluation workplan | ☐ |

**PART 3 Conducting your evaluation**

*(The checklist may be open at this step for many months while the chosen indicators are evaluated, surveys carried out, and reports completed in accordance with the evaluation techniques suggested in Section 2)*

| | | |
|---|---|---|
| ***3-1*** | ***Implement your evaluation workplan*** | ☐ |
| ***3-2*** | ***Collect data*** | |
| 3-2a | Study and understand the data collection methods | ☐ |
| 3-2b | Familiarize yourself with the best practices and principles for collecting data in the field | ☐ |
| 3-2c | Determine the sampling approach | ☐ |
| 3-2d | Ensure everything is in place for data collection | ☐ |
| ***3-3*** | ***Manage collected data*** | |
| 3-3a | Determine who will be the 'data manager' | ☐ |
| 3-3b | Determine how collected data will be submitted to the data manager | ☐ |
| 3-3c | Code the data | ☐ |
| 3-3d | Develop a system for storing and entering the data | ☐ |
| 3-3e | Collate and review the data set | ☐ |
| 3-3f | Determine how to make the data available for analysis and sharing | ☐ |
| ***3-4*** | ***Analyse collected data*** | |
| 3-4a | Review the questions being asked by the evaluation | ☐ |
| 3-4b | Complete a preliminary analysis | ☐ |
| 3-4c | Determine and prepare analyses | ☐ |
| 3-4d | Capture and prepare results | ☐ |
| ***3-5*** | ***Encourage peer review and independent evaluation of results*** | ☐ |

**PART 4 Communicating results and adapting management**

| | | |
|---|---|---|
| ***4-1*** | ***Share results with target audiences*** | |
| 4-1a | Determine which format to use to provide evaluation results and to reach the target audience most effectively | ☐ |
| 4-1b | Develop a strategy and a timeline for delivery of results | ☐ |
| 4-1c | Tell your story! Communicate your findings to the stakeholders | ☐ |
| ***4-2*** | ***Use results to adapt management strategies*** | ☐ |

*(This step should never be closed since adaptive management is an open-ended tool)*

# SECTION 1 *The Evaluation Process*

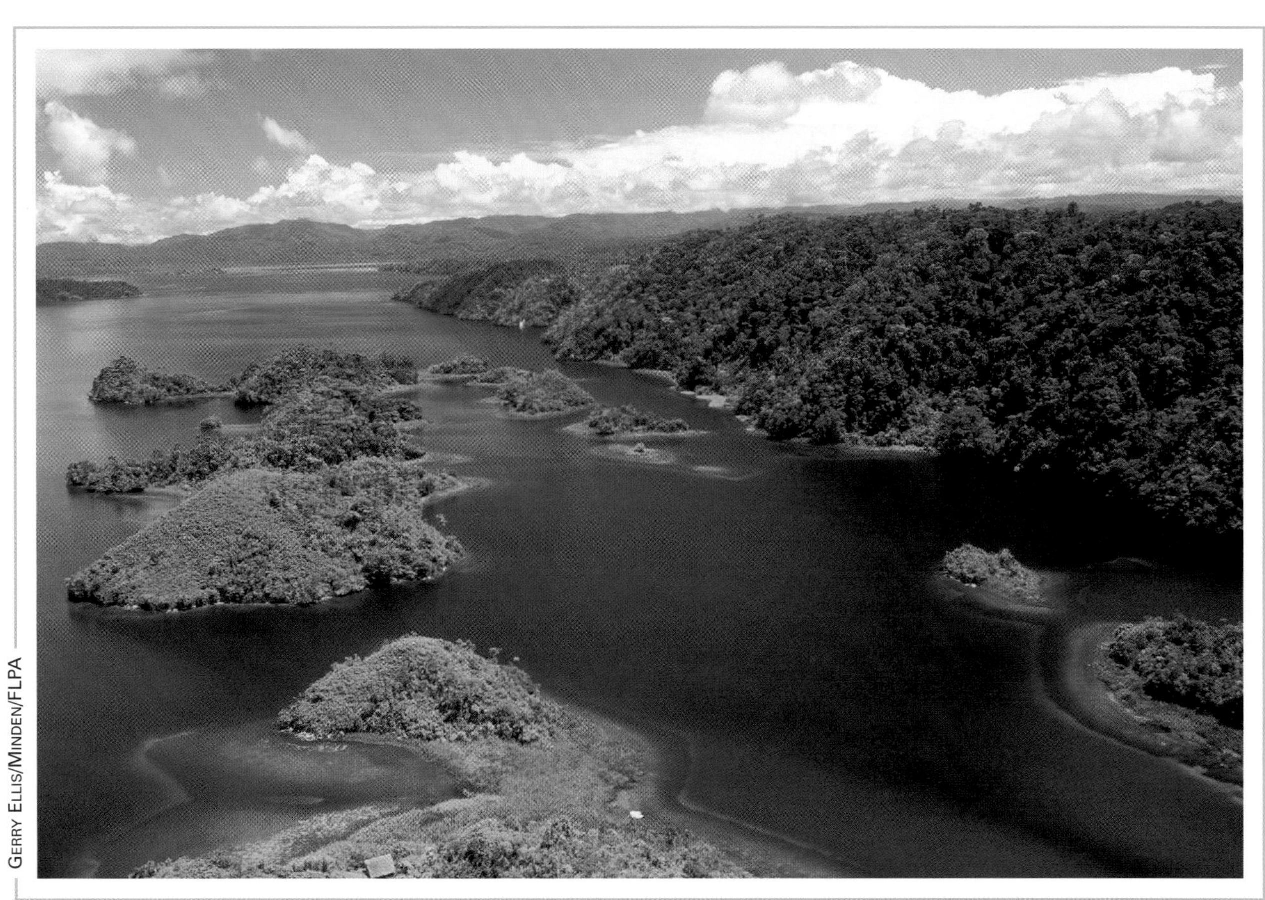

GERRY ELLIS/MINDEN/FLPA

*In nature, land and sea are intimately connected. The evaluation process should highlight the importance of protecting land, coast and sea in a continuum.*

# CHAPTER 1 Selecting your indicators

## Let's start

Selecting indicators that are appropriate for your MPA is the first part of carrying out a management effectiveness evaluation. This includes the following steps:

- ❏ **Step 1-1 Identify your MPA goals and objectives**
- ❏ **Step 1-2 Match relevant indicators to your MPA goals and objectives**
- ❏ **Step 1-3 Review and prioritize the indicators identified**
- ❏ **Step 1-4 Identify how the selected indicators relate to one another**

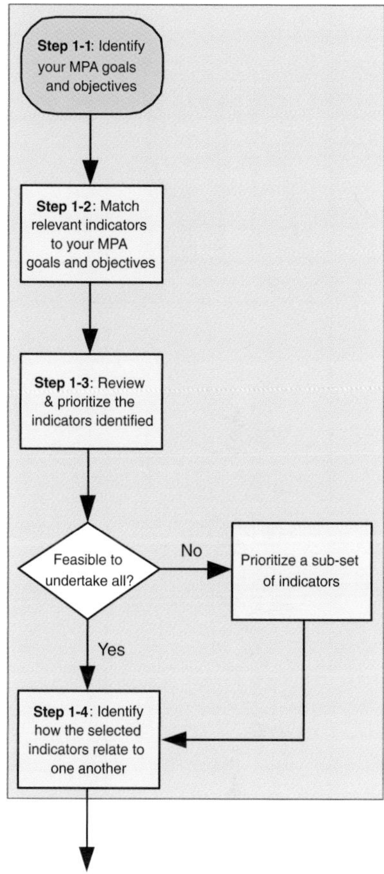


***Chapter 2. Planning your evaluation***

Selecting the most appropriate indicators for your MPA is one of the most critical elements in using this guidebook. Before selecting indicators here are a few key points for you to consider:

- ❏ Clearly stated goals and measurable objectives serve as the basis to identify and select indicators that are most appropriate to your MPA (see Box 4, The Goals and Objectives of an MPA).
- ❏ The process of identifying indicators should be flexible to meet the needs of your MPA.
- ❏ If you identify many indicators, it does not mean that you have to measure all of them.
- ❏ If the goals and objectives of your MPA span biophysical, socio-economic, and governance issues, then your indicators should too.

## Step 1-1 Identify your MPA goals and objectives

You can identify the goals and objectives of your MPA by completing the following tasks:

***Task a Locate the management plan and other relevant information (e.g. accompanying legislation or declarative documents) relating to your MPA.***

***Task b Review the documents and identify the goals and objectives (see Box 4, The Goals and Objectives of an MPA).***

***Task c List the goals and objectives of your MPA on the worksheet provided (Worksheet 2). Some MPAs may have many goals and objectives. In this case, it may be useful to prioritize the goals and objectives and use these to select indicators.***

***Task d Identify the goals and associated objectives of your MPA that overlap with those listed in the summary tables of goals and objectives (see Figures 2, 3 and 4 in Section 2).***

*To learn a few ways to prioritize goals and objectives go to http://effectiveMPA.noaa.gov/guidebook/prioritize.html. If you decide to prioritize goals and objectives, it should be done with consideration of the needs of relevant stakeholders. These prioritized goals and objectives can be recorded in Step 1-1c.*

# Worksheet 2: Form on which to list your goals, objectives and indicator

| **Goals related to your MPA** | **Overlapping goals from summary tables (Figures 2, 3 and 4 in Section 2)** | **Objectives related to your MPA** | **Overlapping objectives from summary tables (Figures 2, 3 and 4 in Section 2)** | **Relevant indica-tors from summary tables (Figures 2, 3 and 4 in Section 2)** |
|---|---|---|---|---|
| | | | | |
| | | | | |
| | | | | |
| | | | | |
| | | | | |
| | | | | |
| | | | | |
| | | | | |
| | | | | |

***Task e List the overlapping goals and objectives on the worksheet (using the numbers and names in the summary tables).***

*The generic goals and objectives in this guidebook are based on real MPA goals and objectives. A survey was done of MPAs from around the world – the list of goals and objectives fell into the three categories of biophysical, socio-economic, and governance. To learn more go to http://effectiveMPA.noaa.gov/guidebook/survey.html*

## *Step 1-2 Match relevant indicators to your MPA goals and objectives*

You can identify and match the relevant indicators by completing the following tasks:

***Task a Look at your overlapping list of goals and objectives from Step 1-1. Identify the indicators that match your list of goals and objectives(see Figures 2, 3 and 4 in Section 2).***

***Task b List the relevant indicators on your worksheet (using the numbers and names in the summary tables).***

*A range of indicators is presented in Section 2, from which you can choose an appropriate set for your site (see Box 5, Introducing the Indicators, for a summary of how the indicators were developed). Every indicator may not be relevant to your MPA.*

*This guidebook is not intended to be used prescriptively. As each MPA is unique, indicators here are not universally applicable or appropriate to all MPAs. Likewise there is no single set of indicators that must be used.*

## *Step 1-3 Review and prioritize the indicators identified*

You can review and prioritize the indicators you identified by doing the following:

***Task a Review each indicator identified from the description in Appendix 1.***

TONI PARRAS

***Task b Determine the feasibility of measuring the indicators identified.***

*Note: Difficulty rankings are provided for each indicator and can be a helpful guide on how much time and effort it will take to measure an indicator.*

TONI PARRAS

***Task c If it is not feasible to measure all indicators, prioritize them.***

***Task d Complete the list of selected indicators.***

This selection process should not become more complex than necessary. In some cases, it should be fairly intuitive to identify the appropriate indicators given the goals and objectives of your MPA.

*To learn ways to prioritize indicators go to http://effectiveMPA.noaa.gov/guidebook/prioritize.html. These prioritized indicators can be recorded in Step 1-3d.*

### *Step 1-4 Identify how the selected indicators relate to one another*

Now that you have selected your indicators, consider how they are related to one another by considering the natural and social conditions of your MPA. It is helpful to draw these relationships on paper in a diagram.

For example, legislation passed in your MPA may influence the types of livelihood activities that are allowed in the area. In turn, these livelihoods influence both the degree of fishing effort and the population size of particular target species present. The status of these species influences the degree to which the biophysical goals and objectives of an MPA are met.

In another example, socio-economic factors, such as stakeholder knowledge of natural history and the number and nature of markets, are directly related to the use of marine resources that influence the ecology of your MPA. Likewise, changes to habitat distribution and community composition in the ecosystem

Box 5

## Introducing the Indicators

#### *What is an indicator and how is it used?*

An **indicator** is a unit of information measured over time that will allow you to document changes in specific attributes of your MPA. An indicator allows you to gauge an aspect that is not directly measurable or is very difficult to measure – such as effectiveness. Because 'effectiveness' is a multi-dimensional concept, a range of different indicators should be used to determine how your MPA is doing. These indicators can provide evidence of whether or not the goals and objectives of your MPA are being achieved. Alone, they are not sufficient proof.

Indicators provide results for several purposes:

- Indicator results feed into the MPA evaluation to measure and demonstrate management effectiveness. The indicators in this guidebook are designed to allow you to regularly diagnose the status of your MPA.
- Measuring, analysing and communicating indicators can promote learning, sharing knowledge, and better understanding of strengths and weaknesses of MPA management actions.
- MPA managers and practitioners can use indicator results to highlight the changes needed in management plans and practices to adapt and improve the MPA. If changes are made in management based on the results of an evaluation, the indicators can help people to better understand how and why changes are made.
- The indicators presented here will help you to learn more about your MPA and the people and resources that are impacted by it.

Go to the beginning of Section 2 to learn more about how the indicators were developed and how they should be used.

influence household occupational structure and enforcement procedures. Also, local values and beliefs about marine resources may influence the level of stakeholder participation in the MPA management process and activities.

*To learn more about how these indicators are conceptually related to each other, visit http://effectiveMPA.noaa.gov/conceptualmodel*

Box 6

## Lessons from Field Tests of the Process

In testing this guidebook, most (82%) of the pilot site teams responded that they found the process of selecting indicators to be useful. A few found it unneccessary to follow the step-by-step process and were able to to match indicators as related to their MPA goals and objectives based on other priorities or methods more suited to their situation.

Also, in working through these steps, several sites reported that their MPAs did not have goals and objectives or found existing ones to be unclear and unmeasurable. They reported that the process of selecting indictors was particularly useful to them because it helped them to identify the need to refine or strengthen their goals and objectives.

To learn more about pilot site testing results, go to http://effectiveMPA.noaa.gov

NOAA Photo Library

***Half of the pilot sites that tested a draft version of this guidebook reported that it needed to be simplified. All sites reported their intention to use it in future.***

Peter Scoones/naturepl.com

*MPAs are increasingly being considered for use offshore, in deeper waters and even beyond Exclusive Economic Zones (EEZs).*

# Planning your evaluation

Conducting a thorough evaluation using the indicators you selected will require planning (see Figure 1, Part 2). This part of the guidebook includes the following steps:

- ❑ **Step 2-1 Assess resource needs for measuring your indicators**
- ❑ **Step 2-2 Determine the audience(s) who will receive the evaluation results**
- ❑ **Step 2-3 Identify who should participate in the evaluation**
- ❑ **Step 2-4 Develop a timeline and a workplan for the evaluation**

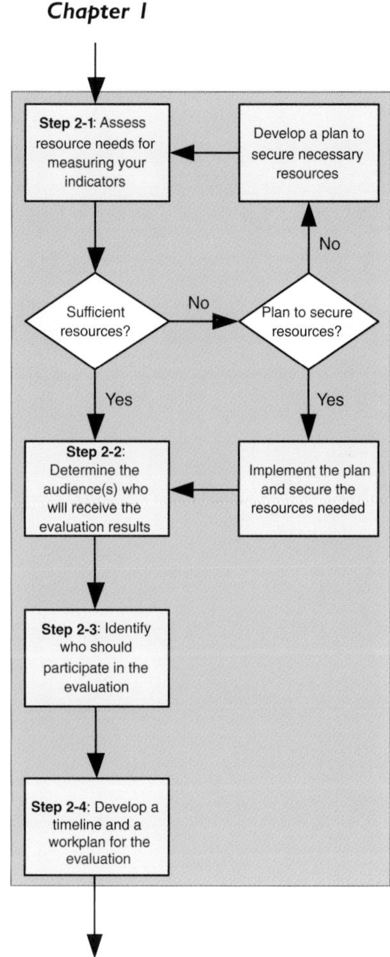


The planning process should be documented in an **evaluation workplan** to provide a record and structure to follow during the evaluation (see Box 7, Developing an Evaluation Workplan).

## *Step 2-1 Assess resource needs for measuring your indicators*

In completing Chapter 1, you selected a set of appropriate indicators and became familiar with them and how to measure them. You now need to estimate the resources required to measure the indicators by completing the following tasks:

### *Task a* Determine the estimated human resources needed to measure and analyse the selected indicators.

For example:

- ❑ How many people will be required to collect data for each indicator?
- ❑ How large an area/population needs to be sampled?
- ❑ How long will it take to complete the evaluation? How much time is needed for each indicator?
- ❑ What level of skills and training are necessary?
- ❑ Do the members of the evaluation team have these skills and training?
- ❑ Will outside technical assistance be required?
- ❑ Which indicators, if any, have similar data collection methods and can be measured concurrently?

### *Task b* Determine the equipment needed to measure and analyse the selected indicators.

For example:

- ❑ What equipment (such as SCUBA gear or hand-held GPS units) and transportation (such as boats, a truck, fuel) are required to measure the indicators?
- ❑ What types of analytical tools (such as **database** and statistical software programmes, or GIS equipment) are needed to generate and analyse results?
- ❑ What types of infrastructure (such as electricity to run computers) are needed on site where the evaluation team will be working?

*To help you, each indicator description in Section 2 contains a list of what is required to measure the indicator. In some cases, measuring an indicator is highly technical and resource intensive. Where appropriate, lower-capacity and cost alternatives are provided.*

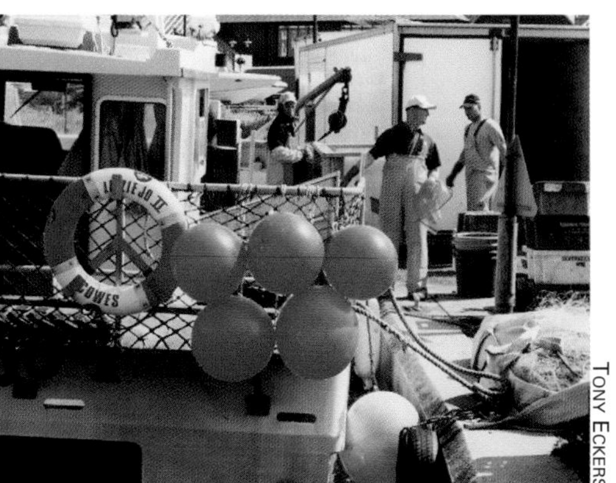

TONY ECKERSLEY

***Task c   Estimate the budget that will be needed for the evaluation.***

For example:

❑ What is the cost of the evaluation team's time?

❑ How much are the consultant and training costs?

❑ What are the equipment and other capital costs?

***Task d   Assess the available human resources, equipment and budget; if not sufficient, develop a plan to secure funds. Secure additional resources as necessary.***

If your MPA has the necessary human and financial resources, and equipment, you can move on to the next step.

If your MPA does not have the necessary human and financial resources, determine if there is a plan to secure these resources. If there is a plan, after you have implemented and achieved it you can move on to the next step.

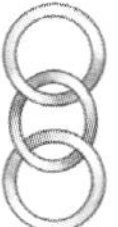

*If you are not ready to undertake this level of evaluation, you can still take steps to work toward adaptive management. Look through the References or go to http://effectiveMPA.noaa.gov for additional references and links.*

**Box 7**

## DEVELOPING AN EVALUATION WORKPLAN

As you work through the chapters in Section 1, you will be gathering information on all aspects of conducting an evaluation. This information will help you to map out what you will need to do from start to finish.

An evaluation workplan should clearly and concisely answer eight planning questions:

- Why is the evaluation being done?
- Who is the audience for the evaluation results?
- Who should participate in the evaluation?
- What methods will be used to measure the indicators?
- What resources (human, financial) are needed to measure these indicators?
- What is the timeline for carrying out the evaluation?
- How are the data to be managed and analysed?
- How will evaluation results be communicated and used for decision-making?

The answers to these questions are pulled together into a single summary workplan document or table. This workplan will help the members of your evaluation team to understand why, how, when, and by whom the evaluation will proceed. Think of it as a map that will allow your evaluation team to get to their final destination – a completed evaluation of management effectiveness at your MPA.

*Be sure to read through all of the guidebook for key information on planning, such as data collection, data analysis, and communications.*

There are a few things to consider when planning your evaluation:

- *Scale* – This guidebook focuses only on conducting evaluations at the single MPA site level, including the immediate surrounding area.
- *System* – Your evaluation will assess the impacts of your MPA on both the natural environment and human aspects at the site.

If you do not have the financial resources or a plan to secure them, you should develop one and implement it. Once you have the necessary resources, you may be in a position to come back to this guidebook.

As you estimate what is required to carry out the evaluation, keep the following in mind:

- ❑ Resource needs will be different at each site, based on factors such as the number of indicators, staff skills, need for outside assistance, and the size of the area.
- ❑ Many of the resources will need to be committed to data collection and analysis.

### *Step 2-2 Determine the audience(s) who will receive the evaluation results*

Before you begin your evaluation, think carefully about the **audience(s)** that you want to reach and develop a plan for communicating and reporting the results. In thinking about this, you may find that there are a number of different audiences.

For example, your primary audience may be whoever requested the evaluation, such as a national agency, programme director, or donor. Keep in mind that there may be others that would find the results useful and that they could bring benefits to your management efforts.

You can determine the most appropriate audiences to receive the evaluation results by completing the following tasks:

#### *Task a Identify the target audience(s).*

To identify the audience(s) for your evaluation results, answer the following questions:

- ❑ Who are the potential audiences that may benefit from or be interested in the evaluation results of your MPA?
- ❑ Which of these audiences are internal stakeholders in the MPA management? Which of these audiences are external to the MPA management?
- ❑ For each audience – what level of influence and interest do they have over the MPA and how it is managed? How important is it for you to stay in communication with each audience?
- ❑ For each audience – what do you know about their preferred method of receiving information? This may be closely related to their technical capacity. For example, do they prefer to read information or listen to a radio or television? Are they computer literate and do they use the Internet regularly? Do they gather together periodically at meetings or conferences? If so, when are these meetings scheduled?
- ❑ What language does each audience speak? What is their average educational level? What style of communications do they prefer – technical and academic or casual and conversational? Where and how are oral communications typically done?

JOHN PARKS

***Audiences vary widely by MPA site and type. Commonly identified audiences (that could be either internal or external audiences, depending on the site) include:***

- Advocacy groups.
- Coastal communities/residents.
- Donors.
- Elected officials.
- Teachers.
- Public.
- Government department heads.
- Native leaders.
- Journalists.
- Fishers.
- Divers and surfers.
- Non-governmental (national, international) organizations.
- Other MPA managers and practitioners.
- Project managers and staff associated with the MPA.
- Researchers and scientists.

Box 8

## Why Think About Communications at the Outset?

For many MPA managers communicating and reporting results is often not given much consideration. The right time to begin thinking about and planning for communications is at the beginning of the MPA evaluation project, not the end of it.

For example, if you understand how your primary audiences take in information you can communicate the evaluation results accordingly and make them more useful. Also, knowing your communications needs at the start of the evaluation will help you to budget for the necessary activities, time and resources.

*The steps to develop a communications plan are discussed in Chapter 4.*

❏ What, specifically, do you expect each audience to do with the results and information you present to them? What actions do you want them to take following the delivery of your results? How are these expectations linked to the goals and objectives of the MPA you are working with?

***Task b Determine and prioritize the primary audience(s).***

You can prioritize primary audiences based on the need to reach them, and how they will use the results, and the types of actions they can take.

*An audience analysis matrix provides a method for identifying and prioritizing the audiences who might be interested in the evaluation results. To learn more about this method, visit http://effectiveMPA.noaa.gov/guidebook/aam.html*

## *Step 2-3 Identify who should participate in the evaluation*

The evaluation team is responsible for planning, implementation and initial analysis. This may or may not include the MPA manager; however it is recommended to have an indiviual who will lead the evaluation and evaluation team.

The following tasks will help you identify who should be involved in conducting the evaluation:

***Task a Determine the level of expertise that is needed to conduct the evaluation.***

The MPA manager and staff, a biologist and a social scientist can do a simple evaluation. A more complex evaluation will require additional people with a diverse set of disciplinary skills, in the fields of marine biology, ecology, oceanography, economics, sociology, anthropology, law and political science.

***Task b Determine which staff or non-staff will conduct the evaluation.***

Some MPAs will not have staff with the full range of disciplinary skills required. As such, external consultants or organizations with the necessary expertise may be required. In this case, determine which parts of the evaluation will be conducted internally versus externally.

There are benefits and limitations with both external and internal evaluators. Table 1 summarises some aspects to consider when deciding who should be involved in the evaluation.

▲ *A large MPA such as the Great Barrier Reef Marine Park in Australia has different needs and resources from a small community-based MPA.*



### *Task c Determine how and when to involve the stakeholders.*

Evaluations should be **participatory** at all stages of the process to capture all issues involved in the management of an MPA. Managers and stakeholders may have very different perspectives on these issues.

Involving stakeholders in the design of the evaluation is crucial because they may be interested in questions that differ from those of the government, managers or scientists. Stakeholders can also be helpful in the data collection and analysis parts of the evaluation process.

For example, local stakeholder participation can provide opportunities for developing stronger relationships between MPA staff and local people. Also, local people may be more aware of cultural complexities and have a natural rapport with others in the community. Training local people to be members of the evaluation team builds capacity and increases the chances that evaluation will continue over time. However, using local people can also create challenges, such as it may be difficult for them to ask certain questions of their neighbours.

*A number of participatory research and action references are available online to assist in planning for stakeholder participation in your evaluation. For more about this, visit http://effectiveMPA.noaa.gov/Bunce.html*

### *Task d Create the evaluation team and determine the people responsible for each task.*

Decide who will lead the evaluation and the responsibilities of each team member based on their skills and experience. Make sure that each member of the evaluation team can complete their activities within the timeline.

Table 1

## Considerations for internal versus external evaluators

| *Internal Evaluators* | *External Evaluators* |
|---|---|
| May have a bias or complex relationships with a community | Often provide impartiality, a fresh perspective, and credibility |
| Have an understanding of the history, experiences and details of the site | May have limited local knowledge, learning is a cost in time and money |
| Often live in or near the site | Usually stay for short visits to the site |
| Tend to focus on issues of relevance to the managers (efficiency and effectiveness of work) | Tend to focus on questions relevant to external groups (stakeholders, funding agencies) |
| May not have all the skills necessary and need technical assistance | Bring technical expertise and perspectives from other sites |
| Are able to enhance the application of results and future work | Take away valuable information, knowledge, perspectives and skills |

*If the members of the evaluation team are not local, they should be briefed on local customs, traditions and behaviours, and particular etiquette so that they can understand as much as possible about the local culture before starting data collection (see http://effectiveMPA.noaa.gov/Bunce.html).*

## Step 2-4 Develop a timeline and a workplan for the evaluation

A timeline should be prepared for the evaluation, identifying specific activities and time periods for starting and completing those activities. A timeline can also provide a means to set up targets and milestones to accomplish along the way. MPA managers and staff have many activities and evaluation is a part of those activities – consider allocating a minimum of 10% of staff time to evaluation annually. Answering the following questions will help you develop a timeline:

### *Task a* Determine the amount of time needed for each activity.

This will depend on the number of indicators selected, the size of your MPA and choice of methods. Consider which indicators have similar methodologies, such as a survey that could be used for several indicators. Also, consider which of these methods are included in existing monitoring programmes at your MPA.

*To see which indicators have similar collection methods see Box 11 in Section 2 on how some of the indicators cluster.*

Consider the amount of data that needs to be collected. This will partly depend on internal and external audience needs and on the type of data being collected.

### *Task b* Determine when the data need to be collected.

Consider factors such as seasonality and frequency. For example, fishing may be seasonal as could the supply of fish for consumption and market needs. There may also be times when it is difficult to do household surveys in a given community because people are away or busy. Data should be collected at the same time of year to ensure comparability over time.

Tony Eckersley

> *The approach to measuring indicators outlined in this guidebook is one that requires periodic but ongoing data collection through time. Some indicators may only need to be measured once every few years, while others may need to be measured once or even twice a year. In either case, planning for the timing of when data are to be collected can be considered in advance by reviewing how often selected indicators are recommended to be measured (see Section 2).*

### *Task c* Develop an evaluation workplan.

Pull together all the components into an evaluation workplan (see Box 7, Developing an Evaluation Workplan). Be sure to include planning elements that are discussed in Chapters 3 and 4. Distribute the evaluation workplan to the evaluation team.

CHAPTER 3 **Conducting your evaluation**

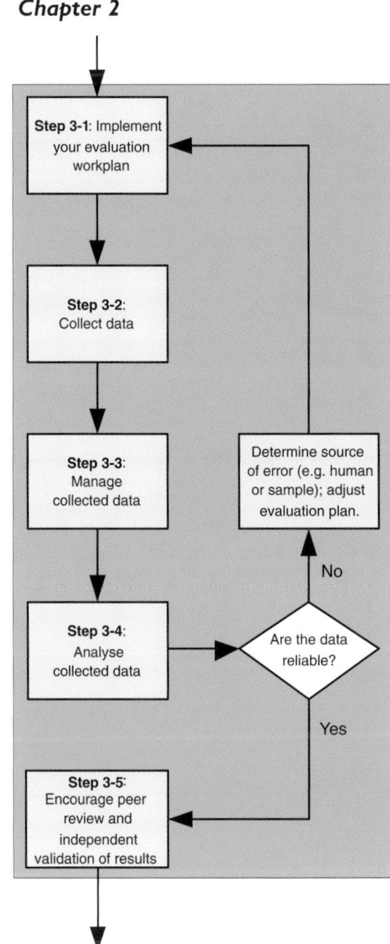


This chapter describes how to collect, manage and analyse the data that are required for conducting your evaluation. The necessary steps, as illustrated in Figure 1, include:

- ❑ **Step 3-1 Implement your evaluation workplan**
- ❑ **Step 3-2 Collect data**
- ❑ **Step 3-3 Manage collected data**
- ❑ **Step 3-4 Analyse collected data**
- ❑ **Step 3-5 Encourage peer review and independent evaluation of results**

## *Step 3-1 Implement your evaluation workplan*

By this point, you have completed an evaluation workplan and have the necessary resources. You are now ready to put it into action and begin your MPA evaluation. Doing this requires much more than just collecting data; it also includes careful consideration as to the timing, logistics and process of data collection, management and analysis.

In implementing the evaluation workplan, the evaluation team must continually consider and be ready to respond to the following questions:

- ❑ Are there timing restrictions? While your evaluation workplan may include considerations on known natural events (e.g. seasons, tides, life history) and social time constraints (e.g. designated national holidays or pre-determined community obligations), the team needs to remain flexible on the timing of its work with respect to unpredictable events that may arise, such as hurricanes, poor water conditions, sudden community emergencies or cancelled flights.
- ❑ Are there new or changing logistical needs? Anticipate and ensure that the necessary logistical arrangements are made and overseen for the evaluation team throughout the implementation of the evaluation. Such arrangements not only relate to fieldwork and data collection, but also to daily needs such as local travel, lodging and meals, access to telephone, fax and e-mail communications, and computer terminals. In some cases, particularly with large evaluation teams who are charged with measuring many indicators, this may require the full-time attention of a logistical officer.
- ❑ Have the resources been made available? Throughout the implementation of the evaluation, the team will need access to the necessary (and previously secured – see Chapter 2) finances and equipment to do data collection. For example, biophysical indicators may require regular access to boats, crew, sampling equipment and fuel. Having safety equipment and finances available for possible medical assistance is also essential. Having someone regularly monitoring that resources are available will allow the evaluation team to focus on the work at hand.
- ❑ Has the team been cleared to do the work? Ensure that all the necessary permits, approvals and permissions are in place to conduct all the work required for the evaluation throughout its duration. Not having the appropriate research and monitoring permits could delay or cancel the work planned for your evaluation.

- ❑ Are you ready to receive the data collected? Ensure that the data collection, management and analysis systems are in place and have been adequately tested and refined. See Steps 3-3 and 3-4 for more details on some of the aspects that will be needed.

ROBERT POMEROY

## *Step 3-2 Collect data*

The following tasks will help you plan for and collect the data.

*The tasks in Step 3-2 need to be considered when planning your evaluation. Key needs for data collection should be addressed in your evaluation workplan. This will help the evaluation team in data collection activities.*

### *Task a Study and understand the data collection methods.*

Data collected are used to answer the specific questions relevant to your evaluation. It is critical that these data are collected accurately. Being trained in, familiar with, and having tested the data collection methods will increase the likelihood that your selected indicators will be measured correctly and consistently. This will help to provide the MPA management team with an accurate and comparable dataset to work with, analyse and refer back to through time.

The methods for measuring the indicators presented in Section 2 have been summarised and simplified. Your MPA may already be monitoring some of the indicators listed, and therefore may have a solid understanding of what is involved in measuring particular indicators. Despite this, keep in mind that for those who have not had relevant training or experience, the data collection methods offered may at first appear challenging. Ideally, your evaluation team will include at least one or two trained and experienced specialists from both the biological and social sciences to conduct the suggested data collection methods.

As discussed in Step 2-2, bringing in external experts can enhance the capacity of the evaluation team. Keep in mind that by building internal capacity to conduct the evaluation it will be easier to continue the evaluation process in the future. Building capacity internally should be done at least several months in advance of the evaluation.

*As discussed within the indicators, many of the biological and social methods require significant experience, time and labour to complete. The evaluation team should review the selected indicators and their methods, be aware of their requirements and difficulty rating, and continually identify and address capacity needs and seek professional assistance well in advance of the start of the evaluation.*

### *Task b Familiarize yourself with the best practices and principles for collecting data in the field.*

The success of data collection efforts will depend in large part on the skills, flexibility and creativity of the evaluation team, as well as on their approach to and the relationships that they establish with the stakeholders involved. For example, some indicators require boat handling and underwater surveys requiring the use of compressed air or mixed gas. In such cases internationally approved and accredited boating navigation and dive safety standards must be followed. This may require training or certification by members within the evaluation team prior to data collection.

***Task c Determine the sampling approach.***

A well-defined sampling approach will ensure that the data collected are accurate and robust. It can provide your team with greater interpretive power and a higher degree of confidence for decision-making.

First, the evaluation team should decide on the sampling units for collecting ecological and social data. For example, the sampling unit for a socio-economic indicator could be an individual, a household or a stakeholder group. Knowing which sampling units are required will help to determine the best approach to data collection.

The following should be considered when developing a sampling approach:

❑ Define the sampling site(s). This should include a spatial definition of the geographic locations within the MPA and nearby local communities, that are being measured. For experimental designs, reference (control) sites outside the MPA or community can be included.

❑ Choose the type of sampling, for example, non-random sampling or random sampling.

❑ When conducting biological surveys, ideally sample within at least three randomly generated replicates at a designated sample site. Maintain similar habitat types and stratify samples along consistent depth/contour profiles. For example, if a biological survey includes two designated sampling sites within the MPA and two designated sites outside the MPA (total of four sites), a minimum of three replicates of the survey must be conducted at random locations within each of these designated sampling sites (12 replicates). The use of replicates is required to minimize variability and increase the confidence level of sampled results reflecting actual conditions. The need and use of replicates within biological surveys is explained further within English *et al.* (1997).

TONY ECKERSLEY

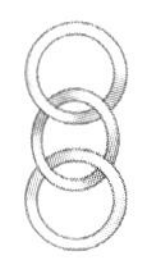

*For additional guidance on sampling approaches go online to http://effectiveMPA.noaa.gov/guidebook/sampling.html. If you are not familiar with sampling or are aiming to conduct statistical analysis on data collected, consult qualified experts prior to implementation.*

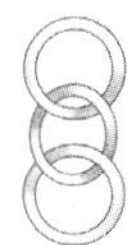

*A list of best practices and guiding principles on how to conduct surveys and interviews is available online at http://effectiveMPA.noaa.gov/guidebook/Bunce.html*

TONY ECKERSLEY

***Task d*** ***Ensure everything is in place for data collection.***

- ❑ Evaluation team is established; each member has clear tasks and training.
- ❑ Evaluation and data collection activities fall within the planned timeline.
- ❑ Logistics, materials and tools are available and ready to use.
- ❑ Sampling unit and area are defined.
- ❑ The measurement methods and techniques (such as interview questionnaires) have been tested.
- ❑ A system to manage, store and analyse information and data is ready for data entry.

## Step 3-3 Manage collected data

Once the selected indicators have been measured the results will need to be processed. This process is commonly referred to as **data management**. This is a critical, and often overlooked, stage of the data collection and analysis process.

Each of the steps in Step 3-3 should be included in the evaluation workplan. This will help the evaluation team understand exactly what happens to data once they have been collected. If the planning information is detailed and not easily summarised, you can create a separate 'data management' document as an appendix to the workplan.

The following tasks provide an overview of the aspects of data management:

***Task a*** ***Determine who will be the 'data manager'.***

Identify a member of the evaluation team to be the 'data manager' who will receive all the collected data for each selected indicator. In some cases this may be the evaluation team leader, or perhaps the same person collecting the relevant information (e.g. the team socio-economist). In other cases there may be a person who is responsible for receiving and handling information, such as a data analyst or a computer specialist.

Tony Eckersley

***Task b*** ***Determine how collected data will be submitted to the data manager.***

This will provide a clear and common understanding for both the person submitting data (data collector) and the person receiving the data (data manager) to know what *type* and in what *form* the data will be submitted. This will greatly improve the accuracy and efficiency of the evaluation.

The *type* of information being collected will depend on the indicator being measured. The types of information include:

- ❑ Numerical (**quantitative**), such as a ranking score, the number of times an organism is observed, a table of numbers, or a total area ($km^2$).
- ❑ Textual (**qualitative**), such as a word, a few sentences, or a story.
- ❑ Graphical, such as a map or a photo.

The *form* in which specific information will be submitted depends on the type of data.

All numerical data may be given to the data manager in the form of a table that the data manager has provided prior to the data collection. Or total areas can be submitted along with the original maps from which the area was calculated.

Textual data may be submitted in the form of a cassette recording, or as an electronic transcript (written) of this recording. Or household survey responses could be original hand-written responses recorded on the data forms or notes taken on notepaper (this would also assume that the data manager has good handwriting recognition skills!).

TONY ECKERSLEY



***Task c Code the data.***

**Data coding** is the process of translating each datum point to prepare for analysis. This translation requires a **code sheet** where the meanings of data collected and their codes are available to the data manager. Identify a member of the evaluation team who will code the data.

In some cases, two or three different words collected as a response to an interview question may be coded (translated) as a single equivalent number. For example, the responses "sometimes", "frequently", and "always" equal "1", whereas "never" equals "0". In other cases, the original datum point and the code may be exactly the same. For example, a numerical ranking ("1", "2", "3") or a single word choice from a respondent survey ("yes", "no") may be the code.

> *As a general rule-of-thumb, collecting data should be done with data coding in mind so as to lessen the amount of coding for the data manager and reduce data management time. The specific data codes should depend entirely on how the data are to be analysed and used. Coding of data should be as simple as possible and, as far as is feasible, it should be consistent.*

***Task d Develop a system for storing and entering the data.***

As each datum point is coded, it should also be entered. **Data entry** is the (often lengthy and tedious) process of moving coded data into a permanent storage location from which to export the data so that it can be analysed. This permanent storage location is known as a **database**.

How data are entered depends on what type of database is being used and the resources, skills and infrastructure available to the evaluation team and data manager. In most cases the data manager will enter coded data generated from the evaluation into a specified, electronic 'MPA management effectiveness' database, using a computer and software. In such cases, coded quantitative data are entered into a spreadsheet or database programme, and coded qualitative and graphic data are entered into a word processing programme. At some sites, a sufficient and appropriate database may be a filing system of paper and folders or a box of index cards kept in a safe place.

© WWF-Canon/Jürgen Freund

*In the case of the evaluation process outlined in this guidebook, a 'MPA management effectiveness' database will need to be created by the evaluation team to permanently store all of the collated, cleaned and coded data for measuring selected indicators.*

*It should be noted that one of the benefits of an electronic database is that it can be easily duplicated (as a backup) and does not take up much physical space (other than a computer).*

Once the system for data entry is developed, begin entering data.

***Task e Collate and review the data set.***

Once data are entered, the data manager is responsible for the collected data and for managing that data.

The data manager collates and reviews the data set in order to check for completeness and errors (accuracy) – this is known as **data cleaning**. If errors (accuracy) or 'gaps' (missing datum points) are found in the data set, the data manager should work with the data collector to correct or understand the problem. In some cases, an incomplete data set will reflect an inability to collect a particular datum point and cannot be filled in afterwards.

***Task f Determine how to make the data available for analysis and sharing.***

The aim of data management is to make retrieving data simple and reliable. Coded and stored data are only as good as the ease with which they can be used for analysis and communication.

Develop a process for someone to contact and request access to data or receive stored information from the data manager and database. Include who is and is not allowed access to the database, and what the responsibilities are of the people who have access.

In some cases the data may be available to anyone, such as on the World Wide Web. In other cases the data may be only accessible to one or two members of the evaluation team.

Include the process and means for making data available to people in the evaluation plan.

## *Step 3-4 Analyse collected data*

Tony Eckersley

Analysis is the process of carefully considering, comparing and contrasting information with the intention of helping to clarify uncertainty or elucidate answers and insight to specific questions being asked. In the case of this guidebook, analysis of data collected during your MPA evaluation will help you to address and respond to the questions that are being asked of the MPA.

Specific analytical tasks for the data collected are dependent on the nature of the information collected and the specified indicator. For each indicator description within Section 2, a few suggested approaches to data analysis are provided to help organize and summarise results.

Results can be viewed in many ways. It is recommended that results be interpreted by a couple of different people and to seek external or expert review as well.

The evaluation workplan should describe which analyses will be done with what data and by whom. Include an explanation of why specific analyses are being done and how they relate to specific questions about the goals and objectives of the MPA and management effectiveness.

The following tasks will help you prepare for and conduct the analysis.

© WWF-Canon/Edward Parker

### *Task a Review the questions being asked by the evaluation.*

A useful starting point in analysis is to go back to your original reason for conducting the evaluation. What are the essential questions that the management team wants to address or fully answer? Make a complete list of these questions, and highlight the ones that are most essential or priorities to address. Which of these questions can be addressed with the evaluation results of which indicators? In most cases, each question will link back to the goals and objectives of the MPA.

### *Task b Complete a preliminary analysis.*

After all data collected have been coded and entered into the database, an explanatory analysis of the data should be completed to investigate their 'strength', or reliability. There are many ways of doing this – the following are common:

- ❑ Simple descriptive analyses of central tendency (median and mode) and variation (range and skewdness) in data collected; and
- ❑ Statistical techniques such as paired **t-tests** and analyses of variance to determine how data sets vary between one another, within a time series or among sites.

Exploratory results address the following:

- ❑ How much variation is there between and within data sets collected inside and outside the MPA?
- ❑ How do data sets compare between one another at different periods of time?
- ❑ How reliably can perceived changes or trends be explained from the data?

If data collected are found to be in error, they should not be used. Identify and address any source of error before continuing the analysis. Common sources of error include both human and sampling error.

### *Task c Determine and prepare analyses.*

Gather all the relevant information obtained throughout the evaluation. This may include data from the database, written notes from evaluation team members, and any results from the preliminary analysis.

Based on the exploratory analysis, you can determine the most appropriate analysis of the data. For example, you may only need to do simple calculations such as sums and percentages. Or, if data are collected from a statistically representative sample, you can apply more advanced descriptive statistics, such as the standard deviation, means and modes, and paired t-tests.

Compare the results of your quantitative analysis with those from other sources and identify any discrepancies and determine why those might have occurred. If a discrepancy cannot be explained, you may need to collect additional data.

You should begin to have an idea of the key results and messages that can be concluded from the analysis. These should help answer the questions and address the objectives of the evaluation.

### *Task d Capture and prepare results.*

When preparing results and conclusions for public dissemination, determine how to orally and visually present results to target audiences, and how to distribute written reports (including graphs and tables of results). For example, with continuous data, spatially plot one set of data (x-axis, as histograms) against another (y-axis). Do any proportional relationships between the data sets appear?

Include stories or anecdotes from stakeholders or the evaluation team that help to illustrate the results.

In some cases, an evaluation team may want to include an **ordinal scale** to help explain the results of an indicator. For example, using a scale of 1–5 to make complex results more easily understood and to observe overall trends. Scorecard methods often present results in this format. There are some downsides to a scaling format in that it can be seen as arbitrary and simplistic; it can take the focus away from interpreting the actual data, and natural background variability makes it difficult to use a scale.

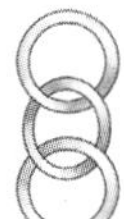

*To learn more about selecting and conducting analyses go to http://effectiveMPA.noaa.gov/guidebook/analyses.html*

Tony Eckersley

## *Step 3-5 Encourage peer review and independent evaluation of results*

It is recommended that you seek out complementary partnerships with research and academic institutions in order to encourage a thorough and independent validation or rejection of the evaluation team's indicator results and analytical findings.

In addition, prior to sharing results with senior management or target audiences, conduct a peer review process of the results and conclusions. Typically, this is a formal process that begins with review by peers who are internal to the evaluation – that is, they are either involved with the evaluation and its process and/or are affiliated closely (e.g. as staff or board members) with the MPA management team that has overseen the evaluation. Ask them to carefully review the evaluation methods, results and findings, and to provide critical and constructive criticism as to how to address any shortcomings, as well as agree with or reject the interpretation and conclusions of the results. In some cases the feedback may require that the evaluation team discard or reconsider certain results or findings and/or go back and re-plan and re-measure certain indicators.

Once an internal review is done, distribute a revised evaluation report for an external review. Select respected and trustworthy experts from both the technical (scientific and policy research) and target audience ends. Invite them to review and comment on the revised evaluation report within an adequate period of time. In some cases, reviewers will be unable to do a review, so prepare a secondary list of reviewers at the outset. It is also important to keep in mind that this external review process may take a bit longer than the internal review. Once you receive comments, have the evaluation team and senior management review them and incorporate changes to the report as appropriate. The end result of a successfully completed internal and external review process is typically an improved product with greater legitimacy and credibility. This will enable you to provide a well-grounded report for target audiences (see Chapter 4).

> *An in-depth peer review process may take as long as four to six months to complete, not counting any revision work or time in re-doing the surveys. It is important that this activity be built into the timeline and workplan.*

DAVID HALL/NATUREPL.COM

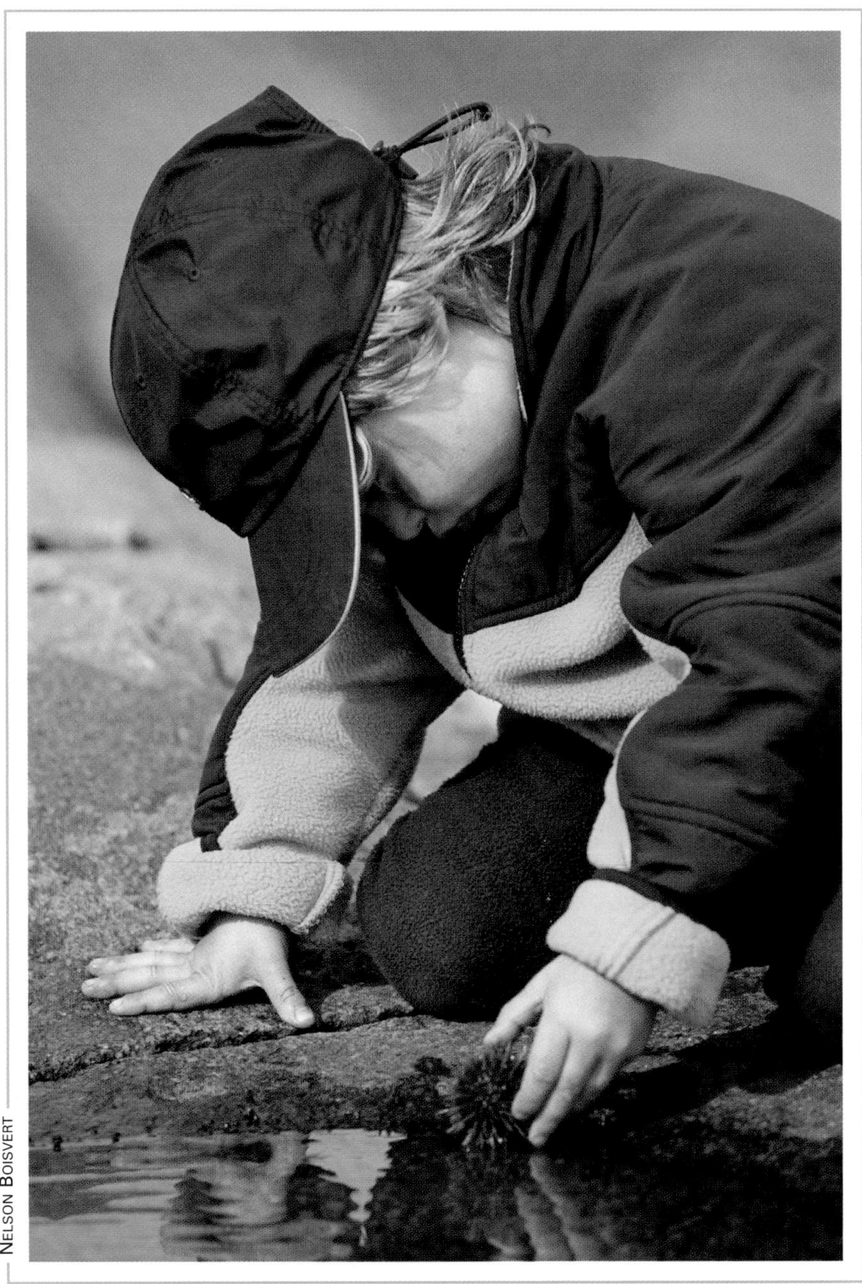

NELSON BOISVERT

*Communicating results can bring new friends and allies to the MPA – including the next generation, vital if MPAs are to survive in an uncertain future.*

# CHAPTER 4 Communicating results and adapting management

This chapter will guide you through the steps needed to take the results from the evaluation and develop an adaptive management strategy. The strategy includes sharing the results and analysis with the identified target audiences and identifying ways to adapt management practices to improve MPA management. These two activities will make the data collection and analyses worthwhile and give them a practical purpose.

The steps taken to communicate results and adapt MPA management practices are illustrated in Figure 2, as follows:

- ❏ **Step 4-1 Share results with target audiences**
- ❏ **Step 4-2 Use results to adapt management strategies**

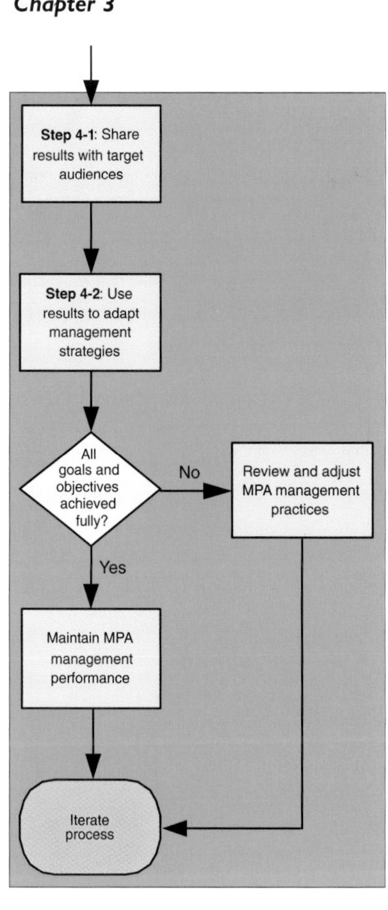


## Step 4-1 Share results with target audiences

To share results with target audiences complete the following tasks:

### Task a Determine which format to use to provide evaluation results and to reach the target audience most effectively.

Use the prioritized target audiences and characteristics that were identified in Chapter 2, Step 2-2. The results of your survey on how target audiences prefer to receive information will help you develop a logical presentation and format (one-way and/or two-way communications) for sharing the evaluation results with the target audiences.

There are several ways to transmit information to people. These include both one-way and two-way communication mechanisms, as presented in Table 2.

**Table 2**

**Types of one- and two-way communication that MPA practitioners can use to communicate the results of their MPA effectiveness evaluation**

| *One-way communications* | *Two-way communications* |
|---|---|
| Written materials (reports, papers) | Group discussion (in-person) |
| Visual materials (posters, pictures) | One-on-one discussion (in-person) |
| Oral presentations (in-person) | Physical and electronic bulletin boards |
| Mass media: newspapers, magazines, radio, television, film | Remote communications: telephone, video phone, web camera |
| Internet: World Wide Web | Internet: e-mail and Internet chat rooms |

*The evaluation workplan should include the main points and concepts in the communications plan (see Box 9, Pulling the pieces together into a Communications Plan). This will ensure that the necessary planning has been done for the coordination and the timing of sharing results with target audiences. You may want to add the communications plan as an appendix to the evaluation workplan as a reference for the evaluation team.*

NOAA Photo Library

In some cases the ideal presentation format may require assistance from communications specialists such as editors, graphic artists, publication designers, journalists and news agencies, community leaders, professional facilitators, lobbyists, statisticians, and Internet and digital solution technicians.

Once you have identified an appropriate format or set of formats for transmitting results to each target audience, list these formats within the audience analysis matrix.

***Task b   Develop a strategy and a timeline for delivery of results.***

A **results delivery strategy** outlines exactly how to conduct the presentation formats identified and assigned to target audiences. Develop a timeline of when to release or deliver these messages using the various presentation formats. This timeline will depend on the type of formats and style in which results are delivered.

Consider how to make the presentation formats most meaningful and thought provoking to your target audiences and include this in your results delivery strategy. For example, what language, tone, style of text, and voice (i.e. passive or active) will most resonate with the target audience?

The results delivery strategy should include which messages and what formats will be used to communicate with different target audiences. Use the audience analysis matrix to identify outreach opportunities.

For example:

- ❑ Is there a particular format that can be used to communicate results to multiple target audiences?
- ❑ Which communication formats should come before others? What is the timing of sharing results both internally and externally?
- ❑ Are there certain communication formats that should be presented simultaneously or within a restricted timeframe?

***Task c   Tell your story! Communicate your findings to the stakeholders.***

This process is referred to as **messaging** – in other words, what story do you want to share with the target audiences? Because the specific content of these messages will not be known until after the evaluation is complete, messaging requires two distinct activities and timeframes.

*A useful discussion of results presentation formats commonly used by conservation practitioners can be found in Margolius and Salafsky (1998).*

- ❑ At the start of the evaluation, prior to obtaining the results – identify the themes and concepts of the marine environment and how it is managed that target audiences are both known to listen to and will want to hear about when results are available. Select the priority messages to share with target audiences.
- ❑ After obtaining the results – identify the results that relate to the priority messages (previously identified) and how they address the themes and concepts that target audiences want to know about.

Messaging allows the evaluation team and MPA managers to keep in mind the critical pieces of information that target audiences will be looking for during the evaluation and as results are generated. For example, look for interesting or illustrative stories that can be used after the evaluation to support or contradict the results. Also, highlight results with real-world examples, stories, and anecdotes – these can be powerful tools with certain audiences to build interest in results and enhance an MPA manager's ability to communicate important messages.

For example, an important message that could be identified and shared with a commercial fishing target audience may be that the MPA is replenishing fish stocks. Having a story of a fishermen saying that he or she is now catching more fish in the MPA/near the MPA/since the MPA was established, will support the quantitative evidence that there is a three-fold increase in fish populations inside the MPA compared to outside. This will make for a much stronger message than only presenting the numbers.

A strategic approach to messaging is to ensure that key messages are communicated in a way that encourages action or behaviour that is desired by

**Box 9**

### Pulling the pieces together into a Communications Plan

The information from the different steps to be undertaken to communicate results can then be used to create a communications plan. This will provide a clear process of how results will be shared and logically and strategically organized.

Think of a communications plan as a 'cheat-sheet' of how to best share your stories. A complete communications plan will contain the following elements:

- An *audience analysis matrix* (see Chapter 2) identifying the range of possible internal and external audiences, their characteristics, and a set of *priority target audiences.*
- A strategy for how and where results will be delivered by identifying which *one-way and two-way presentation formats* will be used with each or groups of target audiences, and the *approach and style of delivery* to be taken.
- A set of *key messages* with illustrative examples and stories that explain the results and that help to focus the attention of particular target audiences.
- A *timeline* of when messages and presentation formats are to be released and delivered to target audiences.

Once these pieces of the plan are pulled together, it will be possible to estimate the time, and human and financial resources needed to complete the plan. Based on this estimate, sufficient time and budgeted resources can be allocated. The resources should be available if the necessary resources were secured at the outset of the evaluation (see Chapter 2).

the MPA manager. The proof that key messages have been successfully communicated is how the target audience takes action after the messages have been delivered.

Put all the pieces together into a communications plan (see Box 9), and put it in motion.

TONI PARRAS

### *Step 4-2 Use results to adapt management strategies*

Adaptive management can be defined as the process of integrating design, management and monitoring to systematically test assumptions, learn and adapt (Salafsky *et al.*, 2001). The idea is that by asking specific questions (testing assumptions), you learn and get results to help make informed decisions and adapt your actions, which can lead to improved performance. This process of asking questions, collecting information to answer them, learning from the results, and adapting behaviour and practices is a cyclical one, that in theory should allow a person or group to increasingly hone in on and refine their abilities and impact with each subsequent revolution through the adaptive management cycle. This creates a positive feedback loop that continually improves on itself as it moves closer to its ultimate goal and sustains itself there. The principle of adaptive management is widely accepted and frequently cited not only within natural resource management and environmental conservation, but also within business, health and human services, public service, and development.

For the purposes of this guidebook, the reason for conducting a management effectiveness evaluation is for MPA staff and decision-makers to use the information generated to adapt and improve the MPA's management, planning, accountability and overall impact. Once results are shared with target audiences, such information can be combined with other data sources and decision-making needs for MPA management processes and underlying contextual issues. Such integration is done in order to enhance the power and relevance of decisions made on future actions and the management strategy.

How information and learning provided by the evaluation process are used by target audiences to adapt management must also be monitored as part of an iterative evaluation process. Observations on how results are eventually used will help design future evaluations.

*The evaluation workplan should include an outline for a strategy applying results so as to adapt and improve ongoing management.*

*There are many good references on adaptive management available, including: Walters, 1986; Hollings, 1978; Hilborn and Walters, 1992; Gunderson, Hollings and Light, 1995; and Salafsky* et al.*, 2001; these are listed in the References.*

Adaptive management is essentially about iteration. That is, repeating the process or steps that bring you successively closer to your desired result. Iteration involves using the results of your evaluation to improve your MPA management. It helps management to adapt and improve through a learning process. As you evaluate the MPA you may find that you are successfully achieving your goals and objectives and that no changes are needed. Or, you may find that things are not going as well as they could and you will need to make some changes.

***Some things to consider when incorporating evaluation results into ongoing planning and the management decision-making process***

- ❏ Complement the evaluation results with other information about the MPA in the decision-making process.
- ❏ Maintain flexibility and be prepared to make changes. If your evaluation reveals that something is not working, find mechanisms to make changes.
- ❏ Be willing to learn from both success and failure, as it will help to strengthen your MPA.
- ❏ Use your common sense, your past experience, and the information that is available to you to make decisions.
- ❏ Use tools for negotiating, reaching agreements, and securing commitments to take actions when deciding to make changes based on evaluation results.
- ❏ Determine the best way to make changes in a participatory manner, such as holding workshops with different stakeholder groups.

***What if the results are not useful?***

There may be cases in which the results that you have obtained from the evaluation are not useful. What can be done? There are several courses of action:

- ❏ Check the data collected and the methods used to ensure that they make sense. Were the correct methods used and used in the correct way for each indicator? Was the data entered correctly? Were the right people interviewed?
- ❏ Review the priority goals and objectives to make sure that they really were the ones that are important to your MPA and revise them as needed.
- ❏ Review the indicators that were selected to ensure that they match the most important goals and objectives and revise them as needed.
- ❏ Return to the evaluation plan and revise it according to adjusted and/or new data collection needs. Make sure that the resources are available to collect this data.
- ❏ Resume data collection using a revised set of indicators and a revised evaluation plan.

TONI PARRAS

Measuring, presenting and discussing the indicators in this guidebook will help you to learn more about your MPA and the people and resources which are impacted by it. The indicators can provide information that can be used in the decision-making process and in working with stakeholders to understand necessary changes in management plans and practices.

> *If the evaluation team finds new ways of applying the indicators in this guidebook to an MPA, take detailed notes of how this was done and why. This can then be shared with other MPA managers and evaluation teams.*

## Other considerations

### Using this guidebook to inform new MPAs

The results of the evaluation and lessons learnt can be shared with other people, with other MPAs, and with the broader conservation and development community. The world is interested in you! New MPAs will be developing and the more that they can learn from your experiences, the better they can plan, the less it will cost, and the sooner they can get up and running. It takes years and even decades to demonstrate impacts. However, incremental learning is a part of adaptive management and can be important new knowledge that is quickly transferred to others. In documenting outcomes, a common mistake is to focus only on success and to ignore or hide failures. Everyone can learn from difficulties and others may have faced the same difficulties. By sharing lessons learned everyone benefits (Margolius and Salafsky, 1998).

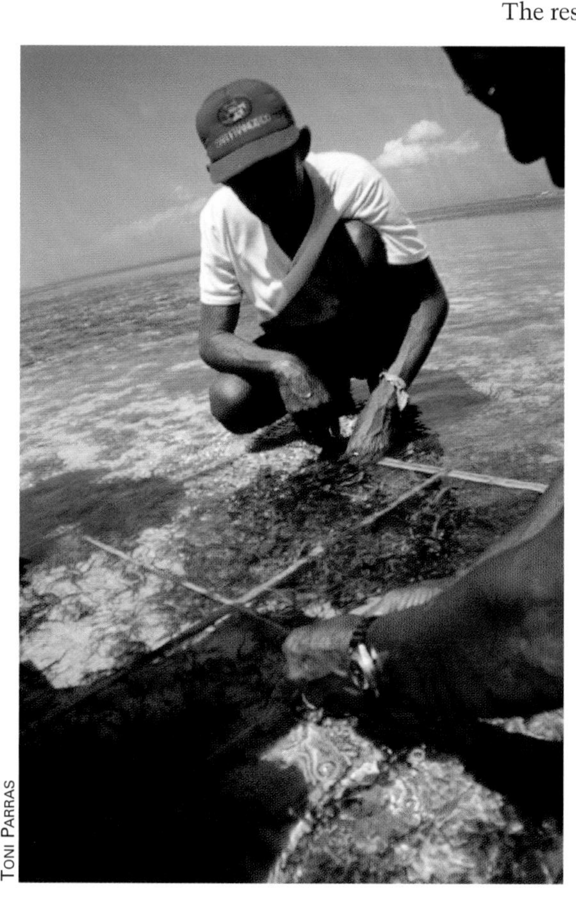

Toni Parras

### Applying management effectiveness evaluations to systems and networks of MPAs

More and more attention is being given to the concept of systems or networks of MPAs in an area or throughout a region or country. One reason for multiple MPAs is to have a representative sample of the types of habitats and organisms that need to be protected. A network also needs to be designed in a way that is socially feasible and acceptable. In the case of networks, using standardized indicators across multiple MPAs in the same area will encourage a more holistic and integrative approach to evaluating how such networked sites are interacting and achieving a common set of goals and objectives. MPA managers working within a network are encouraged to use this guidebook as a common foundation on which to share skills, resources and results. The benefits of this approach can help minimize costs, maximize impacts and build capacity to increase learning and improve MPA management across a network of sites.

### Communicating through MPA systems and networks

Evaluation results should be integrated into national MPA systems, frameworks or national marine conservation strategies where applicable. Learning should be actively shared within the network of other national MPA sites and MPA practitioners.

# References. Works cited in Section 1 and other useful materials


## Marine Protected Areas (including management and evaluation)

Alder, J., Zeller, D., Pitcher, T.J. and Sumaila, U.R. (2002). "A method for evaluating marine protected area management". *Coastal Management* 30(2): 121–131.

Agardy, T. (2000). "Information needs for marine protected areas: scientific and societal". *Bulletin of Marine Science* 66(3): 875–888.

Agardy, T.S. (1997). *Marine Protected Areas and Ocean Conservation.* Academic Press, San Diego, CA and R. E. Landes Co., Austin, TX, USA.

Agardy, M.T. (1995). *The Science of Conservation in the Coastal Zone: new insights on how to design, implement, and monitor marine protected areas.* IUCN Marine Conservation and Development Report. IUCN, Gland, Switzerland and Cambridge, UK.

Day, J.C. (2002). "Marine Park Management and Monitoring: Lessons for adaptive management from the Great Barrier Reef". *In* S. Bondrup-Nielsen, N.W.P. Munro, G. Nelson, J.H. Martin Willison, T.B. Herman and P. Eagles (eds.), *Managing Protected Areas in a Changing World.* SAMPA IV, Wolfville, Canada.

Kelleher, G. (1999). *Guidelines for Marine Protected Areas.* IUCN, Gland, Switzerland and Cambridge, UK.

Kelleher, G., Bleakley, C. and Wells, S. (eds.) (1995). *A Global Representative System of Marine Protected Areas.* The Great Barrier Reef Marine Park Authority, The World Bank, IUCN, Washington, DC, USA.

Kelleher, G. and Kenchington, R. (1992). *Guidelines for Establishing Marine Protected Areas.* A Marine Conservation and Development Report. IUCN, Gland, Switzerland.

Kenchington, R.A. (1990). *Managing Marine Environments.* Taylor and Francis, New York, NY, USA.

Mangubhai, S. and Wells, S. (2004, in draft). *Assessing Management Effectiveness of Marine Protected Areas: A workbook for the Western Indian Ocean.* IUCN, Eastern Africa Regional Programme.

Roberts, C. and Hawkings J. (2000). *A Manual for Fully-Protected Areas.* World Wide Fund for Nature, Gland, Switzerland.

Salm, R.V., Clark, J.R., Siirila, E. (2000). *Marine and Coastal Protected Areas: A Guide for Planners and Managers (3rd Edition).* IUCN, Washington, DC, USA.

Sumaila, U.R. (2002). "Marine protected area performance in a model of the fishery". *Natural Resource Modeling* 15(4): 439–451.

## Management Effectiveness

Hockings, M., Stolton, S. and Dudley, N. (2000). *Evaluating Effectiveness: A Framework for Assessing the Management of Protected Areas.* IUCN, Gland, Switzerland and Cambridge, UK.

Jameson, S.C., Tupper, M. and Ridley J. (2002). "The three screen doors: can marine protected areas be effective?" *Marine Pollution Bulletin* 44: 1177–1183.

## Selecting Environmental Indicators (Chapter 1)

Dixon, J., Kunte A. and Pagiola S. (1996). *Environmental Performance Indicators.* World Bank Environment Department Note. The World Bank, Washington, DC, USA.

Hammond, A., Adriaanse, A., Rodenburg, E., Bryant, D. and Woodward R. (1995). *Environmental Indicators: A Systematic Approach to Measuring and Reporting on Environmental Policy Performance in the Context of Sustainable Development.* World Resources Institute, Washington, DC, USA.

Hunsaker, C.T. and Carpenter D.E. (1990). *Ecological Indicators for the Environmental Monitoring and Assessment Program.* EPA 600/3-90/060. United States Environmental Protection Agency, Office of Research and Development, Research Triangle Park, NC, USA.

Thomas, W.A. (ed.) (1972). *Indicators of environmental quality.* Plenum Press, New York, NY, USA.

Tunsdall, D., Hammond, A. and Henniger, N. (1994). *Developing Environmental Indicators: A report on the World Resources Institute Workshop on Global Environmental Indicators, December 7–8 1992.* The World Resources Institute, Washington, DC, USA.

World Bank (1996). *Performance Monitoring Indicators: a handbook for task managers.* The World Bank, Washington, DC, USA.

## Developing Monitoring and Evaluation Plans (Chapter 2)

Campbell, R.A., Mapstone, B.D. and Smith, A.D.M. (2001). "Evaluating large-scale experimental designs for management of coral trout on the Great Barrier Reef". *Ecological Applications* 11(6): 1763–1777.

Munn, R.E. (1988). "The design of integrated monitoring systems to provide early indications of environmental/ecological changes". *Environmental Monitoring and Assessment* 11: 203–217.

Margolius, R.A. and Salafsky, N. (1998). *Measures of Success: designing, managing, and monitoring conservation and development projects.* Island Press, Washington, DC, USA.

## *Data Collection and Analysis (Chapter 3)*

Bunce, L., Townsley, P., Pomeroy, R. and Pollnac, R. (2000). *Socioeconomic Manual for Coral Reef Management.* Australian Institute for Marine Science, Townsville, Queensland, Australia.

Clarke, K.R. and Warwick R.M. (2001). *Change in marine communities: An Approach to Statistical Analysis and Interpretation. 2nd edition.* Primer-E, Plymouth, UK.

Elliot J.M. (1977). "Some methods for statistical analysis of benthic invertebrates". *Freshw. Biol. Assoc. Sci. Publ., U.K.* 25: 1–156.

English, S., Wilkinson, C. and Baker, V. (eds.) (1997). *Survey Manual for Tropical Marine Resources. 2nd Edition.* Australian Institute for Marine Science, Townsville, Queensland, Australia.

Fairweather, P.G. (1991). "Statistical power and design requirements for environmental monitoring". *Australian Journal of Marine and Freshwater Research* 42: 555–567.

Green, R.H. (1979). *Sampling Design and Statistical Methods for Environmental Scientists.* John Wiley and Sons, New York, NY, USA.

Green, R.H. (1989). "Power analysis and practical strategies for environmental monitoring". *Environmental Research* 50: 195–205.

Hilborn, R. and Walters, C.J. (1992). *Quantitative Fisheries Stock Assessment: Choice, dynamics, and uncertainty.* Chapman and Hall, New York, NY, USA.

Margolius, R.A. and Salafsky, N. (1998). *Measures of Success: designing, managing, and monitoring conservation and development projects.* Island Press, Washington, DC, USA.

McAllister, M.K. and Petermen, R.M. (1992). "Experimental design in management of fisheries: a review". *N. Am. J. Fish. Manage* 3: 586–605.

Schaeffer, D.J., Herricks, E.E. and Kerster, H.W. (1988). "Ecosystem health: measuring ecosystem health". *Environmental Management* 12: 445–455.

Stewart-Oaten, A.W. (1995). "Problems in the analysis of environmental monitoring data". *In* R.J. Schmitt and C.W. Osenburg, *Design of Ecological Impact Assessment Studies: Conceptual Issues and Application in Coastal Marine Habitats.* Academic Press, San Diego, USA. pp. 109–132.

Underwood, A.J. (1995). "On beyond BACI: sampling designs that might reliably detect environmental disturbances". *In* R.J. Schmitt and C.W. Osenburg, *Design of Ecological Impact Assessment Studies: Conceptual Issues and Application in Coastal Marine Habitats.* Academic Press, San Diego. pp. 151–178.

## *Adaptive Management (Chapter 4)*

Gunderson, L.H., Hollings, C.S. and Light, S.S. (1995). *Barriers and Bridges to the Renewal of Ecosystems.* Columbia University Press, New York, USA.

Hollings, C.S. (ed.) (1978). *Adaptive environmental assessment and management.* John Wiley and Sons, New York, NY, USA.

Lee, K. (1993). *Compass and Gyroscope: integrating science and politics for the environment.* Island Press, Washington, DC, USA.

Lee, K. (1999). "Appraising adaptive management". *Conservation Ecology* 3(2). [Online URL:www.consecolo.org/Journal/vol3/iss2/index.html]

Oglethorpe, J. (ed.) (2002). *Adaptive Management: From Theory to Practice.* SUI Technical Series, Vol. 3. IUCN, Gland, Switzerland.

Salafsky, N., Margolius, R. and Redford, K. (2001). *Adaptive Management: a tool for conservation practitioners.* Biodiversity Support Program, Washington, DC, USA.

Walters, C.J. (1986). *Adaptive Management of Renewable Resources.* MacMillian Publishing Company, New York, NY, USA.

Walters, C.J. (1997). "Challenges in adaptive management of riparian and coastal ecosystems. *Conservation Ecology* 1(2). [Online URL: www.consecol.org/Journal/vol1/iss2/index.html]

Walters, C. J. and Hilborn, R. (1978). "Ecological optimization and adaptive management". *Annual Review of Ecology and Systematics* 9: 157–188.

Walters, C. J. and Holling, C.S. (1990). "Large-scale management experiments and learning by doing". *Ecology* 71: 2060–2068.

# SECTION 2 *The MPA management effectiveness indicators*

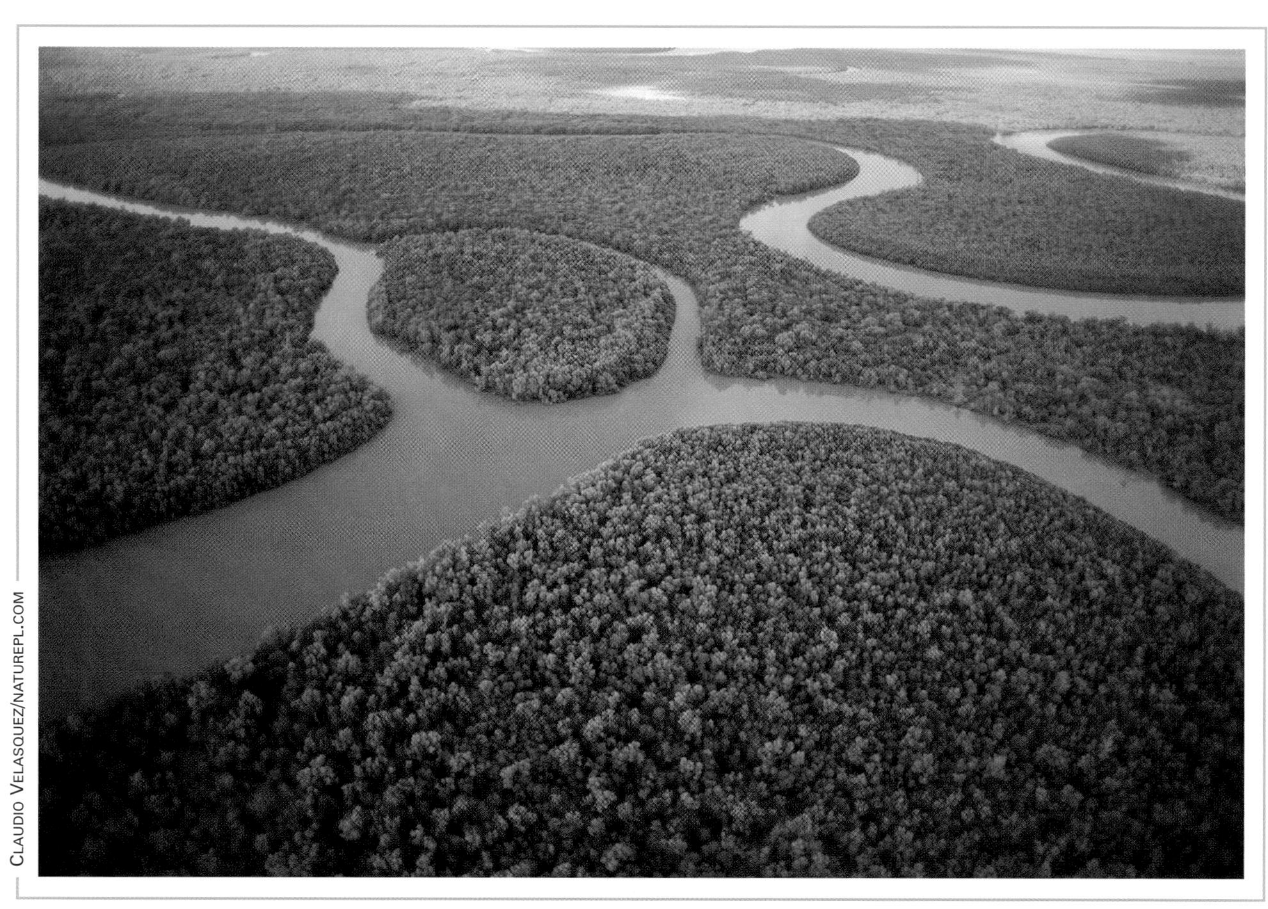
Claudio Velasquez/naturepl.com

*Mangroves, as seen above in Antsiranana, Madagascar, are vital breeding areas for fish and help prevent coastal erosion. Yet many mangrove forests are inadequately protected, leading to reduced success of MPAs.*

# The MPA management effectiveness indicators

## Introduction

There are 42 indicators presented in this Section: 10 biophysical, 16 socio-economic and 16 governance indicators. To make these indicators applicable to a range of MPA goals and objectives, the indicators were developed through a rigorous two-year process of research, expert review and field-testing, and revision.

To be useful and practical, the indicators were developed to meet several criteria. These criteria can be used to select the most appropriate indicators for your site, especially since a given goal or objective can have one or multiple indicators. Following best practices, a good indicator meets five criteria (see Margolius and Salafsky, 1998):

Measurable: Able to be recorded and analysed in quantitative or qualitative terms.

Precise: Defined the same way by all people.

Consistent: Not changing over time so that it always measures the same thing.

Sensitive: Changing proportionately in response to actual changes in the attribute or item being measured.

Simple: Simple indicators are generally preferred to complex ones.

*To learn more about how the indicators were developed (including the process and timeline) go to http://effectiveMPA.2.gov/guidebook/ background.html*

## The difficulty rankings

Each indicator has a difficulty rating. This is to help you understand the relative ease with which the specified indicator can be measured using the most basic methods recommended (in some cases, more complex methods would reflect another one or two points in the difficulty ranking). This ranking takes into account the time, technical skills, finances and other resources necessary to measure the indicator.

1 – the indicator is easy to measure
2 – the indicator is fairly easy to measure
3 – measurement of the indicator requires moderate effort
4 – the indicator is fairly hard to measure
5 – the indicator is hard to measure

Box 10

### Using the Indicators

| *Heading* | *Meaning* |
|---|---|
| Name | Number and name of the indicator. |
| Goal and objective | Which goals and objectives this indicator corresponds with (relating to the larger generic list of MPA goals and objectives developed by the project). |
| Difficulty rating | A rank of how difficult the indicator is to measure (see above). |
| What is "(indicator name)"? | Brief description of the indicator. |
| Why measure it? | The purpose and rationale of the indicator. |
| Requirements | Resources (people, equipment) needed to collect and analyse the information. |
| How to collect the data | The method and approach used to collect information on the indicator. |
| How to analyse and interpret the results | The methods and procedures to analyse the data and suggestions on how to present the results. |
| Outputs | What are the results and how can they be used by the MPA? |
| Strengths and limitations | How useful is the indicator overall and what problems may occur in using the indicator? |
| Example from the field | An example of use of the indicator. |
| Useful references and Internet links | Suggested sources of information on methods, and further explanation of the indicator. |

## *Maximizing time and resources*

Depending on which indicators you have selected, some may be collected concurrently. This requires that either a) the exact same data are collected for two or more indicators, or b) the same or similar methods are used to collect different data for two or more indicators. The box below shows clusters of indicators that could be measured or collected together.

Box 11

### INDICATOR CLUSTERS

***Biophysical clusters***

- B1, B2 – same data collected on focal species counts and lengths.
- B1, B4 – same methods used to measure relative abundance.
- B1, B4, B7 – similar data collected on catch landings and target species.
- B2, B5 – similar methods used to measure recruits.
- B1, B2, B3, B4, B5 – similar survey approach and methods used.
- B1, B3 – similar data collected on habitat utilization.
- B4, B6 – both look at community composition.
- B10, B1 – B8, S3, S1, S5, S10, G1, G4, G14 – all look at human impacts.
- B10, B7 – both look at spill over effects on human activities.
- B7, B4, B6 – all look at trophic levels.
- B9, B10 – similar methods for aerial measures.

***Socio-economic indicator clusters***

- S2, S3, S6, S9, S10, S13, S14 – data can be collected from a household survey.
- S8, S11 – data can be collected from a key informant survey.

***Governance indicator clusters***

- G2, G3, G6, G7, G9, G14, G15, G16 – data are collected from interviews with MPA managers and/or staff.

Please note that while the other governance indicators all require interviews of stakeholders, there are different groups of stakeholders for each indicator.

NOAA PHOTO LIBRARY

# The biophysical indicators

## *Introduction*

Regardless of their many social benefits and aims, MPAs are ultimately a tool for conserving the biophysical conditions of our oceans and coasts. As such, using indicators to measure these conditions is typically of primary interest to managers whose job it is to evaluate the effectiveness of an MPA.

In most cases, the link between the biological state of the marine environment and the livelihoods, income and food security of the people who use and depend upon the resource is explicit and intimate. It then follows that beyond characterizing natural systems, the measurement of biophysical indicators can also be useful when viewed in the context of the socio-economic and governance conditions that operate in and around the MPA. For example, the biological goods (such as fish) and ecological services (such as nutrient cycling) generated from effectively managed MPAs can be thought of in financial terms, where the MPA is a 'bank account' that preserves the natural 'capital' that society depends upon for the future. If this natural capital is left alone and allowed to grow over time, the 'income' generated from this 'principal' may be able to provide ecological goods and services that are of immediate use to people while also offering them future security. Without MPAs, too much of this natural capital may be 'spent' by society, draining away the 'principal' over time. In this regard, six of the biophysical indicators (B1, B2, B3, B4, B6, and B8) can be used to measure how much 'principal' is reserved and available, while the other four (B5, B7, B9, and B10) examine the degree of 'income' that may be influenced as a result of the MPA.

The 10 biophysical indicators included in this guidebook fall into one of three groupings: biotic, abiotic and aerial. The first six indicators (B1 – B6) are used to assess the biotic context in and around the MPA. B1 and B2 are used to examine the status of populations of species. Measurement of these two indicators is moderately difficult, depending on how large the area to be sampled is and how easy it is to observe or catch the organisms to be surveyed. B3 to B6 are used to characterize ecological conditions, and while important, are among the most challenging of all the indicators to measure. In particular, B5 and B6 require a level of capacity, time and labour that may be out of reach of many MPAs around the world. There was much debate and consideration about whether to eliminate B6 because of its complexity and questionable ability to demonstrate effective management in many large, multiple-use MPAs. In the end, consensus was reached to keep B6 because managers and experts felt that better understanding and addressing trophic relationships was critical to the successful design and use of MPAs.

> *Note that the biotic indicators (esp. B1, B2, and B3) rely heavily upon the comparison of data collected from within and outside the MPA. An appropriate approach to sampling in both areas must therefore be ensured.*

B7 is a quasi-biotic indicator that measures the level of some of the biological goods that are generated from the marine environment (both inside and outside the MPA). B7 gauges trends in fisheries exploitation methods, yield, and effort as a reflection of how productive and healthy the exploited stocks are.

B8 is the only indicator offered in this guidebook that is used to assess the abiotic conditions of the marine environment.

Finally, B9 and B10 are spatially defined measures of observed biophysical change. Inclusion of these two 'aerial' indicators within the biophysical category was debated at length throughout their development and testing. Despite being the most closely linked to issues of MPA governance and requiring the collection of similar data, because the direct aim of B9 and B10 is to characterize the biological condition of the MPA, they were not moved into the governance indicator category.

Not all of the indicators will be appropriate for use in every MPA. Some indicators require a higher level of skill, labour, financing, and time to measure than others. Where possible, low-cost, basic methods have been provided for even the most challenging indicators, although such measures can be descriptive, highly subjective, and therefore less accurate and reliable.

> *All but two (B6 and B9) of the biophysical indicators were successfully tested by volunteer MPA sites. Although many of the eight other sets of measures were challenging, their results were nonetheless reported to be of use to the evaluation teams who tested them so as to gauge and report to what degree they were successful in furthering the achievement of the stated biophysical objectives of their MPAs.*

> *Note that in some cases, measurement of the biophysical conditions in and around an MPA may not necessarily demonstrate management effectiveness because it may be outside the influence of even an ideally-managed MPA and beyond the control of its managers. In such cases, these indicators can be used to illustrate this point, allowing managers to openly communicate with decision-makers,*

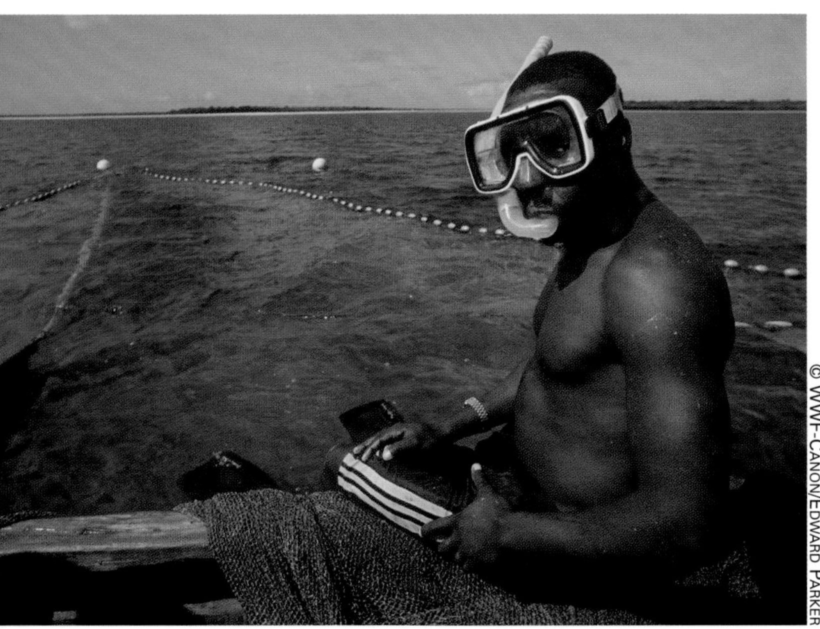


As at 11 other MPA pilot sites, several of the biophysical indicators were tested during 2002 and 2003 at Mafia Island Marine Park in Tanzania. Here a WWF officer tests a new net mesh on Mafia Island.

*the public and donors that influencing some of the environmental conditions may be beyond the ability of the MPA and management team.*

Attempting to adequately but succinctly summarise the numerous monitoring and assessment methodologies available for use by the evaluation team to measure biophysical attributes was not an easy undertaking for the contributors and authors. As most of these methods are thoroughly documented in the scientific literature, the biophysical indicators cannot and do not attempt to review them all. Rather, the indicator descriptions presented here deliberately focus on summarising several of the most basic, widely accepted and actively used methods in practice. A similar approach has been to introduce analytical considerations for the data collected. A few of the more advanced data collection and analysis techniques are acknowledged in the references, but are not the focus of the material summarised in this guidebook.

Also, much consideration was given to whether or not to standardize the methods and citation for measurement of the biophysical indicators, thereby not allowing for methodological choices made by the reader. In the end, most reviewers, test sites and contributors agreed that allowing for multiple measurement options would be the most flexible and inclusive approach given: a) the reality of how site-specific the biophysical characteristics of most MPAs are, and b) the fact that evaluation teams will have differing levels of capacity and access to resources. As a result, this guidebook does not advocate that one method of indicator measurement be used over another. The responsibility to choose the 'right' method is placed on the evaluation team, who is encouraged to use its expertise, judgement and site familiarity to decide which method would be best suited for exploration and use at their MPA given the specifics of the organisms, communities and environment being assessed.

*Note that the basic methods offered for measuring indicators are only a starting point. They may not always provide reliable or adequate evidence as to how effectively your MPA is operating. Rather, the methods listed are offered as a first attempt to assess some of the fundamental biophysical conditions in and around an MPA. Thus, these methods should not be seen as a finite list of how to measure such conditions. In some cases, the methods offered are still undergoing testing and review, continually being refined.*

*Don't celebrate or panic too soon after the results come in! Only through cautious and consistent observation and validation over many years may a team begin to clearly see the ecological effects of an MPA against natural background variability.*

## Useful references


Bell, J.D., Craik, G.J.S., Pollard, D.A. and Russell, B.C. (1985). "Estimating length frequency distribution of large reef fish underwater". *Coral Reefs* 4: 41–44.

Clarke, K.R. and Warwick, R.M. (2001). *Change in marine communities: An Approach to Statistical Analysis and Interpretation. 2nd edition*. Primer-E, Plymouth, UK.

Dartnall, H.J. and Jones, M. (1986). *A manual of survey methods of living resources in coastal areas.* ASEAN-Australia Cooperative Programme on Marine Science Hand Book. Australian Institute of Marine Science, Townsville, Queensland, Australia.

Done, T.J. and Reichelt, R.E. (1998). "Integrated coastal zone and fisheries ecosystem management: generic goals and performance indices". *Ecological Applications* 8 (supplement): 110–118.

Elliot, J.M. (1977). "Some methods for statistical analysis of benthic invertebrates". *Freshw. Biol. Assoc. Sci. Publ., U.K* 25: 1–156.

English, S., Wilkinson, C. and Baker, V. (eds.) (1997). *Survey Manual for Tropical Marine Resources. 2nd Edition.* Australian Institute for

Marine Science, Townsville, Queensland, Australia.

Grumbine, R.E. (1994). "What is Ecosystem Management?" *Conservation Biology* 8(1): 2738.

Hilborn, R. and Walters, C.J. (1992). *Quantitative Fisheries Stock Assessment: Choice, dynamics, and uncertainty.* Chapman and Hall, New York, NY, USA.

Lackey, R.T. (1995). "Ecosystem Management: Implications for Fisheries Management." *Renewable Resources Journal* 13 (4): 11–13.

Ludwig, D., Hilborn, R. and Walters, C.J. (1993). "Uncertainty, resource exploitation, and conservation: lessons from history". *Science* 260: 17–18.

Odum, E.P. (1971). *Fundamentals of ecology.* W.B. Saunders Co., Philadelphia, PA, USA.

Sale, P.F. (2002). "The science we need to develop for more effective management". In Sale, P.F. (ed.), *Coral Reef Fishes: Dynamics and diversity in a complex ecosystem.* Academic Press, San Diego, USA. pp. 361–376.

Tupper, M. (2002). "Marine reserves and fisheries management". *Science* 295: 1233

NOAA Photo Library

Chris Gomersall/naturepl.com

# Figure 2 Biophysical goals, objectives, indicators

## *Biophysical goals (n=5) and objectives (n=26) commonly associated with MPA use*

**GOAL 1 Marine resources sustained or protected**

- 1A *Populations of target species for extractive or non-extractive use restored to or maintained at desired reference points*
- 1B *Losses to biodiversity and ecosystem functioning and structure prevented*
- 1C *Populations of target species for extractive or non-extractive use protected from harvest at sites and/or life history stages where they become vulnerable*
- 1D *Over-exploitation of living and/or non-living marine resources minimized, prevented or prohibited entirely*
- 1E *Catch yields improved or sustained in fishing areas adjacent to the MPA*
- 1F *Replenishment rate of fishery stocks increased or sustained within the MPA*

**GOAL 2 Biological diversity protected**

- 2A *Resident ecosystems, communities, habitats, species, and gene pools adequately represented and protected*
- 2B *Ecosystem functions maintained*
- 2C *Rare, localized or endemic species protected*
- 2D *Areas protected that are essential for life history phases of species*
- 2E *Unnatural threats and human impacts eliminated or minimized inside and/or outside the MPA*
- 2F *Risk from unmanageable disturbances adequately spread across the MPA*
- 2G *Alien and invasive species and genotypes removed or prevented from becoming established*

**GOAL 3 Individual species protected**

- 3A *Focal species abundance increased or maintained*
- 3B *Habitat and ecosystem functions required for focal species' survival restored or maintained*
- 3C *Unnatural threats and human impacts eliminated or minimized inside and/or outside the MPA*
- 3D *Alien and invasive species and genotypes removed from area or prevented from becoming established*

**GOAL 4 Habitat protected**

- 4A *Habitat quality and/or quantity restored or maintained*
- 4B *Ecological processes essential to habitat existence protected*
- 4C *Unnatural threats and human impacts eliminated or minimized inside and/or outside the MPA*
- 4D *Alien and invasive species and genotypes removed or prevented from becoming established*

**GOAL 5 Degraded areas restored**

- 5A *Populations of native species restored to desired reference points*
- 5B *Ecosystem functions restored*
- 5C *Habitat quality and/or quantity restored or rehabilitated*
- 5D *Unnatural threats and human impacts eliminated or minimized inside and/or outside the MPA*
- 5E *Alien and invasive species and genotypes removed or prevented from becoming established*

## *How the biophysical indicators relate to the common goals and objectives*

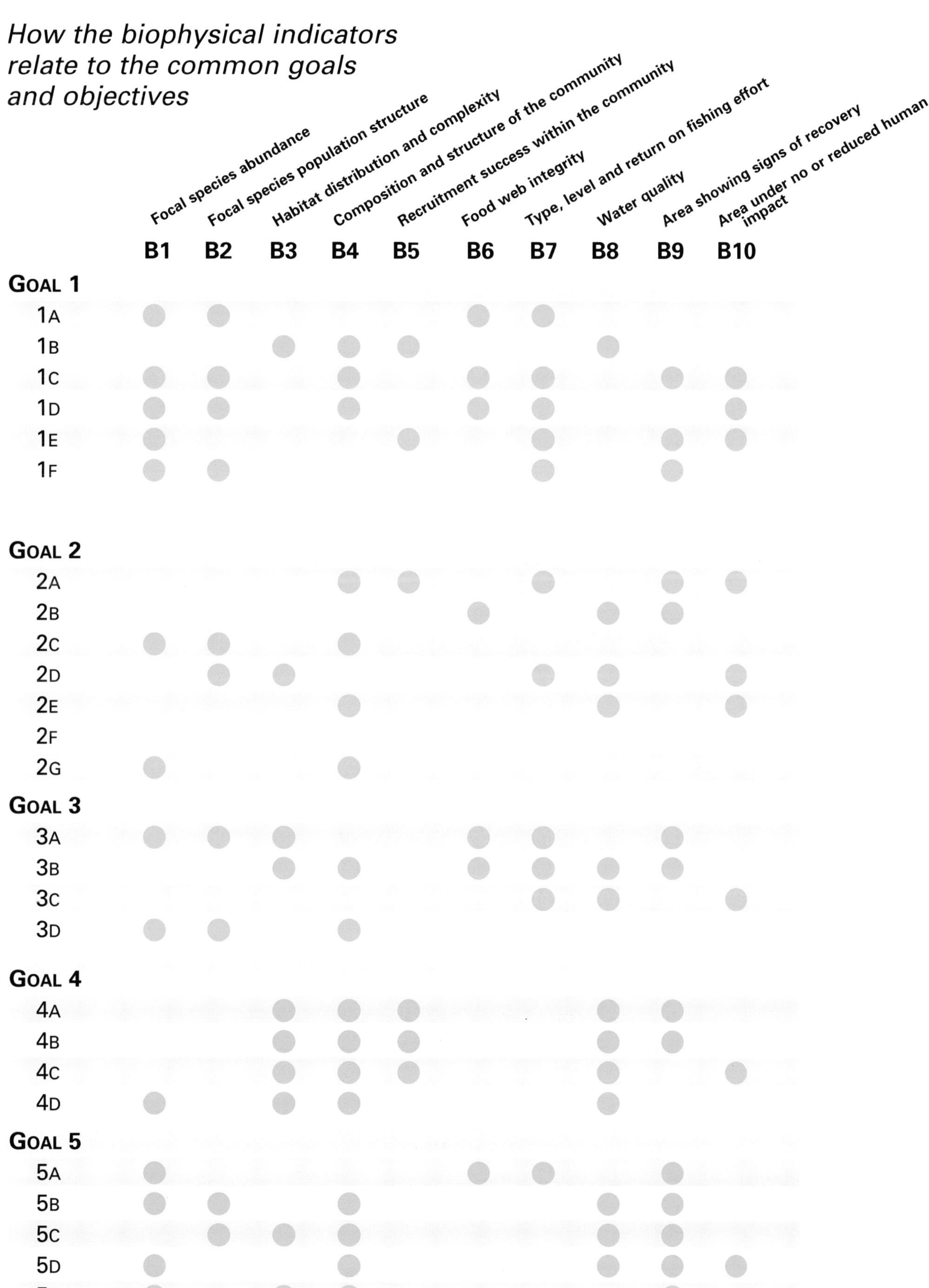

| | Focal species abundance | Focal species population structure | Habitat distribution and complexity | Composition and structure of the community | Recruitment success within the community | Food web integrity | Type, level and return on fishing effort | Water quality | Area showing signs of recovery | Area under no or reduced human impact |
|---|---|---|---|---|---|---|---|---|---|---|
| | **B1** | **B2** | **B3** | **B4** | **B5** | **B6** | **B7** | **B8** | **B9** | **B10** |
| **GOAL 1** | | | | | | | | | | |
| 1A | ● | ● | | | | ● | ● | | | |
| 1B | | | ● | ● | ● | | | ● | | |
| 1C | ● | ● | | ● | | ● | ● | | ● | ● |
| 1D | ● | ● | | ● | | ● | ● | | | ● |
| 1E | ● | | | | ● | | ● | | ● | ● |
| 1F | ● | ● | | | | | ● | | ● | |
| **GOAL 2** | | | | | | | | | | |
| 2A | | | | ● | ● | | ● | | ● | ● |
| 2B | | | | | | ● | | ● | ● | |
| 2C | ● | ● | | ● | | | | | | |
| 2D | | ● | ● | | | | ● | ● | | ● |
| 2E | | | | ● | | | | ● | | ● |
| 2F | | | | | | | | | | |
| 2G | ● | | | ● | | | | | | |
| **GOAL 3** | | | | | | | | | | |
| 3A | ● | ● | ● | | | ● | ● | | ● | |
| 3B | | | ● | ● | | ● | ● | ● | ● | |
| 3C | | | | | | | ● | ● | | ● |
| 3D | ● | ● | | ● | | | | | | |
| **GOAL 4** | | | | | | | | | | |
| 4A | | | ● | ● | ● | | | ● | ● | |
| 4B | | | ● | ● | ● | | | ● | ● | |
| 4C | | | ● | ● | ● | | | ● | | ● |
| 4D | ● | | ● | ● | | | | ● | | |
| **GOAL 5** | | | | | | | | | | |
| 5A | ● | | | | | ● | ● | | ● | |
| 5B | ● | ● | | ● | | | | ● | ● | |
| 5C | | ● | ● | ● | | | | ● | ● | |
| 5D | ● | | | ● | | | | ● | ● | ● |
| 5E | ● | | ● | ● | | | | | ● | |

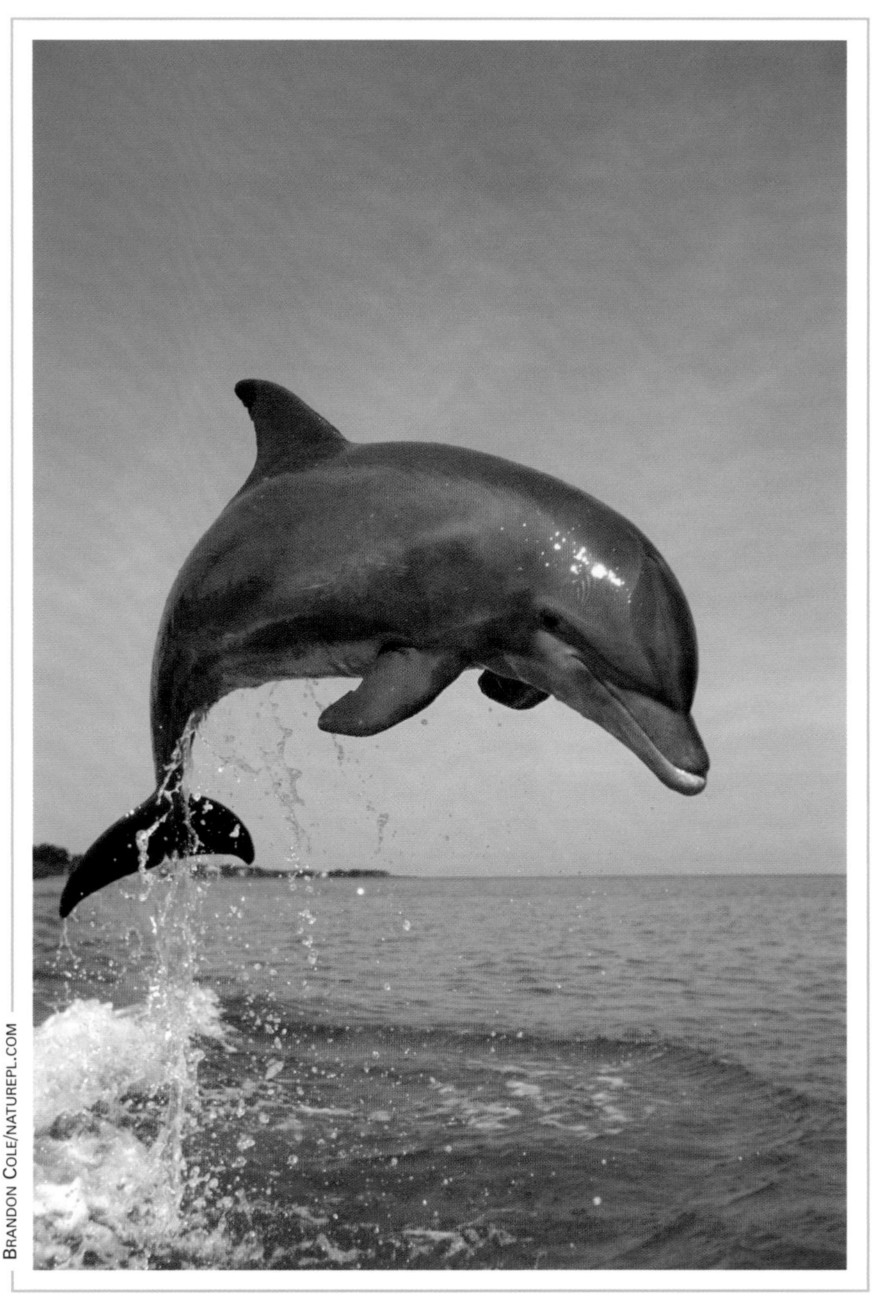

BRANDON COLE/NATUREPL.COM

*A bottlenose dolphin (*Tursiops truncatus*) in the Caribbean leaps from the sea. Marine mammals are useful symbols with which to represent MPAs to the general public.*

## *What is 'focal species abundance'?*

Species **abundance** is the number of individuals of a particular species found to occur within and outside the MPA. Species abundance is a commonly used proxy for population size and is thought to reflect the status of a species' population within a specific location; for example, whether or not the population is growing over time. The density of a species is determined by examining the abundance within a defined (unit) area. Species abundance is one of the most widely used biological 'success' measures of management effectiveness.

A **focal species** is an organism of ecological and/or human value whose management through the MPA is of priority interest. There are several different types of focal species that could potentially be identified for a particular MPA (see Box B1). With many MPAs, their goals and objectives relate directly to the need to protect certain focal species.

*Focal species abundance can also be defined as how commonly a particular species is found relative to other species within the same community, i.e. B4.*

## *Why measure it?*

The protection, enhancement and/or maintenance of populations of focal species are among the most common reasons for using MPAs. Improved and sustained numbers of focal species in the MPA through time is widely seen to indicate effective MPA use. As a result, monitoring changes in the abundance of populations of focal species is one of the most common activities overseen by MPA managers. Fortunately, the basic methods used to compare the number of individuals of a population observed within versus outside an MPA are relatively uncomplicated and easily understood.

As populations of focal species residing within the MPA are protected and allowed to grow, individuals may migrate, or 'spill over', into adjacent, non-protected areas. This increases the biomass avail-

**Relates to goals and objectives**

GOAL 1
1A 1C
1D 1E
1F

GOAL 2
2C 2G

GOAL 3
3A 3D

GOAL 4
4D

GOAL 5
5A 5B
5D 5E

Difficulty Rating 3 (1–5)

**Box B1**

### TYPES OF 'FOCAL' SPECIES

(adapted from Noss, 1990)

- Endemics – species that are only found to occur naturally in the waters near the MPA.
- Exotics – non-native species that are of concern due to their negative effects on the local ecology. For example, introduced algae that aggressively spreads and smothers native habitat.
- Flagships – charismatic species that are of social or cultural significance and are therefore used by managers as symbols of MPA efforts to encourage public interest and support.
- Indicators – species that signal how disturbances may be impacting other organisms within the community. For example, sea otters in kelp forests.
- Keystones – species upon which others in the community directly depend. For example, top fish predators that maintain a coastal food chain, or a coral reef species that provides living space (habitat) for others.
- Targets – species of interest due to their extractive or non-extractive use value. For example, shellfish commonly harvested for local diet needs, or humpback whales that bring tourists to the area. As not all target species will be priorities for management, they will therefore not all be focal species.
- Vulnerables – species that are known to be less resilient to environmental change than others in the community and/or require careful management to sustain. For example, slow-growing organisms or those with few offspring, or threatened, endangered or rare species (such as those on IUCN's Red List of Threatened Species).

NOAA PHOTO LIBRARY

***Sharks such as the white shark (Carcharodon carcharias) often serve as focal species in MPAs. Not only do many serve as keystone species being apex predators, but they are also used as flagship species to boost public interest in MPA management needs and activities.***

able for human use. As a result, many managers are not only responsible for showing how more individuals of focal species can be found within an MPA through time, but also how there are increased numbers of focal species in waters surrounding the MPA.

Also, maintaining healthy populations of charismatic species such as whales or turtles may be of interest to recreation users, visitors and the general public, leading to increased tourism revenues and public support for the MPA's continued existence. Finally, clearly showing decision-makers how an MPA is leading to increased or maintained numbers of focal species can help secure the financial and political support required to sustain and/or expand management efforts into the future.

The indicator can also be a useful gauge of the presence/absence of invasive species and the extent (abundance) of their presence.

## How to collect the data

Before data collection can begin, the evaluation team will need a list of which focal species in and around the MPA need to be observed during the evaluation period. In some cases, neither the evaluators nor the MPA management team may have an accurate understanding of which species these are. If so, a discrete number of focal species must be identified by the team and listed on paper. Reviewing the relevant types of focal species (see Box B1, above) in the MPA can help to do this. This list should be reviewed and approved by the primary stakeholders involved in the management of the MPA prior to the survey.

### Requirements

- A list of the focal species (reviewed and approved by stakeholders).
- Designated sampling sites inside and outside the MPA.
- An adequate number of trained staff and/or volunteers in both survey methods and taxonomic identification.
- A boat (with safety equipment) and engine.
- Survey tools (e.g. tape measure, compass, towline, submersible writing slate).
- SCUBA or snorkelling equipment.
- A handheld global positioning system (GPS).
- Submersible digital camera (to verify species identifications).
- Advanced (if applicable): aerial photography, satellite imagery, and geographic information systems; small airplane or helicopter (for large, wide ranging organisms); tagging and telemetry equipment; and digital video camera and underwater housing.

*Note that there is some ongoing discussion within the scientific community over what taxonomic level abundance measures are best collected. Counts performed at the species (as opposed to genus or family) level are discussed here for organisms of focus within the MPA.*

While some MPAs may have only a handful of focal species to be monitored, other sites may have dozens of them to consider. The number of focal species that can be realistically surveyed to determine this indicator will depend largely on the capacity and resources available to the evaluation team.

There are a number of techniques that can be used to measure the abundance of a focal species population within a specified area. These are thoroughly documented elsewhere in the literature, and are therefore not repeated here. At the end of this section are listed several of the most commonly used citations in practice that can be of use to the evaluation team. Generally speaking however, three common approaches can be used to assess the abundance of populations of focal species:

a) Assessing the number of individuals observed *in situ*;

b) Assessing the extent of the observed population in terms of area (e.g. the total km$^2$ of seagrass beds estimated using GPS) or **biomass** (e.g. basal area or leaf litter of red mangroves) through *in situ* surveys or by using remote technologies (e.g. aerial photographs, satellite technology); and

c) Assessing the landings (fishing catch) of the focal species that has been harvested from the area concerned.

At the most basic level, the evaluation team should estimate the number of individuals observed *in situ* within the survey area according to classes of abundance. With some species, *in situ* observation may only require swimming in the water or being towed behind a boat. With highly mobile species, it may require observation from a boat, airplane or helicopter. An absolute count of individuals is a more precise measure than classes. Provided that

BRANDON COLE/NATUREPL.COM



the evaluation team has the time, labour, and resources to do so, absolute counts should be preferred, particularly for species that lend themselves to this method (e.g. species that occur infrequently, have low population densities or are confined to a small survey area). Depending on the species density and the size of area sampled, absolute counts may be too time consuming and laborious to realistically undertake.

Selecting the appropriate survey technique for *in situ* counts of a particular focal species will largely depend on its behaviour and life history. However, the following rules-of-thumb can be used when considering which method is best:

a) **Sessile**, **sedentary**, and limited-ranging **benthic** species (such as abalone clams or the crown-of-thorns starfish) can be observed within or along a series of (ideally) randomly assigned or systematically and permanently stratified quadrats, plots, transects or point-counts at two or more locations at designated survey sites inside and outside the MPA.

b) Mobile species (such as fishes or sea otters) and wider-ranging benthic species (such as lobster) can be sampled through underwater visual census using multiple point-counts (fixed by GPS), belt transects (particularly for sedentary invertebrates) and timed swims (at a constant rate for 15 minute increments, counting 10m to either side of an imaginary line) along fixed depth profiles in relevant habitats inside and outside the MPA. More than one depth profile (i.e. shallower, deeper) should be surveyed respective to the bottom/habitat type being surveyed. Timed swims may be a preferable survey method for counting large, mobile fish, whereas point-counts and transects may be more useful for smaller fishes.

c) Wide-ranging and highly migratory species (such as sea birds, turtles or mammals) can be observed *in situ* using visual observation or tracked with radio tags and **telemetry**.

d) **Cryptic** and rare species may need to be surveyed using separate techniques from those used for other focal species of interest.

*Measurement of the extent (area or biomass) or landings of a focal species are discussed further in B4 (pp. 76–82) and B8 (pp. 100–103).*

***With highly mobile, wide-ranging focal species, such as the humpback whale, comparison of abundance data inside versus outside the MPA may not apply as individuals could all belong to the same population.***

The methodological specifics for these rules-of-thumb are well documented elsewhere and referenced at the end of this indicator description. Survey replication should be done at multiple, randomly-assigned or systematically distributed sampling sites and depths within both treatment and reference areas.

*Where relevant and feasible, counts of different focal species should be attempted during the same survey to maximize time, labour and funding investments.*

Beyond simple counts of individuals observed, where possible the evaluation team should also try to collect size data for the focal species population. Such information can allow managers to move beyond a simple estimate of how many individuals there are to a better understanding of the distribution of the sizes of individuals observed by size class – that is, how much of the population is comprised of smaller (juvenile) versus larger (adult) individuals. A spread of individuals observed evenly across size classes may indicate that there is

***In the Northwestern Hawaiian Islands, endemic monk seals* (Monachus schauinlandi) *are closely monitored throughout the year in an effort to better understand how the newly designated marine sanctuary is affecting resident populations.***

spawning stock present, and therefore that the abundance of the population may be increased or maintained in the future. The methods used to collect size data are presented in indicator B2. Size classes can be defined by fixed, equal intervals; e.g. 10cm diameter or 1m lengths. It may be easier to collect data on sedentary invertebrates than on mobile vertebrates, as they may lend themselves to handling and sizing. Fairly accurate length estimation can be learned with mobile vertebrates (such as fishes) with some practice (see below for references on this).

Data on measurement of abundance (and size, if relevant) of focal species should be collected regularly, depending on the life history and behaviour of the organism(s) involved. At a minimum, such data should be collected annually or every two years. Ideally, these data should be collected twice a year or quarterly. Data should be collected from both sampling sites inside (treatment site) and outside (reference site) the MPA, including areas immediately adjacent to the boundaries of the MPA to detect 'spill over' effects. The life history and seasonal behaviour of the species being surveyed need to be taken into account when considering the logical timing and frequency of surveys during the year. Repeat surveys should be conducted as close to the same time of month each year as possible.

*Collecting size data from a population of a focal species will also allow evaluators to measure indicator B2.*

If the evaluation team is to assess the abundance of exotic species, providing the evaluation team with an updated checklist of known and suspected invasive species that may inhabit the area being surveyed will help with their identification and perhaps also with the early detection of new species to the area. Information on suspected and known exotics can be obtained from IUCN regional invasive species working groups.

Where applicable, more sophisticated technologies can also allow for the monitoring of focal species abundance. For example, images captured through the use of underwater video and/or photography at fixed distances along a transect can later be analysed on land to carefully calculate frequency observations for focal species. This can be particularly useful in deeper waters where breathing compressed air for extended periods on SCUBA can be dangerous. Radio tags and telemetry may be necessary to track populations of large, migratory organisms. Aerial survey and remote sensing technologies may also assist evaluators to survey large populations of organisms and/or samples adequately across large MPAs. Such advanced techniques will require significantly more resources and capacity to undertake than *in situ* counts.

## How to analyse and interpret the results

Collate, enter and manage data gathered within the MPA's evaluation database. Graph the frequency (y-axis) of individuals of a focal species observed both within and outside the MPA through time (x-axis). Are there any observable trends or changes between focal species within versus outside the MPA through time? Do areas outside but adjacent to the MPA indicate a 'spill over' effect? Using statistical techniques (e.g. student t-tests, analysis of variance), how do sampled populations of the same focal species within and outside the MPA compare against one another, and against themselves, through time? How reliable are perceived changes or trends observed inside the MPA compared to variability occurring outside the MPA? Were known or new invasive species observed during the survey?

Calculate a rough estimate of the density of focal species by dividing the total number of individuals observed (frequency) by the area sampled. Are densities changing through time within compared to outside the MPA? Spatially plot these densities

*If size data is also collected, see B2 for guidance on analysis and interpretation of these data.*

### *Outputs (for each focal species surveyed)*

- A profile of the abundance (either as classes, absolute counts, area or biomass) inside and outside the MPA.
- Estimated population densities inside and outside the MPA.
- An idea of whether or not the population surveyed is clustered or uniformly distributed throughout the survey area.

### *Other outputs (if applicable)*

- A profile of the abundance of smaller versus larger individuals (via size classes) within the focal species population inside and outside the MPA.
- The relative abundance of different focal species observed across the community surveyed.
- Known presence/absence and abundance of invasive species present in the community.

against the area surveyed. Look for patterns in the observed density: are the individuals uniformly distributed across the areas surveyed or are they clustered in certain areas sampled?

Plot the abundance (y-axis) of populations observed across different focal species (x-axis, as histograms) relative to one another within the community. Monitor changes in the relative abundance of these populations of focal species through time. Do any proportional relationships between the relative abundance of populations appear? Are the relative abundances of various focal species observed within the community changing or being maintained through time? Were known or newly arrived invasive species observed during the surveys?

Prepare results and conclusions for public dissemination. Orally and visually present results with target audiences, and distribute written reports (including graphs and tables of results). Encourage independent validation of findings by partners and outside parties within the sampled area in order to confirm or reject results and increase the understanding of the effects of MPA activities on the area. Be sure to include any stories or anecdotes that illustrate the results observed from stakeholders.

### *Strengths and limitations*

The approach and general survey methods for measuring this indicator are relatively uncomplicated and commonly used. However, the degree of overall difficulty in measuring the indicator can range widely. In some cases, collecting abundance data can be done rapidly, inexpensively and with a minimum of specialists. In other cases, it may require several months and a large team to complete. The amount of time, financing, equipment and evaluator skill required for measurement in an MPA will depend in part on:

a) The size of the MPA needing to be surveyed;

b) The number of focal species being sampled;

c) The density with which the focal species occurs;

d) The migratory behaviour and home range size of the population observed;

e) The conspicuousness and degree to which the species is easily observable; and

f) The local/national capacity to conduct the survey and level of skill within the evaluation team.

For example, measuring the abundance of a colourful, sessile organism occurring in the shallow waters of a small MPA will require far less capacity to survey than the measurement of an highly migratory, pelagic species that is known to infrequently visit the seas included within and outside a large MPA.

Abundance observations for a focal species are difficult to infer beyond the sampled area. Large areas must be sampled to confidently characterize large-sized MPAs and surrounding waters. Also, as some populations may occur with a high level of spatial and seasonal variability, they may require a high level of sampling effort in terms of area and time to monitor.

At the most basic level, evaluators must have the capacity to undertake abundance counts or class estimates and be able to correctly identify focal species *in situ*. In some cases, abundance surveys may require a considerable amount of time and labour to undertake. More advanced skills will be needed to do length estimation, biomass estimation, and/or catch-landing surveys.

Finally, counts are limited to depths at which diving can be safely undertaken. To determine the focal species abundance of populations in deeper waters, catch-landing surveys of deep-water species caught should be undertaken.

### *Useful references and Internet links*

Noss, R. F. (1990). "Indicators for monitoring biodiversity: a hierarchical approach". *Conservation Biology* 4(4): 355–364.

### Abundance and length estimation methods

Bell, J.D., Craik, G.J.S., Pollard, D.A. and Russell, B.C. (1985). "Estimating length frequency distributions of large reef fish underwater". *Coral Reefs* 4: 41–44.

Dartnall, H.J. and Jones, M. (1986). *A manual of survey methods of living resources in coastal areas.* ASEAN-Australia Cooperative Programme on Marine Science Hand Book. Australian Institute of Marine Science, Townsville, Queensland, Australia.

English, S., Wilkinson, C. and Baker, V. (eds.) (1997). *Survey Manual for Tropical Marine Resources. 2nd Edition.* Australian Institute for Marine Science, Townsville, Queensland, Australia.

Gunderson, D.R. (1993). *Surveys of Fishery Resources.* John Wiley and Sons, Inc., New York, NY, USA.

Mapstone, B.D. and Ayling, A.M. (1993). *An Investigation of optimum methods and unit sizes for the visual estimation of abundances of some coral reef organisms: A report to the Great Barrier Reef Marine Park Authority.* Great Barrier Reef Marine Park Authority, Townsville, Queensland, Australia.

Mapstone, B.D., Ayling, A.M. and Choat, J.H. (1999). *A Visual Survey of Demersal Biota in the Cairns Section of the Great Barrier Reef Marine Park: A Report to the Great Barrier Reef Marine Park Authority.* Research Publication No. 60. Great Barrier Reef Marine Park Authority, Townsville, Queensland, Australia.

MPA MEI website: useful discussion thread between Tupper and Ellis regarding the appropriate sampling and design for *in situ* observation methods of focal species. [Online URL: effectiveMPA.noaa.gov]

### Underwater visual census methods

Samoilys, M. (ed.) (1997). *Manual for Assessing Fish Stocks on Pacific Coral Reefs.* Training Series QE9700. Department of Primary Industries, Queensland, Australia.

Thompson, A.A. and Mapstone, B.D. (1997). "Observer effects and training in underwater visual surveys of reef fishes". *Marine Ecology Press Series* 154: 53–63.

### Rapid assessment of fishes and habitat

McKenna, Sheila A., Allen, Gerald R. and Suryadi, Suer (eds.) (2002). "A Marine Rapid Assessment of the Raja Ampat Islands, Papua Province, Indonesia". *RAP Bulletin of Biological Assessment 22.* Center for Applied Biodiversity Science, Conservation International, Washington, DC, USA.

The Atlantic and Gulf Rapid Reef Assessment (AGRRA) Program. [Online URL: www.cep.unep.org/programmes/spaw/icri/aggra.htm]

### Timed swim methods

Donaldson, T.J. (2000). Testing the effectiveness of MPAs and other reef fish management strategies using agent-based models. Proposal to the United States National Oceanographic and Atmospheric Administration. Unpublished report. University of Guam Marine Laboratory. Mangilao, Guam. [Online at http://www.uog.edu/marinelab/mpa/abm.pdf]

Box B2

### Example from the Field

At the Far Eastern Marine Reserve, the timing of when the evaluation team measures resident larga seal (*Phoca largha* – right) populations in the Bay of Peter the Great can be tricky. February is the peak breeding season when most individuals of this vulnerable, flagship focal species come onshore, thereby making for rather strict time requirements for performing censuses. Unfortunately this month also often hosts some of the most inhospitable weather and sea conditions of the year. The evaluation team has learned how to conduct their census work from small boats during this time of year, despite average daily temperatures of -10°C and rough seas. The data collected over the past few years indicate that the protected rookeries are helping the species to make a local come-back from near extinction in Russia's South Primorye.

WWF Russia/Far Eastern Marine Reserve

## *What is 'population structure'?*

Population structure is the probability with which different sizes and ages of individuals are likely to occur within a population of a focal species. A population experiencing no or reduced human impacts and influenced largely only by natural conditions is more likely to host the necessary number of reproducers in order to replenish and maintain itself through time than one whose individuals are being removed for human use.

In measuring this indicator, it is possible to go beyond simply assessing how much of a focal species there is at a single point in time (indicator B1) by further characterizing how the individuals in the population are structured by size and age, and by assessing the population's reproductive potential. In this respect, this indicator can be used by managers both as a 'snapshot' at a single point in time of what proportion of the focal species population is made up of reproducers, as well as a 'crystal ball' to help managers forecast population growth rates or predict declines that may occur within the focal species as a result of changes happening in the size/age structure.

Important factors that influence size and age distribution within a population include the regularity of spawning events, the variability in timing, amount and location of larval settlement and recruitment events, and the degree of juvenile survivorship and recruitment in the population.

## *Why measure it?*

For the population of a species to continue to exist through time, an adequate number of reproductive adults must be present. A common rationale in using and supporting MPAs is that they can serve as a safe haven for the breeding stock of a focal species. Therefore, an effectively managed MPA is one that is thought to contain populations of focal species whose individuals are adequately distributed from juvenile to adult size classes so as to allow them to replenish themselves and be viable (i.e. persist in the area through time).

Further, by maintaining spawning stock, effectively-managed MPAs are also thought to:

a) Serve as a source of eggs, larvae and juveniles that are exported to areas outside the MPA; and

b) Increase the number of reproductive adults found in waters outside the MPA as a result of 'spill over' (migration of individuals).

As a consequence, managers are often entrusted not only with the responsibility of showing how the populations found in the MPA have the structure and potential to continue to persist through time, but also with the job of demonstrating how juveniles and adults exported into adjacent waters outside the MPA are helping to stabilize population structures and viability there as well.

In many places, these phenomena are seen as some of the most important benefits arising from MPA use. Therefore, in order to secure and sustain long-term support for MPA efforts, these benefits must be clearly shown.

Note that a network of multiple MPAs may be required to adequately sustain some populations of focal species that exhibit wide-ranging life history characteristics, such as:

- Lengthy larval stages.
- Large home ranges.
- Aggregation from a wide area to a specific site for certain life events.
- Simply being highly migratory in nature.

## *How to collect the data*

The presence and reproductive potential of breeding stock and future viability of populations of a focal species can be assessed by collecting size, age, reproductive potential, and recruitment data from sample areas within and outside the MPA. Because many coastal species occur in various habitats throughout different phases during their lifetime, multiple habitats are likely to require sampling for populations of some focal species. In some cases, distinctive markings and coloration in focal species may also assist evaluators to clearly distinguish between juveniles versus reproductive adults. Also, scientific literature may already exist that shows or suggests the size and/or age of first reproduction of the focal species concerned.

At the most basic level, information on the size of individuals observed within surveyed areas both within and outside the MPA should be collected. Collecting size data on individuals sampled from a

*As the number of individuals found in a population is closely related to its size and age structure, indicators B1 and B2 are closely associated and data can be concurrently collected for both.*

**Relates to goals and objectives**

GOAL 1: 1A 1C 1D 1F

GOAL 2: 2C 2D

GOAL 3: 3A 3D

GOAL 5: 5B 5C

### Requirements

- The same requirements as listed under indicator B1.
- Capture nets, lines, and traps.
- Sizing equipment, such as a fish measuring board, a soft tape measure, sizing sticks, callipers and a set of balances.
- Basic capture-mark-recapture: plastic tagging kit.
- Advanced capture-mark-recapture: radio telemetry tracking system.
- Age: collection and holding equipment for specimens.
- Age: laboratory facilities and equipment to analyse specimens.
- Recruitment: collection plates, nets and traps.

population of a focal species is particularly useful when the organism is both known to have a fixed size to age relationship and when the age (or size) of first reproduction is known. In such cases, a reliable distinction between breeding stock and juveniles can be made based on accurate size data.

The *in situ* survey methods on how to observe and sample individuals for sizing are the same as those described under indicator B1. In most cases, size data can be collected from focal species through *in situ* survey as follows:

a) By estimating the length or size of mobile individuals observed at distance from within the sampled area (both in or on the water or from the air), such as fishes, marine mammals or seabirds;

b) By collecting, handling and measuring actual length or size of live individuals (prior to their release); and

c) By measuring the actual length or size of individuals harvested.

While the collection of age data from individuals surveyed requires a more advanced level of skill, it may be desirable, particularly with focal species where the age of sexual maturation in the organism is known and where size is not a good predictor of reproductive potential. Timed growth studies can be conducted using capture-mark-recapture (CMR) methods on live individuals that have been recaptured after being previously tagged and released. This can be done using simple and inexpensive plastic tags and minimal skill, or through more sophisticated monitored techniques such as submersible radio tags and telemetry equipment. CMR study can not only provide important information on the rate at which individuals grow over

Actual or estimated length/size data are measured differently depending on the type of organism surveyed, for example:

- Fish by their total or caudal length (cm or m).
- Marine mammals by their total length or fluke width (m).
- Bivalves by their dorsoventral length (cm).
- Crustaceans by their carapace length (cm).
- Marine reptiles by their straight line carapace (shell) length (cm).
- Mangroves by their trunk's girth at breast height (cm).

***In Marovo Lagoon in the Solomon Islands, village fishers help local managers monitor focal populations of coral reef fish by allowing them to measure fork length data on individuals caught in waters surrounding several locally managed MPAs.***

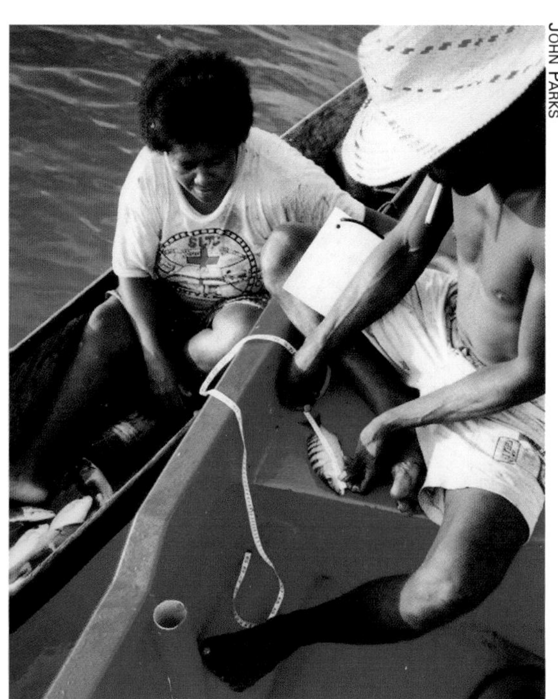

John Parks

time (i.e. the size-age relationship), but also help managers to better understand how populations of focal species move within and outside the MPA.

In many cases, confidently profiling the age structure of a population will require a sophisticated level of scientific study, such as dissection, biopsy, and genetic analysis of the reproductive organs, dissection and analysis of fish otoliths, and study of other morphological characteristics in the species. Such studies can be particularly useful if the size or age of first reproduction are not known for the focal species being assessed.

*Note that with some organisms, such as coral reef fishes, growth rates are not always constant throughout an individual's lifetime. Also, correlations between body size and age may not necessarily be consistent through time. Therefore, an understanding of a population's size structure at a few specific points in time may not allow evaluators to fully or accurately understand population growth rates, ages or reproductive capacity.*

Another measure to assess population structure is to estimate the reproductive potential of a population. This can be characterized in part by:

a) The presence of breeding stock;

b) The amount (biomass, number) of breeders;

c) The timing of spawning behaviour and frequency of breeding events; and

d) The breeding stock's potential fecundity (defined as the number of eggs produced by the population during spawning).

Finally, recruitment and survivorship studies of the focal species can also be conducted to assist in assessing the viability of the population through time. Recruitment data can be collected using visual census or through the capture and sizing of individuals (note that this may lead to specimen mortality). Nets, lines and traps are commonly used to sample juvenile fish and some shellfish. Collection plates, nets and traps can be used to capture smaller individuals of soft- and hard-bodied invertebrate focal species, such as coral recruits and juveniles. Traps are useful for settling lobster, conch, beche-de-mer, or other invertebrate larvae.

*Data collection on larval settlement and juvenile recruitment data can be done concurrently with indicator B5.*

NOAA Photo Library

***Monitoring the timing and frequency of known reproductive events and sites of a focal species can assist the evaluation team to more accurately characterize the structure and viability of the population.***

*Note that because the collection of recruitment data within the MPA may require landing and some mortality of live specimens, this may not be compatible with the goals or rules of your MPA (e.g. in a no-take area).*

Information used to characterize population structure (at a minimum, size data) should be collected ideally once or twice a year, and at least every two years (depending on the focal species). The ideal timing for measurement will depend on the life history of the organism(s) being assessed. Size data should be collected concurrently with abundance data (indicator B1) for each focal species.

## How to analyse and interpret results

The analysis and interpretation of data collected for this indicator are the same as those presented under indicator B1. Enter size and age data into the MPA's evaluation database so that it can be organized and/or exported within defined size or age classes of fixed, equal intervals; for example, 10cm increments, 0.5m lengths, or one year. Enter into a table the frequency with which individuals of each size or age class are observed within and outside the MPA. The distribution of individuals across size/age classes can also be viewed on a graph by plotting the frequency of individuals observed (y-axis) against their respective size/age class (x-axis).

*Note that confidently building an understanding of a population's structure using this indicator will take several years. It is dangerous to attempt to characterize a resident population and/or make management decisions based on a single data set or limited time series of information.*

Using catch data, profile the annual average frequency of sizes (lengths) of organisms harvested through time. From this, plot out a length-converted catch curve on a graph. Use results to form an estimate of the total mortality rate prevailing in successive classes. Compare results with those of other sample populations of the same species.

Compare size/age class structures of the population both within and outside the MPA, through time. Assuming that an adequate and stable number of surviving juveniles and reproductive adults within a population will improve its likelihood of persistence, and allowing for natural variability (which may be high in some cases), try and address the following questions. Are there any observable trends or changes in the size/age class distribution of individuals of a focal species within versus outside the MPA? Do individuals measured outside but adjacent to the MPA indicate a 'spill over' effect of certain size/age classes? If size/age of first reproduction is known, are there any observable changes in the abundance of juveniles versus reproducers within versus outside the MPA? When interpreting size class results, remember that the size structure within many species (such as coral reef fish) is not an accurate gauge of their ages or when reproductive maturity is achieved.

Using statistical techniques (e.g. student t-tests, analysis of variance), how do sampled populations of the same focal species within and outside the MPA compare against one another, and against oneself, through time? How reliable are perceived changes or trends observed inside the MPA compared to variability occurring outside the MPA?

Do the size/age class data gathered provide an improved understanding of whether or not management actions in the MPA are leading to a more balanced population structure compared to outside the MPA? Over time, are size/age 'thresholds' or requirements for the population's sustainability becoming apparent? If so, can this be developed further to inform management needs and processes? Based on the overall results generated for this indicator, how likely does it appear that the population will be able to regenerate itself and be viable through time? When sharing results with primary audiences, it may be useful to provide responses to these questions using a qualitative

NOAA Photo Library

**Blackbar soldierfish (Myripristus jacobus) within a coral reef nook.**

### Outputs (for each focal species)

- A profile of how the population surveyed is structured by size (inside and outside the MPA) at a certain point in time. This may include an understanding of what proportion of the population is sexually mature.
- A graph of the size/class distribution for each focal species studied.
- An improved understanding of how likely the population is able to replenish itself based on hosting adequate spawning stock.

### Other outputs (if applicable)

- The age structure of the population surveyed (inside and outside the MPA).
- Improved understanding of the age of sexual maturation in the focal species.
- A characterization of the reproductive potential (including spawning and breeding ability) of the focal species compared to known life history.
- An improved understanding of how viable, or potentially persistent, the population is based on its ability to replenish itself and host adequate spawning stock.
- A length-converted catch curve and estimated mortality rate.

scale (e.g. lower, unchanged, or higher) and/or quantitative measure (e.g. probability of reproductive capacity or fecundity).

Prepare results and interpreted findings for public dissemination. Orally and visually present results, and distribute written reports (including graphs and tables of results). Encourage independent validation of findings by partners and outside parties within the sampled area in order to confirm or reject results and increase the understanding of the effects of MPA activities on the area. Be sure to include any stories or anecdotes that illustrate the results observed from stakeholders.

Because of the often challenging nature of collecting and analysing biological information and the effects of spatial and temporal variability on interpreting results, it is strongly recommended that if there are no qualified specialists trained to address these issues on the evaluation team or the MPA staff, input and assistance should be sought from outside experts.

Develop a profile of the reproductive potential (if applicable) of the focal species population and how this profile compares against what is known about the life history of the species. How does this profile predict the ability of the population to maintain itself through time? Finally, if applicable, present the number/density of recruits and juvenile sizes resulting from the recruitment survey and discuss how they relate to the observed size class distribution.

### *Strengths and limitations*

Many of the strengths and limitations of this indicator are similar to those described under indicator B1. Size and age class information are accepted and widely understood standards in profiling and better understanding the structure and viability of a population. Also, regular collection of size class information can be useful in understanding and predicting the sustainability threshold of focal species that are targeted for fisheries' harvest within or outside the MPA. In this sense, the indicator can both serve to measure MPA effectiveness as well as improve understanding of *in situ* fisheries management and help to set harvest limits.

Size and age measurement require more skills than merely *in situ* observation. Accurate estimates of individuals' sizes through remote estimation requires skill and experience and is not easily undertaken by novices or managers without existing training. Conducting size measurements of live specimens requires that staff have experience and training in sensitively and non-destructively capturing, handling, sizing and returning live specimens. Scientific age assessments will require: a) staff with a comparatively larger set of technical skills, b) increased time and c) more equipment and finances.

While useful, the capture of reproductive potential and recruitment information will largely multiply the complexity, labour, time and cost requirements of data collection under this indicator.

Also, a useful interpretation of this indicator inherently requires several years of comparable information.

Box B3

## EXAMPLE FROM THE FIELD

A primary objective of Guam's Marine Preserve Network is to restore declining reef fish populations. At the Achang Reef Flat Preserve, an evaluation was conducted of the population structure of the bullethead parrotfish (*Chlorurus sordidus*), one of the most commonly fished species in Guam's inshore reef fishery. The evaluation team's results (right) show how larger and more abundant size classes of bullethead parrotfish were observed within the Achang Reef Flat Preserve than in adjacent control (non-protected) sites. Data collected suggest that this species appears to be experiencing population recovery within the Reef Flat Preserve, which was the Reserve Network's primary objective.

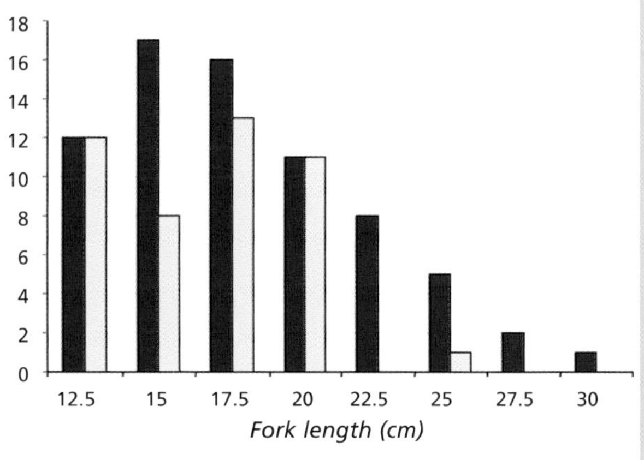


***The observed size class distribution of bullethead parrotfish within (purple bars) and outside (yellow bars) the Achang Reef Flat Preserve.***

### *Useful references and Internet links*


Bell, J. D., Craik, G.J.S., Pollard, D.A. and Russell, B.C. (1985). "Estimating length frequency distributions of large reef fish underwater". *Coral Reefs* 4: 41–44.

English, S., Wilkinson, C. and Baker, V. (eds) (1997). *Survey Manual for Tropical Marine Resources. 2nd Edition.* Australian Institute for Marine Science, Townsville, Queensland, Australia.

Munro, J.L. and Pauly, D. (1983). "A simple method for comparing the growth of fishes and invertebrates". *ICLARM Fishbyte* 1(1): 5–6.


### Age estimation


Choat, J.H. and Axe, L.M. (1996). "Growth and longevity in acanthurid fishes; an analysis of otolith increments". *Mar. Ecol. Prog. Ser.* 134: 15–26.

Ferreira, B.P. and Russ, G.R. (1994). "Age validation and estimation of the growth rate of the coral trout, *Plectropomous leopardus* (Lacepede 1802) from Lizard Island, Northern Great Barrier Reef". *Fish. Bull. U.S.* 92: 46–57.

Fournier, D. and Archibald, C.P. (1982). "A general theory for analyzing catch at age data". *Can. J. Fish. Aquat. Sci.* 39: 1195–1207.

Fowler, A.J. (1990). "Validation of annual growth increments in the otoliths of a small tropical coral reef fish". *Marine Ecology Progress Series* 64: 25–38.

Hilborn, R. (1990). "Estimating the parameters of full age-structured models from catch and abundance data". *Bull. Int. North Pac. Fish. Comm.* 50: 207–213.


### Size-class data in a small MPA


Tawake, A., Parks, J., Radikedike, P., Aalbersberg, B., Vuki, V. and Salafsky, N. (2002). "Harvesting clams and data: involving local communities in monitoring – a Case in Fiji". *Conservation in Practice* 2(4): 32–35.


### Recruitment


Sale, P.F., Doherty, P.J., Eckert, G.J., Douglas, W.A. and Ferrell, D.J. (1984). "Large scale spatial and temporal variation in recruitment to fish populations on coral reefs". *Oecologia* (Berlin) 64: 191–198.

NOAA Photo Library

# Habitat distribution and complexity

## What is 'habitat distribution and complexity'?

**Habitat** is defined as the living space of an organism, population, or community, as characterized by both its biotic and physical properties. Habitat types are distinguished from one another by their distinct biotic and abiotic composition and structure that forms living space.

The **habitat distribution** within a specified area or ecosystem is the structural and spatial characterization of all habitat types represented, based on their:

- Physical location (including depth);
- Configuration (i.e. placement next to one another); and
- Extent in terms of total area (in $km^2$).

> *Habitat distribution varies widely with each MPA. For example, the boundaries of a very small, relatively homogenous MPA may only encompass one or two different habitat types. At the other end, large-scale ecosystem MPAs may host dozens of different habitats.*

Seascapes are dynamic, biotic mosaics comprised of patterns of habitat and characteristic patchiness due to spatial and temporal variability. Some habitat mosaics are more complex than others. **Habitat complexity** is defined as the extent (area in $km^2$) and diversity (number) of habitat types and distinct zones found within a specified area. Higher habitat complexity does not necessarily indicate a 'better' or healthier ecosystem; the 'right' level of complexity all depends on what would occur naturally in the absence of human impacts. However, a highly complex habitat structure hosts a wider variety of habitat types and zones within the ecosystem than one of a uniformly distributed structure of low diversity. Highly complex habitat structures hosting a wide diversity of organisms are commonly cited as priorities for protection by management and conservation groups.

> *Note that under natural conditions, habitat distribution and complexity do not remain static through time and space. For example, reduced habitat complexity observed in an MPA due to increased algal dominance may be within the range of natural variability and not the consequence of human activity.*

**Habitat integrity** can be defined as the likelihood that the distribution and complexity of living space in an area will persist through time. A 'healthy' habitat is therefore one that is considered to have strong integrity and is resilient to pronounced change. Habitat integrity offers a more dynamic perspective to this indicator than simply assessing a 'snapshot' of habitat structure (i.e. at a single point in time).

## Why measure it?

Communities of organisms are dependent on the presence of adequate living space within which to exist and reproduce. Disturbance events in the community, whether natural or man-made, can lead to changes in habitat structure and declines in complexity. Such changes may in turn cause reductions in focal species abundance and changes in population structure and community composition.

MPAs are often used in an attempt to prevent or reduce the frequency and intensity of man-made disturbances in an area so as to arrest deleterious change on the habitat within them. This assumes that such disturbance events are localized within or nearby the MPA and are not outside the influence of management action. 'Broadcast' disturbance events beyond the control of managers, such as a rise in sea surface temperature and downstream sedimentation from inland logging activities, can threaten the effectiveness of MPA management actions. It is not surprising that the maintenance of habitat complexity and 'health' (integrity) is considered a critical measure of success in many MPAs, particularly in large-scale, ecosystem-level MPAs that are representative of multiple habitats. Awareness and an improved understanding of the sources and levels of change to habitat structure can not only allow managers to identify and potentially address them, but also re-evaluate and adjust MPA boundaries and activity zoning intuitively through time to adapt to such change.

***The distribution of habitat and habitat types in an MPA depends on the physical and biological characteristics of the living space. For example, this atoll in Yap, south Pacific, demonstrates zones of habitats associated with coral reef, from onshore out to offshore waters by depth and substrate type. These habitats can include:***

***a) Onshore sandy beach***
***b) Intertidal mud flats and reef rubble zone***
***c) Shallow water patch reef and seagrass meadow***
***d) Inshore back reef flat and reef crest***
***e) Spur-and-groove reef channels and fore reef slope***
***f) Nearshore coastal waters.***

**Relates to goals and objectives**

GOAL 1: 1B

GOAL 2: 2D

GOAL 3: 3A 3B

GOAL 4: 4A 4B 4C 4D

GOAL 5: 5C 5E

NOAA Photo Library

Jurgen Freund /naturepl.com

B3

***Examples of natural disturbance events that are known to lead to changes in habitat distribution and complexity are storms and cyclones (inset). Bottom trawling, dynamite fishing (main picture) and cyanide fishing are examples of localized, man-made events known to reduce habitat complexity.***

*This indicator relates closely to all five biophysical goals identified for MPAs (see Figure B1), particularly goals 4 (habitat protected) and 5 (degraded areas restored).*

## *How to collect the data*

Data collection for this indicator requires an in-depth process of survey and characterization in and around the MPA.

A full inventory of habitats found in and around the entire area of the MPA can be done if the evaluation team has adequate time and resources to do it. Otherwise, a minimum of 20 to 30% of the total area in and around the MPA should be randomly sampled and characterized, with surveys being stratified by depth and substrate type. The evaluation team should at least aim to characterize 'priority' habitat types; that is, those habitats that make up a majority of the total area represented

### *Requirements*

- Designated sampling sites inside and outside the MPA.
- An adequate number of trained staff and/or volunteers.
- Evaluation team ability to recognise, distinguish between and delineate distinct habitat types/zones and **ecotones** (areas of overlapping habitat).
- Evaluation team familiarity with the types and extent of active anthropogenic threats; ability to recognise the effects of man-made disturbance.
- Participation from or access to an experienced community ecologist and/or habitat survey and mapping specialist.
- A boat (with safety equipment) and engine.
- Survey tools (e.g. tape measure, compass, towline, submersible writing slate) for *in situ* characterization of substrate and assemblages of organisms that comprise habitat.
- SCUBA or snorkelling equipment.
- Base maps (ideally digitized) for the larger area being surveyed, at various (high to low) resolutions.
- A handheld global positioning system (GPS).
- Geographic information systems (GIS) software and relevant hardware (e.g. computers, digital plotter and large printer).
- Advanced (if applicable): access to remote sensing technologies (e.g. satellite imagery and/or completed aerial photography); small airplane or helicopter to do aerial photography; digital video camera and underwater housing; remote operated vehicle (ROV) and other robotics; bottom-profiling sonar; evaluation team familiarity with habitat utilization patterns.

within the MPA or are known to be of important conservation and management value for focal species occurring within the MPA (for example, in estuarine habitats where juveniles of focal species recruit to and grow out). Ideally, most MPAs will have the time and resources to conduct an *in situ* inventory and characterization of all habitat types (not just priority ones) represented within and around the MPA. In some cases, all of the habitat types represented within the MPA will be viewed as management priorities and therefore will need to be surveyed.

Habitat characterization is done through *in situ* and/or *ex situ* surveys in and around the MPA. Three categories of data are collected through the habitat characterization survey: 1) habitat composition data, 2) habitat status data and 3) habitat distribution data. Data collection methods for all three categories are described below.

Habitat composition data are collected through a survey of the biotic (species, community composition) and abiotic (substrate, water conditions) characteristics of the sampled area. Allowing for distinctions to be made between patterns of biotic and abiotic characteristics observed, the different habitat types and ecotones occurring can be identified. *In situ* methods of shallow-water surveys to characterize substrate and single- or multiple-species assemblages of organisms are discussed under indicators B1 and B2. Survey methods used to collect data on water conditions are described under indicator B8.

Where these *in situ* sampling methods are not feasible, a qualitative generalization of observed substrate type and species composition can be performed within the area surveyed through timed or random swims with skin diving gear. More advanced technologies for alternative *in situ* habitat profiling may be available at some MPAs, including shallow-water video survey, remotely operated vehicle videography, use of manned submersibles, use of side-scan and bottom penetrating sonar, use of multibeam bathymetry and echo sounding, and bottom sampling. Such alternative *in situ* survey technologies are particularly useful in deep waters.

*In situ data collection methods for this indicator are similar to those of indicators B1, B2, B4 and B5. They should therefore be measured together.*

Characterization of habitat composition can also be done *ex situ* using remote sensing technologies, such as satellite imagery and aerial photography. Such *ex situ* methods may be particularly useful within large or deepwater MPAs where *in situ* sampling is not feasible or efficient. It is recommended that where possible, a minimum level of *in situ* survey should be done to validate data collected through *ex situ* characterization.

In some cases, habitat composition may be difficult to undertake using either *in situ* or *ex situ* methods. In such cases, an approximation of habitat composition, status and distribution should be made using the best available information and knowledge (for example, from the examination of bottom trawl catches outside the MPA and interviews with fishers using the area).

Next, habitat status data should be collected at survey sites. Habitat status is measured as the quantity and quality of live habitat observed within a sampled area. Habitat quantity is typically estimated as the percentage of habitat cover (live or otherwise; e.g. percentage (%) live cover of coral reefs, percentage (%) cover of reef rubble) and/or the density of live organisms (e.g. live seagrass bunches) observed within a sampled area (in $m^2$ or $km^2$). It can also be measured as the volume (grams per $m^2$) of live biomass, such as with kelp or mangrove forests. *In situ* sampling of benthic habitat is often done using transects, quadrats,

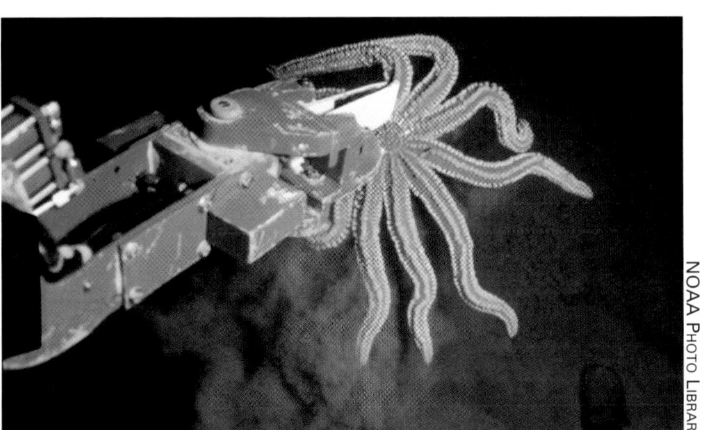

NOAA Photo Library

**Within deep water MPAs,** in situ **habitat characterization may only be possible through the use of technologies such as manned submersibles or remotely operated robotics.**

plots, point-counts or timed swims. Habitat quality is a measure of the robustness or vitality of live habitat encountered during a survey. At a minimum, a subjective characterization of the apparent vitality of the live habitat observed within the surveyed area can be made. A more structured characterization of this would use a standardized

B3

ordinal scale of habitat quality; for example a 3-point scale from "dying" (lowest) to "deteriorating" (middle) and "healthy" (highest). A diagnostic checklist of known indicators related to the health of the habitat type being assessed (e.g. coloration, morphology, frequency or volume) may also be useful to review when live habitat is encountered within the survey area. *Ex situ* methods of habitat status typically involve aerial estimates of habitat quantity (total $km^2$) generated through remote sensing data.

Finally, data on the physical distribution of habitat observed are collected through measurement of the habitat's:

- location (depth and position) within the area surveyed,
- structure (height from the seafloor/substrate, density and volume), and
- configuration (placement relative to other habitats within the area surveyed).

Structure and configuration data collected are measured as units of size ($cm^2$ or $m^2$) or area ($m^2$ or $km^2$). Location data collected are measured as either a unit of depth ($m^2$ or $km^2$) or as geographically referenced coordinates.

These data are collected either:

- *in situ* using a handheld GPS and natural land and sea reference points, or
- *ex situ* via aerial photography or satellite imagery.

Geo-referenced data allow for the demarcation of distinct habitat types observed within the area surveyed. Where the use of a handheld GPS is not possible, compass bearings run from permanent buoys at known and easily referenced locations on a map can serve to help demarcate habitat boundaries. Likewise, the use of land and sea markers can provide a rough estimate as to the distribution and extent of habitat types within the MPA area. Habitat distribution data reflect the physical positions of the various habitat types within the area surveyed, including their structure and zonation across it.

Periodic re-evaluation of the composition, location, quantity and quality of habitat types in the future will help the evaluation team to determine whether or not changes in the distribution and complexity of the habitat are occurring, and if so, to what degree. Ideally, data on habitat characterization should be collected annually, at least within priority habitat types. In many MPAs this may be

*The identification, monitoring and impact of human-induced disturbance events can be documented through the measurement of indicator B10.*

▼ ***Vertically stratified habitats, such as kelp forests, will require more survey effort than habitats which can be characterized simply as seafloor habitat.***

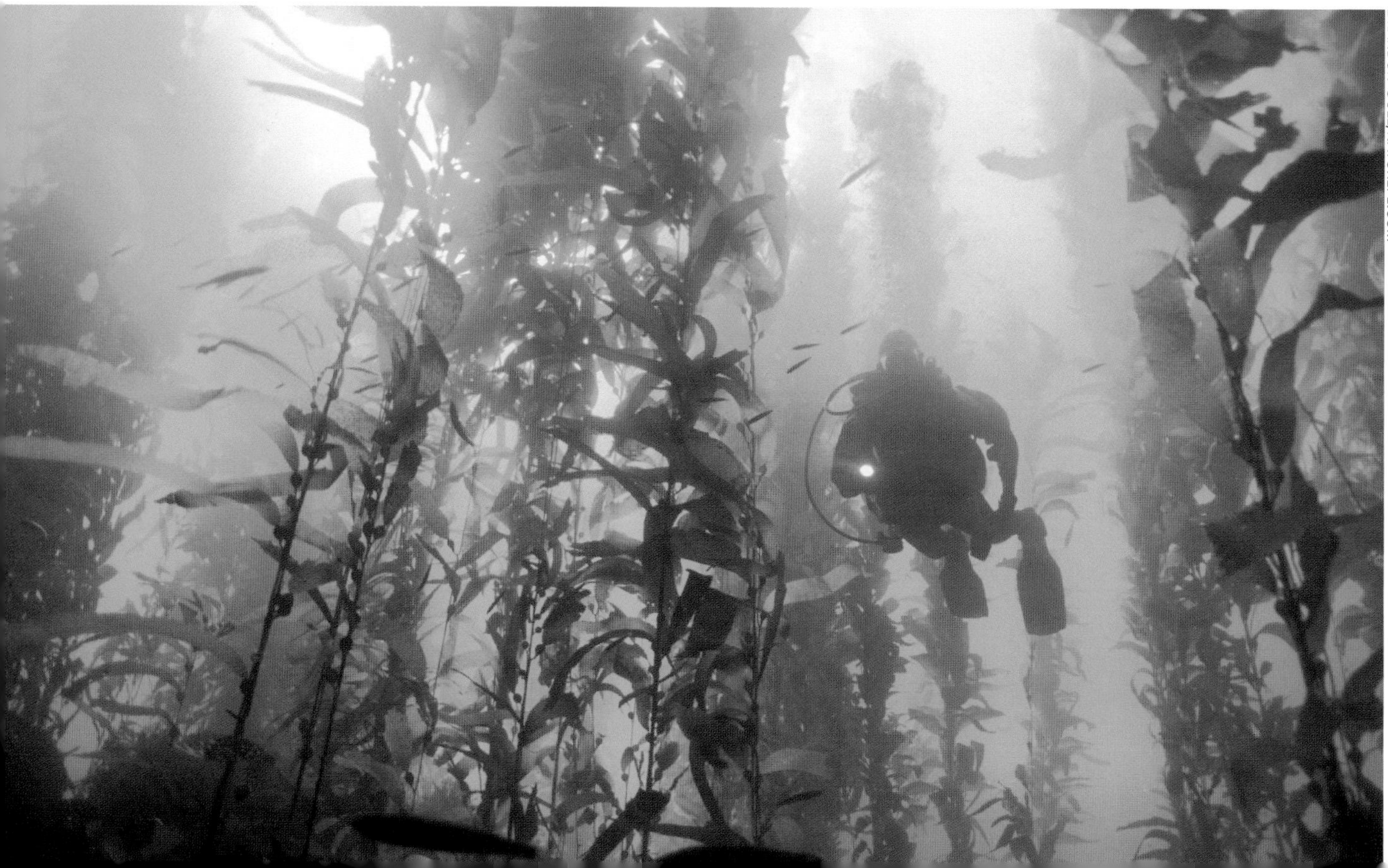

BRANDON COLE/NATUREPL.COM

© WWF-CANON/JÜRGEN FREUND

▲ ***Completing the habitat map for Tubbataha Reef National Marine Park, one of the MPA pilot sites for this book.***

unrealistic. In such cases, repeat surveys can be attempted every two to three years, but no later than five years. Monitoring habitat types with annual or perennial life histories may require more frequent observation. Repeat surveys should be conducted more frequently following natural or human disturbance events that are known by MPA staff and stakeholders to have impacted the area in or around the MPA. Determining the correct timing of when during year the repeat surveys should be conducted may depend on the growth period and **phenology** of the organisms that make up the habitat.

### *How to analyse and interpret results*

The analytical challenge of this indicator is to determine whether or not changes observed in habitat location, composition, quantity and quality inside the MPA are due to naturally occurring phenomena (such as ecological succession) or are enhanced by or a consequence of human perturbation. In order to do this, the habitat types characterized through the survey need to be mapped, labelled and monitored.

Mapping is done by plotting collected habitat characterization data onto a geo-referenced **basemap** of suitable resolution for the entire survey area. The demarcation of observed habitat boundaries onto the basemap is done using the GPS-referenced data that were collected through the habitat

Table B1

**An example table of data entered on the mean % total benthic cover for observed habitat types within coral reef habitat inside and outside the MPA**

| | *MPA* | | | *Control Area 1* | | | *Control Area 2* | | |
|---|---|---|---|---|---|---|---|---|---|
| *Habitat type* | *Mean* | *SD* | *n* | *Mean* | *SD* | *n* | *Mean* | *SD* | *n* |
| Hard corals | 17.64 | 12.59 | 16 | 43.65 | 14.14 | 20 | 36.63 | 8.62 | 16 |
| Coralline algae | 13.07 | 15.61 | 16 | 8.13 | 7.32 | 20 | 2.60 | 2.25 | 16 |
| Fleshy algae | 44.86 | 15.51 | 16 | 10.08 | 6.97 | 20 | 2.28 | 2.26 | 16 |
| Soft corals | 10.05 | 15.22 | 16 | 4.38 | 5.93 | 20 | 39.54 | 13.21 | 16 |
| Sponges | 0.22 | 0.61 | 16 | 2.15 | 2.33 | 20 | 1.09 | 1.13 | 16 |
| Sand | 0.48 | 1.37 | 16 | 0.29 | 0.49 | 20 | 0.15 | 0.30 | 16 |
| Reef rubble and dead rock | 13.68 | 13.78 | 16 | 31.33 | 15.64 | 20 | 17.71 | 10.23 | 16 |

characterization survey. Boundary delineation should be done at a scale that is meaningful for decision-making purposes by the MPA; in some cases this may be as high resolution as a few metres. At a minimum, the boundaries, distribution and overlap of all priority habitat types should be mapped and labelled appropriately against the basemap. Ideally, a precise delineation and labelling of all habitats occurring within and around the MPA should occur using high-resolution basemaps. Boundary delineation should be referenced against other existing habitat maps, if available. Consult MPA staff and local stakeholders to compare generated results against knowledge and experience in order to check for accuracy and identify any potential needs to ground-truth questionable habitat boundaries. Encourage the process of boundary- and fact-checking to be inclusive and participatory.

In some cases, digital basemaps will be available. In other cases, only hard copies of the necessary basemaps will be available, sourced perhaps from government offices or private surveyors. If possible, hard copies of basemaps should be digitally scanned into a computer so that data collected can be exported from database storage and plotted out spatially against the digitized map using image editing or **geographic information system** (GIS) software. Where possible, mapping results should be triangulated through the use of data collected both *in situ* and *ex situ* and validated through stakeholder interviews and discussions. In addition to habitat characterization data, you should attempt to map the spatial extent of known disturbance events and threats.

Other geo-referenced biological and social data collected from other indicators outlined in this guidebook may be useful to overlay against habitat characterization data collected. From such multi-indicator data overlays, patterns between biological processes, human behaviour and habitat distribution may be elucidated spatially. Such spatial overlay and analysis of data from multiple indicators is a process that will not only necessitate access to GIS technologies, but also to additional time, skills and resources.

*Changes observed in habitat distribution and complexity may relate to the abundance of populations of focal species and how they utilize the habitat (e.g. for foraging or nesting). Recognising this, in the absence of existing and sufficient baseline information on populations of focal species and their habitat utilization patterns, this indicator may need to be measured concurrently with indicator B1.*

Where no basemaps, GPS-referenced data or GIS technologies are available, at a minimum spatial data on habitats collected through the use of reference buoys, compass bearings, and land and sea markers can be mapped out by hand on to graph paper. Mapped results created by hand can then be photocopied and checked against MPA staff and/or stakeholder knowledge.

Once mapped, calculate the extent, or the mean % benthic cover of the total area, for each habitat type observed within the overall habitat surveyed. Record these figures for each habitat type in a table (see example table, above), along with their standard deviations and the number of replicate surveys completed within the area sampled. Include data for both the MPA and control areas studied. Periodically update the table as new data are collected through time. Considering the spatial extent and distribution of each habitat type on a regular basis (as repeat data are collected) will allow for comparison and monitoring of changes in the extent of habitats through time.

Compare the extent (total area) of each habitat type through time and determine whether or not there are observable changes or trends in the amount of habitat that is present. Are any trends in the reduction or increase of the total area of a habitat type evident? If so, how can such changes be explained (for example, as the result of a recent cyclone)? In some cases it may take several years to detect observable changes or trends; in other cases it make take only a few months after a disturbance to see marked changes. How do total areas of habitat within versus outside the MPA compare?

In addition to the extent of habitat, are there any observable changes in terms of the spatial distribution and configuration of habitats present within versus outside the MPA? If so, what if anything can be deduced from the apparent movement of these habitat types and their boundaries? If reductions are observed in the extent of certain habitat types, is the area lost being 'replaced' with other habitat types? If so, what could possibly explain this? How are rates of change different between habitats located inside and outside the MPA?

How do the other characteristics of each habitat change through time, if at all? What trends can be observed in terms of the make up (composition) of each habitat type? Are there composition differences within versus outside the MPA? What does the presence or absence of a species that contributes to the composition of the habitat tell you? Are any changes in habitat quality being generally observed? How is the location and distribution of the habitat in the environment changing?

In overlaying the estimated spatial extent of known threats and disturbance events (see indicator B10), how are observed changes in habitat extent and quality related to the location and movement of such threats? If habitat reductions observed are believed to be the result of deleterious human activities, based on the nature and location of such activities, is it realistically within the ability of the management team and the activities of the MPA to reduce or halt them? If not, how will such deleterious activities be addressed, if at all?

Next, estimate the habitat complexity inside and outside the MPA by dividing the diversity (number) of habitat types and distinct zones found within the surveyed area by the total area (in km$^2$) and summing the total length of all boundaries dividing adjacent or overlapping habitat types. Record and monitor changes in these two measures of habitat complexity through time. In viewing the spatial distribution of habitat types and groups of habitat types, do particular patterns, clusters or zones of habitat appear? Through time, is the pattern and diversity of this mosaic being changed or reduced? Is the physical distribution and overlap among groups of habitats becoming more uniform or heterogeneous? In analysing composition data, how are the physical (location, height, area and volume) and biological (composition) dimensions of each habitat type changing in space and time? Are these dimensions becoming more complex or homogenous? Do inter-dependencies appear between constituent dimensions of each habitat type? If so, is it possible to generalize such inter-dependencies across other habitat types? How do habitat complexities compare inside and outside the MPA?

Directly determining habitat integrity is a highly complex process that in most cases would be unrealistic to expect a team to conduct as part of an MPA evaluation. However, estimating the rate of change of habitat extent and complexity within the MPA through time can serve as a proxy for habitat integrity. To estimate the rate of change, calculate the percentage of incremental change observed in the extent, quality (of live cover) and complexity (diversity) between present and last, and present and baseline measures. Score these values as the difference from 100 in observed percentage change and compare them against the rate of average incremental (yearly) change. Qualitatively describe how likely the habitat type will persist based on trends in observed change, observed changes in the rate of change, and as a description of how far away observed habitat distribution and complexity is from what had formerly or could likely be found under only natural conditions. Low rates of change or maintenance of the extent and complexity of habitat may indicate strong integrity. A sustained rate of decline observed in habitat distribution and complexity over a consecutive number of years may be indicative of recent or ongoing disturbance. Such dynamic observations may help to interpret early-warning signals that habitat integrity is deteriorating. On the other hand, documenting only marginal changes in habitat structure and complexity over time within an MPA in comparison to outside it may demonstrate effective management.

As further exploration of habitat integrity, explore correlating results from indicator B1 against habitat quantity and quality results. For example, how do the abundance data collected on a focal species that is known to be an indicator of habitat quality and integrity correlate with data collected on the percentage of live habitat cover observed, if at all? Habitat characterization and mapping results generated from this indicator should be summarized within a habitat inventory report. This report

### Outputs

- A table with % cover of observed habitat types.
- A habitat inventory report: a) delineating the identified habitat types and zones present within and around the MPA (including their location and extent), and b) profiling the biotic and abiotic composition, structure, and quantity and quality of each.
- A geo-referenced map of all habitats observed, their boundaries, and their distribution.
- A description of habitat complexity.
- An improved understanding of habitat integrity.
- For repeat surveys: a spatial analysis of the extent of observed change (if any noticeable) in habitat distribution and complexity over time.

### Other outputs (if applicable)

- A GIS database of data on the location and extent of habitat types and zones, their biotic and abiotic composition, their structure, and their quantity and quality.
- A collection of digital maps generated by GIS with varying levels of overlaid indicator data and analysis.

should identify, biologically and structurally characterize, and spatially delineate the position of all known habitat types occurring within and outside the MPA area. The report should also document any observed changes to the distribution and complexity of habitats through time, and discuss and interpret the analytical findings generated from measurement of this indicator. Review and discuss the results generated from this indicator and summarized in this report with a community ecologist familiar with the ecosystem and habitats involved prior to disseminating or using them for adaptive decision-making.



### *Strengths and limitations*

This indicator requires a significant investment of time, effort and financial resources, particularly within large MPAs hosting entire ecosystems and highly complex habitat structures. Data collection and analysis done at a high spatial resolution and scale can be expensive and tedious. In addition, both GIS analysis and the collection and use of remote sensing data are expensive and time consuming activities that require suitable staff experience, sophisticated equipment, and maintenance in order to be of use to the evaluation team. As a result of the combined technical (both survey and analysis), financial and human resource requirements, this indicator is one of the most cumbersome and resource-intensive ones offered in this guidebook, and may be out of the reach of many MPA operations.

Data must be collected at a geographic resolution that is precise enough to observe changes that occur at a fine scale. If the scale of analysis at which surveys are done is not sensitive to disturbance and biological change, the results of the indicator may be false in that they miss detecting actual changes that are underway. Also, even if adequate resolution and coverage in the survey are provided, there may be insufficient power to explain observed changes.

Despite these challenges, understanding the status and trends in the distribution and complexity of habitats within and around the MPA remains a priority information need and prerequisite to a well designed and adapted ecosystem management effort.

### *Useful references and Internet links*


CSIRO (1998). *Reef Resource Survey and Habitat Mapping of Shallow Reefs in Milne Bay Province, Papua New Guinea*. ACIAR Phase 1 Proposal. Submission by the CSIRO Marine Research to the ACIAR, Canberra, Australia.

Done, T.J. (1982). "Patterns in the distribution of coral communities across the central Great Barrier Reef". *Coral Reefs* 1: 95–107.

Done, T.J. (1995). "Ecological criteria for evaluating coral reefs and their implications for managers and researchers." *Coral Reefs* 14: 183–92.

Fonseca, M.S., Kenworthy, W.J. and Thayer, G.W. (1998). *Guidelines for the conservation and restoration of seagrasses in the United States and adjacent waters.* NOAA Coastal Ocean Program Decision Analysis Series No. 12. NOAA Coastal Ocean Office, Silver Spring, MD, USA.

Mapstone, B.D., Ayling, A.M. and Choat, J.H. (1998). *Habitat, Cross Shelf, and Regional Patterns in the Distributions and Abundances of Some Coral Reef Organisms on the Northern Great Barrier Reef, with Comment on the Implications for Future Monitoring.* Research Publication No. 48. Great Barrier Reef Marine Park Authority, Townsville, Queensland, Australia.

NOAA and Analytic Laboratories of Hawaii (2000). *Benthic Habitat Mapping Program Partnership.* [Online URL: cramp.wcc.hawaii.edu/Overview/5._Cooperative_Programs/NOAAALH_Benthic_Habitat_Mapping_Program/Default.asp]

Tupper, M. and Boutilier, R.G. (1997). "Effects of habitat on settlement, growth, predation risk, and post-settlement mortality of a temperate reef fish". *Marine Ecology Progress Series* 151: 225–236.


#### Index of biotic integrity


Karr, J.R. (1981). "Assessment of biotic integrity using fish communities". *Fisheries* 6(6): 21–27.

Karr J.R., Fausch, K.D., Angermeirer, P.L., Yant, P.R. and Schlosser, I.J. (1986). "Assessment of biological integrity in running waters: A –menthol and it's rationale". *Illinois Nat. Hist. Surv. Spec. Publ.* 5.

United States Environmental Protection Agency (2002). "A brief history of the Index of Biotic Integrity". [Online URL: www.epa.gov/bioindicators/html/ibi-hist.html]


#### GIS introduction


Convis, C.L. (ed.) (2001). *Conservation Geography: Case Studies in GIS, Computer Mapping, and Activism*. Environmental Systems Research Institute (ESRI) Press. Redlands, CA, USA.

© WWF-Canon/Jurgen Freund

*A diver takes vital measurements at the Tubbataha Reef National Marine Park, Philippines.*

Box B4

## Example from the Field

Between the mid- and late-1990s, sharp declines were observed in the percentage of live hard coral cover located within the Tubbataha Reef National Marine Park. In part, this is thought to be due to the massive bleaching experienced throughout much of the world during 1998, contributing to an upsurge in algal cover observed in 1999. Since then, habitat surveys completed up to 2002 indicate that live reef cover appears to be gradually recovering. The protection of Tubbataha from fishing pressures is believed to have contributed to this positive trend, and some are suggesting that the habitat is exhibiting resilience to the disturbances experienced during the 1990s. The ability of the Tubbataha management team to clearly convey this story with target audiences is helping to ensure the area's future support.

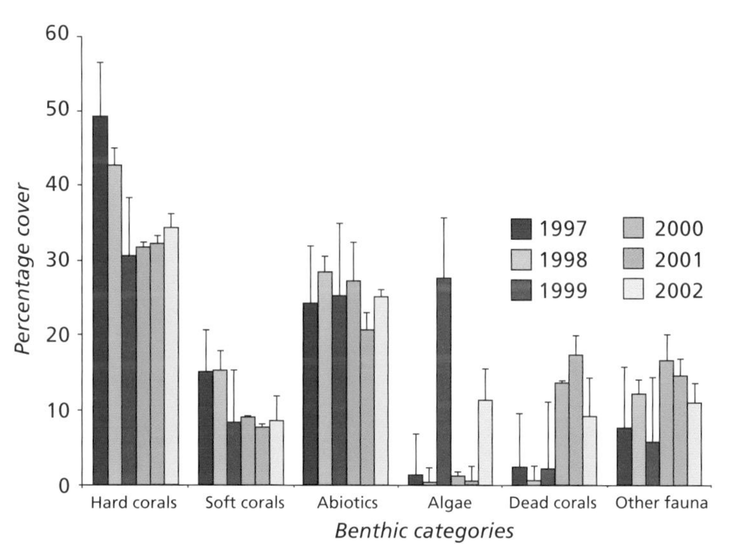


***The observed percentage of live cover from 1997 to 2002 of six major benthic habitat types found within Tubbataha Reef National Marine Park.***

Ripple, W. (ed.) (1994). *The GIS Applications Book: Examples in Natural Resources. A Compendium.* American Society for Photogrammetry and Remote Sensing, Bethesda, MD, USA.

USGS (2002). Geographic Information Systems. [Online URL: www.usgs.gov/research/gis/title.html]

### Remote sensing

Green, E.P., Mumby, P.J., Edwards, A.J. and Clark, C.D. (2000). *Remote Sensing Handbook for Tropical Coastal Management.* Coastal Management Sourcebooks 3. UNESCO, Paris, France. [Online URL : http://www.unesco.org/csi/pub/source/rs.htm]

Green, E.P., Mumby, P.J., Edwards, A.J. and Clark, C.D. (1996). "A review of remote sensing for the assessment and management of tropical coastal resources". *Coastal Management* 24: 1–40.

***Relates to goals and objectives***

GOAL 1
1B 1C
1D

GOAL 2
2A 2C
2E 2G

GOAL 3
3B 3D

GOAL 4
4A 4B
4C 4D

GOAL 5
5B 5C
5D 5E

## *What is 'composition and structure of the community'?*

A **community** is a collection of different and interacting populations of organisms (biota) found living together in a defined geographic area, including indigenous and exotic organisms. Some MPAs will host multiple communities of organisms. This indicator is concerned with the species that both comprise habitat types and the organisms residing in them to form the community – i.e. what is in the community.

> *Note this indicator is primarily used to collect information on multiple populations of species (focal and otherwise) within a community sampled. It is not expected that the evaluation team would realistically be able to measure all populations of organisms that occur within the community.*

**Community composition** is the diversity and makeup of all species present within a community and their relative abundance (respective to one another). Species richness, dominance, diversity, and relative abundance are all characteristics of community composition.

Community structure is a summary description of how the numbers and relative abundance of species occur within a community and are found spatially across the physical environment (form) and habitats in or upon which the members (composition) of the community live. Community structure can therefore be described as the numbers and relative abundances of all species within the community and how they are organized into zones, or strata, of living space. For example, at a basic level the community structure of a coastal ecosystem could be considered within **intertidal**, **neritic** and **benthic zones**. Habitat diversity and relative habitat abundance are both important determinants of community structure. **Abiotic** characteristics (e.g. geology and light) also largely influence community structure.

## *Why measure it?*

This is one of the most commonly identified biophysical indicators of high importance. The maintenance or restoration of the naturally occurring composition and structure of a resident community is often desired to encourage the 'integrity' of an ecosystem, including its health, functioning, and resistance to disturbance. Understanding changes – and the extent and sources (both natural and anthropogenic perturbations) of such changes – occurring within the composition and structure of each community found within and adjacent to the MPA are therefore prerequisites for diagnosing and treating ailing ecosystems. Measurement of community composition and structure through time allows managers to evaluate whether or not their management efforts (in this case, the use of an MPA) are having the desired effects on the target ecosystems.

Additionally, understanding what species comprise a community or organisms and how these organisms are structured within the natural setting allows managers to prioritize and monitor coastal areas requiring management action. For example, by improving the understanding of which near shore areas host the highest levels of species richness and diversity, managers can begin to adaptively prioritize their management efforts and allocate resources accordingly as conditions change. This increases the investment value of management efforts through time and reduces risk.

### *Requirements*

- Similar requirements as listed under indicators B1, B2 and B3.
- A representative sample of survey sites inside and outside the MPA, stratified across known habitat types and zones.
- An adequate number of staff and/or volunteers (respective to the size of the area needing to be surveyed) are needed who are: a) trained in underwater census, b) can accurately identify the species being surveyed *in situ*, and c) willing and committed to undertake the necessary survey work. A minimum team of four people is recommended.
- The necessary survey equipment (e.g. a boat with safety equipment, survey gear and snorkel, hookah or SCUBA equipment) needed to observe the various species and habitats observed within the sampled area (both inside and outside the MPA).
- The ecological knowledge and experience necessary to interpret changes in community composition and structure. This may require consulting the services and/or advice of a professional ecologist familiar with the study area. This caveat comes from recognition that there are rarely simple, universal benchmarks that will describe such changes everywhere they are encountered.

## *How to collect the data*

Where the area to be surveyed under this indicator hosts multiple communities, it may be necessary for the evaluation team to work with management staff to select a set of priority (e.g. two or three) communities that warrant an evaluation of composition and structure based on their ecological role and importance within the overall ecosystem; for example, communities hosting focal species, rare or fragile communities, or communities subjected to strong human impact, such as dive tourism sites or trawling locations.

The methods of data collection for this indicator are described under the *in situ* observation methods for indicators B1, B2 and B3. Data collection for this indicator should be executed simultaneously with indicators B1 and/or B2 in order to maximize the return on the team's investment in monitoring resources. However, unlike B1 or B2 this indicator requires observation of ***all*** (or the visible and vast majority of) living organisms found within the designated community and particular location sampled, as opposed to only a few selected focal species. Therefore the survey is likely to require significantly more energy, time, and capital resources than B1 or B2.

*This indicator is associated with the methods and data collected under indicators B1 and B2. In particular, collection of data on the relative abundance of selected focal species found within a sampled community will be useful under this indicator.*

As a first step, it will be important to identify for each community (or selected priority communities) occurring in and around the MPA, the various habitat types and/or zones found within the areas being managed and contained within the MPA. Next, within each zone/habitat type, a complete inventory should be done of all the types (species) and abundances (frequency) of organisms observed within each community. The precise survey technique used for observing and inventorying the organisms present will depend on the habitat and characteristics of where the survey is being conducted (see indicators B1 and B3 for specifics). Ideally, the evaluation team would have a measure of the area surveyed. Generally speaking, however, randomized timed swims and stationary point counts across the habitat types surveyed will suffice in lieu of visual censuses along transects or within quadrats. These methods are feasible and well documented in detail elsewhere in the literature (see Useful references, below).

Data collected from within the area sampled should reflect the following:

- ❑ A record of each organism (species) observed;
- ❑ A note of which organisms observed are endangered, exotic and rare;

▼ ***In the Philippines, local government managers sometimes train coastal residents in the use of simple assessment techniques to monitor changes in the composition and structure of mangrove forest, seagrass and coral reef communities over time.***

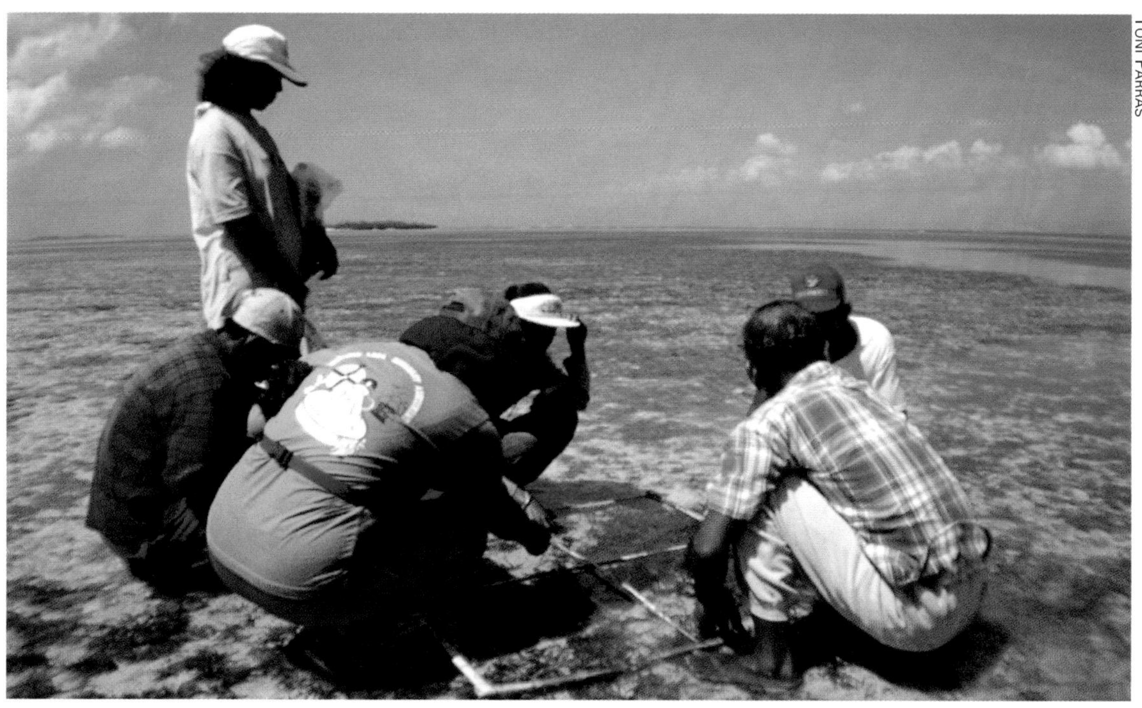

Toni Parras

- The number (frequency) and size (where relevant and feasible) of each individual observed within each species;
- The relative position/depth in the water column where the individual is observed; and
- The habitat type(s) within which they are sampled, including the species that they comprise.

Where possible, the composition and structure of habitats should also be documented through estimation of the percentage of cover and other appropriate measures of abundance. In particular, biotic structural components of habitats (e.g. kelp beds, soft-bottom communities, rocky and coral reefs, seagrasses, mangroves) should be adequately sampled to estimate coverage. Techniques to do this include *in situ* snorkel and SCUBA survey approaches (e.g. manta tow, line intercept transect, quadrats) as well as remote sensing (e.g. aerial photography, satellite imagery, videoed transects) technologies (see indicator B3). The choice of a technique depends largely upon the abilities and resources of the team undertaking the habitat composition study and the type of habitat being inventoried. This may require separate surveys to be conducted from the species inventory described above. Where possible, it is encouraged that the habitat composition surveys be conducted concurrently with other surveys designed to collect other indicator information. For example, during a transect survey across an area of coral reefs sampled, one group of divers may collect species abundance and size data (indicators B1 and B2) concurrently with a second group conducting a line intercept along the transect to provide a profile of the community composition of the coral reef habitat.

Survey of deepwater and pelagic communities will require considerably more time and effort to undertake. In such cases, *ex situ* survey methods (as described under B3) may be useful. Species inventory for deepwater communities is often done through examination of trawl or seine net catches. As such techniques are destructive and not likely to be suitable for regular use within the MPA or under a sustainable monitoring protocol, such destructive survey methods are not recommended.

*Data collection for this indicator can be linked to data collection under indicator B6. Additionally, as this indicator is tied to better understanding the effects of human extraction and other activities on the marine environment, it has links to indicator B10 and several socio-economic indicators.*

Species inventories and habitat cover surveys for each community sampled should be conducted at least every two or three years or ideally annually, particularly if impacts or changes in the community composition are evident. A sufficient number of replicate surveys must be sampled across communities and study sites in order to have confidence in results generated in terms of what is and is not there and in what relative quantities. The timing of inventories undertaken during the year should be repeated consistently and take into account known life history events such as spawning, recruitment, seasonal migration, etc.

> *Note that there are more advanced and some highly technical methods available to the evaluation team to measure community composition. The team will need to have the skills and time necessary to conduct such advanced study, or have access to external expertise and resources to do so.*

## How to analyse and interpret results

Collate, enter and manage data gathered within the MPA effectiveness-monitoring database.

There are several simple analyses that can be undertaken by calculating species composition (i.e. diversity in terms of richness and evenness) and structure (i.e. relative abundance and physical distribution) using the data that have been collected. In particular, a minimum of two attributes must be calculated in order to measure this indicator:

- species richness, and
- relative species abundance.

Two additional attributes can be optionally calculated:

- species evenness (using the Shannon and Simpson's indices), and
- habitat diversity.

Species richness is measured as the total number of species present within the community. To determine this, generate a list of all species observed within the managed area and categorize each by habitat type/zone surveyed. Generating a profile (matrix/diagram and description) of the habitat composition and structure of species found within and outside the MPA will also be useful. The total number of species present from this list can be monitored through time to keep track of changes/trends. Note that it will be necessary to keep abreast of any relevant taxonomic changes or new understandings related to speciation, particularly with marine organisms where new informa-

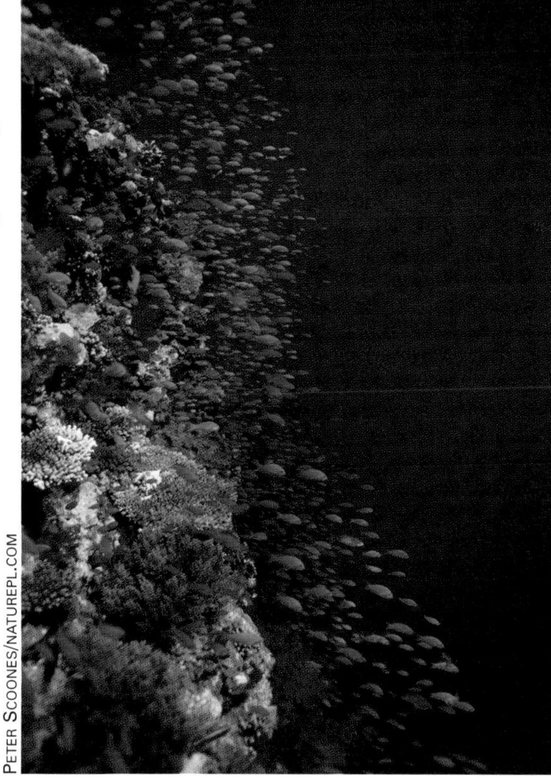


**An example of a vertically structured community from the Red Sea, Egypt.**

tion is continually updating taxonomic relationships such as with coral reef fishes.

Next create a graph showing the relative species abundance (or create a relative abundance index) by plotting the commonness (grouped from most to least on the x-axis, and listed by name) of species present in the community against the frequency with which they were observed (y-axis) relative to one another. This can further be analysed at a habitat-specific level. Highlight/identify exotic, rare, endangered and commonly found organisms within this description. Characterize the community structure by determining and describing the relative abundance of various species present within the community.

Also, from this point species evenness can be measured as the proportion of individuals among species based on relative abundance respective to the degree that a species dominates a community (dominance ranking). Calculate a measure of dominance (that is those that biologically control a community by most influencing the surrounding environment) using the Simpson's Index of concentration (see Useful references, below). Using this index, determine which species most dominate the community. Species evenness can be calculated using a Shannon Diversity Index, a relatively simple calculation well documented in the literature (see Useful references, below). Comparisons between indices can be analysed using a modified t-test method to compare Shannon indices (see Magurran, 1988). The Morisita-Horn Index allows for comparisons between baseline and time series results (see Magurran, 1988).

In addition, a habitat profile can be developed through a Habitat Diversity Index using Shannon calculations for the area surveyed. A map characterizing habitat types, diversity and coverage across the managed area and within the MPA can be built from the results of this analysis. Changes in habitat composition through time can be monitored using these results, and results can be compared against previous spatial data (if possible, overlaid using geographic information systems) to determine the location, extent and degree of observed habitat change underway.

In terms of fish assemblages, a common test for comparing composition observations of fish communities through time is the Czekanowski's Proportional Similarity measure (see Schoener, 1968, for methods).

Characterization of the relative abundance of species within the community can optionally be identified as either **log-normal**, **broken stick**, or ecological dominance. Distribution of these patterns of relative abundance can be plotted and analysed. These analytical methods are well documented in the literature (see Useful references, below).

Based on the community structure (relative abundance, dominance shifts, and physical distribution) data collected for each community surveyed within and outside the MPA and the resulting evidence generated, is the community studied within the MPA experiencing a notable shift (large shifts away from normal structure in relative abundance or dominance) in terms of its structure? Do data suggest that the community studied within the MPA is experiencing a notable increase (presence of more than three species previously absent and/or increase in the relative abundance of a several species) in terms of its diversity?

Discuss results between indices across and between habitats and communities sampled. What patterns in local and regional diversity can be elucidated? How do communities compare relative to the species that are found in them and their abundances? Are there any changes observed through time regarding the relative abundance of native versus invasive species, and if so, what correlated changes in species richness and abundance are observed with the presence of these invasive organisms?

If changes are observed in community composition and structure (such as a reduction in the diversity of species present or shifts in dominance of certain species), or if the presence of new or exotic species is detected, these changes may necessitate

### Outputs

- List of the species and habitats composing the community.
- Description of how these species and habitats are structured within the community.
- Profile of the relative abundance of selected species present within the community.
- Profile of species dominance.
- Profile of species diversity (richness and evenness).
- Profile of habitat diversity.
- Habitat composition/type map.

increased effort to monitor these specific observations more regularly (annually or twice a year).

Note that confident interpretation of changes observed in community and diversity require sufficient time and an adequate dataset. Drawing credible conclusions within the short-term may be a challenging task, and should not be underestimated. Short-term changes observed in biodiversity can lead to misinterpretation of results; for example, the number of species in a community may rise with or shortly after the onset of a disturbance, not dropping until a later time period. Finally, ecological attributes can suggest or contribute toward observed changes in community composition shifts, such as with interactions between populations of organisms or in patterns and gradients of community-habitat utilization.

## Strengths and limitations

The basic methodological strengths and limitations of the *in situ* survey techniques identified here are described under indicators B1 and B2. Additionally, not all the habitat types need to receive the same survey effort. For example, coral reef monitoring may be prioritized over seagrasses or other soft-bottom communities based on threat, value and risk assessment.

An adequate understanding of changes in community composition and structure is critical to achieve optimal management and fully understand the extent of impacts that management interventions have on the environment concerned. Establishing empirical causality between community composition changes and/or stability and implementation of an MPA is notably challenging, but nevertheless critical to improving MPA use and replication should such causality be established.

This indicator is one of the more challenging biophysical indicators to measure. The actual survey methods involved are relatively straightforward and approachable with a modest level of training and experience. However, due to the indicator's scope of data collection, a thorough and comprehensive understanding of community composition and structure will require considerably increased staff time, effort and financial resources beyond what is required for simply monitoring the abundance and structure of populations of selected focal species. Beyond data collection, this indicator also requires substantially increased analytical and interpretive complexity. With this complexity there is also a higher degree of uncertainty involved in accurately interpreting results and drawing valid conclusions. Given these increased requirements, there is the risk that this indicator may be seen as a secondary priority in terms of

**Box B5**

### Example from the Field

To characterize the composition and structure of the extensive (110km long) coral reef community of Mexico's Sian Ka'an Coastal Biosphere Reserve, the species diversity of fish, algae and scleractinian corals was assessed across several monitoring stations. In comparing data collected over the past several years, fluctuations observed in species richness within the community appear to be occurring in a cyclical manner. Moreover, these changes to the community have not appeared to be overtly influenced or exacerbated by natural disturbances, such as hurricanes. Instead, recreational use, such as boat traffic, fishing and diving are increasingly attributed as the cause of change to the community structure.

Toni Parras

management effectiveness data collection when in actuality it is of primary importance given the priority goals and objectives of the MPA.

It should also be noted that the comparability of community composition results between a managed area (i.e. within the MPA) against adjacent, unmanaged areas undergoing both natural and man-made change may be difficult to interpret accurately due to "shifting baseline" effects. This effect is where the extent of changes in the community structure and composition that would naturally occur within the MPA if it were not experiencing human management intervention are not detected or are confused as "reductions" in changes observed in adjacent, unmanaged areas. The consequences of this effect can lead to errors in interpretation and conclusions when comparing reference and treatment (MPA) data. Given these potential problems, it would be wise to collect 5–10 years of data, rather than two or three, before attempting to interpret the results.

**Box B5 (cont.)**

***Changes observed within the composition of coral reef fish communities in Sian Ka'an over the past ten years***

| | Pedro Paila | | Yuyum |
|---|---|---|---|
| | back reef | reef crest edge | inner fore reef |
| **SPECIES RICHNESS** | | | |
| 1991 | 33 | 23 | 31 |
| 1996 | 24 | 30 | 26 |
| 1997 | 15 | 41 | 29 |
| 1998 | 11 | 20 | 28 |
| 1999 | 20 | 27 | 18 |
| 2000 | – | 19 | 15 |
| 2001 | – | 15 | 16 |
| 2002 | 14 | 15 | 10 |
| **DENSITY (individuals/m$^2$)** | | | |
| 1991 | 0.90 | 0.39 | 0.60 |
| 1996 | 2.78 | 7.95 | 1.75 |
| 1997 | 0.80 | 2.85 | 5.43 |
| 1998 | 1.18 | 1.08 | 14.13 |
| 1999 | 0.38 | 1.13 | 0.60 |
| 2000 | – | 0.60 | 1.13 |
| 2001 | – | 0.93 | 0.98 |
| 2002 | 1.80 | 0.65 | 2.23 |
| **DIVERSITY (H)** | | | |
| 1991 | | | |
| 1996 | 2.2836 | 1.3274 | 2.7996 |
| 1997 | 2.3257 | 2.9356 | 2.1094 |
| 1998 | 1.3143 | 2.1973 | 0.5419 |
| 1999 | 1.7670 | 2.1341 | 0.8862 |
| 2000 | – | 2.4166 | 2.4585 |
| 2001 | – | 2.1214 | 2.3013 |
| 2002 | 1.7489 | 1.9241 | 0.8390 |
| **EVENNESS (J)** | | | |
| 1991 | | | |
| 1996 | 0.8060 | 0.4592 | 0.9196 |
| 1997 | 0.9699 | 0.8810 | 0.6474 |
| 1998 | 0.5708 | 0.8326 | 0.2181 |
| 1999 | 0.9081 | 0.8320 | 0.9071 |
| 2000 | – | 0.9422 | 0.9079 |
| 2001 | – | 0.7834 | 0.9261 |
| 2002 | 0.6627 | 0.8757 | 0.3644 |

## *Useful references and Internet links*


Done, T.J., Ogden, J.C., Wiebe, W.J., Rosen, B.R. (1996). "Diversity and ecosystem function of coral reefs". *In* H.A.Mooney, J.H. Cushman, E. Medina, O.E. Sala, E.D. Schulze (eds.), *Functional Roles of Biodiversity: A Global Perspective*. SCOPE 55. John Wiley & Sons, Chichester, UK. pp. 393–423.

Green, D.G., Bradbury, R.H. and Reichelt, R.E. (1987). "Patterns of predictability in coral reef community structure". *Coral Reefs* 6: 27–34.

Schoener, T.W. 1968. "Sizes of feeding territories among birds". *Ecology* 49: 123–141.


## Methods


English, S., Wilkinson, C. and Baker, V. (eds) (1997). *Survey Manual for Tropical Marine Resources. 2nd Edition.* Australian Institute for Marine Science, Townsville, Queensland, Australia.

Samoilys, M. (ed.) (1997). *Manual for Assessing Fish Stocks on Pacific Coral Reefs*. Training Series QE9700. Department of Primary Industries, Queensland, Australia.


## Fish community composition


Helfman, G.S. (1978). "Patterns of community structure in fishes: summary and overview". *Env. Biol. Fish.* 3: 129–148.

Sale, P.F. and Douglas, W.A. (1981). "Precision and accuracy of visual census technique for fish assemblages on coral patch reefs". *Environmental Biology of Fishes* 6:333–339.

Sale, P.F. and Douglas, W.A. (1984). "Temporal variability in the community structure of fish on coral patch reefs, and the relation of community structure to reef structure". *Ecology* 65:409–422.

Sale, P.F. (ed.) (1991). *The ecology of fishes on coral reefs*. Academic Press, San Diego, CA, USA.

NOAA Photo Library

## Diversity


Connell, J.H. (1978). "Diversity in tropical rain forests and coral reefs". *Science* 199: 1302–1310.

Dallmeier, F. (1996). "Biodiversity inventories and monitoring: essential elements for integrating conservation principles with resource development projects". *In* R.B. Szaro and D.W. Johnston (eds.), *Biodiversity in Managed Landscapes: Theory and Practice*. Oxford University Press, New York, NY, USA. pp 221–236.

Magurran, A.E. (1988). *Ecological Diversity and Its Measurement.* Princeton University Press, Princeton, NJ, USA.

Reid, W.V., McNeely, J.A., Tunstall, D.B., Bryant, D.A. and Winograd, M. (1993). *Biodiversity Indicators for Policy-Makers*. The World Resources Institute and IUCN. The World Resources Institute, Washington, DC, USA.

Monitoring and Assessment of Biodiversity Program (2002). Conservation and Research Center of the National Zoo's of the Smithsonian Institution. [Online URL: www.si.edu/simab/]

Saunders, D., Margules, C. and Hill, B. (1998). *Environmental Indicators: Biodiversity.* Australia State of the Environment Indicator Report. Environment Australia, Canberra, Australia.

Simpson, E.H. (1949). "Measurement of diversity". *Nature* 163: 688.

Szaro, R.B. and Johnston, D.W. (eds.) (1996). *Biodiversity in Managed Landscapes: Theory and Practice*. Oxford University Press, New York, NY.

World Bank (1998). *Guidelines for Monitoring and Evaluation for Biodiversity Projects.* Environment Department Paper No. 65. Global Environment Coordination, The World Bank, Washington, DC, USA.

## *What is 'recruitment success within the community'?*

**Recruitment success** within the community is the degree of larval input, settlement, and juvenile recruitment and **survivorship** experienced across populations of organisms that exist within a community. The degree of recruitment success is thought to serve as a proxy for the ability of the community to persist through time and be viable (i.e. the likelihood of continued persistence). Through the observation of changes in recruitment success, this may assist in describing how the relationships between populations in the community are or may be changing. This indicator therefore aims to provide some reflection on assessing the probability of a community of organisms being able to maintain itself through time.

This indicator is used to measure changes in the recruitment levels of multiple populations in a community so as to better understand how the community is doing overall. It is not expected that recruitment success can be monitored for all populations of species occurring within the community. It is hoped that from data collection on this indicator, MPA managers and other practitioners may improve their ability to predict whether or not the diversity and amount of surviving recruits observed in the community indicate recovery of the community toward what it was prior to threat exposure, or whether or not the recruits indicate that the community is merely being maintained or perhaps being degraded. In this sense it is intended to be a dynamic indicator, serving as a forecasting indicator of trends occurring in the community rather than simply a 'snapshot' of how the community is composed and structured (indicator B4). However, recognising the natural fluctuations in recruitment and seasonal population variability, the indicator must be considered from a long term perspective.

*As the composition and relative abundance of species within a community is in part a function of a community's ability to replenish its constituent populations, this indicator is closely related to and associated with indicator B4.*

*This indicator is sometimes used as a proxy for ecosystem health (B3, B4) and food web integrity (B6). It therefore has important meaning for managers who are concerned with maintaining ecosystems function and resiliency through MPA use.*

This indicator aims to enable rapid collection of information on multiple populations of species (including focal species) within the community across the relevant habitat types or zones, it is not realistically expected to measure every population occurring within the community. This indicator focuses on measuring the regularity (periodicity) and extent of general species larval settlement and recruitment as well as rates of juvenile survivorship within multiple populations in the community. It does not measure true reproductive capacity and viability.

## *Why measure it?*

While a community's composition and structure serve to provide a periodic or static understanding of the overall health and status of the community and its ecology, this indicator attempts to serve as a dynamic measure or proxy of a community's potential and ecological resiliency. For example, it is not enough to argue that a community is healthy and will be resilient based only on a stable and balanced community composition. Managers must also have some understanding of the potential for this community to persist, based on the regularity of spawning and recruitment events, an adequate abundance of recruits across populations to the community, and survivorship of an adequate number of these recruits to adult sizes. In this regard, this indicator is a community-level corollary to indicator B2.

**Relates to goals and objectives**

GOAL 1
1B 1E

GOAL 2
2A

GOAL 4
4A 4B
4C

B5

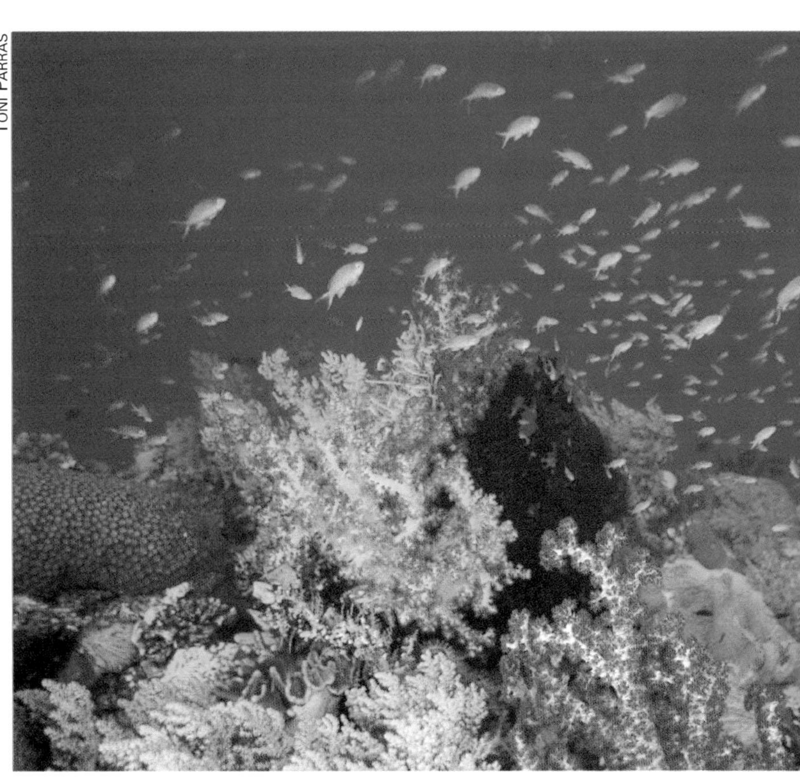
TONI PARRAS

B5

### Requirements

- Same requirements and equipment as listed under indicators B2 and B4.
- The necessary equipment to conduct non-specific collection of juveniles and recruits, including trawls, seines and gill nets.
- A list of all of the species within the community needing to be studied (from B4).
- Knowledge of the larval settlement stages for the species concerned.
- Knowledge of how to visually identify larval stages and juveniles for the species concerned.
- Knowledge of the reproductive biology and recruitment process for the species concerned.
- Knowledge of larval settlement patterns within the community.
- Knowledge of known recruitment areas located within the community.
- Knowledge of larval settlement stages and recruitment areas for juvenile representatives of the community.
- Knowledge of the breeding event seasons (timing) and spawning locations.
- An understanding of basic oceanographic patterns and processes as they relate to physical effects on larval import and export distribution and patterns.
- Dyes or simple drogues (for monitoring oceanographic patterns).

## How to collect the data

*This is one of the most complex and advanced management effectiveness indicators offered in this guidebook. In addition, there is much debate over the use and reliability of recruitment data to interpret ecological health due to the high spatial and temporal variability associated with recruitment. As such, measurement of this indicator should only be conducted by highly qualified individuals and within unique biological communities that host numerous focal species, represent rare or threatened communities, and/or face an acute level of human stressors.*

While highly challenging and somewhat controversial to attempt, recruitment success can be examined through the following parameters: a) the presence and relative abundance of relevant size classes (recruits/juveniles and reproductive adults) of populations within the community, b) the breeding or spawning potential and event regularity, and c) the settlement and recruitment potential and event regularity. Due to the fact that recruitment success is also a function of larval input and dispersal, this attribute may also need to be taken into account for a full understanding of recruitment potential.

Should it be decided to attempt this indicator, the recommended minimum data collection is the capture of size class information of focal species within the community surveyed, with a particular focus on juveniles and recruits. The survey methods used to sample species (relative abundance and size classes) across the community are the same as those described for *in situ* survey under indicator B2. The collection of age structure data across all species within the community is not mandatory under this indicator, although such information could be collected concurrently under indicator B2.

Ideally, the size class and age structure of many species within the community should be studied. Sampling the community is previously discussed under B4. The relative abundance and sizes of all species' individuals (juveniles) captured in the recruitment survey should be recorded. Assuming some basic reproductive biology is known for members within the community, size class structure results may also serve to calculate the abundance of juvenile versus adult individuals across species within the community and begin to build a profile through time of survivorship rates of recruits and juveniles to adult stages.

Monitoring the regularity and extent of known spawning and recruitment events should also be conducted under this indicator. Visits to known spawning locations and estimation surveys of spawning biomass should be attempted for focal species within the community. In addition, validation of the occurrence of these events should be demonstrated through:

*The data collection of size information on observed focal species recruits and juveniles under this indicator can be collected concurrently with indicator B2.*

- ❑ *in situ* collection of spawn (eggs and sperm) during and following known spawning events at aggregation sites, and
- ❑ *in situ*, low-impact collection (e.g. light traps, collection plates/tiles, water column stations) of settling larvae and established recruits within known recruitment/settlement centres (e.g. mangroves and seagrass communities).

Recruitment via asexual reproduction (e.g. fissure of soft-bodied invertebrates or coral reef fragmentation and grow out) is not measured under this indicator.

Placement of small floats and drogues can assist in tracking water movement during and directly after spawning events to provide a sense of where the eggs and larvae are going. Current meters deployed in relation to tidal activity can be useful to make predictions about the timing of spawning daily or seasonally.

Fixed visual census stations or timed swims (using either snorkel or SCUBA) can be used to account for post-settlement juveniles when collecting other indicator (one through three) data, depending on the species and their life history. The specific steps in undertaking a juvenile/recruit capture survey and spawning collection techniques are documented elsewhere in the literature (see English *et al.*, 1997, for a good starting point). References for the identification of larvae and post-larval stages of many species are also available in the literature. While more sophisticated larval settlement and recruitment studies are possible, they are quite time and labour intensive and are therefore not considered minimum requirements for data collection under this indicator.

TONI PARRAS

*Note that the use of trawl, seine and gill nets to collect recruits/juveniles will likely lead to indiscriminate (non-specific) mortality and may be considered destructive. Therefore, such sampling techniques may not be permitted and/or suitable for regular use under a sustainable monitoring protocol.*

Note that fish aggregation and spawning sites often occur at discrete locations that may or may not be included within the area delineated by the MPA. If a known site is located adjacent to the MPA or in the general area, it will be important to monitor it as fishes within the MPA may likely migrate to the aggregation site at certain times during the year to spawn there and then return back to their home range territory within the MPA.

Data should be captured at least annually, and ideally timed to coincide with the completion of survey work for indicators B2 and B4. Timing of data collection will depend largely on the known timing and frequency of spawning and recruitment events.

More advanced biological studies of breeding (reproductive biology) or spawning (reproductive behavioural) potential are also possible to gauge with this indicator. Such methods will require significantly more labour, finances and time than discrete studies of size classes and juvenile settlement and recruitment patterns in selected focal species within the community.

### *How to analyse and interpret results*

Collate, enter and manage the data gathered in the MPA effectiveness-monitoring database. Create a community profile of the relative abundance of each population of species observed within the community and what proportion of observed individuals of each species are juveniles versus adults. Plot the relative abundance (y-axis) of juveniles versus adults (x-axis); using size class data to distinguish between species observed and sampled within the community. Are there more or less juveniles and reproductive adults present across the represented populations than observed previously. Cross-reference these findings with the results of indicator B2. Track the age structure (juvenile versus adult) and relative abundance of species observed through time.

Write up results and interpretation for public dissemination. Orally present results using graphs and tables, and discuss with selected stakeholder groups, decision-makers and peers. Encourage independent validation of results by outside parties within the sampled area in order to confirm or reject findings and improve the understanding of the effects of management action on the area. Be sure to include any stories or anecdotes that illustrate the results observed from stakeholders.

Generally speaking and holding all things equal, an adequate and stable number of surviving juveniles and reproductive adults across populations within the community will increase the community's ability to be viable through time. At what level are surviving recruits in populations studied within the MPA experiencing a decline (reductions in the number of recruits across a majority of the populations studied) in the community? How have the timing, frequency and output of observed spawning and recruitment events changed?

Describe qualitatively (low, unpredicted or high) and/or quantitatively (probability based on reproductive potential across species within community) whether or not the community appears to be viable into the future. If not, how can these results inform adaptive management decision-making to address these concerns?

Finally, present the relative abundance (number/density) results of recruits and juvenile sizes resulting from the recruitment survey and discuss how these figures compare to previous observations.

### Outputs

- A community profile of the relative abundance of recruits/juveniles to the community following known larval settlement and juvenile recruitment events.
- A summary profile of the contribution of immature (juvenile) versus mature (reproductive adults) size classes to each species observed within the community.
- A confirmation of the frequency of known spawning events and estimate of spawning biomass.
- An estimate of the reproductive potential and resiliency of the community in the near future.
- A profile of the biomass of eggs, sperm and larvae released during such events.

### Optional outputs may include

- Age class structure (through otolith analysis) across populations of species present within the community.
- A profile of the reproductive potential (including spawning success and estimate of reproductive output) of species present in the community.
- An improved understanding of the reproductive biology and spawning behaviour of species within the community.

## Strengths and limitations

This is a complex indicator to measure. Collection of size class and recruitment data across many species within the community (difficulty rating 5) will require considerably more time, skill, equipment and financial resources to complete than the study of a selected group of focal species within the community (difficulty rating 4). In either case, an appropriately skilled team of evaluators will be necessary. If a suitably qualified team of individuals is not available from within the MPA management team, universities and research centres may be the best positioned to assist in developing a partnership for data collection and training MPA staff in survey techniques. Such specialists will need to fully meet the stated knowledge, equipment and skill requirements.

Moreover, the value of 'snapshot' recruitment studies is highly contested, as the data generated are known to be highly unreliable due to their inability to take into perspective the notorious effects of temporal and spatial variability. Even if they are found to be reliable, results of juvenile recruitment rates and spawning regularity may not be sufficient to confidently provide for a complete or accurate interpretation of the reproductive potential within a community of organisms. Many years of data collection will be required to draw conclusions about recruitment success with confidence.

Recruitment study techniques using nets, seines and trawls can lead to indiscriminate mortality and should therefore be avoided, minimized or conducted very carefully so as not to be highly destructive.

All of this being said, this indicator is sometimes viewed as the closest suggestion of how managers can encourage a more complete understanding of the dynamic nature of community ecology and reproductive potential.

## *Useful references and Internet links*

### Introduction, including variability issues


Caley, M.J., Carr, M.H., Hixon, M.A., Hughs, T.P., Jones, G.P. and Menge, B.A. (1996). "Recruitment and the local dynamics of open marine populations". *Annual Review of Ecology and Systematics* 27: 477–500.

Carr, M.H. (1991). "Habitat selection and recruitment of an assemblage of temperate zone reef fishes". *Journal of Experimental Marine Biology and Ecology* 126: 59-76.

Doherty, P.J. (1991). "Spatial and temporal patterns in the recruitment of a coral reef fish". *In* P.F. Sale (ed.), *The Ecology of Fishes on Coral Reefs.* Academic Press, San Diego, CA, USA. pp. 261-293.

Sale, P.F. (1999). "Recruitment in space and time". *Nature* 397: 25–26.

Sale, P.F., Doherty, P.J., Eckert, G.J., Douglas, W.A. and Ferrell, D.J. (1984). "Large scale spatial and temporal variation in recruitment to fish populations on coral reefs". *Oecologia* (Berlin) 64: 191–198.

Victor, B.C. (1983). "Recruitment and population dynamics of a coral reef fish". *Science* 219: 419–420.

Walters, C.J. and Collie, J.S. (1989). "Is research on environmental effects on recruitment worthwhile?" *Canadian Journal of fisheries and Aquatic Sciences* 45: 1848–1854.

Williams, D. McB., Russ, G. and Doherty, P.J. (1986). "Reef fish: large-scale distribution and recruitment". *Oceanus* 29: 76–82.


### Juvenile survey


English, S., Wilkinson, C. and Baker, V. (eds) (1997). *Survey Manual for Tropical Marine Resources. 2nd Edition.* Australian Institute for Marine Science, Townsville, Queensland, Australia.


### Larval survey


Choat, J.H., Doherty, P.J., Kerrigan, B.A. and Leis, J.M. (1993). "Sampling of larvae and pelagic stages of coral reef fishes: a comparison of towed nets, purse seine and light-aggregation devices". *Fishery Bulletin* 91: 195–201.

Doherty, P.J. (1987). "Light-traps: selective but useful devices for quantifying the distributions and abundances of larval fishes". *Bulletin of Marine Science* 41: 423–431.


Box B6

## EXAMPLE FROM THE FIELD

Surveys of newly settled yellowstripe goatfish (*Mulloidichthys flavolineatus*) and other coral reef fish within and outside marine preserves located in Guam were undertaken during 2002. Fish observed were enumerated along four replicate, 25 x 2m transects at each study site (these smaller 50m$^2$ transects were used because newly settled fish are small and often cryptic, requiring additional time to obtain an accurate count). Three months later, the evaluation team revisited the transects and performed repeat counts of surviving recruits known to fall within a specific range of sizes after three months of grow-out time. Results indicate that despite settlement rates for *M. flavolineatus* between sample sites being indistinguishable (nested ANOVA, F = .04, p = 0.840; see Figure, left), three months later recruitment success was significantly lower within harvested areas (F = 9.5, p = 0.004; see Figure, right). This difference can be partially explained by the fact that newly settled goatfish are a prized catch by local fishers, who prefer eating juveniles. Therefore, lower rates of recruitment success outside the preserves are due in part to fishing pressure.

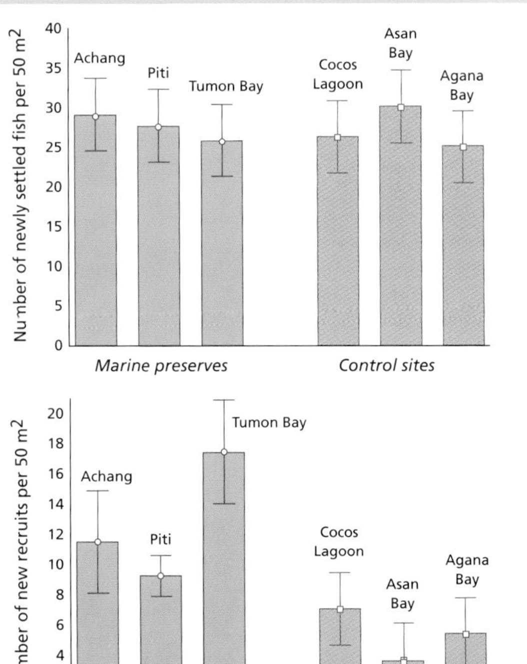


***The observed settlement rate (top) and recruitment success (bottom) of yellowstripe goatfish experienced over several months in protected (blue) versus non-protected (red) sites sampled in Guam.***

Relates to goals and objectives

GOAL 1
1B 1C
1D

GOAL 2
2B

GOAL 3
3A 3B

GOAL 5
5A

B6

## *What is 'food web integrity'?*

A **food web** is a representation of the energy flow through populations in a community. The 'web' of relationships within this representation illustrates the many distinct but interconnected food chains, or linear sequences of organisms that indicate prey items and predatory relationships among them. A small proportion of the energy stored by the biomass within a position in the food chain is passed on to the next **trophic level** (position in the food chain) when this biomass is consumed.

**Food web integrity** is a measure of how supportive (for the members of the community) and reliable the trophic relationships are within the interconnected food chains of a community. When a food web loses its integrity, it indicates that the relationships between trophic levels have been disturbed or lost. This may occur, for example, if a species within the food web is eradicated through over-harvesting, thereby changing or eliminating the feeding relationships that were dependent on its position in the food web – that is, elimination of its influence on prey items and removal of its biomass for those predators which relied on feeding on it. It is important to note that even if a food web is stable, it does not necessarily mean that it is supportive of the overall community or is a desirable state of predator-prey relationships.

Trophic position in a food chain is a functional classification and is not determined by taxonomy (although phylogeny can be used to make predictions about trophic function). The trophic relationship concept allows a hierarchical perspective to emerge within community ecology. At the most basic level, individuals hold positions within food webs either as producers (photosynthetic organisms) or consumers. Consumers can be further categorized as herbivores (feed on producers), carnivores (feed on herbivores and/or other carnivores), or detritivores (feed on decomposed or decomposing organic matter). In turn, groups of individuals within the same trophic position form functional 'guilds' within the community (e.g. herbivorous fishes or apex predators). Finally, the network or 'web' of functional guilds and food chains culminates in a mass balance of energy exchange and biomass that comprises an ecosystem. It is this highest level, where the energy exchange and biomass contained within the ecosystem is manifested within a food web, that this indicator seeks to assess and monitor.

## *Why measure it?*

MPAs are hosts to single or multiple ecosystems, including their constituent communities of organisms and food webs. A healthy and stable ecosystem is one that is able to sustain the energy flow between trophic levels within a food web. Therefore, describing the food relationships between populations of organisms within the community is an essential feature in the effective management of an MPA.

When positions in the food web are eliminated (for example, from over-fishing), trophic relationships are lost or jeopardised and the ecosystem may experience imbalance and negative cascading effects throughout the food web. Measuring, understanding and monitoring such changes through time are important to assess the impacts of effective MPA management in coastal ecosystems. Also, detecting changes in trophic relationships and observing reductions in food web integrity may serve as an 'early warning' signal for managers to predict troubled trophic relationships, remedy deteriorating ecological conditions, and increase management efforts in the area. As such, it can be useful in diagnosing large-scale ecological variations.

One of the most important potential services that MPAs can provide is re-establishment of natural conditions and predator-prey relationships. This indicator can be used to document important and

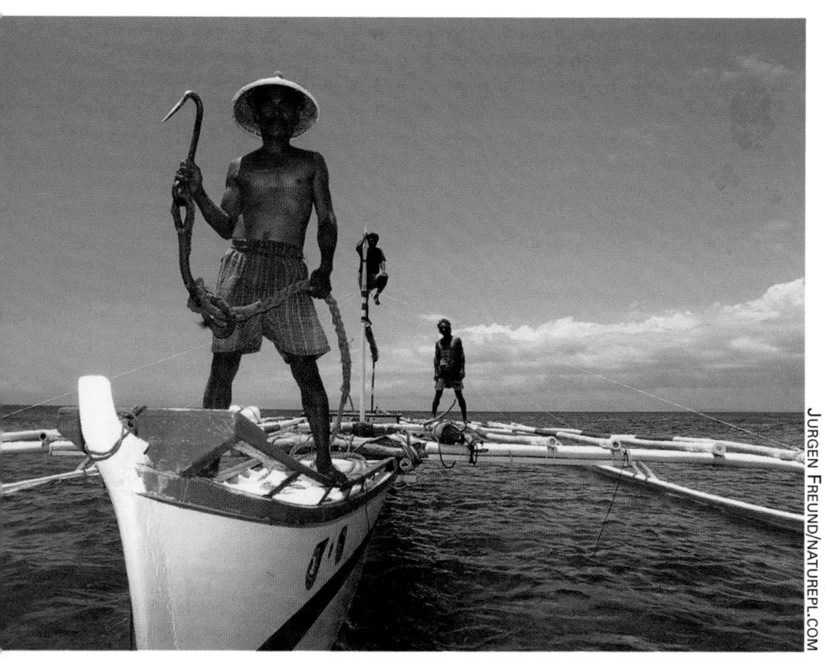
Jurgen Freund/naturepl.com

***A shark hunter near Bohol, Philippines, in 1997. The systematic extirpation of top-level predators, such as sharks, can result in 'cascading' negative impacts down through the trophic chain of organisms threatening the overall integrity of the food web.***

complementary evidence of progress towards the achievement of re-establishing such natural conditions, and can be a powerful tool for demonstrating and characterizing how these natural feeding relationships exist where (as is often the case) such baseline information is not available. Given that we understand only a few food webs in the marine environment, the potential for contributed knowledge is very important. This indicator therefore also aims to collect evidence of restored or strengthened food web relationships, and not merely detect when food relationships are awry.

Detecting changes in food web relationships provides managers with the opportunity to highlight such changes publicly, investigate their source, and determine whether or not they are the result of activities occurring within or outside the MPA. In the case where changes are within the control or political and legislative influence of the MPA manager, this detection may provide an opportunity to reconcile or address the causes of change. In some cases however, food web changes observed within the MPA may be due to exogenous (outside) influences that are well beyond the control of the MPA managers and/or unrelated to the MPA goals and objectives. For example, increased predation on threatened focal sea otter populations in an MPA by orca may be identified as a result of over-fishing using purse seines of orca prey fish populations hundreds of miles away from the MPA. In such instances, the awareness of the changing feeding relationships due to outside factors may:

a) Provide managers with the necessary knowledge and protection against unjustified criticism of MPA performance due to changes observed within the MPA; and

b) Provide an opportunity to lobby for reconciliation beyond the jurisdiction and goals of the MPA.

In this sense, such outside influences on food relationships can help MPA managers illustrate how external, non-MPA related actions have direct effects on MPA management effectiveness. This can help managers identify how to distribute (or re-distribute) human, financial and policy resources toward other external interventions in order to improve the health of the area being protected. This being said, it is important to determine the scale of the evidence collected under this indicator so that it is used to address only questions/issues relevant to the scale at which they are being asked/raised. Therefore, changes in food relationships that are the result of higher scales of ecological change (e.g. global climate change) are beyond the scope of the MPA or its ability to influence such relationships and should be identified as such.

### Requirements

- Same requirements listed under indicator B1.
- Set of scales or balances (measurements in grams).
- Knowledge of the species present within the community or ecosystem.
- An understanding of predator-prey relationships between resident species.
- A calculator.
- Mathematical skills.
- Advanced: mathematical and ecological modelling skills; access to an individual who can consult with the evaluation team and is familiar with the measurement and analysis techniques used; access to mathematical trophic modelling software.

Finally, in theory food webs possess characteristics that allow them to be considered excellent ecological descriptors (Winemiller, 1990). As a consequence, food web integrity is considered an important determinant of ecosystem health and functionality, both of which are difficult parameters to concretely demonstrate. Illustrating a functional and resilient food web therefore may serve as a proxy for a healthy ecosystem.

## How to collect the data

Data collection to fully measure this indicator is not a discrete or easily approachable task. However, as an approachable starting point (or at a very minimum) a descriptive data collection process can be initiated. To do this, the team should conduct interviews and hold focus group discussions with knowledgeable individuals (e.g. research scientists, fishers, MPA scientific staff) in order to map out and characterize (functionally) the known roles and niches organisms occupy within various trophic levels, including their multiple predator-prey relationships and how or why these may be changing through time. As part of this process, a focused examination can be made into a single 'chain' (discrete thread) of particularly relevant relationships within the overall food web, from single or specific bottom- through top-level trophic occupiers. This relevance may be as a result of a biological attribute (such as the chain hosting relationships between multiple focal species or being of known ecological cornerstone value), or because the food chain has some socioeconomic importance (such as providing livelihood opportunities). Information collected should include a discussion on the status of and between occupiers (species) at various trophic levels based on as much empirical evidence as possible (data collected from indicators B1 and B2 may be useful here). For example, the characterization and modelling of the following chain of trophic relationships could be conducted: phytoplankton – krill – fish – seals – polar bears. Under this example, close monitoring of the abundance of krill or seals and their trophic relationship status to fish or polar bears could serve as a proxy for the overall integrity within the food chain. Collecting descriptive and empirical information to characterize a few of these cornerstone chains, including the degree of interconnectedness between them, would act as a surrogate for the complete characterization of the entire web and all of its constituent trophic relationships.

Alternatively, examination of top and bottom points in a single food chain (e.g. apex predators and lowest-level producers) may serve as proxies for the overall chain.

In some cases, MPAs may have the staff, expertise and time necessary to characterize and monitor the full gamut of trophic positions and relationships within a community's food web. In such cases, a more rigorous and in-depth evaluation can be done. First, the various organisms occurring within the system should be identified and aggregated into their trophic positions and guilds within the community's overall food web. This process will result in assigning each species single or multiple roles, between producers, herbivores, first-level carnivores, second-level carnivores, etc. up to top-level carnivores. This should result in the characterization of a completed set of interconnected food chains between all members in the community.

Next, the average weight (g/m$^2$) and relative biomass of populations or organisms found within the community should be directly measured and recorded using *in situ* capture and release or fish catch surveys. Relative biomass (g/m$^2$/species) can be determined for each population by collecting the weight and size of individuals observed in addition to calculating the area from which these observations are taken. Average species biomass records should be listed by trophic guild in ascending order. This can be done either from a book of species with trophic guild membership that can be consulted or from a baseline study of digestive tract contents found in the relevant species concerned.

*The collection of data for this indicator can build seamlessly from other data collection activities and surveys under indicators B1, B4 and B7.*

JOHN PARKS

From here, the relative abundance (number) of organisms found within the area and surveyed using data collected under indicators B1 and B4 should be identified. The relative biomass (g/m$^2$) of each trophic guild can then be calculated by multiplying the average biomass of individuals in a population by the total number of individuals (abundance) observed within the trophic level. The total biomass of each guild should be listed in ascending order, along with the constituent species that make up the level. Note that in some cases (depending on the objectives of the MPA), managers may only be concerned with understanding food relationships between herbivorous and carnivorous species, and may focus data collection accordingly.

Data collection should ideally occur annually or twice a year. An inter-annual time series data collection approach is recommended. Note that because trophic relationships and structures vary widely by geography and community composition, biomass and abundance data must be collected (and analysed – see below) at site- and/or community-specific levels.

## How to analyse and interpret results

First, create an illustration of the assumed food web being represented within the community. Specifically, highlight distinct food chains of species observed and interconnections between these food chains. Also, identify and aggregate the various organisms into trophic positions and guilds within the food web: i.e. producers, herbivores, first-level carnivores, second-level carnivores, etc.

Next, using the total biomass results obtained for each trophic guild observed within the food web, determine the trophic ratios (or proportions) between guild levels and assign rankings. The trophic ratio is the relationship of the biomass values among the different trophic guilds (e.g. the producer:herbivore ratio or the producer:tertiary carnivore ratio (Arias-Gonzalez, 1998).

Then, assign trophic levels as either integer (1, 2, 3...) or fractional (1.3, 2.7, etc. as determined through a weighted average of prey item trophic levels) rankings across specific guilds within the communities present in the ecosystem(s) (see Lindeman, 1942; and Odum and Heald, 1975). A good summary of the specific steps in how to go about trophic level assignment can be found in Christensen and Pauly (1992).

A very simple trophic level index (TLI) can now be calculated weighing both integer and fractional trophic level by the trophic guild biomass. For example, in a system that is characterized as 30% herbivorous (trophic level = 1), 40% first-level carnivorous (trophic level = 2), and 30% second-level carnivorous (trophic level = 3), the TLI will be: 1 (0.30) + 2 (0.40) + 3 (0.30) = 2.

Ecological efficiency is the percentage of biomass produced by one trophic level that is incorporated into the biomass of the next higher trophic level. Generally speaking, this is approximately 10% of the total energy available within any one trophic level. Based on this rule, each trophic level that is assigned for guilds present is weighted 10 times the one below it. Of equal or greater importance may be that it reflects progress towards the stated goal of maintaining abundance and large size among species of high trophic levels. Create a table of the resulting values in order of increasing trophic assignment.

Finally, calculate a trophic structure index using the summary results generated to this point (see Done and Reichelt, 1998; Christensen and Pauly, 1992).

Observe changes and shifts in trophic structure/position and the index through time. Determine (based on index results) whether or not the food web observed is stable, in decline or improving. Use observed results to predict trophic trends and inform management decision-making and priority setting. Do data suggest that food webs within the MPA are undergoing changes? If so, are changes observed indicative of food web deterioration or strengthening, in terms of how close the relationships are from the desired state?

### Outputs

- A descriptive profile of the trophic relationships and status between members of at least a single food chain within the overall food web.
- An illustration of the food web and the interconnected food chains.
- A profile of average species and relative biomass, grouped by trophic guild.
- A profile of total biomass within observed trophic guilds.
- A list of trophic ratios between guilds to be monitored through time.
- A trophic structure index.

Rigorous ecological analysis and advanced modelling will be necessary to confirm or reject with confidence the results of this indicator. It should be noted that numerous, more advanced mathematical modelling techniques exist and are available through which to gauge the stability and reliability of trophic relationships found within the target ecosystem. For example, some models enable a prediction of the effects of species exploitation at varying levels of maturity on the overall food web. For the purposes of meeting this indicator such advanced modelling techniques are not required, as it may not be feasible for the MPA project team to undertake them.

## Strengths and limitations

This is not an easy indicator to measure. Data collection can be time-consuming, depending on the number of species being considered (i.e. a single chain of species versus an entire food web) and the complexity and overlap between and among individual and clusters of trophic relationships within the area surveyed. Should an evaluation team determine that this indicator must be measured, the team should be aware that it will likely take additional time to secure the necessary human and financial resources to develop the capacity to measure this indicator. Given the difficulties in collecting data for this indicator, evaluation teams need to think carefully about how closely justified data collection for this indicator is against the MPA goals and objectives.

Incrementally, capture of weight data for this indicator may, at first glance, appear relatively simple and straightforward given existing data collection investments made under related indicators (e.g. B1 or B7). However, such incremental time investments will require more than a minor amount of additional time and manpower. Based on real-world experience, even modelling of a single food chain of relationships can become time consuming and labour intensive. Furthermore, incremental data collected (such as weight) are not necessarily always easily and quickly obtained. Finally, a comfort level and familiarity with mathematics is required.

The full potential of this indicator is theoretically achieved through comparison of data collected from food webs within the MPA against those found under 'pristine' ecosystems. As 'pristine' conditions and reference data are difficult to come by, in the absence of such benchmark locations this indicator loses some of its analytical power. For example, since a 'pristine' food web that would be found to occur naturally under no human impacts is not possible to characterize, how can the restoration of food web integrity to such a level be defined? What food webs would be considered 'normal' given current conditions in the world?

This indicator has limited accuracy and poor inference beyond the sites and communities where trophic information is modelled. As the level of analysis of food web relationships grows, its accuracy is decreased significantly. Further, establishing causality between trophic changes observed in the food web and use of management interventions (or the lack thereof) is not possible. The indicator may function as more of an educational and illustrative tool about the state of the community ecology being managed, than as a proven measure of management effectiveness.

Despite the limitations and uncertainties, food webs and their role in ecosystem resilience are now widely recognised as critical components of successfully managed marine areas. While the methods for measuring this indicator are still being tested, refined and expanded, the topic of food web integrity was widely accepted by contributors to and reviewers of this guidebook to be of critical enough a nature for inclusion. This is particularly relevant given that the indicator is accepted as a potential macro-descriptor of changes occurring within an ecosystem and of its overall health.

### *Useful references and Internet links*

Botsford, L.W, Castilla, J.C. and Petersen, C.H. (1997). "The management of fisheries and marine ecosystems". *Science* 277(5325): 509–515.

Christensen, V. (2003). "Using Ecopath with Ecosim for ecosystem based management of fisheries". *In* H. Jákupsstovu (ed.), *Workshop on Ecosystem Modelling of Faroese Waters, Tórshavn, September 2002*, FRS 2003: 73–75.

Christensen, V. and Pauly, D. (1992). "ECOPATH II - A software for balancing steady-state models and calculating network characteristics". *Ecological Modelling* 61: 169–185.

Christensen, V. and Pauly, D. (eds.) (1993). *Trophic Models of Aquatic Ecosystems.* ICLARM Conference Proceedings 26. International Center for Aquatic Living Resources Management, Manila, Philippines.

Done, T.J. and R.E. Reichelt (1998). "Integrated coastal zone and fisheries ecosystem management: generic goals and performance indices." *Ecological Applications* 8 (suppl.): 110–118.

Hutchings, J.A. (2000). "Collapse and recovery of marine fishes". *Nature* 406(6798): 882–885.

Jackson, J.B.C., Kirby, M.X. *et al.* (2001). "Historical overfishing and the recent collapse of coastal ecosystems". *Science* 293(5530): 629–638.

Jennings, S., Kaiser, M.J. and Reynolds, J.D. (2001). *Marine Fisheries Ecology*. Blackwell Science, London, UK.

Lindeman, R.L. (1942). "The trophic-dynamic aspect of ecology". *Ecology* 23: 399–418.

Myers, R. A. and Worm, B. (2003). "Rapid worldwide depletion of predatory fish communities". *Nature* 423: 280–283.

Odum, W.E. and Heald, E.J. (1975). "The detritus-based food web of an estuarine mangrove community". *In* L.E. Cronin (ed.), *Estuarine research, Vol. 1.* Academic Press, New York. pp. 265–286.

Pauly, D., Christensen, V., Guénette, S., Pitcher, T.J., Sumaila, U.R., Walters, C.J., Watson, R. and Zeller, D. (2002). "Towards sustainability in world fisheries". *Nature* 418: 689–695.

Pauly, D., Palomares, M.L., Froese, R., Sa-a, P., Vakily, M., Preikshot, D. and Wallace, S. (2001). "Fishing down Canadian aquatic food webs". *Canadian Journal of Fisheries and Aquatic Sciences* 58: 51–62.

Sainsbury, K. and Sumaila, U.R. (2003). "Incorporating ecosystem objectives into management of sustainable marine fisheries, including 'best practice' reference points and use of Marine Protected Areas". *In* M. Sinclair and G. Valdimarson (eds.), *Responsible Fisheries in the Marine Ecosystem*. CAB International, UK. pp. 343–361.

Winemiller, K.O. (1990). "Spatial and temporal variation in tropical fish trophic networks". *Ecological Monographs* 60(3): 331–367.

Box B7

## Example from the Field

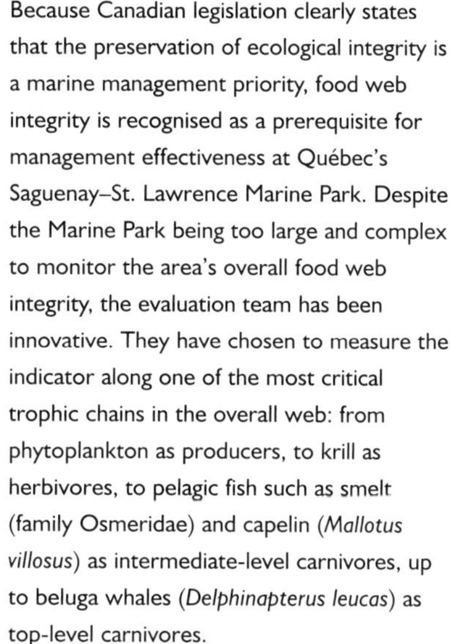

Because Canadian legislation clearly states that the preservation of ecological integrity is a marine management priority, food web integrity is recognised as a prerequisite for management effectiveness at Québec's Saguenay–St. Lawrence Marine Park. Despite the Marine Park being too large and complex to monitor the area's overall food web integrity, the evaluation team has been innovative. They have chosen to measure the indicator along one of the most critical trophic chains in the overall web: from phytoplankton as producers, to krill as herbivores, to pelagic fish such as smelt (family Osmeridae) and capelin (*Mallotus villosus*) as intermediate-level carnivores, up to beluga whales (*Delphinapterus leucas*) as top-level carnivores.

Parks Canada

***The endangered Beluga whale* (Delphinapterus leucas) *is the flagship species of Saguenay-St. Lawrence Marine Park. The St. Lawrence population numbers less than 500 individuals.***

**Relates to goals and objectives**

GOAL 1
1A 1C
1D 1E
1F

GOAL 2
2A 2D

GOAL 3
3A 3B
3C

GOAL 5
5A

## What is 'type, level, and return on fishing effort'?

The type of fishing effort is a description of the kind and degree of extractive power used during fishing activities, both in terms of technology and skilled labour.

The level of fishing effort is a measure of the amount of total labour (number of people) and time (number of hours/days) used during a fishing activity.

The return on fishing effort is a measurement of the efficiency with which the harvesting activity is undertaken. Efficiency in fishing effort is measured as the number (of individuals) or weight (biomass) of a species caught per unit effort (day or hour per person or team of people) of harvest invested across each fishing method and technology used. The catch per unit effort (CPUE) is a profile of the relative efficiency of a particular fishing technology. CPUE can be measured in harvest areas outside the MPA, in areas immediately adjacent to its boundaries (to measure 'spill-over' effects), and/or in areas within it (where zoned relevantly, or for catch-and-release comparison data). CPUE data are typically collected either *in situ* during fishing operations, or during a creel survey of catch landings when brought ashore (see below).

## Why measure it?

Often MPAs are established explicitly because of the high importance that fisheries extraction has in sustaining human societies. Increased fishery yields (via spill-over of biomass from no-take zones and MPAs) and improved livelihoods (via improved income and food availability from increased fisheries yields) are therefore common and important objectives of MPA use throughout much of the world. This indicator is a direct attempt to quantify and track trends in fisheries yield, technological uses, and livelihood opportunities through time.

Despite the importance of measuring the impacts of MPA use on fishing catches, it is important to note that only in relatively few cases has this type and level of analysis been done in the literature on MPAs.

This indicator is indirectly linked to measuring the spill-over effects from areas of no or reduced human activity (indicator B10). In addition, catch levels can also strongly influence community structure (indicator B5) and trophic relationships (indicator B6); for example, through the collateral effects of by-catch volume that are associated with some overly-efficient fishing technologies or the systematic extirpation of high-level predators, such as grouper.

> *Note that within MPAs whose aims may be to reduce or eliminate fishing effort in and around the MPA, reduction of fishing effort will not be sought for the purpose of maximizing yields to fishers but rather as evidence of strengthened focal species populations.*

*This indicator relates thematically (human use) to several of the socio-economic and governance considerations, and so data collected here may be useful for consideration under some of these indicators (e.g. S1 and G1).*

Tony Eckersley

The word 'fishing' is broadly defined here as including any activity involving the extraction of living marine resources, either for commercial or non-commercial (e.g. subsistence) use. As such, it includes:

- Harvesting of skipjack tuna by commercial fleet purse seine vessels.
- Shallow-water harvesting of charismatic gastropods and echinoderms for curio sale to tourists.
- Gleaning of cockles, seaweed and other edible marine invertebrates by hand at low tide for home consumption (below, right).
- Hunting of seabirds and seals for sale as meat at a local market.

### *Requirements*

- Clipboard and paper.
- Pencil or pen.
- Creel (landing) survey forms.
- CPUE observation data sheets.
- General knowledge of the number of resource harvesters and their fishing activities.
- Knowledge of locations of relevant marinas, boat ramps and public access points.
- Knowledge of locations.
- The amount of time (hours/days) each person spends harvesting resources.
- How efficient the technology is at catching the desired species.
- The physical impact (if any) of the fishing technology on the habitat.
- List of survey locations including: points of entry and landing, key fishing areas, and (where relevant) multiple-use zones for each gear type allowed in and around the MPA.

## *How to collect the data*

At a minimum, the following information about the type and level of fishing effort should be collected through creel (landing) surveys and interviews with randomly sampled boats and fishers (or other resource users) at known landing locations:

a) What species is/are being targeted for catch,

b) Which species are actually being caught (full catch composition),

c) Where the catch was taken, either outside and adjacent to the MPA or within it (where applicable),

d) A general description of the harvest method(s) used,

e) The type(s) and number of fishing gears used,

f) The support technology available (e.g. a hydraulic winch),

g) The number, type(s), and size(s) of the boats used to land the catch,

h) The number of people (fishers) involved in landing the catch, including boat crew, and their individual roles,

i) The number, type, and size (horsepower) of engines involved in landing the catch,

j) The amount of time (hours/days) required to land the catch, including transit time,

k) The size of individuals landed per species,

l) The total weight of the catch (in kg, estimated if necessary), and

m) The total monetary value of the catch (in local currency) needed to be captured and recorded.

Random sampling is done by randomly selecting a specified number of individual boats or fishers within a known population of currently active vessels or harvesters.

Beyond simple landing surveys, a more advanced level of data collection requires the capture of detailed CPUE observations made *in situ* (on board

*Measurement of this indicator is closely linked to that of indicator B1 (for 'target' focal species), and is likewise one of the most commonly used indicators. Increased CPUE is often observed as being correlated to increased focal species abundance.*

Tony Eckersley

While the principal focus of this indicator is to assess fishing effort related to income generation and dietary consumption, the indicator can also be easily adapted to assess the non-commercial, non-food effort related to:

- recreation fishing, and
- catch-and-release sport fishing.

In addition, data can be collected under this for non-extractive commercial uses of living marine resources, such as:

- dive tourism,
- whale watching, and
- aquaculture.

In all such cases, the rate of 'return on effort' from these activities can be measured in terms of income.

B7

or in the water) by the evaluator in real time during fishing activities. Precise times (hours, minutes) and locations (ideally using GPS coordinates and a geo-referenced basemap of the harvest area) of observed fishing effort and landings are recorded as they occur. Such CPUE data must be accompanied by completion of a comprehensive frame survey that details the power (e.g. boats, engines, fishers and gears) employed across spatial (total fishing area, in km$^2$) and temporal (time expended, in days, hours and minutes) effort. Such frame surveys must be regularly updated.

The specific process and forms used in performing creel and CPUE surveys are well documented elsewhere in the literature and are not repeated here (see Useful references, below). It is not recommended that the evaluation team request harvesters to record their own CPUE data *in situ*. However, if appropriately trained and willing, harvesters may be in a position to record simple fields of catch data into a log book for specific target species; e.g. catch volume and individual sizes, the total time spent fishing, the number of boats and people involved, etc.

Fishing effort is employed differently depending on the target species. Likewise, fishing effort affects each species differently. Therefore, measures of fishing effort must be species-specific, even within an ecosystem-level monitoring framework. Each species must be individually parsed out and measured separately from the others, with data collected on it specifically and analysed as such.

JOHN PARKS/WWF

***Catch surveys can take a lot of time, particularly when the catch of an individual fisher is large. For example, data collection for this one person's catch of mixed reef fish caught outside a small MPA in West Papua, Indonesia, took one hour.***

For example, if multiple species of deepwater fish caught are simply grouped together and recorded as "a mixed catch of 150 fish" within a single day's catch survey, this may mask the fact that one of the species included in the catch is an increasingly uncommon species. This could lead to the inadvertent and systematic extirpation of rare species whose decreasing frequency in catch (and decreased CPUE) has been masked by the presence of other, commonly (or increasingly) occurring species of fish. The rationale and logic behind this argument is well documented in the literature (Polunin and Roberts, 1995; Russ, 1991).

Supplementary catch and effort information may be available for review via national or regional fisheries statistics. Governmental agencies and/or non-governmental organizations may be a source of such information, providing the evaluation team with data from which to triangulate direct observations and completed interview surveys.

Tangential but related information that may also be useful includes:

*Where possible, supplemental interview data on catch effort can also be collected from fishers during household surveys conducted under relevant socio-economic indicators (e.g. approximately how often they go to harvest target species, how long they need to go out to secure an adequate catch, and what their typical catch composition and sizes are like).*

a) licensing records held by a government bureau about registered industrial or medium- to small-scale commercial fishing operations, and

b) a description of the trade and market attributes of the fisheries in question, including the market value and annual tonnage/value of catches using government bureau statistics.

These data should be triangulated with relevant socio-economic indicators presented after the biophysical category.

Information should be collected on the types and numbers of destructive fishing gears operating, the prevalence (frequency or popularity) of such use, and the amount of destructive fishing effort (people, time) being employed. This information can be collected (or estimated) through direct observation (patrols, number of recorded incidents) or through talking with key informants (including users, management staff and enforcement officials). Because many destructive fishing techniques are illegal, note that it may be difficult to collect reliable information. Therefore key informants should be carefully selected, and evaluators should be aware of any potential biases (see IMA, 2000).

Data should be collected on a regular basis throughout the year (weekly, monthly) or during seasonal harvest or reproductive event periods. Creel surveys should ideally be randomly sampled or uniformly stratified across all relevant landing sites with respect to the day of the week and time of month (moon phase) when harvest is active.

> *To measure precisely the return on fishing effort expended for each target species would require a highly sophisticated and deep level of fisheries-independent data collected through advanced measurement and analysis techniques than is feasible and practical for MPAs under this indicator.*

### *How to analyse and interpret results*

It is possible to begin to develop an understanding of the trends in fisheries extraction effort and methods by monitoring changes over time in:

- the type and popularity of fishing gears used,
- the power of gears,
- the level of and return on fishing effort in and around the MPA,
- the incidence in destructive fishing technology use,
- changes in the size and species composition of catch,
- changes in the number and volume/weight of target species caught.

With data on the level of effort collected, calculate the catch per unit effort using the weight of key species caught per day per person spent harvesting for each fishing method/technology: CPUE = total weight (kg) of target species catch per unit time (day).

Examine the relative efficiency between fishing methods in terms of their competitive returns on effort, total labour investments (number of fishers, hours or days fished), and total volume of catch. Which technologies are the most efficient? Which are clearly overly efficient relative to the others? What are the trends with respect to the prevalence in use of different gears available? Are some increasingly being used over others, and how does this relate to their catch efficiency ratings? If data are available, is the incidence of destructive technology use (such as cyanide fishing, dynamite fishing and fine mesh nets) declining, unchanged or on the rise? How do observed changes or trends in fishing gear types being used and efficiency relate to management actions in the MPA? Based on results, do data suggest that the level of fishing effort around the MPA has changed (declined/ improved)? If so, to what degree?

For each target species and gear type, calculate the following figures over a specified interval of time (e.g. three months, a fortnight, or a year) for the following:

- the total amount of catch (by weight, volume, and/or number individuals),
- the total species richness (diversity) of the catch,
- the total effort (# of boats, # of fishers, # hours/days),
- the average catch,
- the average size of individuals caught, and
- the average CPUE.

Enter these data into a table, where the columns are the categories of calculations and the rows the time intervals. Next, plot these attributes through time (across specified intervals) for each target species, and then overlay the various results. Are there observable trends or inverse relationships

*This indicator is closely associated with other socio-economic (S1, S5, S10) and governance (G1, G4, G15) indicators, in addition to being linked to B1 and B6.*

between any of these attributes? If so, what does this mean? Do increased catch sizes and effort inversely relate to the average size of individuals caught?

One caveat is that differential interpretation of results may arise based on the life history of the population being fished and the timing of the catch survey done. For example, data may be skewed (false positive) to look as if a tremendous increase in CPUE is observed when in reality this is simply due to undertaking the landing survey at a time when fish migration, aggregation or recruitment is underway.

### Outputs

- A record of the gear types being used.
- A record of the power being invested.
- A record of the size and composition of catches.
- A record of catch-effort efficiency and CPUE calculations for target resources removed by local stakeholders across all gears and technologies used.
- Time series graphs of total catch size, total effort, average sizes of individuals landed, and the CPUE for each species.
- A map of key representative fishing sites across habitat types in and outside the MPA and locations of key points of entry (parks, boat ramps) to the MPA.

## Strengths and limitations

Data in this indicator are relatively straightforward to collect, although it may appear simpler than it really is and can often be time consuming and labour intensive. Measurement of this indicator is not as simple as it may appear, and it is important to be aware that accurate catch data collection for the predominant species (those caught most often) and for focal species (those of interest to the MPA and its goals and objectives) will require notable additional time and man-power. CPUE surveys also require relatively well-trained staff and must be done consistently for at least a full year in order to acquire an accurate idea of what catch rates are. Furthermore, scientific consultants and staff (who may need to be hired out and are expensive) will be necessary to develop catch-effort databases and analyse baseline data.

With sufficient training, CPUE and creel surveys can be undertaken by project staff and community volunteers for relatively little cost or logistical investment. However, technical oversight and scientific review of results by qualified and experienced fisheries biologists is important, and so the collection of CPUE data may not be appropriate or feasible in every MPA site. Visual or creel/vessel based surveys are fairly accurate in terms of estimating return on fishing effort invested.

Changes in the type of fishing gears being used and the number of boats and fishers may be both more easily measured and more useful in terms of identifying fishing pressure issues and increases. Likewise, changes in the size and composition of catch are as or more important as how many fish are being caught.

CPUE is not necessarily a good indicator of ecological change and therefore alone is not sufficient to identify and prevent imminent collapses for all fishery stocks. Also, the long-term, consistent monitoring perspective required for CPUE data makes it very difficult to correlate CPUE with environmental change.

The evaluation team should check for accuracy in fishing effort and CPUE reporting submitted from volunteer fishers and, if possible, check for and factor in the falsification or misreporting of data. Data accuracy related to submitted catch reports from all fishers should not be assumed.

## Useful references and Internet links

Dulvy, N.K., Metcalfe, J.D., Glanville, J., Pawson, M.G. and Reynolds, J.D. (2000). "Fisheries stability, local extinctions and shifts in community structure of skates". *Conservation Biology* 14: 283–293.

Gulland, J.A. (1975). *Manual of Methods for Fisheries Resources Survey and Appraisal: Part 5 - Objectives and Basic Methods.* FAO Fisheries Technical Paper No. 145. United Nations Food and Agriculture Organization, Rome, Italy.

Gulland, J.A. (1983). *Fish Stock Assessment: A Manual of Basic Methods.* Wiley Interscience, Chichester, UK.

Gunderson, D.R. (1993). *Surveys of Fishery Resources*. John Wiley and Sons, Inc., New York, NY, USA.

Hilborn, R. and Walters, C.J. (1992). *Quantitative Fisheries Stock Assessment: Choice, dynamics, and uncertainty.* Chapman and Hall, New York, NY, USA.

Box B8

## EXAMPLE FROM THE FIELD

In the Galapagos Islands Marine Reserve, there are two dominant commercial lobster fisheries in operation: blue or green lobster (*Panulirus gracilis*) and red lobster (*P. penicillatus*). Fishing for these species is permitted only during a specified 4-month season. Data collected over the past six years illustrate an interesting story for the MPA. During the late 1990s, total catches rose to new highs (see Figure, below). This prompted the entry of many new fishers into the fishery during 2000 and 2001, thereby leading to a decline in the stocks and reduced harvests in 2001 and 2002. In 2002, fewer active fishers were reported (due to lowered catches the year before), leading to reduced effort. Some speculate that this may lead to increased catches in the coming years, likely followed by another influx of fishing effort. Such high-and-low cycles in commercial fisheries are not uncommon, and have prompted managers and stakeholders in similar situations to discuss the need for further limitations on fisheries in order to set a scientifically-sustainable level of catch by a limited level of effort.

### Total lobster fishery catches (T) per annum from the Galapagos 1997–2001

| *Year* | *Commercialized Catch (tons)* |
|---|---|
| 1997 | 65.3 |
| 1998 | 31 |
| 1999 | 54.4 |
| 2000 | 85 |
| 2001 | 64.1 |
| 2002 | 51.4 |
| ***Average*** | ***58.55*** |

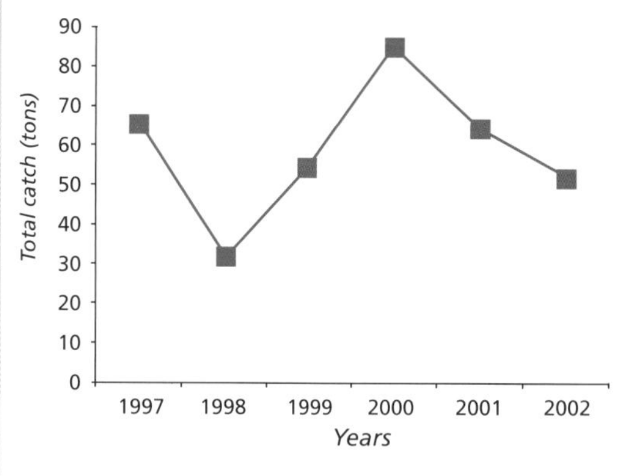


Jennings, S., Kaiser, M.J. and Reynolds, J.D. (2001) *Marine Fisheries Ecology*. Blackwell Science, London, UK.

Munro, J.L. and Pauly, D. (1983). "A simple method for comparing the growth of fishes and invertebrates". *ICLARM Fishbyte* 1(1): 5–6.

Pauly, D. (1978). "Fish population dynamics in tropical waters: a manual for use with programmable calculators". *ICLARM Stud. Rev.* (8): 325p.

Pauly, D. (1983). "Some simple methods for the assessment of tropical fish stocks". *FAO Fish. Tech. Pap.* (234): 52 p.

Polunin, N.V.C. and Roberts, C.M. (eds.) (1996). *Reef Fisheries*. Chapman and Hall, London, UK.

Russ, G.R. (1991). "Coral reef fisheries: Effects and yields." *In* P.F. Sale (ed.), *The Ecology of Fishes on Coral Reefs*. Academic Press, New York, NY. pp. 600–635.

Schnute, J.T. (1985). "A general theory for analysis of catch and effort data." *Can. J. Fish. Aquat. Sci.* 42: 414–429.

Sparre, P. and Venema, S.C. (1992). *Introduction to Tropical Fish Stock Assessment. Part 1 – Manual.* FAO Fisheries Technical Paper No. 306, Rev. 1. United Nations Food and Agriculture Organization, Rome, Italy.

# Water quality

**Relates to goals and objectives**

GOAL 1
1B

GOAL 2
2B 2D
2E

GOAL 3
3B 3C

GOAL 4
4A 4B
4C 3D

GOAL 5
5B 5C
5D

## What is 'water quality'?

Water quality is an abiotic and biotic (in the case of bacterial pollution) measure of the ambient environmental parameters present within the water column. Parameters of water quality include temperature, salinity, oxygen content, turbidity, sedimentation rate, nutrient loading, and presence (suspension) and density of toxins, bacteria and other particulate matter.

## Why measure it?

Water quality is a limiting factor to biological processes within the organisms, populations of organisms, and habitats present within the project site and MPA. Water quality is therefore a key determinant of overall community health and viability. As such, it is an important indicator to measure, one which will be necessary to maintain a respectable level of scientific credibility.

Water quality can be easily and negatively influenced through multiple sources of human activities in or near the coastal zone, particularly in the case of marine pollution. Some examples of human activities that negatively influence water quality include point and non-point discharge of human and other solid and liquid wastes, dumping of trash and refuse into the sea, oil and toxic spills within coastal waters, storm water run-off from urban areas, upland erosion of sediments and their transport and deposition/siltation on downstream coastal environments, fertilizer presence from agricultural run-off, and bilge water discharge.

### Requirements

- Adequately trained staff.
- Knowledge of physical oceanography.
- An understanding of local currents, tides, and water dynamics.
- Thermometer.
- Refractometer.
- Collection bottles for water samples.
- Secchi disc.
- Light meter.
- Other standard hand-held and laboratory water quality monitoring equipment.
- Advanced: specialized equipment, such as instrumentation for analysis of phenol, heavy metals and other toxics; partnerships with universities, environmental quality government agencies, and/or other research institutions; assistance to analyse complex parameters of water quality; programmatic links to and support from baseline national environmental quality assessments or long-term monitoring protocols; remote sensing technologies.

JURGEN FREUND/NATUREPL.COM

TONI PARRAS

***Sediments washed out to sea as a result of deforestation and erosion in the Philippines can endanger marine ecosystems like coral (inset).***

One objective of MPA use is to protect coastal waters from or minimize the impacts of marine pollution and activities that are known to reduce water quality. This is particularly true for MPAs which contain habitat types that serve as land-sea interface areas, such as wetlands and mangrove swamps that act as important filters in mitigating marine pollution and maintaining an adequate level of water quality for the wider community and coastal ecosystems present within the surrounding areas.

This indicator should particularly be measured in MPAs with goals and objectives tied to tourism, diving and other economic activities requiring high water quality. Further, MPAs with goals and objectives linked to improvement of water quality and water or waste management practices should prioritize data collection for this indicator.

It should be noted that the link between effective MPA management and improved water quality may not necessarily be causal. However, it is assumed that through the designation and management of the MPA, in many cases this will include a reduction in known *in situ* activities that pollute the marine environment and/or changes in land-based activities that have downstream impacts on the marine environment. In such cases, an improvement in (or maintenance of) water quality over the long-term could be reasonably expected from effective MPA management.

Understanding the effects of land-based activities and water quality on the nearshore marine environment, focal species therein, and even human health can also provide important public educational opportunities for redirecting social behaviour related to marine pollution and waste disposal.

### How to collect the data

Much has been written about how to undertake water quality surveys within the coastal water column (at varying depths), and so these techniques are not repeated here (see references listed at the end of this section). However, the following parameters and measurements are recommended for collection under this indicator on a regular basis (weekly, monthly, or quarter-annually, depending on the parameter) across sampling locations:

- *Sedimentation rate*: downstream sediment traps can be used to measure particulate presence, composition, and suspension density (parts per thousand) from water samples taken; measure loads and changes in densities and attempt to identify sources.
- *Temperature:* a marine-rated mercury thermometer in protective casing or inexpensive electronic probes can be used; for longer-term deployment (particularly in known areas at risk to sea surface temperature warming), submersible, retrievable temperature loggers whose data readings can be downloaded after a fixed period of time and then re-deployed can be used.
- *Salinity and freshwater input* (particularly useful in sensitive estuarine habitat): a durable refractometer should be used.
- *Oxygen content:* a number of hand-held electronic devices exist to measure dissolved oxygen content and monitor eutrophication areas.
- *Turbidity:* a secchi disk at various sampling locations can be used.
- *Standard water analysis*: presence of known pathogens such as *E coli* (biological indicator) should be checked, and presence and loading rates (amount) of oil, petroleum, nutrients (especially nitrogen, phosphorous) and fertilizers, pesticides and other toxins, and heavy metals should be screened and measured.
- *pH levels.*
- *Biological agents:* such as chlorophyll and phytoplankton levels.

*Some water quality parameters (particularly those that are land-driven) may not necessarily be realistically influenced by the management actions be taken at the MPA. In such cases, measurement of such non-linked parameters – while perhaps interesting – should not be conducted as an indicator of the MPA's management effectiveness. Instead, the evaluation team should be encouraged to focus on these abiotic conditions, which arguably are effected through the effectiveness of the MPA being managed.*

Scientific validation of findings and study trends (literature) that demonstrate relationship(s) between environmental (in this case, water quality) parameters and species and habitat abundance and viability is also needed over the long term to provide a firm understanding of causality. Therefore, the evaluation team will likely need baseline data on the history and trends of various environmental factors within the area.

Also, accounting for natural perturbations (particularly those related to water temperature and salinity changes) will be important to accurately gauge impacts related to management (inside the MPA) or unmanaged human use (outside the MPA). This may necessitate undertaking broader, long-term monitoring programmes of study with project partners in the government and academic institutions. For example, monitoring upland agricultural development impacts including pesticide/fertilizer and nutrient loading in the watershed, estimating runoff volume and sedimentation rates may be necessary to fully understand and predict upper and lower limits of water quality parameters during certain times of the year (e.g. during the rainy versus dry seasons).

> *Note that in MPAs where water movement is highly dynamic and variable (such as within highly fluctuating tidal areas or areas exposed to river currents), the simple water sampling methods offered here may be insufficient to accurately characterize the effects of the MPA and its management on water quality levels.*

The seasonality of water quality (e.g. rainy seasons and frequency of river basin flooding) must be accounted for when considering an appropriate timeframe within which to collect such information.

More advanced evaluation of water quality and its links to the biotic system may also be useful to evaluation teams that have the necessary skills, time, and resources to undertake them. For example, remote-sensing technologies may be available to profile relevant abiotic parameters and how they relate to biological events. Or perhaps sampling for the presence and degree of bioaccumulation (amount) of heavy metals or contamination of persistent organic pollutants within the tissues of focal species (such as molluscs or dead sea mammals) may be an important activity to undertake in an MPA located downstream of upland agricultural activities given its goals and objectives. Or perhaps tracing the path and monitoring the levels of heavy metal bioaccumulation through various trophic levels of the resident food web are important to people living near an urban MPA who rely on local fishery spill-over from a no-take area for food and income.

## How to analyse and interpret results

Summarize and disseminate results with resource users and stakeholders. Analyse the results generated in terms of two components:

- ❑ identification of the water quality issues and specific parameters needing to be addressed, and
- ❑ assessment of what is causing/sourcing these changes.

*Collection of data for this indicator can be linked to the collection of information related to assessment of indicator B10.*

In this regard, the scale-dependency of the parameters investigated becomes more evident.

Monitor observed changes and trends in the environmental parameters measured for water quality and disseminate findings. Correlate these findings against the results of B1 and B4 to see if any relationships or patterns emerge.

Encourage a community-organized water quality monitoring system to take responsibility for regular monitoring and analysis activities. Simple computer software packages (e.g. PRIMER ecological statistics) and the use of friendly, specific procedures to interpret water quality (e.g. the BIOENV procedure) could also be useful for community interpretation of results.

> *The seasonality of water quality (e.g. rainy seasons and frequency of river basin flooding) must be accounted for when analysing and interpreting results.*

A water and environmental quality specialist should review results, and ideally, the specialist should carry out independent spot-checking to confirm or reject measurements taken.

Do data suggest that the water quality within the MPA is changing? If so, to what degree have parameters shifted away from the desired water quality state across the majority of parameters measured?

## Strengths and limitations

Equipment and training costs for the full suite of measures (outlined below) will require moderate to significant financial resources. More technical equipment and measurements do exist for evaluating water quality, but are in all probability not necessary to sufficiently profile this indicator.

### Outputs

- An index of water quality parameters.
- Graphs of parameter results plotted across time.
- Advanced: scatterplots of parameter measures correlated against natural phenomena and biological data.

For most of the measures outlined above, relatively simple methods of water quality testing can be undertaken with some labour investment (two to three persons) and an adequate commitment of staff time. The data collected under this indicator are easily collected and can involve trained community volunteers to complete them. The frequency with which these measures are taken necessitates a relatively high turn over in monitoring equipment, which can add up through time. However, because of the relative ease and importance that this indicator carries as it relates to the biophysical environment (particularly in terms of abiotic factors), this indicator should be easily undertaken.

Water quality is a highly complex issue to address and control with many sources of influence that often arise from outside the jurisdiction and mandate of the MPA and its managers. In this situation, MPA water quality may be strongly influenced by on- and upland development and environmental management practices that lie well outside the influence of the MPA team. For example, an MPA objective to improve water quality may be unfeasible based on poor upland agricultural practices that lead to downstream sedimentation and the introduction of fertilizers into the marine environment of the MPA. In such cases, the indicator can be used to highlight the extent and persistence of such problems by MPA managers to the public and decision-makers. Also, MPA managers can use such opportunities to raise issues about the appropriate siting and design of the MPA.

Because it may be difficult to accurately or definitively link the water quality status in an MPA to the success or failure of the MPA to achieve the stated goals and objectives, in some cases it may be dangerous to claim a direct correlation between this indicator and 'proof' of effective MPA management. Despite this shortcoming, the measurement of water quality against stated MPA goals and objectives will be an important indicator to measure in many MPAs, and thus is being included in this guidebook.

Also note that hydrophobic compounds are difficult to measure in water.

## *Useful references and Internet links*

Sheehan, P.J. (1984). "Effects on community and ecosystem structure and dynamics". *In* P.J. Sheehan, D.R. Miller, G.C. Butler, and P. Boudreau (eds.), *Effects of pollutants at the ecosystem level.* John Wiley and Sons, New York, NY, USA.

Box B9

## Example from the Field

This indicator is the only biophysical indicator focusing on 'environmental' conditions and basic monitoring of micro-scale and abiotic factors. This being said, in many MPAs it is increasingly being recognised that red tide events, heavy metal and toxin bioaccumulation, eutrophication, and fish kills are all prevalent phenomena linked to the types of abiotic parameters being assessed under this indicator. During the process of developing the original set of indicators, several separate abiotic indicators were generated and then collapsed under this single, 'umbrella' environmental indicator by participating experts and managers. Despite this, some pilot sites expressed that given the nature of some MPAs created to address highly abiotic goals and objectives, it may be useful for evaluation teams to split out the multiple measures collapsed under this single indicator into several discrete indicators; for example: chemical and biological compound presence (water composition); rates of sedimentation and siltation; toxin presence; or temperature and turbidity.

### Standard survey methods

Strickland, J.D. and Parsons, T.R. (1972). "A practical handbook of seawater analysis". *Bull. Fish. Res. Board Can.* 167: 310.

United States Geological Survey (1999). *National Field Manual for the Collection of Water-Quality Data: U.S. Geological Survey Techniques of Water-Resources Investigations.* USGS Information Services, Washington, DC, USA. [Online URL: water.usgs.gov/owq/FieldManual]

United States Virgin Islands Coastal Zone Management Program (2001). *Coastal Water Quality Monitoring Manual: Parameters and Techniques.* Department of Planning and Natural Resources, Division of Coastal Zone Management. National Oceanic Atmospheric Administration, Washington, DC, USA. [Download online URL: www.ocrm.nos.noaa.gov/PDF/USVI_Monitoring_Manual.pdf]

**Relates to goals and objectives**

GOAL 1
1C 1E
1F

GOAL 2
2A 2B

GOAL 3
3A 3B

GOAL 4
4A 4B

GOAL 5
5A 5B
5C 5D
5E

B9

## What is 'recovery'?

Recovery is measured as the proportion of the total MPA area (km$^2$, or % of total area) or focal species population (abundance, biomass, or % of total population) that has experienced or 'been restored' to assumed 'original' (target) levels of either:

- Community composition or habitat distribution deemed representative of 'ideal' (i.e. relatively undisturbed by human activity) or 'natural' conditions (i.e. non-human influenced); or
- Viable population levels and stock integrity, such as the return of 60% or more of the original standing spawning stock that is assumed would occur in the absence of human impact.

Whether the recovery target requires that the MPA return biotic characteristics 'back' to some state of 'natural condition', or if it is simply to achieve some identified level below this state, is dependent on the definition of what 'recovery' is. This 'recovery' target may be defined previously within the MPA's recovery-related goals and objectives, in which case it requires them merely to be adopted. But in some cases, a measurable target for 'recovery' has not been specified under the aims of the MPA. In this situation, the MPA management team may need to think carefully about setting measurable aerial restoration targets annually and incrementally through time. From such clearly defined aerial targets, this indicator can be more easily measured. For example, an MPA goal whereby "focal species populations are restored to levels where they can replenish themselves through time within 40% of state waters" is a more measurable definition than one that simply states that "focal species are to be restored back to naturally occurring levels".

It should be noted that in some MPA locations that frequently experience natural disturbances (e.g. cyclones) which limit/prevent the restorative capacity of the project, this indicator may not easily be applicable. In such cases, the 'natural conditions' restoration target may not be realistic and instead may need to give way to a compromise restoration level that is sub-natural conditions.

*There is room for much subjectivity and bias in creating definitions for 'natural' conditions or 'restored' levels. What is more important than the words used is the ability for these words to be measurably defined, even at the expense of substantial debate. If it is not possible for the evaluation team to agree on a measurable definition of what the state of 'recovery' or 'natural condition' is, then this indicator cannot be measured, nor likely will progress made toward the associated MPA objectives be able to be evaluated.*

Finally, this indicator may not be relevant at all MPA sites, depending on the extent (or even presence) of restoration targets within the MPA goals and objectives.

## Why measure it?

This indicator is a discrete measure of the amount of area (with constituent biotic and abiotic attributes) that has been returned to target operational conditions, that is, has been fully restored to natural conditions from some defined level below this. As such, it attempts to act as a concrete success measurement of MPA performance against the stated restoration target. It is a universally understood indicator of interest to stakeholders, decision-makers, donors and researchers.

Note that this indicator should not be measured by MPAs where the goals and objectives of the area do not include 'restoration' (either back to natural state or sustainable fishing levels). However, if 'restoration' is a clearly defined management objective in an MPA, this indicator is a direct measurement of the extent to which this aim is being achieved.

The indicator is used to determine and highlight whether or not a 'restoration' objective for an MPA has been fully achieved. Partial achievement of a

### Requirements

- Same requirements as those listed under B1 to B6, particularly B4 and B5.
- An accurate basemap of the project area, MPA delineation, and habitat types.
- A hand-held GPS unit is needed to delineate areas.
- Clearly defined, measurable definition of 'recovery'.

*Note that while both aerial indicators (B9 and B10) may be collecting similar types of information as those data collected under the enforcement-related governance indicators (G13 to G16), the distinction is that here the data collected are used to address questions relating to biophysical aims, as opposed to compliance ones.*

defined and measurable restoration objective may be laudable progress overall, but this incomplete success will be reflected clearly within the indicator's measurement.

### How to collect the data

To document the recovery of fish or mobile invertebrate focal populations, a visual census should be used to estimate and document the threshold level of population recovery (as a percentage change in population size and structure). Such recovery thresholds may likely have little grounding in scientific literature or fisheries biology, but for the purposes of the indicator they must serve as a 'best guess' that can be adjusted and refined. For areas ($km^2$) that are closed and fully-protected to allow recovery of focal fish and invertebrate populations, their recovery in the closed area can be sensibly expressed as the proportion of the overall population in which the local sub-populations have exceeded the assumed (designated) recovery thresholds.

On the other hand, within an area not fully closed but under restoration, it is the proportion of that area, or the proportion of sample stations in the area, that have exceeded a 'recovery milestone'. The 'recovery milestone' is defined as the exceeding of a known reference point for:

- focal species abundance and population structure (B1 and B2),
- community composition and structure (B4),
- habitat distribution and complexity (B3),
- food web integrity (B6), and
- recruitment success (B5).

These indicators could be derived based on a frequency analysis of areas exceeding the recovery milestone or threshold at a large enough number of samples in the designated area (within and outside the MPA). A stratified or randomized sample of observation stations would be made throughout the designated area at which ratings or estimates of these indicators would be captured through time. Therefore, the extent of area restored could be expressed not only in terms of area ($km^2$), but also as the proportion (%) of stations at which the observed index exceeds a pre-defined level (e.g. recovery milestone).

*In some respects, this indicator can be thought of as an embodiment or filter of other relevant biophysical indicators, most notably B1 to B6. As such, data collected under these other indicators may be useful in making a 'case' toward an articulated level of 'recovery'.*

Samples for this indicator could be measured between every two to five years throughout observation stations across the project area. In order to sample an adequate number of stations within larger MPAs, this may require investment of more time.

### How to analyse and interpret results

Disseminate results of the proportion or 'recovery milestone' frequency within the total project area and quantify the total area restored ($km^2$). Keep in mind that such discrete measurements (number of recoveries, total area) are effective and popular communication tools with stakeholder, public, decision-making, and donor audiences.

#### Outputs

- Total project area ($km^2$) restored fully (100%) versus partially (as % of change in structure, biomass, density/ abundance, or total cover).
- Estimated proportion (% change in population density, structure, or biomass) of recovery within focal species population against specified target.
- Estimated frequency with which 'recovery milestones' are met across focal species populations within the community.

### Strengths and limitations

With a clearly defined 'restoration' target and supporting data (from B1 through B6) available for use, this indicator can be a relatively simple measure to attempt and done with low incremental investment in terms of time and labour.

However, the setting of 'recovery milestones' and sustainable population levels is challenging scientifically, and often poorly understood or documented. As a result, the reliability of results generated from this indicator may be questionable in terms of measuring population recovery thresholds.

## Box B10

## Example from the Field

During the expert group development and pilot site testing of this indicator, there was much discussion and controversy expressed over the illogical definition of what 'restoration' or 'recovery' is in the absence of sufficient evidence to indicate what 'naturally'-occurring levels for the biological attributes involved would be. Several people felt that this indicator suggests the nearly impossible task of attempting to aim for, characterize, and measure true 'recovery'. Given the global reach and multiple levels of human impacts on the Earth's ecosystems, even as far back as several hundred years ago, people saw the use of the term 'restoration' as disingenuous and dangerous. As such, the term 'recovery' was allowed (providing it was used in the content of uncertainty) and 'restoration' discarded as a value-laden and impractical term that presupposes that the evaluation team actually knows what a population, community, or ecosystem looks like in it's 'natural' state. As a result of this stigma, this was one of only two biophysical indicators not tested by the pilot sites.

### *Useful references and Internet links*

Sousa, W.P. (1984). "The role of disturbance in natural communities". *Annual Review of Ecology and Systematics* 15: 53–391.

***Mangrove swamps, vital for replenishment of fish stocks, can be good areas to restore in an MPA.***

Jeff Foott/naturepl.com

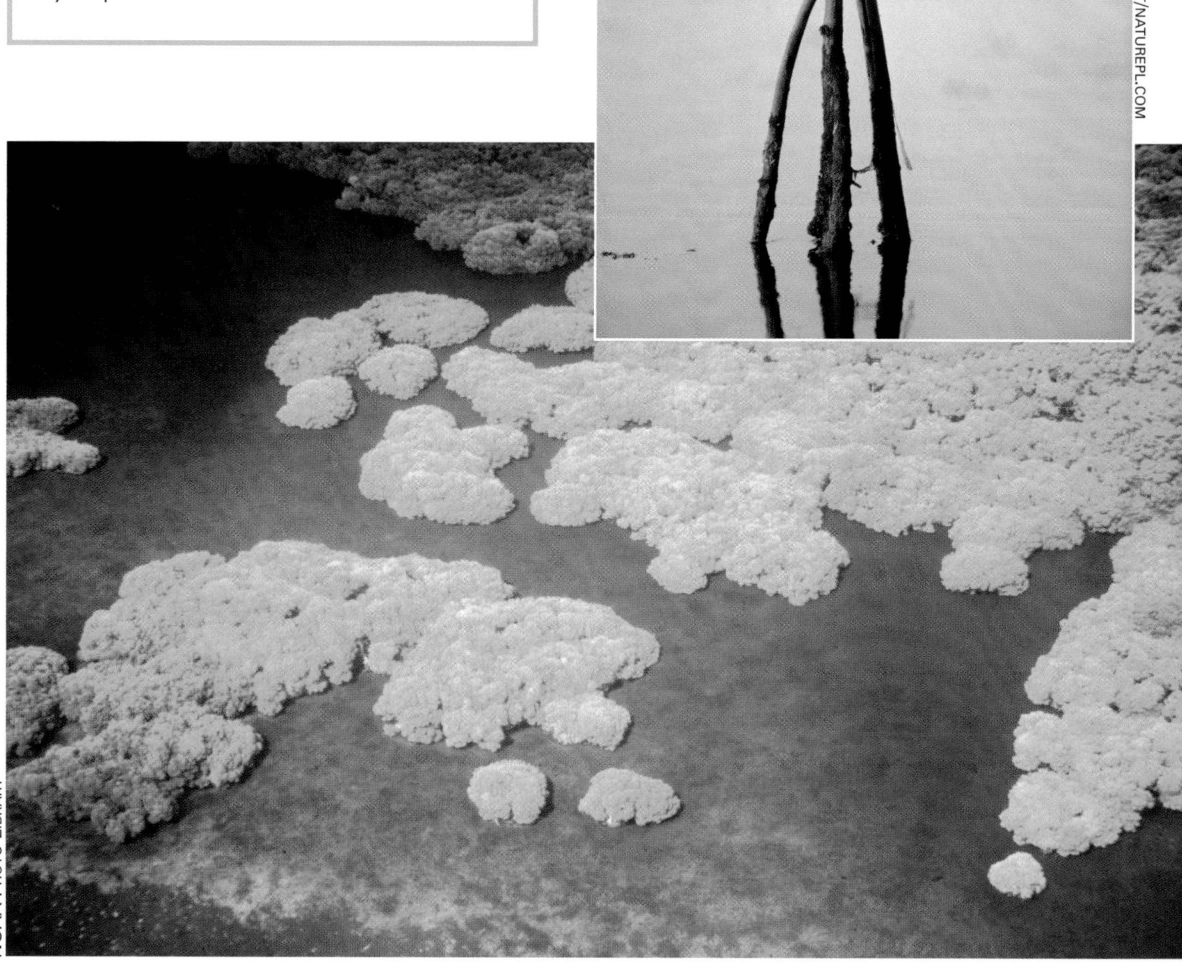

NOAA Photo Library

## What is 'human impact'?

Human impact is defined as the cumulative environmental effect of all extractive and non-extractive uses of living and non-living marine resources located within a specified area (in this case, within and outside the MPA). Examples of extractive and non-extractive human uses within coastal waters include fishing, tourism, aquaculture, coastal development, seabed drilling and mining, transportation, and trade. Varying levels of human use of marine resources can result in varying levels of impact. For example, the type and number of certain fishing gears (such as bottom trawls, purse seines, and gill nets) are known to have significantly higher impacts on ecosystems than others (such as pole and line and cast nets). Some extractive uses (such as dynamite fishing) are well documented as having highly destructive impacts associated with them.

An area under no impact is defined as one that is completely free of all extractive or non-extractive human uses that contribute impact. Not all MPAs include such areas. These areas are commonly referred to as 'reserves' or 'fully-protected areas', and are often delineated as distinct, 'no-take' zones within a larger MPA. Some 'no-take' zones are time bound; for example, the seasonal prohibition of access within known spawning grounds of a focal species. One frequent exception to the prohibition of all human activity within 'no-take' zones is the allowance of MPA monitoring and scientific research activities.

> *Note that areas under 'no' human impact are assumed to experience broadcast impacts of human activities that occur outside the MPA, such as a rise in sea surface temperature contributed by global warming effects. The focus on 'no' impact under this indicator is specific to human activities within the MPA.*

## Why measure it?

Reducing the level of human impact experienced in an area of waters is a common aim of MPAs. It is assumed that if an MPA experiences reduced or no human impact, the focal species, habitats, and communities therein have a greater probability of being able to replenish and maintain themselves through time than ones outside the MPA that are experiencing a higher level of human impact. It is also assumed that the greater the level of restriction on extractive uses within an MPA, the less total human impact will occur.

Measuring the scale and pattern of human uses through time and their cumulative effect is therefore needed to test and legitimise these assumptions. Understanding the level of and changes to human use within and outside the MPA can also help managers to identify and proactively address **threats** (i.e. natural or human activities that do or could negatively contribute to the overall impact experienced in the area).

> *Note that simply having an area declared free from human use does not necessarily mean that the area is effectively free from such activity.*

## How to collect the data

This indicator is measured by: a) characterizing the presence, level, and impact of various human activities and threats through time; and b) quantifying the total area under no or reduced human impact, as the result of the degree of compliance with prohibitions or restrictions on user activity.

At the simplest level, a qualitative characterization of the presence, level, and impact of human activ-

### Requirements

- Clipboard, paper, and pencil.
- A map of the delineated MPA boundaries (and fully-protected zones, if applicable) and the surrounding waters/area.
- The desired degree to which human activities and threats are to be reduced or eliminated within the MPA. Such a target may be able to be derived based on the MPA's goals and objectives. In other cases it may require careful thought by the management team with regard to setting measurable impact reduction targets annually and incrementally through time.
- Knowledge of the types of extractive and non-extractive activities and technologies being used within and around the MPA, including threats.
- Stakeholders who are willing to openly share their observations, experiences, and beliefs about human activities and threats.
- Literature and other data sources on the scale and impacts of human activities and threats.
- Advanced: a handheld GPS unit; a boat and engine.

**Relates to goals and objectives**

GOAL 1: 1C 1D 1E

GOAL 2: 2A 2D 2E

GOAL 3: 3C

GOAL 4: 4C

GOAL 5: 5D

ities and threats (both upland and coastal) should be done through manager interview (with supporting evidence regarding enforcement and compliance) and stakeholder triangulation. Key informant interviews with MPA staff and across stakeholder groups can help to initially identify and characterize the presence and number of human uses (both extractive and non-extractive), and which of these are or should be considered threats to the MPA (i.e. activities that are leading or could lead to increased negative impacts within the area).

The next step is to assess and describe all threats found to be operating in and around the MPA. Specifically, for each threat identified, the level of its impact using the following three parameters needs to be described: a) the intensity of the threat (i.e. level of operation and degree of overall human effort involved), b) the extent of the threat (i.e. the total area across which the threat is distributed and active), and c) the urgency of the threat (i.e. the frequency, timing, and acuteness of the threat). These three threat parameters should be quantitatively assessed along with their descriptions; for example, the number of users or boats per threat per harvest unit, the frequency of activities, and the spatial extent (expressed in $km^2$) of the total area in which threats are observed. Data for these parameters can be collected through structured and semi-structured interviews and focus group discussions of MPA management staff and stakeholder groups. Supplemental information can be taken from secondary data sources and/or direct observation of user activities, levels, and impacts. For example, the intensity (number of fishers), area (in $km^2$), and urgency (trends in frequency of activity) of a particularly threatening extractive activity (such as dynamite fishing) could be collected through harvester interview, and supplemented with existing studies and survey results from direct observations (such as the number of times blasts are heard in a day).

Characterization of human activities and trends can also be described in terms of: a) the types and numbers of extractive gears and technologies that are used, particularly with regard to the extractive efficiency of such technologies and their destructive effects, and b) changes in the power of extractive and non-extractive effort, particularly in terms of the number of fishers, number of boats, number of gears, etc.

During the baseline characterization inside and outside the MPA, the nature and level of physical, chemical, biological, and other environmental effects that are known to occur as a result of extractive and non-extractive uses should be documented. The uses that are known to have deleterious impacts on species, habitats, and community ecology should be highlighted. The threats (both human induced and natural) may already be identified and previously prioritized for management action (such as with the designation of the MPA) with the aim of eliminating or minimizing these threats over time.

An estimation of the physical location (placement) and extent (area) of threats and other human activities observed within and around the MPA should also be made as part of the characterization.

In terms of collection of data on the extent of destructive fishing methods used within the managed area, it is important to estimate the total area known where such technologies are used. Additionally, the percentage of area ($km^2$) within the MPA where destructive fishing technologies and other fishing techniques are prohibited should be calculated. Destructive technologies include the use of poisons (e.g. potassium and sodium cyanide, bleach, plant toxins), dynamite, bottom trawling, physical destruction with tools etc., and fine mesh nets for extraction.

A much more in-depth, time consuming, and accurate method of characterizing the presence, level, and impact of human activities is to directly observe all human activities operating in the area in and around the MPA, measuring the three parameters of user behaviour and impacts mentioned above through *in situ* survey. In addition to this, additional impact data about threats and other human activities can be further characterized through the measurement of other biophysical indicators, particularly B1 to B7. In addition to a qualitative discussion of impacts, the results of these indicators can provide supporting evidence as to the nature and extent of environmental impacts associated with the human uses operating within the area surveyed.

> *B10 is not a 'true' biophysical indicator in that it does not assess biotic or abiotic states, trends, or outputs. Rather it is a contextual indicator that assesses activities known to impact biophysical conditions. However, results collected from the measurement of indicators B1 to B7 can be used to provide supplementary evidence to data collected on B10.*

Quantification of the total area under no or reduced human impact requires six steps. First, the total area (in $km^2$) bounded by the MPA through the use of previously delineated boundaries on a basemap or the *in situ* collection of GPS data from which to quantify the total area should be calculated. Second, the total area (in $km^2$) of all locations within the MPA that have been designated as 'no-take' or 'fully-protected' zones (i.e. areas free from all human activity) must be gauged. If the entire area within an MPA is fully protected, the totals will be the same. If an MPA does not contain any areas zoned for no human activity, the total will be zero. Note that both of these areas may already have been delineated and calculated within existing documentation, such as in the MPA management plan and/or accompanying legislation. In this case, it still may be useful to validate these totals through *in situ* GPS delineation.

Third, it is necessary to subtract the area designated to be free from human activity from the total MPA area to determine the area within the MPA that has *not* been designated to be free from human activity. These totals should then be converted into percentages, and the three areas and percentages should be recorded in an annotated table. Fourth, the results of the human activity characterization and the spatial estimates of the extent ($km^2$) of threats operating in the MPA (taken from the threat reduction assessment – TRA) should be revisited. Using these results, it should be possible to estimate the total area in the MPA that is not actually free from human activity. If the characterization results and TRA suggest that human activities may be underway in areas designated as 'fully protected' or 'no-take', an attempt should be made to estimate how much of this designated area is actually being violated versus that being respected (in $km^2$ and as a percentage).

Fifth, for *each* human use occurring in the MPA, the total area ($km^2$) of the MPA that was designated for reduction should be estimated, defined by how each human use (or groups of uses) are to be measurably reduced within the MPA. In some cases, a human use will have been designated to be reduced throughout the entire area of the MPA. In other cases, this reduction will have been designated to occur only in a specific habitat type or zone. Finally, for each human use, the results of the human activity characterization and TRA index should be reviewed and an estimate carried out of how much (in $km^2$ and as a percentage) of the area is actually under reduction compared to how it was originally designated for reduction.

Answering the following questions about the designated versus actual area under no or reduced human impact may be of interest to the evaluation team during its investigation: 1) how was the specific delineation of the no-take area defined? Was it demarcated on the basis of biological parameters or political convenience? 2) How effective is fisher compliance with the no-take area? Are there any reported/confirmed (or unreported/unconfirmed) violations of extractive activities taking place in the area? 3) What forms of surveillance and enforcement are being conducted in the area? How certain are those who police/enforce the area that the area truly is being observed as 'no-take' zone? Manager and stakeholder responses to such questions will assist the evaluation team in determining the degree to which the designated areas under no or reduced human impact are being effectively managed, and the degree to which violations (if any) are occurring in the area (see relevant governance indicators).

Data on human activities as well as natural and man-made threats should be collected twice a year or annually, including all information needed to demarcate the area(s) where they are operating, depending on how active and changing they are. Threat reduction data should be collected twice a year. Calculations of the total area under no or reduced human impact should be made every year, unless needed sooner (for example, if new threats arise or if changes to the existing boundaries are made during the year).

> *Note that the synergistic and dynamic effects among and between threats are not captured under the methods outlined here. As a result, observed feedback loops and synergistic impacts resulting from threats operating on one another should be documented qualitatively.*

### How to analyse and interpret results

Theoretically (and ideally in practice), if an MPA is successful in reducing human threats – or prohibiting them altogether – then the actual area under no or reduced human impact should equal the area designated as such. In viewing the calculated area results, how closely do designated (on paper) areas of no and reduced human use compare to actual (in reality) areas of no or reduced human use? Do real-world observations reflect the reduction or prohibition of human activities that, on paper, are supposed to be occurring? How are extractive technology and power (effort) changing through time? Have all human activities halted within fully protected areas? To what degree have human activities and impact been reduced in designated areas, across each activity?

One way to analyse an estimated degree and area of human impact reduction using data collected for this indictor is through the threat reduction assessment (TRA) index (reference guides on how to use the TRA index are listed at the end of this

*Data collected under this indicator are closely associated with several other socio-economic (local use patterns and occupational structure) and governance (user conflicts, understanding of rules and regulations, and enforcement) indicators, and should be conducted accordingly. The distinction on B10 is that data collected are used to evaluate biophysical aims of the MPA.*

indicator description). Working with management team and stakeholder representatives, the relative progress to date made in abating each threat identified can be estimated as the percentage of total threat reduction in comparison to total threat potential. While subjective, the TRA is undertaken so that meaningful comparisons can be made across different areas as to the degree with which human use impacts have been mitigated over a period of time. The logic behind the TRA is that if the management team can identify the threats facing their MPA and its surrounding waters, then they can also assess their progress through time in achieving no or reduced human impact through measuring the degree to which each of these threats is reduced. Threats can also be visually diagrammed and discussion can take place as to how they conceptually relate to one another through causal relationships. Compare threat reduction scores across all identified threats annually or every two years. Based on the spatial extent of how human activities and threats are operating within and outside the MPA, are there any observable trends (increases or decreases) in the area with respect to the level and scale of these activities and threats? Are key threats and destructive human activities being halted successfully through time within the MPA? Are rates of threat reduction of specific activities steady or changing?

> *As there is increasing international attention and promotion in using fully-protected MPAs (reserves), results generated from such areas will be of interest to many managers and stakeholders beyond your MPA site.*

Results from this indicator will be of most relevance and use when linked with other biophysical assessment results, and when describing the history and contextual background of threats operating at the MPA site. Pair results of other biophysical indicators with results in human impact reduction, do any relationships appear? Are results within areas free from all human activity significantly different from results in other reduced but multiple human use areas of the MPA? For example, are changes observed in the same focal species' abundance in the MPA and within relatively adjacent areas significantly different between reserve and non-reserve waters within the MPA? Through time, is a greater or reduced percentage of total MPA area found under full protection? Finally, is there an optimum percentage (20%, 50%) of reserve versus non-reserve waters found within multiple-zone MPAs being achieved through time? If so, on what grounds (why) can this be argued?

Disseminate summary results of threats profiled and changes observed in threats with various stakeholders, managers, and decision-makers. As data collected on this indicator can be conducted in tandem with governance indicators (e.g. surveillance and enforcement, number of violations), interpretation of how effectively the area of no or reduced human impact is being policed by enforcers and complied with by fishers may also be of interest to target audiences of results.

### Outputs

- A descriptive and quantitative characterization of the human activities and threats (both natural and human) present in and around the MPA.
- Total area of the MPA.
- Total area (and percentage) of the MPA designated as being under no human activity.
- Total area (and percentage) of the MPA actually under no human activity.
- Total area (and percentage) of the MPA designated as under reduced human activity.
- Total area (and percentage) of the MPA actually under reduced human activity.
- GPS coordinates for these areas.
- Threat assessment profile and prioritization.
- Threat reduction index (score of 1–100%).
- Map of threat activity within and outside the MPA; areas of destructive fishing technology use.
- Map of the boundaries of the MPA at the site and the reserve area(s) within or overlapping with it.

## Strengths and limitations

This indicator may prove to be useful as a rapid, qualitative assessment tool to guage how the biophysical environment, or specific attributes, within and outside the MPA may be being impacted by human activity and experiencing change. However, due to the highly subjective nature of the methods involved (being based in large part on manager and stakeholder perceptions), this indicator should only be measured in conjunction with other biophysical indicators, as the results generated from this indicator cannot be considered accurate on their own or viewed as stand-alone evidence of MPA management effectiveness. Results from this indicator should be considered only as signposts and proxies, and may be of most use when linked contextually with other biological indicator results and when describing the background to the threats operating.

While the indicator may appear conceptually simple, data are not always simply or easily collected. Because of the complexity that occurs where multiple human uses occur in and/or around the MPA, an accurate and repeatable measure becomes difficult to construct. Even the most basic level of data collection on human activities and threats requires adequate time and staff to interview the necessary number of managers and stakeholders, conduct focus group discussions, and source secondary data. The nature of TRA methods may also be difficult to approach and measure with many stakeholders, even at a highly subjective level.

## *Useful references and Internet links*


Schmitt, R.J. and Osenburg, C.W. (1995). "Detecting ecological impacts caused by human activities." *In* R.J. Schmitt and C.W. Osenburg (eds.), *The Design of Ecological Impact Assessment Studies: Conceptual Issues and Application in Coastal Marine Habitats*. Academic Press, San Diego, USA. pp. 3–16.

Underwood, A.J. (1995). "On beyond BACI: sampling designs that might reliably detect environmental disturbances". *In* R.J. Schmitt and C.W. Osenburg, *Design of Ecological Impact Assessment Studies: Conceptual Issues and Application in Coastal Marine Habitats*. Academic Press, San Diego, USA. pp. 151–178.

Warwick, R.M. (1993). "Environmental impact studies on marine communities: pragmatical considerations". *Australian Journal of Ecology* 18: 63–80.


### TRA Methodology


Margolius, R. and Salafsky, N. (2001). *Is Our Project Succeeding? Using the Threat Reduction Assessment Approach to Determine Conservation Impact*. Biodiversity Support Program, World Wildlife Fund, Washington, DC, USA. [Download online URL: www.BSPonline.org]

Salafsky, N. and Margolius, R. (1999). "Threat reduction assessment: A practical and cost-effective approach to evaluating conservation and development projects". *Conservation Biology* 13: 830–841.


### No-take areas


Roberts, C. and Hawkings, J. (2000). *A Manual for Fully-Protected Areas*. World Wide Fund for Nature, Gland, Switzerland.

Tupper, M. (2001). "Putting no-take marine reserves in perspective". *MPA News* 26: 2.


### Promotion of no-take areas


National Center for Ecological Analysis and Synthesis (2001). *Scientific Consensus Statement on Marine Reserves and Marine Protected Areas.* Annual Meeting of the American Association for the Advancement of the Sciences, February 2001.


Box B11

## Example from the Field

How easy is it to track human impacts, you might ask? In Tanzania's Mafia Island Marine Park, measuring all human impact throughout the MPA was determined to be "very demanding, verging on impossible". To overcome this, the evaluation team decided to modify and limit the measurement of this indicator to focus on a single human activity (fishing, vis-à-vis total effort) and within only a fraction of the total MPA area (30 of 822 km$^2$, defined by a regulated fishing zone). The evaluators found that even this restricted measurement of human impact was still labour intensive, requiring 6 people and 3 boats working 10–12 hours per day for 9 days per month over a 4 month period. Even with this level of significant investment in data collection, the issue of the evaluation team's inability to adequately monitor and sample illegal and night fishing activity was quickly identified. To overcome this, the team partnered with innocuous-looking dive tourism boats, who volunteered to record observed incidences of illegal fishing in the zone sampled while they passed through the zone on a daily basis to and from dive sites. While this helped, the team then found that the tourism personnel were not reliable in filling out their data forms. With a bit of training, they have begun to improve with time. The Mafia team are still creatively seeking means to adequately sample night diving.

***MIMP wardens George Msumi and WWF Project Community Officer Hisluck Mambosho at Park HQ, Mafia Island.***

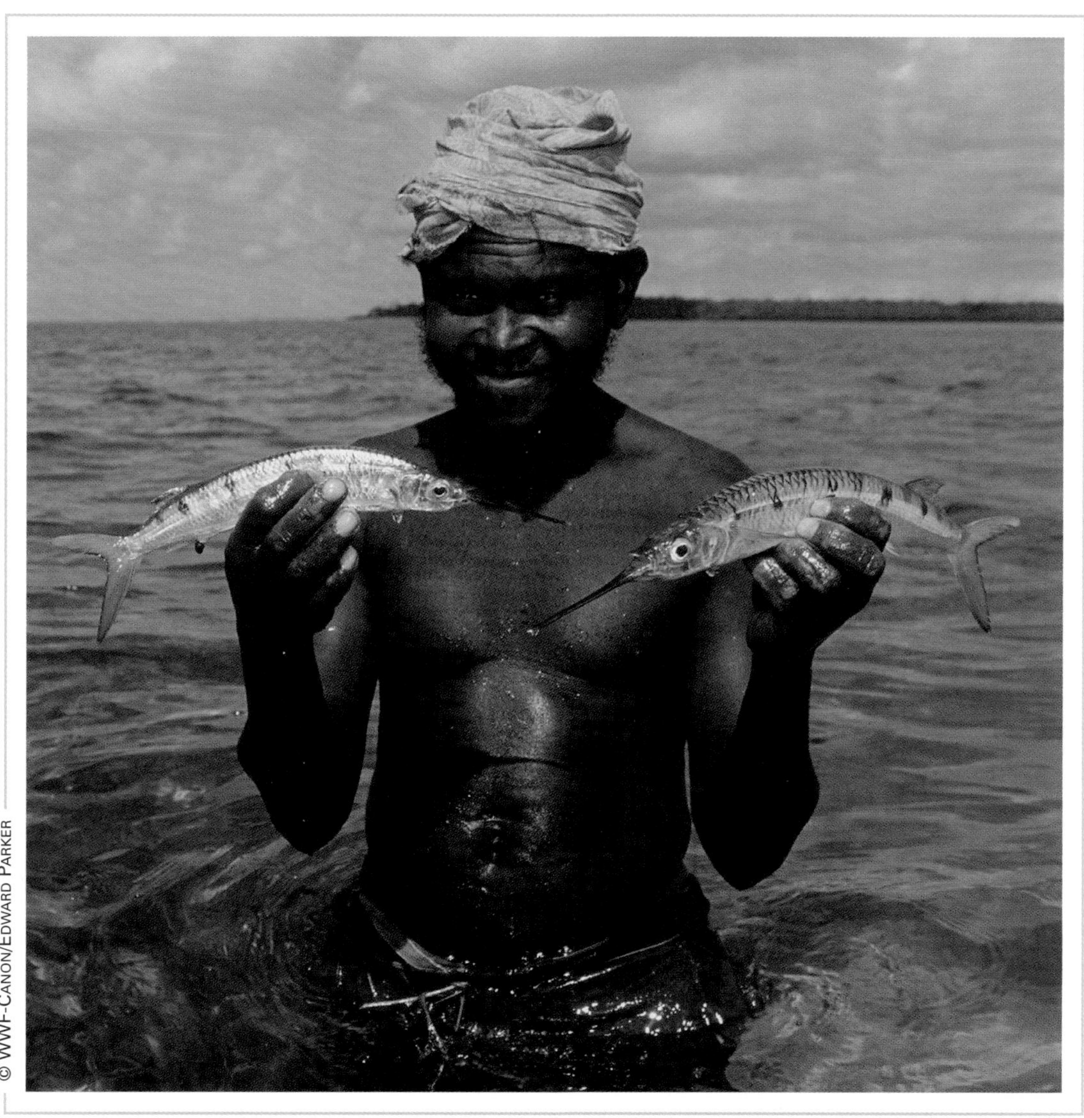



*In and around most MPAs, locally caught fish find a ready market with buyers and so provide valuable income to local people – the focus of the socio-economic indicators presented in this book.*

# The socio-economic indicators

## *Introduction*

Experience shows that social, cultural, economic and political factors, more than biological or physical factors, shape the development, management and performance of MPAs (Fiske, 1992; Kelleher and Recchia, 1998; Mascia, 2002; Roberts, 2000). MPAs affect and are affected by people. For this reason, the goals and objectives of many MPAs include socio-economic considerations such as food security, livelihood opportunities, monetary and non-monetary benefits, equitable distribution of benefits, compatibility with local culture, and environmental awareness and knowledge. Understanding the socio-economic context of stakeholders involved with and/or influenced by the MPA (individuals, households, groups, communities, organizations) is essential for assessing, predicting and managing MPAs. The use of socio-economic indicators allows MPA managers to: a) incorporate and monitor stakeholder group concerns and interests into the management process; b) determine the impacts of management decisions on the stakeholders; and c) demonstrate the value of the MPA to the public and decision-makers.

The socio-economic indicators in this guidebook address the overall value of the MPA, in addition to being focused on the achievement of social and economic goals and objectives. Several of the indicators, such as S4, S5 and S6, measure people's perceptions. People's perceptions are known to have an impact on conservation, so while the measurement of perceptions may be imprecise, their use can be of real value to the MPA manager. Several of the indicators, such as S2, S3, S13, rely on interviewing household members and fishers. Interviews provide access to a wealth of valuable information relating to such issues as natural history, resource use and income. With this opportunity in mind, and recognising how busy household members and fishers are, if interviews are to be conducted, questions from several selected indicators should be collected at the same time to capture overlapping information needs more efficiently. Indicators S2, S3, S13 and S14 are concerned with aspects of understanding people's values and understanding marine resources at the broader community level.

It should be noted that there is no one indicator which captures the total economic value of the MPA. Consideration was given to such an indicator but it was felt that the methods for collecting such information were beyond the capability of most MPAs. However, several of the indicators can be used to measure components of total economic value such as use and non-use values of the MPA. These include indicators S6 (perceptions of non-market and non-use value), S7 (material style of life), S8 (quality of human health), S9 (household income distribution by source), S10 (occupational structure), S11 (community infrastructure and business), and S12 (number and nature of markets). While not direct measures of total economic value, used together, these indicators can provide information on benefits and costs associated with the MPA and can adaptively inform MPA managers in their planning and management decision-making.

Collectively, coastal and marine ecosystems provide food, building materials, firewood, recreational opportunities, protection and buffering from coastal hazards, economic development opportunities, and important life support functions. Valuation of MPAs and their associated natural resources necessitates the estimation of benefits and costs of using the natural assets. The total economic value of a natural system is the sum of all net benefits from all compatible uses, including non-use values. Conceptually, it is the amount of resources, expressed in common units of money, by which society would be worse off if the natural resource or environmental amenity were lost. It consists of 1) use value and 2) non-use value. Use values include direct use (fishing, diving), indirect use (coastal hazard protection), and option value (potential future direct and indirect use of a natural system). Non-use values represent values that are not associated with any use and include existence value (the value of knowing that the resource exists in a certain condition), option value (the value of being able to use the resource in the future) and bequest value (the value of ensuring the resource will be available for future generations).

It should be noted that indicator S6 – perceptions of non-market and non-use value – suggests the use of scale analysis rather than more advanced non-market and non-use economic valuation methods. This is due to the complexity of using these methods and the need for advanced economic analysis skills which are usually not found among MPA staff.

## *Useful references*


Bunce, L., Townsley, P., Pomeroy, R. and Pollnac, R. (2000). *Socioeconomic Manual for Coral Reef Management*. Australian Institute of Marine Science, Townsville, Queensland, Australia. Available on www.reefbase.org

Berkes, F., Mahon, R., McConney, P., Pollnac, R. and Pomeroy, R. (2001). *Managing small-scale fisheries: alternative directions and methods*. International Development Research Centre, Ottawa, Canada. Available on www.idrc.ca/booktique

Fiske, S.J. (1992). Sociocultural aspects of establishing marine protected areas. *Ocean and Coastal Management* 18: 25-46.

Grigalunas, T.A. and Congar, R. (eds.) (1995). *Environmental economics for integrated coastal area management: valuation methods and policy instruments*. Regional Seas Reports and Studies No. 164. United Nations Environment Program, Nairobi, Kenya.

Kelleher, G. and Recchia, C. (1998). Lessons from marine protected areas around the world. *Parks* 8(2): 1-4.

Kempton, W., Boster, J.S. and Hartley, J.A. (1995). *Environmental Values in American Culture*. MIT Press, Boston, USA.

Langill, S. (compiler) (1999). *Stakeholder Analysis. Volume 7. Supplement for Conflict and Collaboration Resource Book*. International Development Research Center, Ottawa, Canada.

Lipton, D.W., Wellman K., Sheifer, I.C. and Weiher, R.F. (1995). *Economic valuation of natural resources – a handbook for coastal resource policymakers*. NOAA Coastal Ocean Program Decision Analysis Series No. 5. NOAA Coastal Ocean Office, Silver Spring, Maryland, USA.

Mascia, M. (2002). *The social dimensions of marine reserve design and performance*. Draft manuscript submitted for inclusion in the book J. Sobel (ed.) Marine Reserves: their science, design and use. Center for Marine Conservation. Washington DC, USA.

McClanahan, T.R., Glaesel, H., Rubens, J. and Kiambe, R. (1997). The effects of traditional fisheries management on fisheries yields and the coral reef ecosystems of Southern Kenya. Environmental Conservation. 24(2): 105–120.

Pollnac, R. (1998). *Rapid assessment of management parameters for coral reefs*. Coastal Resources Center Coastal Management Report # 2205. Coastal Resources Center, University of Rhode Island, Narragansett, Rhode Island, USA. Available at www.crc.uri.edu

TONI PARRAS

Pollnac, R.B. and Crawford, B.R. (2000). *Assessing behavioral aspects of coastal resource use*. Proyek Pesisir Publication Special Report. Coastal Resources Center, Coastal Management Report #2226. Coastal Resources Center, University of Rhode Island, Narragansett, Rhode Island, USA. Available at www.crc.uri.edu

Pomeroy, R.S. Economic valuation: available methods. *In* Chua, T.-E. and Scrua, L.F. (eds.) (1992). *Integrative framework and methods for coastal area management*. ICLARM Conf. Proc. 37. International Center for Living Aquatic Resources Management, Manila, Philippines.

Pomeroy, R., Pollnac, R., Katon, B. and Predo, C. (1997). Evaluating factors contributing to the success of community-based coastal resource management: The Central Visayas Regional Project 1, Philippines. *Ocean and Coastal Management* 36 (1–3): 97–120.

Roberts, C.M. (2000). Selecting marine reserve locations: optimality versus opportunism. *Bulletin of Marine Science* 66(3): 581–592.

# Figure 3 Socio-economic goals, objectives, indicators

## *Socio-economic goals (n=6) and objectives (n=21) commonly associated with MPA use*

**GOAL 1** **Food security enhanced or maintained**

- 1A *Nutritional needs of coastal residents met or improved*
- 1B *Improved availability of locally caught seafood for public consumption*

**GOAL 2** **Livelihoods enhanced or maintained**

- 2A *Economic status and relative wealth of coastal residents and/or resource users improved*
- 2B *Household occupational and income structure stabilized or diversified through reduced marine resource dependency*
- 2C *Local access to markets and capital improved*
- 2D *Health of coastal residents and/or resource users improved*

**GOAL 3** **Non-monetary benefits to society enhanced or maintained**

- 3A *Aesthetic value enhanced or maintained*
- 3B *Existence value enhanced or maintained*
- 3C *Wilderness value enhanced or maintained*
- 3D *Recreation opportunities enhanced or maintained*
- 3E *Cultural value enhanced or maintained*
- 3F *Ecological services values enhanced or maintained*

**GOAL 4** **Benefits from the MPA equitably distributed**

- 4A *Monetary benefits distributed equitably to and through coastal communities*
- 4B *Non-monetary benefits distributed equitably to and through coastal communities*
- 4C *Equity within social structures and between social groups improved and fair*

**GOAL 5** **Compatibility between management and local culture maximized**

- 5A *Adverse effects on traditional practices and relationships or social systems avoided or minimized*
- 5B *Cultural features or historical sites and monuments linked to coastal resources protected*

**GOAL 6** **Environmental awareness and knowledge enhanced**

- 6A *Respect for and/or understanding of local knowledge enhanced*
- 6B *Public's understanding of environmental and social 'sustainability' improved*
- 6C *Level of scientific knowledge held by the public increased*
- 6D *Scientific understanding expanded through research and monitoring*

## *How the socio-economic indicators relate to the common goals and objectives*

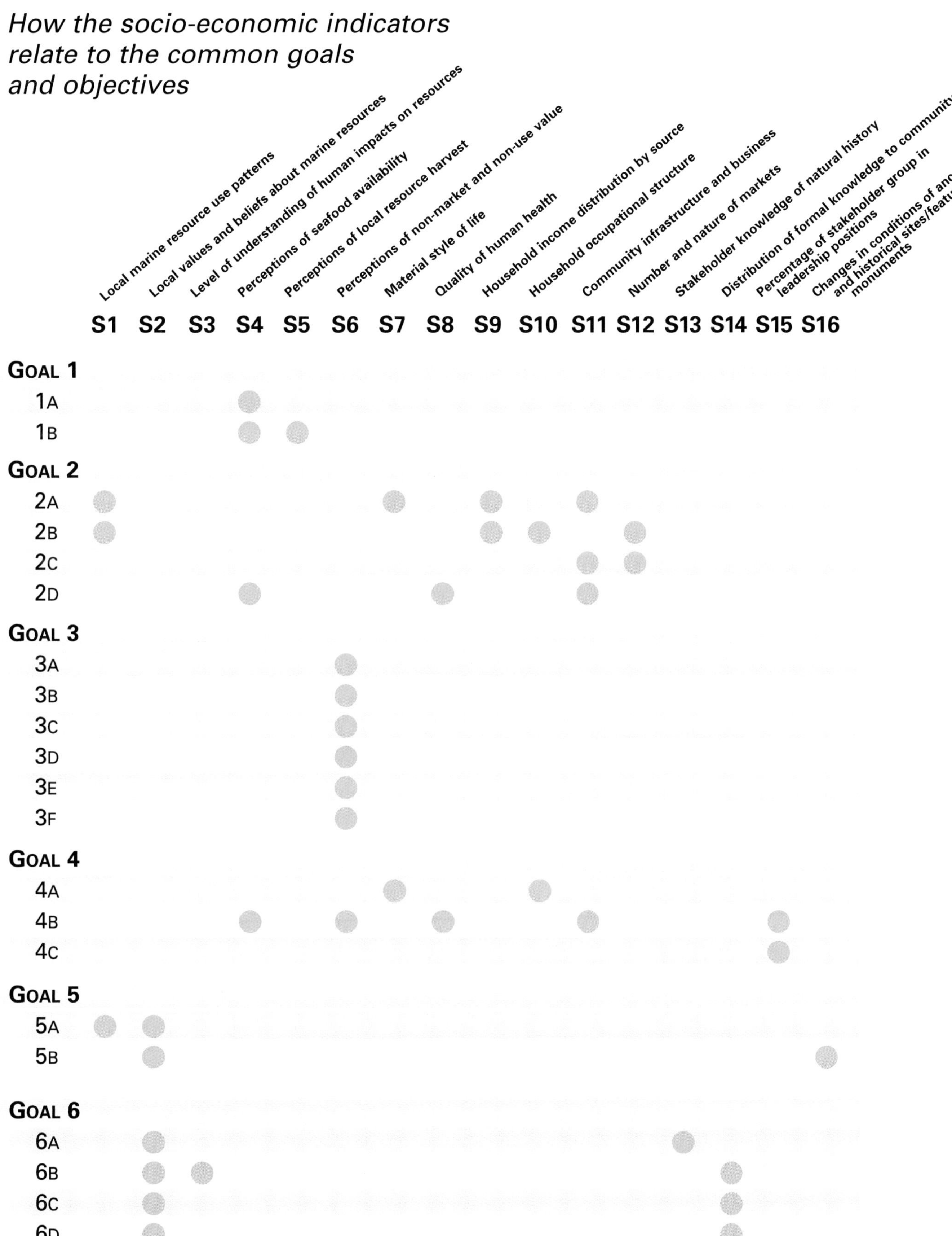

| | Local marine resource use patterns | Local values and beliefs about marine resources | Level of understanding of human impacts on resources | Perceptions of seafood availability | Perceptions of local resource harvest | Perceptions of non-market and non-use value | Material style of life | Quality of human health | Household income distribution by source | Household occupational structure | Community infrastructure and business | Number and nature of markets | Stakeholder knowledge of natural history | Distribution of formal knowledge to community | Percentage of stakeholder group in leadership positions | Changes in conditions of ancestral and historical sites/features/monuments |
|---|---|---|---|---|---|---|---|---|---|---|---|---|---|---|---|---|
| | **S1** | **S2** | **S3** | **S4** | **S5** | **S6** | **S7** | **S8** | **S9** | **S10** | **S11** | **S12** | **S13** | **S14** | **S15** | **S16** |
| **Goal 1** | | | | | | | | | | | | | | | | |
| 1A | | | | ● | | | | | | | | | | | | |
| 1B | | | | ● | ● | | | | | | | | | | | |
| **Goal 2** | | | | | | | | | | | | | | | | |
| 2A | ● | | | | | | ● | | ● | | ● | | | | | |
| 2B | ● | | | | | | | | ● | ● | | ● | | | | |
| 2C | | | | | | | | | | | ● | ● | | | | |
| 2D | | | | ● | | | | ● | | | ● | | | | | |
| **Goal 3** | | | | | | | | | | | | | | | | |
| 3A | | | | | | ● | | | | | | | | | | |
| 3B | | | | | | ● | | | | | | | | | | |
| 3C | | | | | | ● | | | | | | | | | | |
| 3D | | | | | | ● | | | | | | | | | | |
| 3E | | | | | | ● | | | | | | | | | | |
| 3F | | | | | | ● | | | | | | | | | | |
| **Goal 4** | | | | | | | | | | | | | | | | |
| 4A | | | | | | | ● | | | ● | | | | | | |
| 4B | | | | ● | | ● | | ● | | | ● | | | | ● | |
| 4C | | | | | | | | | | | | | | | ● | |
| **Goal 5** | | | | | | | | | | | | | | | | |
| 5A | ● | ● | | | | | | | | | | | | | | |
| 5B | | ● | | | | | | | | | | | | | | ● |
| **Goal 6** | | | | | | | | | | | | | | | | |
| 6A | | ● | | | | | | | | | | | ● | | | |
| 6B | | ● | ● | | | | | | | | | | | ● | | |
| 6C | | ● | | | | | | | | | | | | ● | | |
| 6D | | ● | | | | | | | | | | | | ● | | |

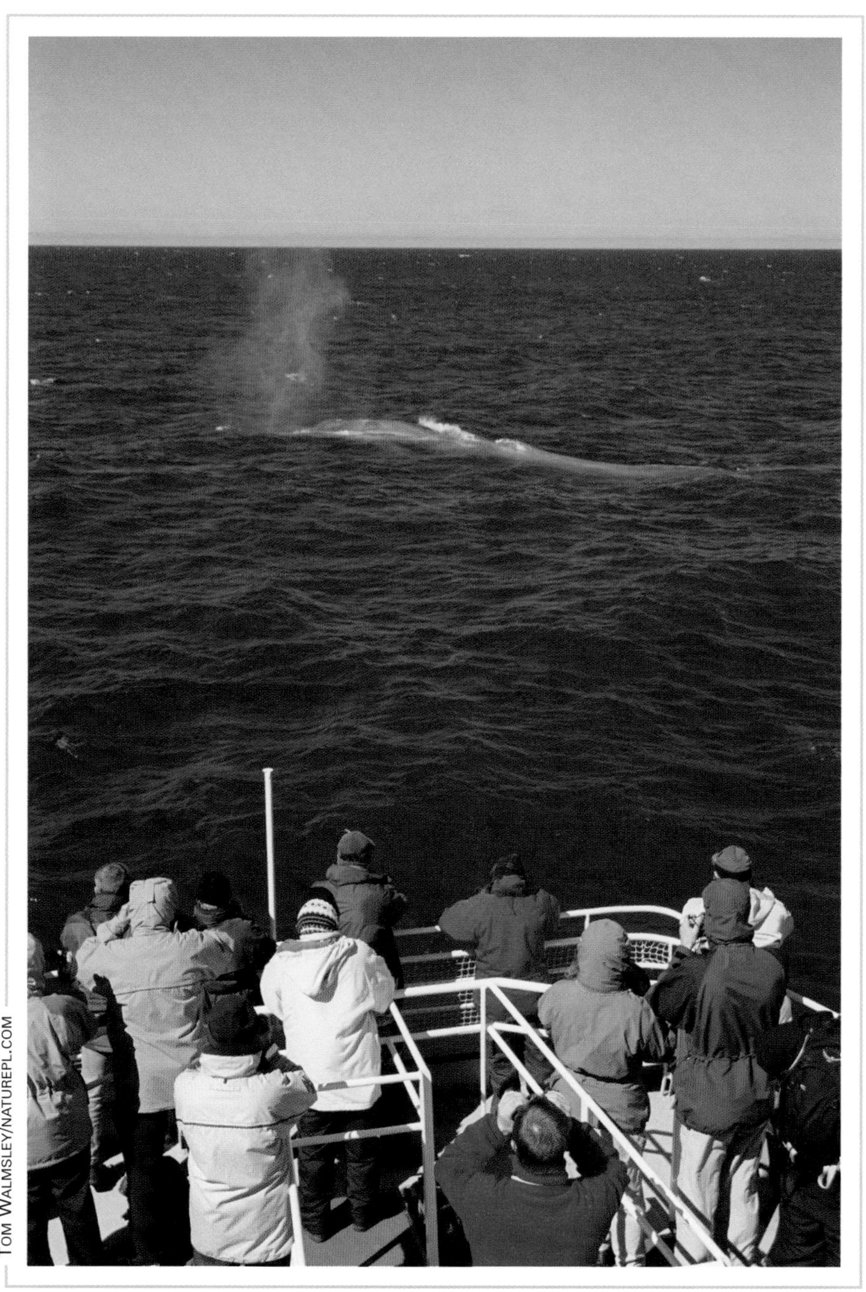

TOM WALMSLEY/NATUREPL.COM

*Wildlife enthusiasts watch a Blue whale (*Balaenoptera musculus*) blowing in the Atlantic Ocean. Ecotourism is a source of income for many MPAs and an activity that can be monitored and measured as part of the evaluation of management effectiveness.*

S1

## *What are 'local marine resource use patterns'?*

Local marine resource use patterns are the ways people use or affect coastal and marine resources.

## *Why measure it?*

By understanding local marine resource use patterns it is possible to determine whether or not management strategies are impacting income and livelihood patterns and cultural traditions. MPA managers can also use this information on local marine resource use patterns to determine what coastal and marine related activities have been affected by the MPA and consequently who may benefit and who may lose from the MPA. This information can be used to try to minimize impacts on the MPA. This information also provides an understanding of potential threats to the MPA.

The degree of compliance and MPA success is influenced by the patterns of local use present within the area. Consequently, understanding local use patterns will help the MPA manager increase support for the MPA and minimize the impacts on resource users by ensuring the formal MPA design is consistent with existing informal patterns of marine resource use.

## *How to collect the data*

The 'area' for identifying marine resource use patterns is defined as the MPA and the immediately adjacent coastal and marine zone.

The data on local marine resource use patterns should be collected first through secondary data from government sources, including village and town offices; and national agency reports, maps, statistical reports, and official regulations. Then through primary data collection from focus groups, semi-structured interviews, structured surveys and observations. Visualization techniques are also useful and include:

- ❑ Local classifications – to clarify the marine resource uses and associated species;
- ❑ Maps – to show the location of activities, residence of stakeholders, and use rights;
- ❑ Timelines – to show when activities occur and the seasonality of events; and
- ❑ Drawings – to show different marine resource-related activities.

The data collection begins with the gathering of information on marine-related activities, which include activities that directly or indirectly affect marine resources (both land- and sea-based activities). This information will help in understanding the other sub-parameters. Key questions that should be addressed include:

- ❑ What marine related activities are taking place at sea?
- ❑ What reef related activities are taking place on land?
- ❑ What impacts are these activities having on marine resources?

Next, the stakeholders, including the type and number of primary and secondary stakeholders, and their basic characteristics need to be understood. Important questions include:

- ❑ Who is involved in these activities?
- ❑ How many people are involved in each activity?
- ❑ What are their basic characteristics (e.g. gender, residency status, age)?

**Relates to goals and objectives**

GOAL 2
2A 2B

GOAL 5
5A

### *Requirements*

- Interviewers.
- Notebook and pen.
- Handheld GPS device.
- Basemap of area.

***A Grey whale 'spy hops' in Baja California, Mexico – and excites participants on a whale-watching trip.***

TOM WALMSLEY/NATUREPL.COM

The manner in which marine-related activities are carried out needs to be understood including technology used, techniques for applying the technology, and ways people organize themselves in these activities. Key questions include:

- How are the uses conducted?
- What technology is used and how much is used?
- How is the equipment constructed and who owns it?
- How do these methods affect the marine resources?
- How are people organized to use marine resources?

The boundaries of the community area need to be understood. This involves asking where are the political, biological/ecosystem, physical/ oceanographic, fishing areas, social/cultural, and traditional/customary boundaries.

The location of marine related activities and stakeholders is also important to understand. Key questions include:

- Where do these marine related activities occur?
- Where do stakeholders live and work?
- Where are the marine resources located for comparison?

Finally, it is important to understand the timing and seasonality of activities, including the daily, weekly and monthly patterns of resource use, seasonal changes and long-term trends in resource use. Key questions include:

- When do the uses take place and what changes occur at particular times?
- Why do these changes in use occur?

## *How to analyse and interpret results*

Present the results in a narrative form with accompanying tables, figures, and diagrams to clarify and highlight points. The focus of the data analysis and presentation should be on the major marine-related activities identified through the data collection. Summarize the relevant information on the other sub-parameters for each activity. Diagrams can be drawn from the visualization techniques. The descriptions may also include quantitative data.

***Fishers use marine resources for a number of livelihoods and cultural activities.***

PETE OXFORD/NATUREPL.COM

### Strengths and limitations

The major limitation of this indicator is that it involves a great deal of preparation and use of several data collection methods. Furthermore, it is time consuming and costly. However, if done well, the indicator can provide very useful and important information for management.

### Useful references and Internet links

Bunce, L., Townsley, P., Pomeroy, R. and Pollnac, R. (2000). *Socioeconomic Manual for Coral Reef Management*. Australian Institute of Marine Science, Townsville, Queensland, Australia. Available at www.reefbase.org

#### Outputs

- A narrative report describing the major marine related activities, with tables, figures, and diagrams to clarify and highlight points.
- Summaries of other sub-parameters with tables, figures, and diagrams to clarify and highlight points.

Box S1

### Example from the Field

The Channel Islands National Marine Sanctuary in California is currently engaged in a five-year management plan review process. As part of this process, the Sanctuary will be proposing broad-based changes to its management plan. As required by the National Environmental Protection Act, CINMS has developed a Draft Environmental Impact Statement (DEIS) including a chapter on the *Description of Affected Area*. The *Description of Affected Area* identifies physical, biological, geological and cultural resources throughout the study area. The study area is from Pt. Sal in the north to Pt. Dume in the south, an area of over 6,000 nautical miles, nearly six times the size of the current Sanctuary boundaries. In addition to the description of the ecosystem, all human use activities, including upland activities in the watershed, are described. These human use activities were prioritized as part of the management plan review process and identified as key resource management issues to be addressed over the next five years. The human uses profiled in the DEIS include: oil and gas development; commercial and recreational fishing; harbour activities; military use; vessel traffic; recreational use; urban and rural land use; tourism activities; and point and non-point source discharge.

Relates to goals and objectives

GOAL 5
5A 5B

GOAL 6
6A 6B
6C 6D

## *What are 'local values and beliefs'?*

Local values and beliefs about marine resources are measures of how people make choices and undertake actions related to marine resource use and management based on their values about what is good, just and desirable and their beliefs of how the world works. A value is a social more or norm manifested as a result of history and culture. It is a shared understanding among people of what is good, desirable or just. A belief is a shared understanding by members of a group or society of how the world works.

## *Why measure it?*

In an MPA context, managers are interested in how values and beliefs related to marine resources, their use, and management practices influence behaviour within the stakeholder group or society. Local values and beliefs therefore influence people's behaviour and assist in forming customary practices. Depending on the structure and orientation of values and beliefs they may undermine or enhance management efforts and the success of the MPA. Consequently, understanding this indicator can help a manager to more effectively integrate people's local values and beliefs into the MPA management structure and thereby minimize adverse effects of management.

## *How to collect the data*

Through a survey of households, respondents should be asked a series of questions about their perceptions related to their values and beliefs on marine resources, their use, and management.

To understand values and perceptions about use and management respondents might be asked questions such as:

- ❑ Why is/are the sea/mangroves/coral reefs important to you?
- ❑ Why is/are fishing/diving/other activities important to you?
- ❑ Does (destructive activity – e.g. bomb fishing) hurt the resource?
- ❑ Why do people conduct this (destructive activity)?
- ❑ What do you think of current MPA management strategies?
- ❑ Do the current MPA management strategies complement local cultural beliefs and traditions?

Any stories or anecdotes that illustrate their thoughts should be recorded.

As an example, Pollnac and Crawford (2000) questioned households in North Sulawesi, Indonesia about their perceptions of bomb fishing and why they use this technique. Respondents were asked:

- ❑ Does bomb fishing hurt the resource?
  Yes___ No___
- ❑ Why do fishers bomb fish?

To further assess values and beliefs about the resources, the respondents can be asked to indicate the extent to which they agree with the following statements:

**Fishers and coastal communities have a variety of differing values and beliefs about their marine resources.**

#### Requirements

- Survey forms.
- List of households to survey.
- Interviewers.
- Notebook and pen.

- ❑ We have to take care of the land and the sea or they will not provide for us in the future.
- ❑ We do not have to worry about the sea and the fish; God will take care of it for us.
- ❑ We should manage the sea to ensure that there are fish for our children and their children.

Respondents should be asked if they very strongly agree, strongly agree, agree, neither agree nor disagree (neutral), disagree, strongly disagree, or very strongly disagree. This will result in a scale with a range of one to seven.

### How to analyse and interpret results

Calculate the percentage distribution of responses. For the example on bomb fishing above, prepare a table showing percentage distribution of responses (see Tables S1 and S2). Prepare a narrative explanation of the results. For example:

Table S1

**Percentage distribution of responses on whether bomb fishing hurts the resource**

| | *Yes* | *No* |
|---|---|---|
| Bentenan | 88 | 12 |
| Tumbak | 96 | 4 |
| Rumbia | 94 | 6 |
| Minanga | 94 | 6 |

Table S2

**Percentage distribution of the perception that bomb fishers fish that way because it is a quick/easy way to obtain fish/money**

| *N=224* | *Yes* | *No* | *Total* |
|---|---|---|---|
| Bentenan | 61 | 39 | 100 |
| Tumbak | 64 | 36 | 100 |
| Rumbia | 56 | 44 | 100 |
| Minanga | 62 | 38 | 100 |
| Total | 61 | 39 | 100 |

*A large majority of respondents agree with the statement that bomb fishing hurts the resource. The largest percentage of respondents who said it did not hurt the resource was from Bentenan. As to why fishers use the technique, the most frequent response is that it is a quick and/or easy way to obtain lots of fish and/or money (39% of respondents gave this response).*

*The local values and beliefs of the stakeholders with regard to marine resources and their management are illustrated by a high degree of compatibility between local values and beliefs and the goal and objectives of the MPA. A high level of compatibility is indicated by local values and beliefs being reflected in the MPA goal and objectives, developed in a participatory manner and with local support for the MPA.*

#### Outputs

- Tables of percentage distribution of perception of values and beliefs.
- Narrative explanation of statistical results.

### Strengths and limitations

As with any indicator, it is useful to observe and analyse changes in local values and beliefs about marine resources over time to determine, for example, if participation in and activities of the MPA are having an impact on peoples values about conservation.

### Useful references and Internet links


Bunce, L., Townsley, P., Pomeroy, R. and Pollnac, R. (2000). *Socioeconomic Manual for Coral Reef Management.* Australian Institute of Marine Science, Townsville, Queensland, Australia. Available at www.reefbase.org.

Kempton, W., Boster, J.S. and Hartley, J.A. (1995). *Environmental Values in American Culture.* MIT Press, Boston, USA.

Pollnac, R.B. and Crawford, B.R. (2000). "Assessing behavioral aspects of coastal resource use". *Proyek Pesisir Publication Special Report. Coastal Resources Center, Coastal Management Report #2226.* Coastal Resources Center, University of Rhode Island, Narragansett, Rhode Island, USA.

Mafia Island, Tanzania, with young mangrove trees in the foreground, viewed from Chole Island.

Box S2

## Example from the Field

At Mafia Island Marine Park in Tanzania, an important issue in the Islamic country is the extent to which people regard the availability of natural resources as a consequence of human activities of one kind or another, as opposed to the traditional attitude that everything in nature stems from the will of God/Allah. Respondents in the survey were asked to characterize a number of factors in respect of their impact on the availability of fish in the sea, including dynamite fishing, fisher density and the will of God.

The results show that only 25% of all respondents regard the effect of the will of God as either great or very great. This is the case across all strata, more or less evenly, though interestingly the group attributing the highest effect to God's will was fishers (33%). The percentage of respondents rating the other factors as being of great or very great importance to fish availability is as follows:

- Dynamite fishing – 90%
- Small mesh seine nets – 63%
- Number of fishers – 31%

The relevance to management is encouraging in that there do not appear to be deeply entrenched religious beliefs that preclude people from accepting the connection between human actions and fish availability.

# Level of understanding of human impacts on resources

Relates to goals and objectives

GOAL 6

6B



Difficulty Rating 3 1–5

## What is 'level of understanding of human impacts on resources'?

Level of understanding of human impacts on resources is a measure of the degree to which local stakeholders understand basic ecological relationships and the impacts that human activities have on the natural environment.

## Why measure it?

An understanding of individual perceptions of factors influencing the status of marine resources can be used to identify the distribution of faulty, as well as accurate, perceptions. The knowledge about these distributions can then be used to structure interventions designed, for example, to involve the community in the management of its resources, and to evaluate the resulting changes. This could lead to improved human use patterns and help to target environmental education programmes at user groups and stakeholders.

### Requirements

- Survey forms.
- Interviewers.
- List of households to survey.
- Notebook and pen.

## How to collect the data

Measuring this indicator involves conducting an assessment of stakeholder perceptions about the extent to which they believe their own activities affect the natural environment. Questions should be asked using a semi-structured interview or focus group, which addresses threats to the natural environment and changes in the natural environment due to the threats. The questions might include:

- What events, activities or changes do you feel have affected or are affecting the natural environment?
- What changes in the natural environment do you attribute to these threats?
- How do you compare the threats in terms of levels of impact?

Visualization techniques are particularly important when assessing stakeholder perceptions because they provide visual and oral ways of communicating ideas. Several visualization techniques can be used, including maps and transects, decision trees, Venn diagrams, and flow charts.

## How to analyse and interpret results

Prepare narrative text descriptions of the answers to the questions based on the relevant data and responses. These data will often be qualitative and include anecdotes, stories, historical accounts and legends, informant observations of apparent causes and effects, and opinions on how the natural environment should and should not be used. Illustrate important points in the text with diagrams using visualization techniques to ensure that stakeholder perceptions are being accurately presented.

**Fishing boats, Indonesia. Unchecked human use of coastal resources, such as the public's over fishing of an open access fishery, can lead to long-term, negative impacts on the marine environment and its ecology.**

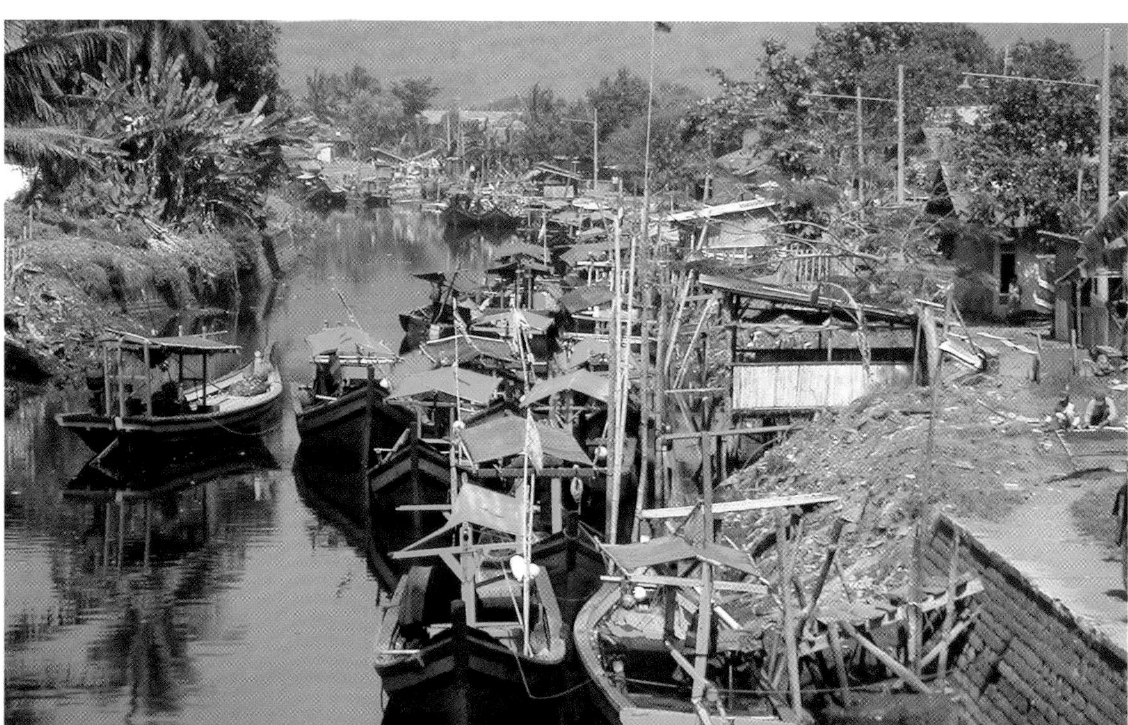

ROBERT POMEROY

## Outputs

- Narrative text.
- Maps and transects.
- Decision trees and flow charts.
- Venn diagrams.



Measure and describe the level of understanding of the extent to which stakeholders believe their own actions affect the natural environment and their level of environmental awareness.

## Strengths and limitations

Stakeholder perceptions are difficult parameters to assess because people's perceptions, opinions and attitudes are highly variable and often there are few secondary data on stakeholder perceptions.

## Useful references and Internet links

Bunce, L., Townsley, P., Pomeroy, R. and Pollnac, R. (2000). *Socioeconomic Manual for Coral Reef Management.* Australian Institute of Marine Science, Townsville, Queensland, Australia. Available at www.reefbase.org

Box S3

### Example from the Field

At the Sian Ka'an Biosphere Reserve in Mexico, a survey, semi-structured interviews, focus groups, informal communications and observations provided information on the stakeholders' level of understanding of human impacts on the resource. Members of the Punta Allen community identified the main threats and problems listed below.

It was expected that most resource users would think that negative environmental conditions, such as hurricanes and storms, had the most serious impacts on marine resources. But when it came to human impacts, results from the questionnaire showed that tourism development is the human impact that most concerns the population. In order to simplify the analysis, tourism development here considers different kinds of responses, including permit supply, infrastructure, foreign investments, and introduction of bigger boats. When the focus groups were asked why they considered tourism development a threat to their community, they said that they are afraid of being displaced by big international companies. With regard to marine resources, they mentioned that more development for tourism activities will bring more tourists to the community and with that, big hotels. All this, they said, will damage their mangroves and beaches; there will be more boats in the water and more oil will be spilled; and also more waste will be generated.

| | COMMUNITY | | MARINE RESOURCES | |
|---|---|---|---|---|
| N=153 (3 answers by respondent) | Responses | Percentage | Responses | Percentage |
| **Threats** | Hurricanes and storms | 17% | Hurricanes and storms | 13% |
| | Tourism development | 24% | Tourism development | 17% |
| | Blank spaces | 23% | Blank spaces | 30% |
| | Uncontrolled fishing | 6% | Uncontrolled fishing | 23% |
| | Waste and pollution | 9% | Waste and pollution | 15% |
| | Population growth | 9% | Lack of surveillance | 2% |
| | Others | 12% | | |
| **Problems** | Roads | 22% | Uncontrolled tourism | 24% |
| | Power and water supply | 14% | Uncontrolled fishing | 6% |
| | Waste and pollution | 25% | Waste and pollution | 17% |
| | Blank spaces | 24% | Blank spaces | 47% |
| | Lack of participation | 5% | Lack of participation | 3% |
| | Feral fauna | 6% | Lack of surveillance | 3% |
| | Others | 4% | | |

### *What is 'perceptions of seafood availability'?*

Perceptions of seafood availability is a measure of what the primary food purchaser/preparer in the household thinks about the local availability of seafood for the household.

### *Why measure it?*

This indicator is important for understanding the contribution of the MPA to food security in the local community. Household food security can be defined as "that state of affairs where all people at all times have physical and economic access to adequate, safe and nutritious food for all household members, without undue risk of losing such access" (FAO).

This indicator is especially important if one of the stated objectives of the MPA is to improve local nutrition or the availability of local seafood. For example, households may respond that the availability of seafood was reduced right after the establishment of the MPA, but two years later they may respond that seafood availability has increased. If household perceptions of availability of local seafood does not improve or if it drops in the MPA community, and if similar trends do not appear in the control communities, one could suspect that the MPA is negatively impacting seafood availability. If this is so, and if this is not a desired impact, the MPA management plan and management measures must be adjusted.

This indicator is also useful for responding to complaints from the local community about the MPA. If households perceive an increase in the availability of local seafood over time, then this information can be used in support of the MPA.

Several questions must be asked of households in the MPA community to measure perceptions of seafood availability. In particular, the household primary food purchaser/preparer should be interviewed. Questions can be asked in a separate survey or as part of a larger survey that includes questions from other indicators. The questions might include:

- ❑ How many days during the past month did your family have an insufficient amount of food?

Never____, Once a week____, Twice a week_____, More than twice a week______ Specify number of days: _______

(This question should be asked for the same period (season, month) every year since there are seasonal differences in food and seafood availability.)

- ❑ How many days during the past month did your family have an insufficient amount of local fresh seafood due to lack of availability?

Never____, Once a week____, Twice a week_____, More than twice a week______ Specify number of days: _______

(Again this question should be asked for the same period (season, month) every year.)

### *Requirements*

- Survey of food purchaser/preparer in the households in the MPA community.
- Interviewers.
- List of households to be surveyed.
- Paper/pencil.
- Optional: ladder-scale diagram.

**Relates to goals and objectives**

GOAL 1
1A 1B

GOAL 2
2D

GOAL 4
4B

Difficulty Rating 3 (1–5)

S4

***The public may assume that a sufficient supply of seafood caught outside the MPA remains to meet their needs, but in reality the supply may have decreased, driving prices up and reducing food security.***

Toni Parras

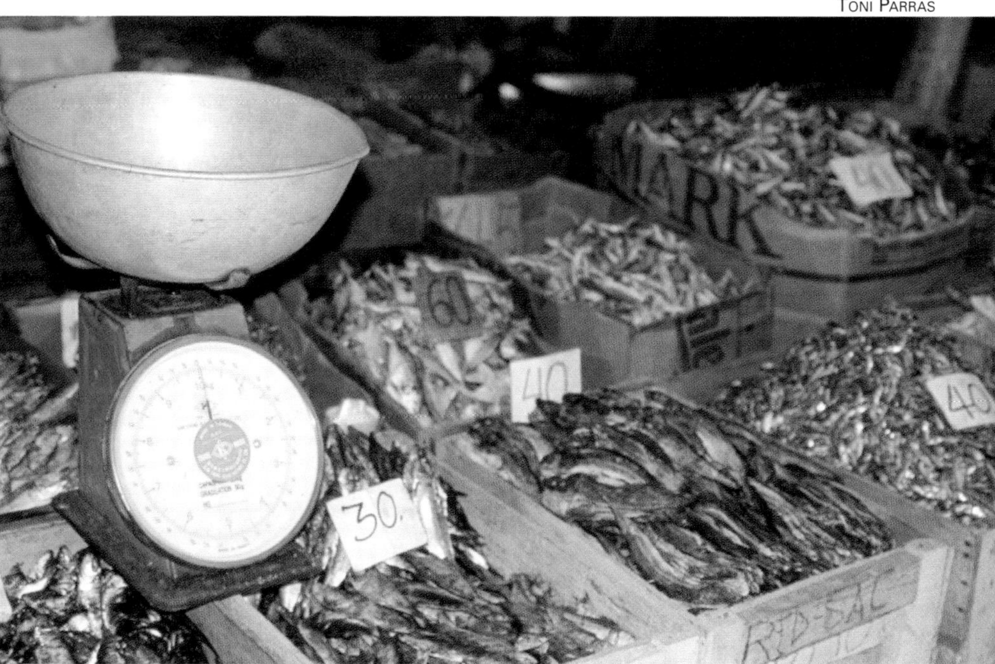

- ❑ How many days during the past year did your household have an insufficient amount of local fresh seafood due to lack of availability? Never____, Specify number of days________, Specify month(s) or season______________
- ❑ Have you observed changes in the availability of local seafood since the MPA was established? Increase___ Same____ Decrease_____ Why?
- ❑ Do you feel that the MPA is having an impact on the availability of local fresh seafood? Yes/No. Why?

An alternative to these questions is to use a self-anchoring scale. This approach utilizes a ten-point ladder-scale where the bottom step indicates no seafood at all and the top step indicates the availability of more than enough seafood for the family throughout the year. The respondent is asked to identify on the ladder-scale the situation at the present time and the situation at some time period in the past (such as before the MPA). The number of and direction of changes in the steps is a measure of the perceived change.

TONY ECKERSLEY

### Outputs

- Tables of the availability of food and seafood in the local community.
- Strengths and limitations.

## How to analyse and interpret results

Present the data in a table showing percentage distribution of the responses to each question.

Analysis of the data from the self-anchoring method involves calculating mean values for the differences between each indicator for today (T2) and the pre-project period (T1). Conduct a paired comparison t-test to determine whether the mean differences between the two time periods are statistically significant.

## Strengths and limitations

The strength of this indicator is having data to compare over time so that trends in responses can be measured.

The usefulness of this indicator will depend upon the availability and cooperation of the household food purchaser to respond to the questions. Also, it is assumed that when using this indicator to evaluate food security, specifically improvements in local nutrition, that availability and consumption of local fresh seafood contribute positively to nutrition.

## Useful references and Internet links

Bunce, L., Townsley, P., Pomeroy, R. and Pollnac, R. (2000). *Socioeconomic Manual for Coral Reef Management.* Australian Institute of Marine Science, Townsville, Queensland, Australia. Available at www.reefbase.org

Berkes, F., Mahon, R., McConney, P., Pollnac, R. and Pomeroy, R. (2001). *Managing small-scale fisheries: alternative directions and methods.* International Development Research Centre, Ottawa, Canada. Available at www.idrc.ca/booktique

Pollnac, R.B. and Crawford, B.R. (2000). "Assessing behavioral aspects of coastal resource use". *Proyek Pesisir Publication Special Report. Coastal Resources Center, Coastal Management Report #2226.* Coastal Resources Center, University of Rhode Island, Narragansett, Rhode Island. Available at www.crc.uri.edu

# Perceptions of local resource harvest

## What is 'perceptions of local resource harvest'?

Perceptions of local resource harvest is a measure of what local fishers think about the availability of target fish species and changes in the availability of fish.

## Why measure it?

This indicator provides information on fishers' perceptions of changes in the availability of target species, which is useful for determining if the MPA management is achieving its objective of increasing harvests of seafood and consequently the availability of locally caught seafood. If the perceptions are a positive increase, then the fishers may be more receptive to MPA management. If the perceptions are negative, then the fishers may be less receptive to MPA management, and changes in MPA management may be necessary. The indicator is also a useful measure of fish abundance, availability and size, and species composition.

## How to collect the data

Information on this indicator is collected by conducting a survey of fishers. They may be asked:

> Compared to ten years ago, what is the quantity of available (target species)?
>
> A lot less____ less_____ same_____ more_____ a lot more______

The responses produce a five-point scale ranging from a lot less to a lot more with same in the middle.

As an alternative, a self-anchoring scale can be used. This approach utilizes a ten-point, ladder-scale where 1 is the worst situation and 10 is the best situation. The respondent is asked to identify on the ladder-scale the situation at the present time and the situation at some time period in the past (such as before the MPA or a period of years ago). The number of and direction of changes in the steps is a measure of the perceived change. For this approach the fisher is provided the following scenario and question:

> Given a scale where 1 indicates a situation where none of the target species are available and a 10 indicates a situation where there are so many fish that the fisher can catch as many as he/she wants in a very short period of time, how would you rank conditions:
>
> Today_______ Before the MPA_________

## How to analyse and interpret results

Present the data from the first question dealing with comparison in a table showing percentage distribution of the responses to each category (i.e. a lot less, less).

To analyse the data from the self-anchoring method, calculate mean values for the differences between each indicator for Today (T2) and the pre-project period (T1). Conduct a paired comparison t-test to determine whether the mean differences between the two time periods are statistically significant.

| *Indicator* | *T1* | *T2* | *T2-T1* | *P* |
|---|---|---|---|---|
| Availability of target species | 4 | 6 | 2 | <0.01 |

## Strengths and limitations

A limitation of this indicator is that fishers who have fished on target species in an impacted (target) area over the time period being evaluated must be present and willing to respond to the questions. Also, every individual's baseline for assessing

Relates to goals and objectives

GOAL 1

1B

Difficulty Rating 3 (1–5)

S5

### Requirements

- Survey form.
- List of fishers to be surveyed.
- Interviewers.
- Paper/pencil.
- Ladder-scale diagram.

### Outputs

- Table of graded ordinal judgement of local fisher perception of fish harvest.
- Strengths and limitations.

© WWF-Canon/Meg Gawler

S5

*The people who know the most about the marine environment in and around the MPA are often those whose livelihoods and dietary needs are dependent upon the resources found nearby. However, their observations and assumptions regarding the state and trends in the resources do not always mirror reality.*

status and changes in fish catch is personal and not really intergenerational. As a result, historical over-fishing is often not evaluated in this assessment of people's perceptions of the status of the fishery.

Box S4

## Example from the Field

At the Sian Ka'an Biosphere Reserve in Mexico, a survey was conducted of 53 inhabitants in Punta Allen, representing 24% of the total productive population, about perceptions of local resource harvest. The questionnaire responses revealed the following information about the perception of Punta Allen community members on lobster catches:

| N=51 | % |
|---|---|
| Much higher | 0% |
| Higher | 4% |
| Same | 18% |
| Less | 69% |
| Much less | 10% |

Results were discussed and confirmed during interviews with key informants. They said that lobster catches decreased considerably after Hurricane Gilbert in 1988. They explained that other hurricanes, such as Roxanne in 1995, also caused serious damage to the reef and other marine environments, resulting in important decreases in catches.

The strength of this indicator is having data to compare over time so that trends in responses can be measured.

Since this indicator uses a survey to obtain information from fishers, it can provide a wealth of other types of information, such as natural history of living marine resources.

### Useful references and Internet links


Bunce, L., Townsley, P., Pomeroy, R. and Pollnac, R. (2000). *Socioeconomic Manual for Coral Reef Management*. Australian Institute of Marine Science, Townsville, Queensland, Australia. Available at www.reefbase.org

Berkes, F., Mahon, R., McConney, P., Pollnac, R. and Pomeroy, R. (2001). *Managing small-scale fisheries: alternative directions and methods*. International Development Research Centre, Ottawa, Canada. Available at www.idrc.ca/booktique

Pollnac, R.B. and Crawford, B.R. (2000). "Assessing behavioral aspects of coastal resource use". *Proyek Pesisir Publication Special Report. Coastal Resources Center, Coastal Management Report #2226*. Coastal Resources Center, University of Rhode Island, Narragansett, Rhode Island, USA. Available at www.crc.uri.edu

NOAA Photo Library

## *What is 'perceptions of non-market and non-use value'?*

Perceptions of non-market and non-use value of the MPA is a measure of how individuals think about the value of coastal resources that are not traded in the market (non-market) and the value of the resources to those who do not use the resources (non-use). It provides information on community members' perceptions of the value of the MPA and coastal resources.

## *Why measure it?*

Non-market values are the economic value of activities that are not traded in any market, which includes direct uses, such as divers who have travelled to the MPA by private means; and indirect uses, such as biological support in the form of nutrients, fish habitat and coastline protection from storm surge. Non-use values represent values that are not associated with any use and include existence value (the value of knowing that the resource exists in a certain condition), option value (the value of being able to use the resource in the future) and bequest value (the value of ensuring the resource will be available for future generations).

This information is useful in order to:

- Understand the value of the MPA in non-monetary terms, which can be used to evaluate the tradeoffs between alternative development, management and conservation scenarios;
- Demonstrate the importance of the MPA to the larger population by calculating the value of the resources to people; and
- Understand the changing value of the MPA to stakeholders over time.

### *Requirements*

- Survey form.
- List of households to survey.
- Simple statistical analysis (computer and spreadsheet software).
- Interviewers.
- Paper/pencil.
- Optional: economist to provide specialist assistance.

## *How to collect the data*

The concepts of non-market and non-use values are largely abstract and theoretical. The economic methods used to obtain this information are too complex to be carried out without thorough training. The use of economic valuation methods such as travel costs and contingent valuation require an economist experienced in the use of the methods. When an economist is not available, an alternative approach using scale analysis is recommended.

The approach is to obtain community members' perceptions of the value of the MPA and coastal resources. A sample of households in the community is interviewed. Each respondent is asked to indicate the degree of their agreement or disagreement with a series of statements. These could include statements about beauty, about looking after the sea for their children's children, about "enjoying time on the water", and about other non-extractive goods and services that a 'healthy' marine environment can provide. Each individual MPA will need to decide the specific wording of the questions. An example of questions that involve some aspect of relationships between coastal resources and human activities include:

- The reefs are important for protecting land from storm waves (indirect non-market value).
- In the long-run fishing would be better if we cleared the coral (indirect non-market value).
- Unless mangroves are protected we will not have any fish to catch (indirect non-market value).

**Relates to goals and objectives**

GOAL 3

3A 3B
3C 3D
3E

GOAL 4

4B

S6

***Nearshore homeowners are often the first to recognise the benefits of a healthy coastline. For example, coastal forests can serve to buffer homes from the full effect of natural threats such as storms and increased wave action.***

- Coral reefs are only important if you fish or dive (existence non-use value).
- I want future generations to enjoy the mangroves and coral reefs (bequest non-use value).
- Fishing should be restricted in certain areas even if no one ever fishes in those areas just to allow the fish and coral to grow (existence value).
- We should restrict development in some coastal areas so that future generations will be able to have natural environments (bequest value).
- Seagrass beds have no value to people (existence value).

Note that the statements are written such that agreement with some indicates an accurate belief, while agreement with others indicates the opposite. This was done to control for responses where the respondent either agrees or disagrees with everything. Statements are randomly arranged with respect to this type of polarity. Respondents are asked if they: very strongly disagree, strongly disagree, disagree, neither disagree nor agree (are neutral), agree, strongly agree or very strongly agree with each statement. This results in a scale with a range from 1 to 7.

Table S3

## Example of percentage distribution of scale values

| *Statement number* | *One* | *Two* | *Three* | *Four* | *Five* | *Six* | *Seven* |
|---|---|---|---|---|---|---|---|
| 1 | - | 06 | - | 18 | 05 | 45 | 26 |
| 2 | 03 | 11 | 03 | 23 | - | 33 | 27 |
| 3 | - | - | - | 06 | 03 | 61 | 30 |
| 4 | 06 | 35 | - | 39 | 02 | 17 | 02 |
| 5 | 14 | 32 | 06 | 17 | 02 | 18 | 12 |
| 6 | 18 | 44 | - | 06 | 02 | 17 | 14 |
| 7 | 03 | 11 | - | 35 | - | 36 | 15 |
| 8 | - | 08 | - | 29 | 06 | 39 | 18 |

### *How to analyse and interpret results*

Calculate percentage distribution of responses to the statements and report them in a table. Polarity of the statement is accounted for in the coding process, so as a score value changes from 1 to 7 it indicates an increasingly stronger and more accurate belief about the content of the statement.

A more complete analysis can be conducted on the data using more advanced statistical methods. The scale values associated with the eight attitude statements about relationships between coastal resources and human activities can be factor-analysed, using the principal component analysis technique and varimax rotation. The scree test can be used to determine the optimum number of

***The aesthetic beauty and mere fact of existence of natural areas along the coastline is of great value in many societies. Several studies of particular places have clearly documented how the total of such non-market values exceeds the total income generation from such areas.***

MIKE READ/NATUREPL.COM

### Outputs

- Table on percentage distribution of scale values.

factors to be rotated. Factor scores were created to represent the position of each individual on each component.

Where resources are available, it may be possible to use more advanced economic methods to value coastal and marine resources. A number of methods are available depending upon the situation and the data needs. The main methods and approaches can be categorized as: generally applicable, potentially applicable, and survey-based. Generally applicable methods are directly based on market prices or productivity. Potentially applicable methods use market information indirectly. Use survey-based methods in the absence of data on market or surrogate-market prices.

### Strengths and limitations

The main limitation of this indicator is that the concepts of non-market and non-use values are largely abstract and theoretical. As a result, the economic methods usually employed are too complex to be carried out without thorough training. The approach presented above is a simpler technique for obtaining information on people's perceptions of value of the MPA and coastal resources, although conducting it still involves a certain level of advanced analytical skills. The indicator may require infrequent specialist studies, such as by an economist.

### Useful references and Internet links


Bunce, L., Townsley, P., Pomeroy, R. and Pollnac, R. (2000). *Socioeconomic Manual for Coral Reef Management.* Australian Institute of Marine Science, Townsville, Queensland, Australia. See page 224, "Non-market and non-use values". Available at www.reefbase.org

Grigalunas, T.A. and Congar, R. (eds.) (1995). *Environmental economics for integrated coastal area management: valuation methods and policy instruments. Regional Seas Reports and Studies No. 164.* United Nations Environment Program, Nairobi, Kenya.

Lipton, D.W., Wellman, K., Sheifer, I.C. and Weiher, R.F. (1995). Economic valuation of natural resources – a handbook for coastal resource policymakers. *NOAA Coastal Ocean Program Decision Analysis Series No. 5.* NOAA Coastal Ocean Office, Silver Spring, MD, USA.

Pomeroy, R.S. "Economic valuation: available methods". *In* Chua, T.-E. and Scrua, L.F. (eds.) (1992). "Integrative framework and methods for coastal area management". *ICLARM Conf. Proc. 37.* International Center for Living Aquatic Resources Management, Manila, Philippines.


Table S4

## Economic valuation measurement and valuation techniques

| *Generally applicable* | *Potentially applicable* | *Survey-based* |
|---|---|---|
| Those that use the market value of directly related goods and services:<br>▪ change in productivity<br>▪ loss of earnings<br>▪ opportunity cost<br>▪ marketed goods as proxies | Those that use surrogate-market values:<br>▪ property values<br>▪ wage differential<br>▪ travel costs | Contingent valuation |
| Those that use the value of direct expenditures:<br>▪ cost-effectiveness<br>▪ preventive expenditures<br>▪ shadow project | Those that use the magnitude of potential expenditures:<br>▪ replacement cost | |

Box S5

## Example from the Field

As one means of obtaining some information about community members' perceptions of the non-market and non-use value of marine resources, a sample of household members in Matalom were requested to indicate the degree of their agreement or disagreement with five statements. The following five statements were used, each of which involves some aspect of non-market or non-use value.

1. The reefs are important for protecting land from storm waves.
2. In the long-run fishing would be better if we cleared the coral.
3. Unless mangroves are protected we will not have any fish to catch.
4. Coral reefs are only important if you fish or dive.
5. I want future generations to enjoy the mangroves and coral reefs.

Respondents were asked if they agree, disagree, or neither (are neutral) with respect to each statement. If they indicated either agree or disagree, they were asked if they agree (disagree) strongly, agree (disagree), or agree (disagree) just a little with each statement. Percentage distribution of responses to the statements are in the table below.

Toni Parras

Table S5

### Example of percentage distribution of scale values

| *Statement number* | *One* | *Two* | *Three* | *Four* | *Five* | *Six* | *Seven* |
|---|---|---|---|---|---|---|---|
| 1 | - | 06 | - | 18 | 05 | 45 | 26 |
| 2 | 03 | 11 | 03 | 23 | - | 33 | 27 |
| 3 | - | - | - | 06 | 03 | 61 | 30 |
| 4 | 06 | 35 | - | 39 | 02 | 17 | 02 |
| 5 | 14 | 32 | 06 | 17 | 02 | 18 | 12 |

## What is 'material style of life'?

Material style of life is an indicator of the relative social status of a community and is often used as an indicator of wealth. It involves assessing household structures (e.g. roof, walls) and furnishings (e.g. television, radio).

## Why measure it?

Material style of life is important for determining the extent of equity of monetary benefits through the community. It is also important for understanding the economic status and relative wealth of coastal communities. It is particularly useful for determining changes in wealth where it is difficult or impossible to obtain accurate income data.

Positive economic impact of the MPA should be indicated by increasing material style of life items present in the community households. If the MPA has a positive impact on improving economic or social status or relative wealth, it should be indicated by increasing material style of life scores over time in the MPA community. Increases should be larger in MPA communities than in control communities. Likewise, if MPAs have an equitable impact, increases in material style of life scores should occur for all identified social groups, especially poorer and disadvantaged groups in the community. If this has not occurred, then the MPA project manager should compare findings with the control community. If changes are less negative in the MPA community, the MPA is probably not responsible for the negative change.

### Requirements

- Survey form.
- Interviewers.
- List of households to survey.
- Paper/pencil.

Relates to goals and objectives

GOAL 2

2A

GOAL 4

4A

## How to collect the data

As a first step, the appropriate assets to assess need to be determined based on locally derived items associated with wealth and poverty. This list should include items that are likely to be purchased or upgraded within a reasonable time period, such as five years. The list will usually include items about type of roof, structural walls, windows, and floors.

These lists are not simple to construct. For example, house structure indicators might include four roof types: thatch, wood, tin and tile. It is possible to select only the most expensive type and use it in the list, but that would leave out all the gradation available in the different types. If the different types are used, how are values assigned to each type? The addition of different wall, floor, and window types, as well as appliance and other furnishings, greatly complicates the problem. The measure cannot be a simple addition of items. Items must be evaluated, accepted or rejected, and given

**Housing quality has been found to be a useful measure of the relative level of household wealth within coastal communities.**

TONY ECKERSLEY

TONI PARRAS

weights based on scale construction which deals with these problems. Techniques such as Guttmann scale analysis and factor analysis have been developed. Accurate scale construction is needed to make meaningful comparisons between individuals and groups of individuals (occupational subgroups, communities), as well as to make comparisons between different time periods, such as pre- and post-MPA.

Most importantly, the lists of assets to be measured should be appropriate to conditions of wealth within the target areas, to facilitate comparisons and measure change. For example, in one area a television may be considered by the local people as the top household asset representative of wealth, while in another area a radio is considered to be the top asset of household wealth.

The list of household structures and furnishings might include:

- ❑ Type of roof: tile ___ tin ___ wood ___ thatch ___
- ❑ Type of outside structural walls: tiled ___ brick/concrete ___ wood ___ thatch/bamboo ___
- ❑ Windows: glass ___ wooden ___ open ___ none ___
- ❑ Floors: tile ___ wooden ___ cement ___ thatch/bamboo ___ dirt ___
- ❑ Toilet: flush ___ pail flush ___ outdoor ___
- ❑ Water: inside tap ___ pump ___ outside tap ___
- ❑ Electricity: yes ___ no ___
- ❑ Household furnishings: fan ___ refrigerator ___ radio ___ television ___ wall clock ___

Table S6

## Example of percentage distribution in Village A

| *Item* | *Village A* |
|---|---|
| Bamboo wall | 30 |
| Cement wall | 57 |
| Wooden wall | 15 |
| Glass window | 55 |
| Wooden window | 45 |

### *Outputs*

- Table of percentage of distribution of material items in the community.

The actual collection of material style of life data during the survey is not difficult. A list is prepared and the interviewer simply checks off the items by observation or by asking the respondent if they are present or not.

### *How to analyse and interpret results*

Calculate the total number of items and the percentage distribution of each item and present them in a table.

Box S6

## Example from the Field

As part of the baseline survey conducted in Bentenan and Tumbak and the control sites of Rumbia and Minanga, the presence or absence of several aspects of house construction, considered by the research team to be indicative of differential social status, were recorded for each household included in the survey. The items and their percentage of distribution in the control and pilot project sites are found in the table below.

| *Item* | *Bentenan/Tumbak* | *Rumbia/Minanga* |
|---|---|---|
| Bamboo walls | 30 | 31 |
| Cement walls | 57 | 49 |
| Wooden wall | 15 | 24 |
| Glass window | 42 | 39 |
| Open window | 26 | 37 |
| Wooden window | 33 | 39 |
| Cement floor | 73 | 73 |
| Dirt floor | 7 | 31 |
| Tile floor | 1 | 0 |
| Wooden floor | 22 | 4 |
| N | 81 | 51 |

*Source*: Pollnac R.B. and B.R. Crawford (2000).

## *Strengths and limitations*

One of the major difficulties with this indicator lies in properly identifying household items indicative of relative wealth/poverty in the community. In addition, it is often difficult to separate impacts of the MPA from impacts of other economic changes in the household caused by general economic and community development. To address this issue, it is recommended that a control be used. For example, a control site may be a neighbouring community that has similar characteristics to the community near the MPA but that has no relation to or impact from the MPA. Alternatively, it may be possible to use control groups, such as people in the community associated with the MPA (fishers) and compare them with those with no association with the MPA. By comparing the control site or group with those impacted by the MPA it is possible to account for impacts caused by the MPA versus those from general economic and community development.

## *Useful references and Internet links*

Berkes, F., Mahon, R., McConney, P., Pollnac, R. and Pomeroy, R. (2001). *Managing small-scale fisheries: alternative directions and methods.* International Development Research Centre, Ottawa, Canada. Available at www.idrc.ca/booktique

Pollnac, R.B. and Crawford, B.R. (2000). "Assessing behavioral aspects of coastal resource use". *Proyek Pesisir Publication Special Report. Coastal Resources Center, Coastal Management Report #2226.* Coastal Resources Center, University of Rhode Island, Narragansett, Rhode Island, USA. Available at www.crc.uri.edu

Pomeroy, R., Pollnac, R., Katon, B. and Predo, C. (1997). "Evaluating factors contributing to the success of community-based coastal resource management: The Central Visayas Regional Project 1, Philippines". *Ocean and Coastal Management, 36 (1-3):97-120.*

DAVID SHEPPARD/IUCN

Relates to goals and objectives

GOAL 2

2D

GOAL 4

4B

## *What is 'quality of human health'?*

The quality of human health is a measure of the general nutrition and health of people in the community.

## *Why measure it?*

Information on the quality of human health is used to indicate the general nutrition and health of people in the community and the quality of life and relative wealth of people in the community. It has been stated, for example, of one measure of quality of human health, infant mortality rate, that, "No statistic expresses more eloquently the differences between a society of sufficiency and a society of deprivation than the infant mortality rate". If the MPA is providing improvements in livelihood and income, and overall improvements in wealth in the community, then it could be expected that the quality of human health should increase.

### *Requirements*

- Information on infant mortality rate, health services, child weight, diseases, vaccinations (from secondary sources).
- Paper/pencil.
- Interviewer.

## *How to collect the data*

A variety of measures of quality of human health can be used. These include infant mortality rate, availability of health services, child weight, variety and rate of diseases, type and number of vaccinations.

Secondary sources, such as the local health department, community nurse or doctor, or local hospital or health care centre, provide this information for the local context, but it is most likely aggregated for some larger area. Regional health services may have the disaggregated data which could be used to calculate an index for the local context. National statistics offices and reports may also have the data. At least a five-year series of data should be used to analyse trends. Key informants (mayor, doctor, nurse, midwife, health department, hospital) can be contacted to provide an explanation of reasons for and changes in the measures.

When secondary sources are not available, the information could be collected by interviewing key informants (mayor, doctor, nurse, midwife, health department, hospital) and asking them to provide a general description about the selected measure in the community.

For example, data can be collected on the occurrence of diseases in the area. Key informants (mayor, doctor, nurse, health department, hospital) are interviewed to identify major and minor diseases in the area. They might be asked:

- ❑ What are the five major diseases in the community?
- ❑ What were the five major diseases in the community ten years ago?
- ❑ If there is a change, what was done to address the disease problem?
- ❑ What is being done to address the disease problem?

## *How to analyse and interpret results*

Collate the data and present it in a narrative format. For example:

***Human health measures, including the availability of health services, nutritional levels and infant mortality rates, can be proxies for the relative wealth within a community.***

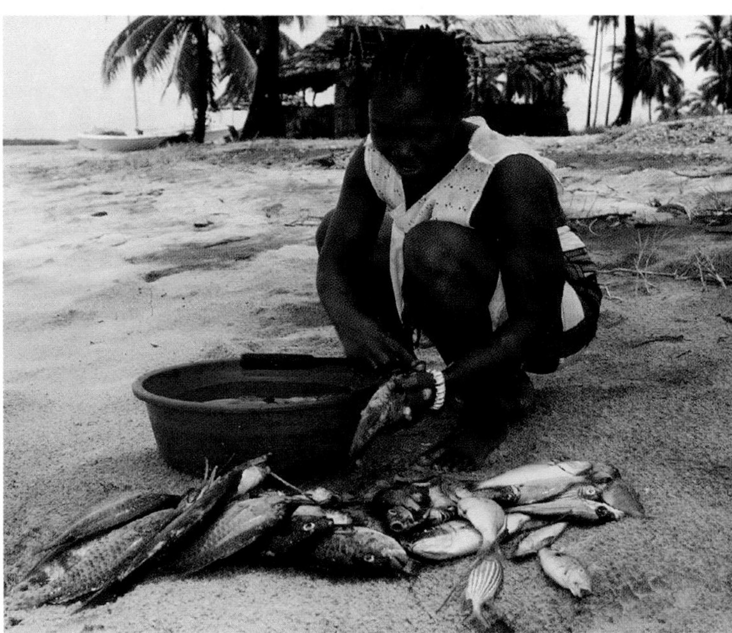

Box S7

## EXAMPLE FROM THE FIELD

The infant mortality rate in Placencia was one in 200 births in 1990. The MPA was implemented in 1994. As a result of the MPA, new occupations were created in Placencia such as dive master, fly fishing guide, and boat guide. These new occupations have raised the income level of households in the village and a doctor arrived in the community in 1998. In the 2000 national census, the infant mortality rate had improved in Placencia to one in 400 births.

The town of Bontoc had an infant mortality rate of 10 infant deaths per 1,000 births in 2001. Five years ago (1996), the infant mortality rate was 18 infant deaths per 1,000 births. In 1999, a health clinic staffed by a nurse was established in the community. The nurse provides minor medical care and midwife services. A doctor visits the clinic one day per week. The people of the community pooled their own time and funds to build the health clinic.

#### *Outputs*

- Narrative presentation on quality of human health in the community.

### *Strengths and limitations*

It may be difficult to obtain the secondary data at a village/community level as data is often reported in an aggregated form. The original source of the data will need to be contacted.

### *Useful references and Internet links*

Bunce, L., Townsley, P., Pomeroy, R. and Pollnac, R. (2000). *Socioeconomic Manual for Coral Reef Management*. Australian Institute of Marine Science, Townsville, Queensland, Australia. Available at www.reefbase.org

Pollnac, R. (1998). "Rapid assessment of management parameters for coral reefs". *Coastal Resources Center Coastal Management Report # 2205*. Coastal Resources Center, University of Rhode Island, Narragansett, Rhode Island, USA. Available at www.crc.uri.edu

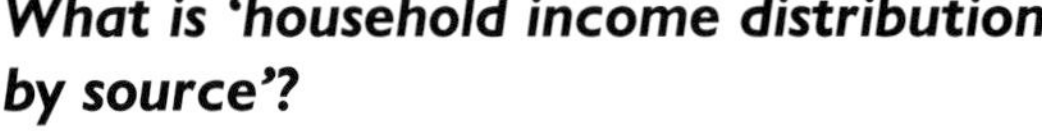

Relates to goals and objectives

GOAL 2

2A 2B

## What is 'household income distribution by source'?

Household income distribution by source is a measure of the principal sources of income for households in the community.

## Why measure it?

An important part of understanding stakeholder characteristics are household livelihood and sources of income, which include the way people combine the resources and assets at their disposal to make a living for themselves and their families. An understanding of these livelihood and income sources will allow the MPA manager to better measure and understand the impacts of the MPA on local households. It will allow the MPA manager to understand who is winning and losing, following shifts in household income sources, as a result of the MPA. Shifting sources of income may indicate a positive or negative impact of the MPA on households. Understanding income sources will also enable the manager to determine levels of community dependency on the resources, which can be used to make changes in MPA management to diversify occupational and income structures. For example, if more than 90% of the community are fishers, then the MPA might offer aquaculture training so they are less dependent on one income.

Also, if households perceive a decrease in the sources of household income over time, then this information can be used to make changes in MPA management to ensure that local households are obtaining adequate livelihoods and incomes. Finally, if households perceive an increase in the sources of household income over time, then this information can be used in support of the MPA.

## How to collect the data

Secondary data is first collected to determine the main sources of income for households and to sort out a few broad groups of people dependent on particular income sources, such as fishing, farming or dive operations. These data may be available from census bureaus and local government offices. The following secondary data are most often available:

- ❑ Economic status (ownership of key assets such as land, fishing boats) and aspects of social status (particularly membership of formal organizations).
- ❑ Sources of livelihood of community members, which often only cover the principal economic activity of individuals or households (specific information on stakeholder households is often available).

Primary data may need to be collected using a survey or a semi-structured interview to gather data from a sample of households in the community on different sources of household income and different sources of livelihood for households. Questions might include:

- ❑ What are the different sources of income in your household? List all.
- ❑ What is the relative importance of each source of household income in the community? Provide percentages.
- ❑ What are the different types of livelihood of the household? List all.
- ❑ What is the relative importance of each livelihood activity to overall household income? Provide percentages.

This data is collected from a sample of households in the community over time to assess shifting sources of income, especially those related to the MPA, such as fishing, dive operations, and tourism.

### Requirements

- Survey form.
- Sample of community households to be surveyed.
- Interviewers.
- Notebook and pen.

## How to analyse and interpret results

Prepare tables of percentages showing the different sources of household income, relative importance of each source of household income in the community, different types of livelihood of the household, and relative importance of each livelihood activity to overall household income. Prepare a narrative text to explain the quantitative results.

### Outputs

- Narrative presentation on quality of human health in the community.

## *Strengths and limitations*

A limitation is that the usefulness of this indicator will depend upon the availability and cooperation of the household informant to respond to questions about source of income, often a sensitive topic.

## *Useful references and Internet links*

Bunce, L., Townsley, P., Pomeroy, R. and Pollnac, R. (2000). *Socioeconomic Manual for Coral Reef Management.* Australian Institute of Marine Science, Townsville, Queensland, Australia. Available at www.reefbase.org

*Note that this indicator (S9) and S10 (occupational structure) both use a survey to collect data and may be conducted at the same time.*

***Many, but not all, households generate revenues through multiple sources and family members. Decreased reliance on a single income stream, for example from fishing, means that a household will be more resilient to any change that might occur within the fishery occupation as a result of adapted management efforts.***

DAVID SHEPPARD/IUCN

Box S8

## Example from the Field

At the Sian Ka'an Biosphere Reserve in Mexico, a census was used to gather information about the monthly average income by productive activity. Results show that women, who represent 23% of the economic force of the community, are earning the same amount of income as many men involved in tourism activities and even more when it comes to their own businesses.

Average income comes from dividing the total amount reported for each activity, by the number of men/women that provided information on their monthly income.

At Tubbataha Reef National Marine Park in the Philippines, the mean income level in Cagayancillo is 3,812 pesos per month or 45,744 pesos per annum. This is below the poverty threshold level in the Philippines which is set at 92,500 pesos per year (National Statistics Office, 1998). Only 10% of the households are above the poverty threshold, leaving 90% below. The main occupations in Cagayancillo are seaweed farming and fishing. Farming becomes a supplementary occupation to provide staple food for home consumption. The table (right) shows that most households engage in multi-occupation – 35% of the households engage in farming, fishing and seaweed farming, 17% engage in fishing and seaweeds, 16% engage in fishing and farming, and 11% engage in farming and seaweeds. Small percentages engage in fishing only (4%), seaweed farming only (3%) and farming only (15%). The remaining 1% is in non-agri/fisheries activities such as services and government employment. Mat weaving is also a popular supplementary source of income among women. They use pandan and buri as raw materials.

### Distribution of respondents by income source

| | *Income source percentage* | *No. of respondents* |
|---|---|---|
| Fishing only | 4 | 8 |
| Farming only | 15 | 30 |
| Seaweeds only | 3 | 5 |
| Fishing & Farming | 16 | 32 |
| Fishing & Seaweeds | 17 | 33 |
| Farming & Seaweeds | 11 | 21 |
| Farming, Fishing & Seaweeds | 35 | 69 |
| Non-Agri or Non-Marine | 1 | 2 |
| TOTAL | 100 | 200 |

**Average income by productive activity per month in USD**

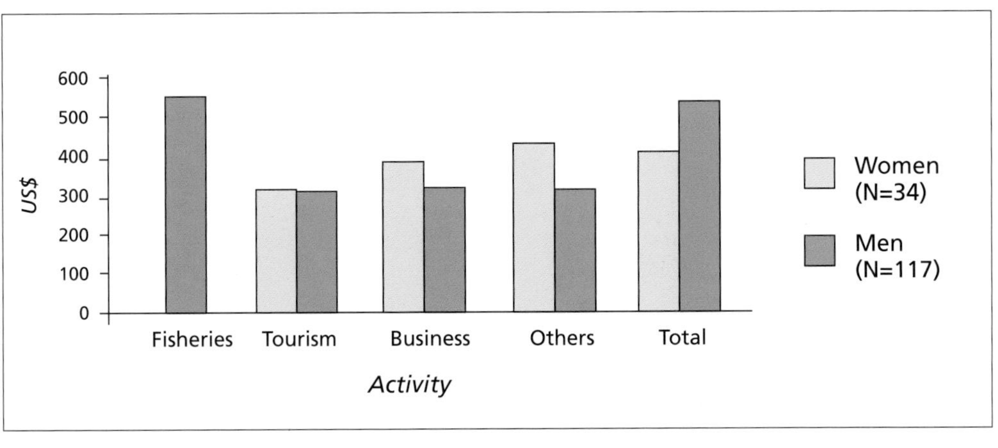

## *What is 'household occupational structure'?*

Household occupational structure measures the distribution of productive activities (occupation, sources of income, both monetary and non-monetary) across households and social groups (age/gender) in the community. It is a list of all the household members, and each member's occupation. It can also include the gender, age, ethnicity and religion of each household member.

## *Why measure it?*

Household occupational structure is an important aspect of social structure as well as an indicator of the relative importance of the different uses of coastal resources. It is an indicator of stabilization or diversification of occupations and level of resource dependency. The indicator is used to determine the percentage of households dependent on coastal resources for livelihood, changes in household occupations as a result of the MPA, and to identify and determine the acceptance and relative importance of alternative (non-target resource based) livelihood activities.

This indicator is useful for determining if the MPA and associated activities, such as alternative livelihood activities, are impacting upon households in the community. It is possible to determine, for example, that fishers in the community are shifting from fishing as a primary occupation to fly fishing guides or dive boat operations as a result of the MPA. It will allow for a measure of the dependence of households on coastal resources for livelihood and income and changes over time on that dependence. The indicator results in a measure of impact of the MPA on household occupational structure in the community.

Ideally, the value of all coastal activities that contribute to the household should be obtained, for example, the income earned from fishing, the value of fish brought home for food. The problem is that most primary producers in developing countries do not keep records of income, and income from fishing, for example, varies so much from day to day that it is difficult to provide an accurate figure for weekly or monthly income. It not only varies from day to day, but also from season to season. The difficulty with estimating income is further compounded by the occupational multiplicity. Household occupational structure is a realistic alternative means of understanding the relative importance of these activities to the individual household.

JOHN PARKS/WWF

*In many parts of the world, three or four generations all live together under the same roof. In such situations, each household member typically contributes to the whole by engaging in a wide variety of specific roles and productive activities.*

### *Requirements*

- List of households to survey.
- Secondary data on household occupational structure.
- Survey form.
- Interviewer.
- Paper/pencil.

## *How to collect the data*

Secondary data is an inadequate source of information about occupations, since most published statistics only include the full-time or primary occupation. Most coastal communities, especially in rural areas, are characterized by occupational multiplicity – a given individual or household may practice two, three, four or more income or subsistence-producing activities. The only way to determine the distribution and relative importance of these activities is by the use of a sample survey.

| Household member | Age | Gender | Education level | Primary occupation | Secondary occupation | Tertiary occupation |
|---|---|---|---|---|---|---|
| 1 | | | | | | |
| 2 | | | | | | |
| 3 | | | | | | |
| 4 | | | | | | |

A survey form can be administered to a sample of households in the community. Respondents are asked to list all the members in the household. They then are asked the age and gender of each person and then their primary, secondary and tertiary occupations. A table such as that above can help organize these data.

In addition, the respondent should be asked about the overall primary and secondary sources of income. This is particularly important to determine the range of household sources of income that may not be noted by occupation, such as remittance. The questions might include:

- What is the primary source of household income?
- What is the secondary source of household income?

### How to analyse and interpret results

Calculate the distribution of occupations in the community. During the testing process, as shown in the following sample table, the number of household members throughout the community that were noted as farming for their primary occupation was calculated, then the same for fishing, fish trading and so on. The same calculations were then done for secondary occupations and then tertiary occupations. Once the raw numbers were noted, the percentages could be calculated as noted in parentheses in the sample table.

Construct a similar table for primary and secondary sources of household incomes.

Construct a final table noting the distribution of age, gender and education.

### Outputs

- Table of percentage distribution of ranking of occupational activities in community.
- Table of primary and secondary sources of household incomes.
- Table of distributions of age, gender and education.

*Note that this indicator (S10) and S9 (household income distribution by source) both use a survey to collect data and may be conducted at the same time.*

Table S7

**Number of household members in each occupation (percentage distribution)**

| *Occupation* | *Primary* | *Secondary* | *Tertiary* |
|---|---|---|---|
| Farming | 0 (0%) | 10 (17%) | 0 |
| Fishing | 70 (63%) | 17 (28%) | 15 (17%) |
| Fish trading | 25 (23%) | 7 (12%) | 10 (11%) |
| Carpentry | 15 (14%) | 6 (10%) | 0 |
| None | 0 | 20 (33%) | 65 (72%) |
| **Total** | **110 (100%)** | **60(100%)** | **90(100%)** |

## Strengths and limitations

This indicator can be an accurate measure of dependence on coastal and marine resources if appropriate methods are used. Respondents must know the sources of household income and be able to rank them in terms of relative importance. The interviewers must make it clear to the respondent that the list of activities and ranking must relate to the full year of activities. This is especially important where there are seasonal differences. Another complication is that defining the household may be challenging in certain locations due, for example, to an extended family living in the house.

## Useful references and Internet links


Berkes, F., Mahon, R., McConney, P., Pollnac, R. and Pomeroy, R. (2001). *Managing small-scale fisheries: alternative directions and methods.* International Development Research Centre, Ottawa, Canada. Available at www.idrc.ca/booktique

Pollnac, R.B. and Crawford, B.R. (2000). "Assessing behavioral aspects of coastal resource use". *Proyek Pesisir Publication Special Report. Coastal Resources Center, Coastal Management Report #2226.* Coastal Resources Center, University of Rhode Island, Narragansett, Rhode Island, USA. Available at www.crc.uri.edu


Box S9

### EXAMPLE FROM THE FIELD

At the Sian Ka'an Biosphere Reserve in Mexico, a census was conducted in Punta Allen to collect data on occupational structure. The census was conducted in 113 households, containing a total of 433 inhabitants.

For over 30 years the primary source of income of the men of Punta Allen was lobster fishing (*right*). Nowadays, tourism activities and services are growing fast, as a consequence of the increasing massive tourism developments in the north of Quintana Roo.

Women of Punta Allen are still dedicated to housekeeping, but in the past six years, they have been incorporated into economic activities, particularly in the tourism sector, where they participate in a wide variety of activities: members of tourism cooperatives, owners of boats, chefs, waitresses, housekeepers in guesthouses, secretaries, etc. Other significant sources of income for these women are their own businesses, including supermarkets, restaurants and guesthouses.

JOHN PARKS/WWF

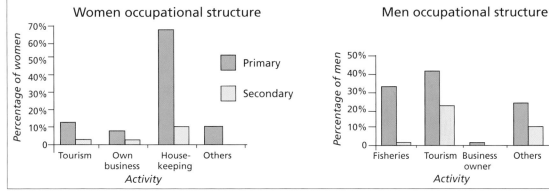

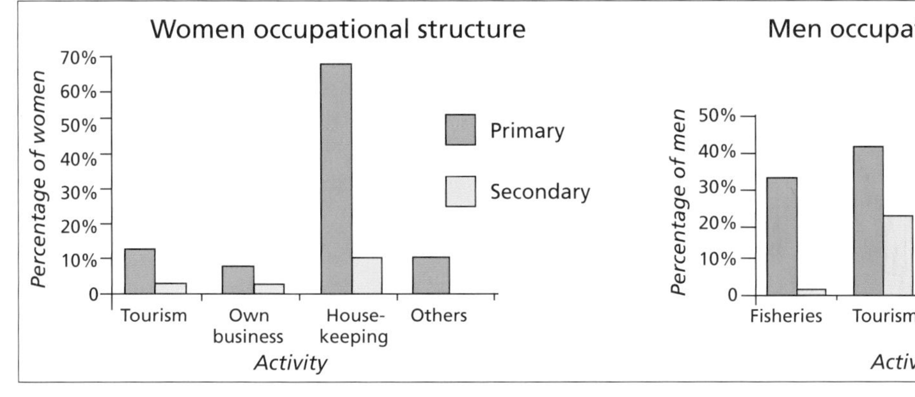

# Community infrastructure and business

**Relates to goals and objectives**

GOAL 2
2A 2C
2D

GOAL 4
4B

## What is 'community infrastructure and business'?

Community infrastructure and business is a general measure of local community and economic development. It is a description of the level of community services (e.g. hospital, school), and infrastructure (e.g. roads, utilities), which can include information essential for determining sources of anthropogenic impacts on coastal resources (e.g. sewage treatment). It is also a description of the number and type of commercial businesses in the area, especially those associated with activities related to the MPA.

## Why measure it?

If measured over time, community infrastructure and business is useful for determining changes in economic status and relative wealth and development of the community, as well as access to markets and capital. A positive change in community infrastructure and services (e.g. improved roads, hospital) indicates an increase in the relative wealth of the community, resulting, in part or wholly, from economic gains obtained from the MPA. A negative change in community infrastructure and services may indicate no or limited changes in the relative wealth of the community being obtained, in part, from the MPA. An increase in commercial business, such as dive shops, hotels and restaurants for tourists, indicates an increase in overall community economic development resulting from activities associated with the MPA.

TONY ECKERSLEY

### Requirements

- Baseline information on community infrastructure and services and businesses.
- Survey form and check list.
- Interviewers.
- Paper/pencil.

## How to collect the data

This information is collected by interviewing key informants (e.g. mayor, town engineer), reviewing secondary data and/or observing the community. A checklist needs to be developed to enumerate and determine the existence of community infrastructure items. The checklist of items might include the items listed opposite.

Other items may be added to the list depending on the infrastructure, services and businesses in the area. This checklist may also include information on the condition of the item (e.g. roads: smooth, few pot holes, or many potholes). It may also be useful to ask business people about the number of employees, number of locally hired employees, and if the business is locally owned. This information will provide an indication of the impact of local businesses on the economy.

## How to analyse and interpret results

Collate the data and present it in a narrative format. For example:

> Matalom has 1km of asphalt road (3km of stone and 0.5km of dirt), as well as one bridge, which reportedly needs maintenance. The town has water piped to all homes and businesses. There are telephones and electricity.

◀ ***Businesses that generate revenues based on the presence of an effectively managed MPA, such as boat trips for visitors, provide additional jobs and livelihood opportunities for those within the coastal community.***

There is a primary school and a health clinic. In the last two years, three guesthouses been established, one dive shop and two restaurants to serve the increasing number of divers coming to the MPA.

Data can also be presented quantitatively by making a table showing the presence and/or number of each item. Changes in type of items, number and characteristics, either new or gone out of business, should be noted over time.

TONY ECKERSLEY

### Outputs

- Narrative presentation of community infrastructure and business.
- Table showing presence and/or number of each item.

### Strengths and limitations

A challenge with this indicator is accurately identifying significant infrastructure and business items in the community. Similar to material style of life, it is often difficult to separate impacts of the MPA on level of community infrastructure and business development, such as a paved road or sewage treatment, from impacts of other economic changes in the community caused by general economic and community development. As noted in S7 – Material style of life – a control could help account for these changes and impacts.

### Useful references and Internet links

Berkes, F., Mahon, R., McConney, P., Pollnac, R. and Pomeroy, R. (2001). *Managing small-scale fisheries: alternative directions and methods.* International Development Research Centre, Ottawa, Canada. Available at www.idrc.ca/booktique

Pollnac, R.B. and Crawford, B.R. (2000). "Assessing behavioral aspects of coastal resource use". *Proyek Pesisir Publication Special Report. Coastal Resources Center, Coastal Management Report #2226.* Coastal Resources Center, University of Rhode Island, Narragansett, Rhode Island, USA. Available at www.crc.uri.edu

### Checklist of items that might be included in the survey of community infrastructure and business

| | | | |
|---|---|---|---|
| Hospitals | yes___ | no___ | #____ |
| Medical clinics | yes___ | no___ | #____ |
| Resident doctors | yes___ | no___ | #____ |
| Resident dentists | yes___ | no___ | #____ |
| Secondary schools | yes___ | no___ | #____ |
| Primary schools | yes___ | no___ | #____ |
| Water piped to homes | yes___ | no___ | |
| Sewer pipes and canals | yes___ | no___ | |
| Sewage treatment facilities | yes___ | no___ | |
| Septic/settling tanks | yes___ | no___ | |
| Electric service hook-ups | yes___ | no___ | #____ |
| Telephones | yes___ | no___ | #____ |
| Public transportation | yes___ | no___ | |
| Paved roads | yes___ | no___ | |

#### Businesses

| | | | |
|---|---|---|---|
| Food markets | yes___ | no___ | #____ |
| Hotels | yes___ | no___ | #____ |
| Guesthouses | yes___ | no___ | #____ |
| Resorts | yes___ | no___ | #____ |
| Restaurants | yes___ | no___ | #____ |
| Food stalls | yes___ | no___ | #____ |
| Gas stations | yes___ | no___ | #____ |
| Banks | yes___ | no___ | #____ |
| Specialty shops | yes___ | no___ | #____ |
| | type________ | | |
| Gift shops | yes___ | no___ | #____ |
| Dive shops | yes___ | no___ | #____ |
| Tour operations | yes___ | no___ | #____ |
| Fishing guides | yes___ | no___ | #____ |

Box S10

## EXAMPLE FROM THE FIELD

Tumbak has 1km of asphalt road (3km stone and 0.5km dirt), as well as one bridge, which reportedly needs maintenance. Microlets and boats link the community to nearby towns. The town nearest to Tumbak with full services (bank, gas stations, markets, government offices) is Belang, the seat of the kecamatan (district government), which is about two hours and 28km to the south. People and products can also be transported by the three automobiles, one motorcycle and 20 bicycles, and numerous boats recorded in the village statistics. The pipe meant to deliver fresh water to the community is out of service, so residents must travel by boat to the river for fresh water, which is transported back to the village in plastic jerry cans. Approximately 8% of the households have septic or settling tanks and 26% are officially connected to the national electric company lines. The survey indicates that 85% of households have electricity, many of them unofficially connected to the neighbour's supply. There are no telephones, gas stations, markets, restaurants, or accommodation for visitors. There is one elementary school.

*Source*: Pollnac, R.B. and Crawford, B.R. (2000).

Relates to goals and objectives

GOAL 2

2B 2C

## *What is 'number and nature of markets'?*

The number and nature of markets is a measure of the number and types of markets where marine products from the area of the MPA are purchased and sold. The market is the connection between the producer (e.g. fisher, mangrove harvester) and the consumer (e.g. resident, tourist, hotel owner). The market serves both a physical function (i.e. buying, selling, storage, processing) and an economic function (i.e. price, behaviour).

## *Why measure it?*

Since the livelihoods and incomes of people in the community are linked to markets, it will be important to understand the changing nature of markets. This indicator is particularly useful in determining coastal resident access to markets and capital, which contribute to livelihood opportunities. The MPA can have both positive and negative impacts on markets for coastal resource goods (e.g. fish, mangrove) and services (e.g. tourism, recreational fishing, diving). The positive impacts will be shifts in markets resulting in increased income as demand changes for different goods and services provided by the MPA. The negative impacts will be a reduction in the number of markets as goods and services from the MPA are reduced due to management and potential loss of income.

This indicator allows for measurement of the impact of the MPA on markets for major marine products from the area. It allows for an analysis of changes over time in the supply and demand of major marine products and market channels as a result of MPA management. It is important to recognise that market demands also have an impact on the MPA through economic incentives to participate in illegal and/or unsustainable activities.

### *Requirements*

- List of key informants to interview.
- Survey form.
- Secondary data on major marine products and markets.
- Paper/pencil.

***Locally caught fish outside MPAs are often sold at a number of different markets, including local (town/village), provincial/state, national, and international.***

## How to collect the data

The data can be collected through either a key informant survey of representative fishers and traders or through a survey of fishers and traders. Secondary data on these major marine products may be available in the MPA management plan, economic studies of the region, and from government agencies such as fisheries, environment and natural resources or tourism departments.

Since the market may vary from product to product, there is a need to identify each one. For example, the market for lobster may be different from that for finfish.

As a first step, the major marine products (i.e. fish, shellfish, crabs, mangrove) in the area of the MPA need to be identified. The key questions might include:

- ❑ What are the ten most important vertebrates harvested? Note local and scientific names.
- ❑ What are the ten most important invertebrates harvested? Note local and scientific names.
- ❑ What are the five most important flora harvested? Note local and scientific names.

The data collection should only focus on the major marine products as the analysis can get complicated the more products that are included.

For each resource, it is important to understand the harvest patterns, importance and marketing. Important questions to ask might include:

- ❑ What time of year is the resource harvested (month)?
- ❑ Where is the resource harvested (inshore, reef, offshore, distant waters)?
- ❑ What is the importance, in terms of value and quantity, of each resource? Rank from 1 to 10.
- ❑ What is the resource primarily gathered for? Household consumption, trade/barter, or sale in the market.
- ❑ If the resource is sold, where is the market located (local, regional, national, export)? And to whom (wholesaler, retailer, transporter, processor)?

To supplement the information collected above, for each product, the key informants should be asked to rank the degree of demand for the product using the following scale:

1 = little or no established market exists for the product; never sold or traded

2 = limited demand for the product; can occasionally sell some

3 = some demand for the product; can sometimes sell it

4 = strong demand for the product; can usually sell it

5 = very strong demand for the product; can always sell it

## How to analyse and interpret results

Prepare a written narrative for each product describing the harvest patterns, importance and marketing system. Prepare a summary table that compares important market characteristics for each product. This information can be presented on a map showing the flow or movement of each product from harvest to consumer along the market channel.

## Strengths and limitations

Ranking the major marine products will be important as there may be a long list generated by the key informants.

## Useful references and Internet links

Bunce, L., Townsley, P., Pomeroy, R. and Pollnac, R. (2000). *Socioeconomic Manual for Coral Reef Management.* Australian Institute of Marine Science, Townsville, Queensland, Australia. Available at www.reefbase.org

### Outputs

- A narrative identifying the major marine products in the area and harvest and marketing for these products.
- Summary table of important market characteristics of each product.
- Map showing market channel flow or movement of each product.

Box S11

## EXAMPLE FROM THE FIELD

At Tubbataha Reef National Marine Park in the Philippines, the market outlets for fishery products, including dried seaweeds from Cagayancillo, are either Puerto Princesa City or Iloilo City. There are wholesale buyers stationed in the islands who deliver in bulk to outside markets. Prices are dictated by these buyers who exact patronage by offering advance sums of money for the producers' daily consumption of basic goods which they themselves supply. A foreign operator of live fish products (lapu-lapu) markets directly to Taiwan through its own network.

Agricultural products are sold locally or consumed by the producing households. Likewise, mats are sold locally or through individual contacts who visit the islands. Products are transported to the markets by 4 boats (10-20 gross tons) that ply the Iloilo and Puerto Princesa routes. Except for the summer months (March to May) there is no regularity in the schedule of these boats. Schedules are highly dependent on weather. The regular fare for passengers is 350 pesos going to Puerto Princesa City and 300 pesos going to Iloilo City. These include food for the entire duration of the trip. For cargoes, a bag of rice or cement costs 50 pesos each.

TONI PARRAS

TONI PARRAS

TONI PARRAS

GOAL 6

6A

Difficulty Rating 3 1–5

## What is 'stakeholder knowledge of natural history'?

Stakeholder knowledge of natural history (referred to here as local knowledge) is a measure of the knowledge held by stakeholders that is not based on scientific research but comes from stakeholder observations, experiences, beliefs and perceptions of cause and effect. It is also the degree to which local stakeholders pass on to next generations local knowledge and beliefs about the natural environment and the effects of human use.

## Why measure it?

MPA compliance and success may be influenced by changes in the distribution of local knowledge and awareness among the stakeholders of natural history and biological event timing across generations, gender, and community roles and positions. In order for people to take action to protect and manage the environment, they need to understand how the natural ecosystem works. Those with higher levels of knowledge of natural history tend to be more receptive to management initiatives, such as an MPA, and provide more support for the MPA.

Stakeholder knowledge of natural history can be used by MPA managers to:

- Contribute to their scientific understanding of marine resources, e.g. local fishers may advise on reef fish behaviour, habitat and migration patterns.
- Facilitate interactions with stakeholders by ensuring the managers know as much as the stakeholders, since fishers may not respect a manager if he or she is not as knowledgeable about marine resources as the locals.
- Facilitate accurate communication and data collection by ensuring that managers, scientists and stakeholders use the same terms.
- Determine if the MPA is enhancing community respect and/or understanding of local knowledge.

***Resource users have varying degrees of knowledge about the life history and behaviours of target marine organisms. Such knowledge can both hinder and assist MPA management.***

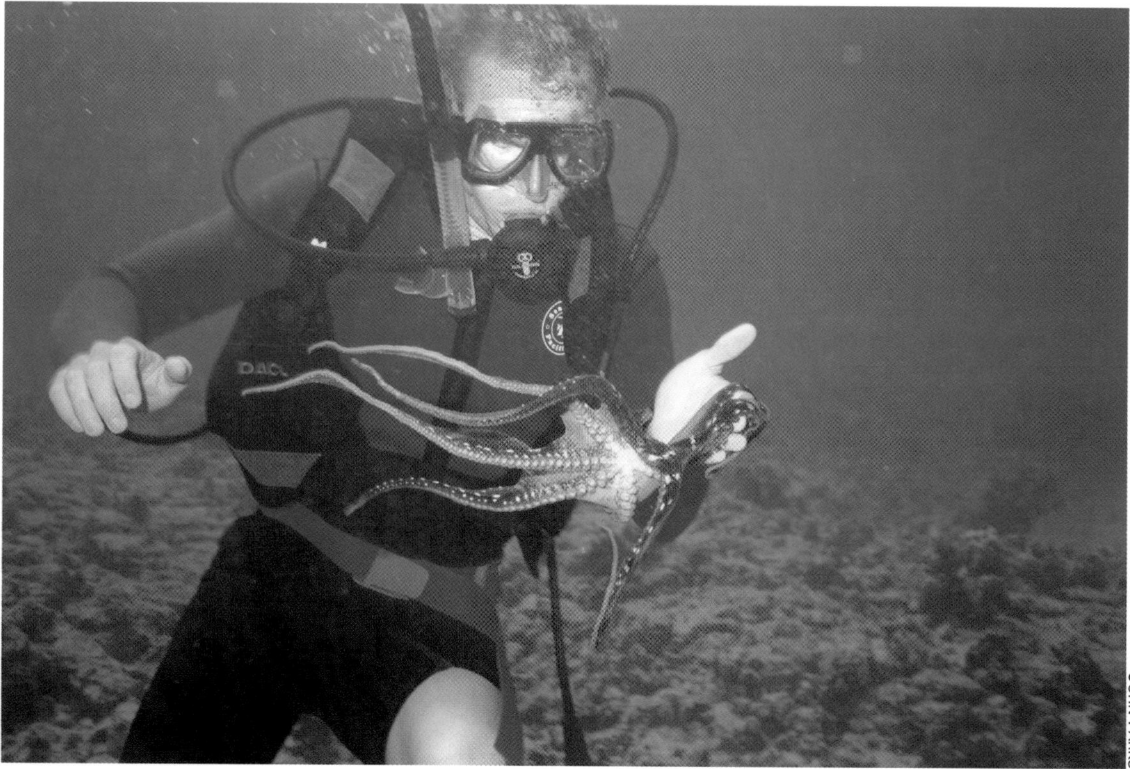

JOHN PARKS

### Requirements

- Survey form.
- Interviewer.
- Notebook and pen.
- Map of area.

## How to collect the data

The focus of this indicator is folk taxonomy and local knowledge of resources. Folk taxonomy involves understanding the local names of marine aquatic resources, locations of the resources and related activities, particularly significant places such as fishing grounds and landing sites, and related activities around the resources. Important questions to address when assessing local knowledge may include:

❏ What are the local names of the marine resources?

❏ What are the local names of the places where they are located?

❏ What are the local names of particularly significant places related to the resources (e.g. spawning sites)?

❏ What are local names of activities related to the resources?

This involves understanding how these items are classified, e.g. while scientists may divide fauna into families and species using scientific criteria, stakeholders may use very different groups such as edible/non-edible, species that live in similar environments, seasonal availability, etc.

Local knowledge refers to stakeholder understanding of the marine aquatic resources including: the location of resources, their mobility, quantity, interactions among resources, feeding behaviours, and breeding behaviours and locations. Key questions may include:

❏ Where are the resources located?

❏ What is the extent of their mobility?

❏ What is the population size of each resource?

❏ What kinds of interactions are there among resources?

❏ What are feeding behaviours of the resources?

❏ What are the breeding behaviours and locations?

This knowledge also involves understanding how these characteristics have changed over time and why. Local knowledge may be limited to commercially important species, with which stakeholders are often most familiar.

Variations in local knowledge may occur. This refers to the range of perceptions among different stakeholders, e.g. fishers may know more about changes in the fish populations because they harvest these resources; whereas divers may be more familiar with coral conditions since they see the corals while diving.

Folk taxonomy should be assessed first because it will provide important information for local knowledge and variations in knowledge. It will probably be found that there is little secondary data on local knowledge, which is often passed on by word of mouth from generation to generation.

A range of data collection methods and visualization techniques can be used. Semi-structured interviews, oral histories, surveys, observations and focus group interviews are all important for collecting information. During the data collection it is particularly important to record who the informants are and their characteristics (e.g. age, gender), which will be used to assess variations among people and stakeholder groups.

Visualization techniques include:

❏ Local classifications to identify local taxonomies;

❏ Ranking matrices to assess variations among individuals and stakeholder groups; and

❏ Ranking matrices and timelines to encourage discussion and analysis of changes in resource abundance or other features of local knowledge where relative quantities are important.

It is also important to measure through semi-structured interviews with MPA managers:

❏ Their awareness of stakeholder knowledge of natural history;

❏ Their use of this knowledge; and

❏ The interaction and consistency of local stakeholder knowledge and scientific knowledge.

## How to analyse and interpret results

Summarise the data into descriptive text based on the qualitative information and quantitative data. Use tables and figures to clarify and illustrate variations and trends, e.g. knowledge of place names and beliefs about distributions of flora, fauna and minerals can be put on maps; ranking matrices and timelines created by informants during field data collection can be included to show stakeholder knowledge and perceptions of resource conditions and changes.

Analysis of variations is unique and involves comparing responses from informants to determine the basis of their differences. By comparing the responses on local taxonomies and local knowledge with the informants' basic characteristics, it will be possible to determine the socio-economic basis of their differences, e.g. variation may be related to area of residence or work experience.

### Outputs

- A narrative text on each sub-parameter such as folk taxonomy and local knowledge.
- Summary table of important market characteristics of each product.
- Maps showing location of resources.
- Ranking matrices and timelines showing stakeholder knowledge and perception of resource conditions and changes.

## Strengths and limitations

An appreciation of local knowledge by managers and scientists is needed.

It is important to note that local knowledge is variable. For example, a spear or hand line fisher usually has greater knowledge than a deck hand on a trawler. While some local resource users may have an extensive knowledge of marine organism life history and behaviour, a lot of local knowledge is based in (or flavoured by) mythology, religion, etc. and is inaccurate. Local knowledge often includes a lot of spurious reasoning for observed patterns. While local knowledge is important and can be very useful, caution must be used and the information should be checked with others in the community and with scientific experts.

## Useful references and Internet links

Bunce, L., Townsley, P., Pomeroy, R. and Pollnac, R. (2000). *Socioeconomic Manual for Coral Reef Management. Australian Institute of Marine Science, Townsville,* Queensland, Australia. pp. 202-204 in Chapter 6, "Traditional Knowledge". Available at www.reefbase.org

Box S12

### EXAMPLE FROM THE FIELD

At the Galapagos Marine Reserve, a survey of 348 individuals in three inhabited islands was conducted to measure stakeholder knowledge of natural history. The table below provides results of the survey showing the percentage of stakeholders in the different islands with knowledge of natural history.

| | Santa Cruz | San Cristobal | Isabela |
|---|---|---|---|
| Origin of the archipelago | 45% | 44% | 43% |
| Weather of the archipelago | 38% | 35% | 21% |
| Marine currents | 35% | 32% | 38% |
| Evolution of the species | 38% | 33% | 37% |
| Concept of endemic species | 47% | 44% | 46% |
| Fisheries resources | 18% | 16% | 20% |
| Vegetation | 21% | 16% | 20% |
| Danger of extinction | 25% | 17% | 37% |
| Alien species | 38% | 33% | 52% |
| ***Average*** | ***34%*** | ***30%*** | ***35%*** |

There is a relatively higher degree of stakeholder knowledge of terrestrial natural history than marine due to a greater effort on environmental education about terrestrial systems. There is a need to improve stakeholders' knowledge of marine systems.

## What is 'distribution of formal knowledge to community'?

Distribution of formal knowledge to community is a measure of the degree of awareness of information generated by the scientific community held by stakeholder and user groups about MPA use and ecosystem impacts.

## Why measure it?

The information generated by this indicator can help to contribute to improved scientific understanding of local ecosystems and to facilitate interactions with stakeholders by ensuring the stakeholders have confidence in the scientific information. It can also facilitate accurate communication and data collection by ensuring that managers, scientists and stakeholders use the same terms. As a result, rewritten, interpreted, translated, disseminated/communicated, and ideally understood scientific information can lead to meaningfully applied and managed MPAs.

***Scientific knowledge and techniques can be a valuable asset to local users and coastal communities.***

JOHN PARKS

## How to collect the data

A list of scientific information provided to the community by MPA management and scientists is prepared. This may be material on expected impacts of the MPA, expected changes on resources from the MPA, and impacts from changes in certain use patterns provided at meetings, in publications, or through television and radio. Second, each respondent is asked whether they are aware of this information or not. Third, they are asked to describe the types of scientific information provided to them. Any stories or anecdotes that illustrate their thoughts should be recorded.

Based on these conversations, the following scale should be used to rank the awareness they have about scientific information.

1 = no awareness of information generated by the scientific community about MPA use and ecosystem impacts.
2 = limited awareness of information generated by the scientific community about MPA use and ecosystem impacts.
3 = moderate awareness of information generated by the scientific community about MPA use and ecosystem impacts.
4 = extensive awareness of information generated by the scientific community about MPA use and ecosystem impacts.
5 = complete awareness of information generated by the scientific community about MPA use and ecosystem impacts.

A follow-up question should be asked about why they do or do not have confidence in the scientific information: to what extent do you believe the scientific information?

Also, a question to be asked about how to improve the information provided to them is: how can this information be improved?

**Relates to goals and objectives**

**GOAL 6**

**6B 6C 6D**

### Requirements

- Survey form.
- Interviewers.
- List of households to survey.
- Notebook and pen.
- Map of area.

### Outputs

- Narrative report with text boxes on anecdotes and stories.
- Tables and figures to clarify and illustrate important points.

## How to analyse and interpret results

Summarise the data into descriptive text based on the qualitative information and quantitative data. Use tables and figures to clarify and illustrate variations in the scale ranking of confidence. Include anecdotes and stories, and opinions about the scientific information.

## Strengths and limitations

This indicator can provide valuable information for improving MPA education programmes and scientific research.

## Useful references and Internet links

Bunce, L., Townsley, P., Pomeroy, R. and Pollnac, R. (2000). *Socioeconomic Manual for Coral Reef Management*. Australian Institute of Marine Science, Townsville, Queensland, Australia. Available at www.reefbase.org

***Scientific information can be combined with local knowledge of the marine resources to improve management.***

TONI PARRAS

S14

Box S13

## EXAMPLE FROM THE FIELD

In Mafia Island Marine Park in Tanzania, respondents were asked to gauge the extent to which they felt they had acquired information on the marine environment from various information sources disseminated by MIMP, with the following results:

***Information gained through discussions/meetings with MIMP workers in the village***

| | *Elders* | *Fishers* | *Farmers* | *Other* | *Women* | *Youth* | *Students* | *Total* |
|---|---|---|---|---|---|---|---|---|
| Very much | 9 | 15 | 7 | 5 | 13 | 10 | 7 | 66 |
| Average | 8 | 15 | 11 | 11 | 5 | 10 | 5 | 65 |
| Little | 8 | 15 | 5 | 9 | 7 | 5 | 7 | 56 |
| None | 12 | 30 | 22 | 25 | 28 | 46 | 54 | 217 |
| **Total** | **37** | **75** | **45** | **50** | **53** | **71** | **73** | **404** |

***Information gained through the booklet called Bahari (for primary school)***

| | *Elders* | *Fishers* | *Farmers* | *Other* | *Women* | *Youth* | *Students* | *Total* |
|---|---|---|---|---|---|---|---|---|
| Very much | 2 | 4 | | 3 | 2 | 3 | 4 | 18 |
| Average | | 1 | | 1 | 2 | 4 | 7 | 15 |
| Little | | 4 | | 3 | 3 | 3 | 4 | 15 |
| None | 35 | 66 | 45 | 45 | 46 | 61 | 58 | 356 |
| **Total** | **37** | **75** | **45** | **50** | **53** | **71** | **73** | **404** |

***Information gained through calendars, leaflets and meetings conducted by the Mafia Turtle and Dugong Project***

| | *Elders* | *Fishers* | *Farmers* | *Other* | *Women* | *Youth* | *Students* | *Total* |
|---|---|---|---|---|---|---|---|---|
| Very much | 4 | 12 | 5 | 5 | 8 | 10 | 23 | 67 |
| Average | 1 | 17 | 4 | 6 | 4 | 6 | 16 | 54 |
| Little | 5 | 10 | 11 | 12 | 8 | 13 | 9 | 68 |
| None | 27 | 36 | 25 | 27 | 33 | 42 | 25 | 215 |
| **Total** | **37** | **75** | **45** | **50** | **53** | **71** | **73** | **404** |

These results indicate that about 30% or so of villagers feel that they have received information thanks to the awareness-raising methods described above and that more than 50% of people feel that they have had no information at all. It is notable that even amongst primary school children only 15% have acquired information from a booklet on the marine environment (Bahari) that was specifically circulated to primary school teachers. Given the size of the resident communities within the marine park (over 15,000) these results are not as negative as they otherwise seem, nonetheless they illustrate the wide scope for further awareness-raising and will provide a baseline for ongoing environmental education efforts.

At the Far East Marine Reserve in Russia, the following groups were polled during 2002: local inhabitants, visitors to the museum, dive tourists and schoolchildren. They were requested to give an estimate of the quality of scientific information provided by the MPA specialists, to say whether they trust them when they recount the actual threats from unregulated human activity in the Peter the Great Bay (i.e. poaching, unregulated tourism on the coast, land-based pollution), and to express their expectations about the information provided by the reserve. Of particular interest is the level of trust in the reserve's information on environmental threats and the importance of the MPA. The results are summarised below:

| ***Group*** | ***Number of people polled*** | ***Level of trusting (%)*** |
|---|---|---|
| Local people | 50 | Limited - 35<br>Moderate - 55<br>Extensive - 10 |
| Outside visitors | 500 | Moderate - 15<br>Extensive - 70<br>Complete - 15 |
| Dive tourists | 70 | Moderate - 10<br>Extensive - 85<br>Complete - 5 |
| School children | 60 | Extensive - 35<br>Complete - 65 |

# Percentage of stakeholder group in leadership positions

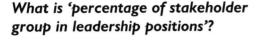

Relates to goals and objectives

GOAL 4

4B 4C

## What is 'percentage of stakeholder group in leadership positions'?

The percentage of stakeholder group in leadership positions measures the number of individual stakeholders from the various stakeholder groups who have been or currently are in a leadership position related to MPA management.

## Why measure it?

This indicator is important to measure because it provides an understanding of the degree of equity among social groups associated with the MPA. If a range of stakeholders (especially those from minority groups) are involved in leadership positions in MPA management, a broader representation of ideas and interests is achieved; a more democratic and equitable management structure is in operation; and a greater level of participation in management is achieved. If all stakeholder groups are not represented, recommendations can be made to include non-represented stakeholder groups in a leadership position in MPA management.

## How to collect the data

First, a copy of the organizational structure of the MPA management should be obtained and reviewed.

Second, the representative structure of stakeholder groups from the organizational structure should be identified.

Next, through a key informant interview of MPA management, the stakeholder groups and the representatives of the stakeholder groups to MPA management, both previous and current, should be identified.

Then through key informant interviews of MPA managers and known stakeholder groups, a listing of all stakeholder groups associated with the MPA can be prepared. The list should be cross-checked with information provided by the stakeholder groups to identify leaders and representatives.

*Note that if you have difficulty in identifying the stakeholder groups using key informant interviews, a stakeholder analysis can be conducted using the methods described under indicator G12.*

### Requirements

- Survey form.
- Interviewers.
- List of leaders and representatives of stakeholder groups to survey.
- MPA management plan and organizational chart.
- Paper/pencil.

Each leader and representative should be interviewed in order to describe their stakeholder group history and the role of their group in MPA management.

Finally, a check should be made to see if all stakeholder groups identified through the stakeholder analysis are represented in MPA management. If a stakeholder group is not represented in MPA management it should be asked why not and whether there are plans for it to be represented. It is important to measure this indicator over time as stakeholder groups and representatives may change.

## How to analyse and interpret results

Identify the total number of stakeholder groups associated with the MPA and present this in a table. Calculate the total number of stakeholder groups that have been, or currently are, in leadership positions and present these in a table. Prepare a narrative report to accompany the tables that describes the history and role of stakeholder group representation and leadership in MPA management.

### Outputs

- Table of total number of stakeholder groups that have been, or currently are, in a leadership position in MPA management.
- Accompanying narrative describing the history and role of stakeholder group representation and leadership in MPA management.

## *Strengths and limitations*

One strength of this indicator is that it provides a measure of the percentage of stakeholder groups represented in leadership positions in MPA management. However, the indicator will not measure the 'power' that each stakeholder group has in MPA management. It should be noted that some stakeholder groups may not have defined representation procedures to select their representatives or may not be organized enough to have representation.

## *Useful references and Internet links*

Langill, S. (compiler) (1999). *Stakeholder Analysis. Volume 7. Supplement for Conflict and Collaboration Resource Book.* International Development Research Centre, Ottawa, Canada.

Box S14

### Example from the Field

At Tubbataha Reef National Marine Park in the Philippines, the Tubbataha Protected Area Management Board, which is the policy-making body for the park is composed of 15 members, four of which are from non-governmental organizations and 11 from branches of government. With the assumption of office of the new set of local government officials in Cagayancillo last July 2001, department officers of the government have become more active. Most of the development and conservation activities are initiated by these officers under the Coastal Resource Management Programme. However, participation of fisherfolk and farmers is encouraged through the activation of various groups like the Municipal Fisheries Resource Management Council composed of Barangay Councils. These organizations are constituted by about 60% fishermen and farmers and 40% elected government officials. A Livelihood Committee was also recently formed involving representatives from farmers, fishermen and women's groups. The committee is composed of four members from government and two from private groups.

***The local community participates in management at Mafia Island Marine Park, Tanzania. Stakeholders external to the management team often actively participate or can be recruited to serve as community leaders in support of MPA management efforts.***

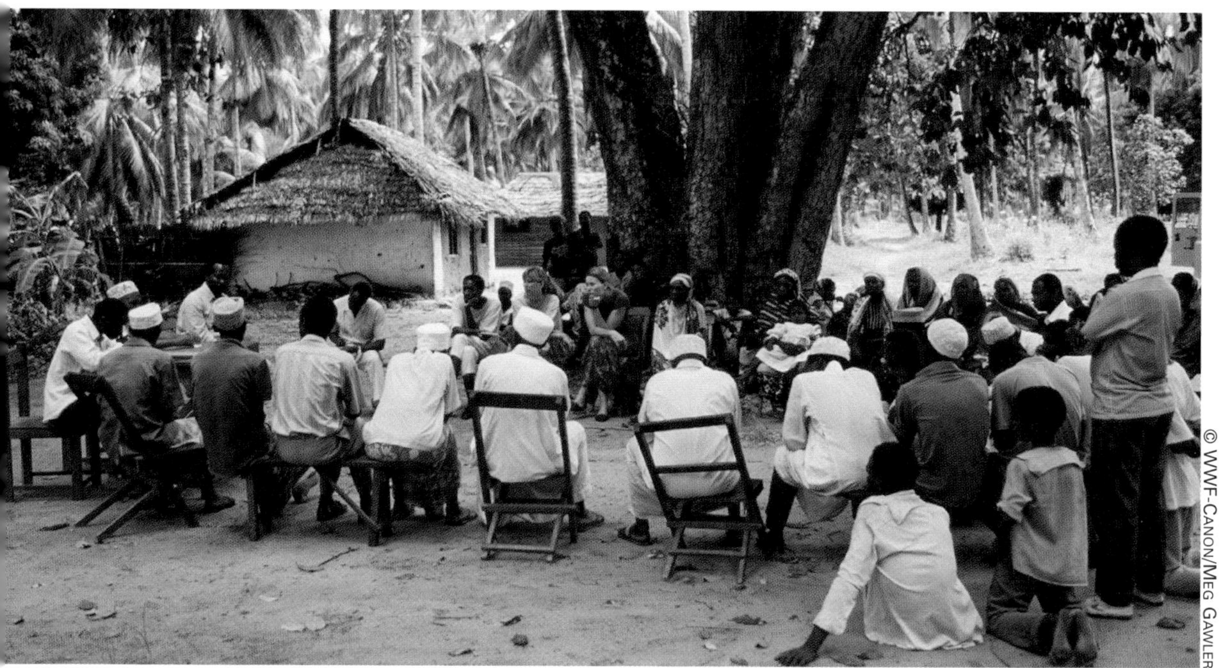

# Changes in conditions of ancestral and historical sites, features, and/or monuments

Relates to goals and objectives

GOAL 5

5B

## What is 'changes in conditions of ancestral and historical sites, features, and/or monuments'?

Changes in conditions of ancestral and historical sites/features/monuments is a measure of the significance, presence and use of material features that have at some point in time become significant for a society's culture and history.

## Why measure it?

This indicator can be used to measure impacts of the MPA and its activities, such as increased tourism, on the ancestral and historical site/feature/monument. This is important for maximizing compatibility between the MPA management and local culture.

### Requirements

- Basemap of area.
- Camera.
- Survey form.
- Interviewers.
- Notebook and pen.
- Handheld GPS device.

The information generated by the indicator can be used for interpretive programmes and for raising cultural awareness and/or sensitivity.

This indicator also provides feedback on the level of knowledge about any site/feature/monument, as well as its condition to assess how well the MPA contributes to preserving the community's and society's culture and history.

***If appropriately designed, MPAs can provide protection not only to living marine organisms and habitat, but also to valuable cultural resources such as historic sites and shipwrecks.***

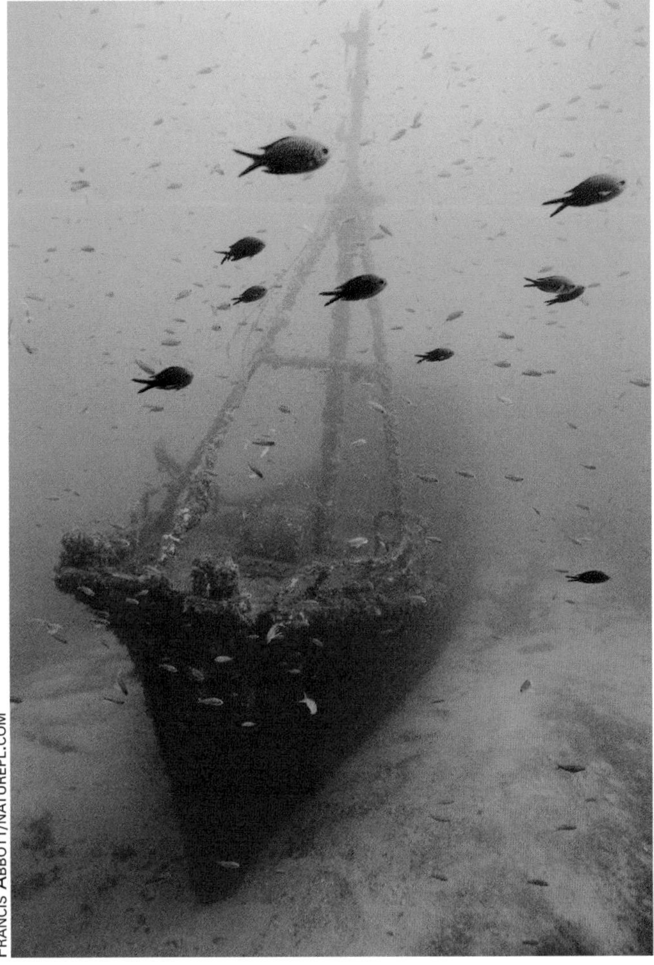

FRANCIS ABBOTT/NATUREPL.COM

## How to collect the data

First, a basemap of the land and sea area around the MPA should be prepared. Second, all ancestral and historical sites/features/monuments on the land and sea should be identified on the map. Third, historical profile information should be collected. This involves addressing the following questions:

- ❑ What is the historical importance of the site?
- ❑ What local folklore is associated with the site?
- ❑ What is the condition of the site?
- ❑ What is the level of restoration of the site?
- ❑ What is the level of access to the site?
- ❑ What is the level and availability of interpretive materials?

Information on these sites/features/monuments can come from many sources. Secondary data on the history of the area is available in libraries. Interviews should be conducted with local government officials, national museums, community historians, and national or university archaeologists. Interviews should also be conducted with key local informants, such as elders and traditional leaders, to identify these sites/features/monuments. Local fishers may need to be interviewed to locate sites/features/monuments at sea. It should be noted that many traditional sites in the community, such as burial grounds, will need to be identified.

In addition, photographs should be taken from all angles and sufficiently close to show details of wear and tear. A scale can be used to rank the condition of the site/feature/monument. A scale of 1 to 10 can be used where 1 is very poor/deteriorating condition and little knowledge of the site/feature/monument and 10 represents excellent condition and high knowledge about site/feature/monument.

A survey of the site/feature/monument should be conducted at least every five years unless a major event, such as a natural event (hurricane, flooding), change in access, or change in cultural attitude, has occurred.

## How to analyse and interpret results

Prepare a narrative text describing the sites/features/monuments. It should include location on the map, detailed photographs, and copies of significant secondary source publications/documents (e.g. brochures, historic documents).

## Strengths and limitations

A limitation to this indicator is that access to the site may be difficult. Another challenge is identifying all the important sites/features/monuments. This may require understanding the local culture and talking to knowledgeable local residents about these areas. This indicator may have limited application in many places, but be useful in other places, such as a World Heritage Site, where culture is a major factor.

### Outputs

- Narrative text describing the site/feature/monument.
- Basemap with locations of cultural resources and historic sites.
- Photographic documentation.

It will be important to work with an archaeologist and a historian as much as possible to make sure that all sites are identified. Older members of the community should be identified and interviewed as they may have knowledge of such site/features/monuments.

## Useful references and Internet links

McClanahan, T.R., Glaesel, H., Rubens, J. and Kiambe, R. (1997). "The effects of traditional fisheries management on fisheries yields and the coral reef ecosystems of Southern Kenya". *Environmental Conservation* 24(2): 105–120.

Mascia, M. (2002). "The social dimensions of marine reserve design and performance". Draft manuscript submitted for inclusion in the book by J. Sobel (ed.) *Marine Reserves: their science, design and use.* Center for Marine Conservation. Washington, DC, USA.

Fiske, S.J. (1992). "Sociocultural aspects of establishing marine protected areas". *Ocean and Coastal Management* 18: 25–46.

Kelleher, G. and Recchia, C. (1998). "Lessons from marine protected areas around the world". *Parks* 8(2): 1–4.

Roberts, C.M. (2000). "Selecting marine reserve locations: optimality versus opportunism". *Bulletin of Marine Science* 66(3): 581–592.

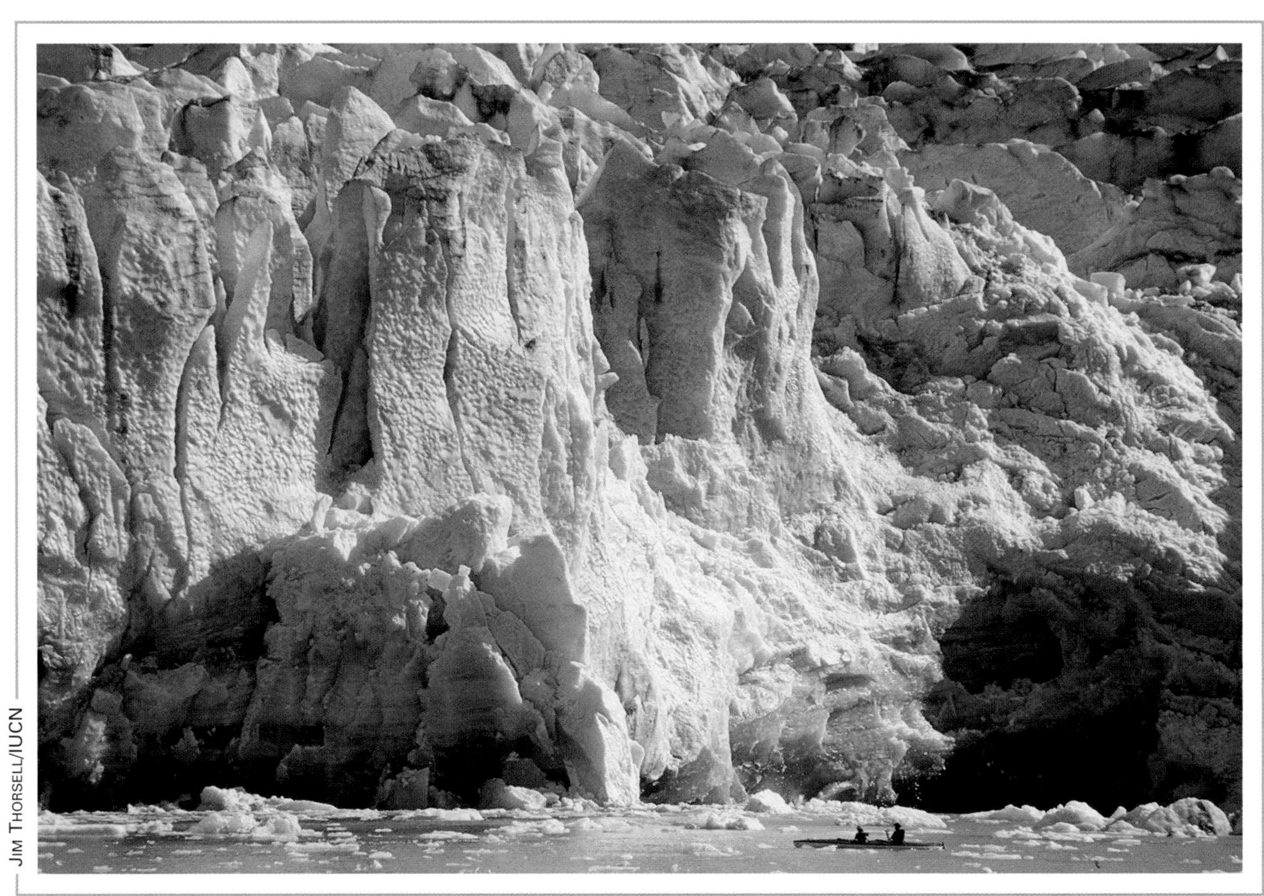

JIM THORSELL/IUCN

*The St Elias World Heritage site is a transboundary MPA with sections in Yukon (Canada) and Alaska (USA). Transboundary sites can present challenges to governance.*

# The governance indicators

## *Introduction*

By definition, an MPA is a governance tool. It limits, forbids or otherwise controls use patterns and human activity through a structure of rights and rules. Resource governance is the way in which users and their intentions are managed through a set of rights, rules, and shared social norms and strategies. This includes enforcement mechanisms, such as policing measures and punishments, as well as incentives to direct human behaviour and use. Resource governance can include: a) formal and informal forms of resource ownership; b) use rights and the laws that support these rights; and c) the rules, rights and regulations that dictate how resources can and cannot be used. Resource governance is defined by formal organizations and law, traditional bodies, and/or accepted practice. Resource governance takes place at four related levels: local, provincial/state, national, and international. In this guidebook, we are particularly interested in the governance of the MPA and marine resources.

MPAs may be managed under a variety of arrangements. The three most general arrangements are centralized, community-based (or locally managed), and collaborative (or co-management). The differences between the three primarily relate to the degree of stakeholder participation in the process and the location of management authority and responsibility. Centralized management tends to involve limited participation by stakeholders and management authority and responsibility are located in a central agency or office of government. Community-based or locally managed tends to involve a great deal of local stakeholder participation and management authority and responsibility are located at the community or local organization level. Co-management is a sharing of authority and responsibility between government and local stakeholders, which may take many forms, and involves a high degree of stakeholder participation. This guidebook has been written to allow for MPA evaluation under any of these three arrangements.

This guidebook has a large focus on participation in MPA management, as experience has shown that the imposition of an MPA located near human settlements and without broad stakeholder participation, consensus and acceptability can lead to failure. Where local stakeholders have a high degree of participation in MPA planning and management, there is greater sense of ownership by them of the MPA and this leads to stronger and longer-term conservation success. This is not to say that all MPAs have or should have a high degree of stakeholder participation, as many centrally managed MPAs have also been successful. It is crucial, therefore, to understand the social, economic, political and governance context of the MPA. For this reason, the indicators should be analysed together so that linkages between the socio-economic and governance indictors can be identified and examined. Among the 16 governance indicators, several measure stakeholder participation, particularly G9, G11, G12 and G13. Each indicator measures a distinct aspect of stakeholder participation in MPA management.

Most of the governance indicators attempt to measure the goals and objectives, and in many cases are true 'process' and 'input' indicators (e.g. G14 and G15 for enforcement and G10 and G11 for training). A few are 'output' indicators (e.g. G3 for management plan and G12 for stakeholder satisfaction), but none are 'outcome' indicators.

A marine protected area by definition imposes new property rights arrangements at the site by restricting or forbidding access. As such, no individual indicator on property rights has been developed. The MPA may cause shifts in property rights in areas surrounding it but it was felt that the methods to identify changes in property rights were too complex and beyond the scope of the MPA manager. If necessary, a side research study could be conducted on property rights in the area of the MPA.

Transaction costs, the costs of gaining information about the resource and what users are doing with it, the costs of collective decision-making, and the costs of operation, are integral to the MPA management arrangement. Transaction costs of MPA management can increase or decrease over time depending upon the administrative arrangements, the functions of management, and the efficiency with which the MPA is managed. While an important indicator of management effectiveness, again, no indicator has been developed due to the complexity of measuring transaction costs. However, as a proxy, shifts and trends in the MPA budget can be analysed through information from indicator G6 – Availability and allocation of MPA administrative resources.

# Figure 4 Governance goals, objectives, indicators

## *Governance goals (n=5) and objectives (n=21) commonly associated with MPA use*

**GOAL 1** **Effective management structures and strategies maintained**

1A *Management planning implemented and process effective*
1B *Rules for resource use and access clearly defined and socially acceptable*
1C *Decision-making and management bodies present, effective, and accountable*
1D *Human and financial resources sufficient and used efficiently and effectively*
1E *Local and/or informal governance system recognised and strategically incorporated into management planning*
1F *Periodic monitoring, evaluation, and effective adaptation of management plan ensured*

**GOAL 2** **Effective legal structures and strategies for management maintained**

2A *Existence of adequate legislation ensured*
2B *Compatibility between legal (formal) and local (informal) arrangements maximized or ensured*
2C *National and/or local legislation effectively incorporates rights and obligations set out in international legal instruments*
2D *Compatibility between international, national, state, and local rights and obligations maximized or ensured*
2E *Enforceability of arrangements ensured*

**GOAL 3** **Effective stakeholder participation and representation ensured**

3A *Representativeness, equity, and efficacy of collaborative management systems ensured*
3B *Resource user capacity effectively built to participate in co-management*
3C *Community organizing and participation strengthened and enhanced*

**GOAL 4** **Management plan compliance by resource users enhanced**

4A *Surveillance and monitoring of coastal areas improved*
4B *Willingness and acceptance of people increased to behave in ways that allow for sustainable management*
4C *Local ability and capacity built to use resources sustainably*
4D *User participation in surveillance, monitoring, and enforcement increased*
4E *Application of law and regulations adequately maintained or improved*
4F *Access to and transparency and simplicity of management plan ensured and compliance fostered*

**GOAL 5** **Resource use conflicts managed and reduced**

5A *User conflicts managed and/or reduced: 1) within and between user groups, and/or 2) between user groups and the local community or between the community and people outside it*

## *How the governance indicators relate to the common goals and objectives*

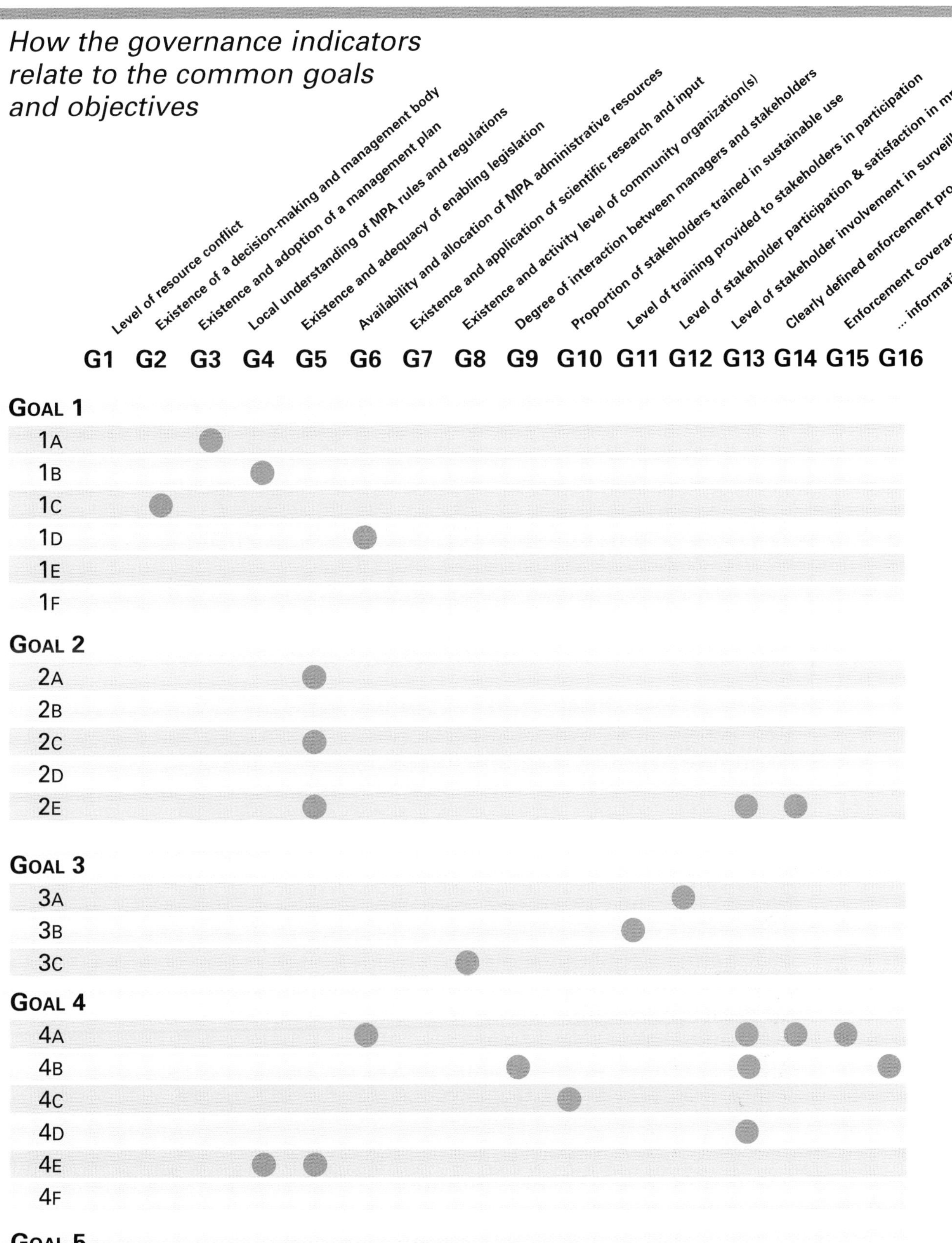

| | G1 Level of resource conflict | G2 Existence of a decision-making and management body | G3 Existence and adoption of a management plan | G4 Local understanding of MPA rules and regulations | G5 Existence and adequacy of enabling legislation | G6 Availability and allocation of MPA administrative resources | G7 Existence and application of scientific research and input | G8 Existence and activity level of community organization(s) | G9 Degree of interaction between managers and stakeholders | G10 Proportion of stakeholders trained in sustainable use | G11 Level of training provided to stakeholders in participation | G12 Level of stakeholder participation & satisfaction in mngt .... | G13 Level of stakeholder involvement in surveillance, .... | G14 Clearly defined enforcement procedures | G15 Enforcement coverage | G16 ... information dissemination ... |
|---|---|---|---|---|---|---|---|---|---|---|---|---|---|---|---|---|
| **Goal 1** | | | | | | | | | | | | | | | | |
| 1A | | | ● | | | | | | | | | | | | | |
| 1B | | | | ● | | | | | | | | | | | | |
| 1C | | ● | | | | | | | | | | | | | | |
| 1D | | | | | | ● | | | | | | | | | | |
| 1E | | | | | | | | | | | | | | | | |
| 1F | | | | | | | | | | | | | | | | |
| **Goal 2** | | | | | | | | | | | | | | | | |
| 2A | | | | | ● | | | | | | | | | | | |
| 2B | | | | | | | | | | | | | | | | |
| 2C | | | | | ● | | | | | | | | | | | |
| 2D | | | | | | | | | | | | | | | | |
| 2E | | | | | ● | | | | | | | | ● | ● | | |
| **Goal 3** | | | | | | | | | | | | | | | | |
| 3A | | | | | | | | | | | | ● | | | | |
| 3B | | | | | | | | | | | ● | | | | | |
| 3C | | | | | | | | ● | | | | | | | | |
| **Goal 4** | | | | | | | | | | | | | | | | |
| 4A | | | | | | ● | | | | | | | ● | ● | ● | |
| 4B | | | | | | | | | ● | | | | ● | | | ● |
| 4C | | | | | | | | | | ● | | | | | | |
| 4D | | | | | | | | | | | | | ● | | | |
| 4E | | | | ● | ● | | | | | | | | | | | |
| 4F | | | | | | | | | | | | | | | | |
| **Goal 5** | | | | | | | | | | | | | | | | |
| 5A | ● | | | | | | | | | | | | | | | |

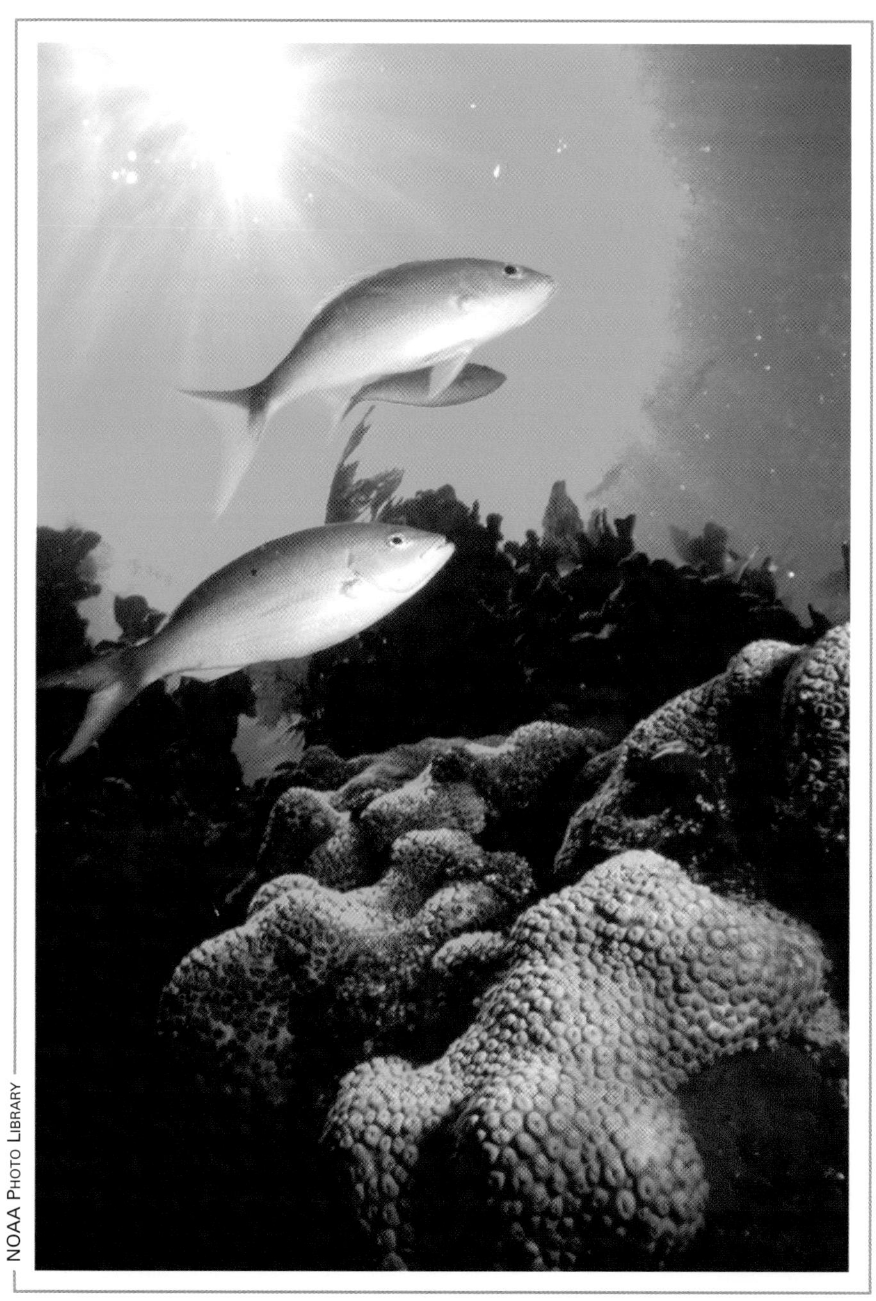

NOAA Photo Library

*The colourful life of a coral reef epitomises the diversity and attraction of marine protected areas.*

Relates to goals and objectives

GOAL 5

5A

## *What is 'level of resource conflict'?*

Level of resource conflict associated with the MPA is a measure of the nature and characteristics of conflict associated with planning, management and decision-making for the MPA.

Therefore, the term 'conflict' can be taken to mean just about any situation in which there is a clash of interests or ideas. In the context of an MPA, it usually means that there is a group or groups whose interests are in opposition to those of the MPA. It is often very difficult to precisely define the limits of MPA conflicts because they are frequently rooted within a particular cultural, economic, political and social context. It is important to realize that, to the extent that conflict represents the productive interaction of competing interests and values, it is a useful and ever-present function in a dynamic society.

## *Why measure it?*

The use of this indicator will enable a determination of whether or not conflicts associated with the MPA are increasing or decreasing over time, as well as the nature and characteristics of the conflicts. This information can be used to determine how well MPA management is responding to conflicts associated with the MPA.

MPA staff face the challenge of trying to respond to conflicts so that unproductive consequences can be avoided while human well-being and the natural environment are protected. Conflicts involving MPAs are inevitable as, for example, an area is taken out of production, new rights and rules for use of marine resources are implemented, and individual and group interests in the marine resources are affected.

## *How to collect the data*

A conflict assessment is the systematic collection of information on conflicts associated with the MPA. Conflict is dynamic, with new conflicts arising and conflicts being managed or resolved continuously over time. As such, the conflict assessment process must be dynamic, where key informants are interviewed periodically to identify the existence and characteristics of conflicts associated with the MPA.

The first step in the conflict assessment process is to identify if a conflict exists. This may not be as easy as it seems at first, as conflicts may be very public or may be kept relatively quiet within a small group of stakeholders. Also, conflicts may surface through traditional systems of conflict management, such as fishers going to a senior fisher or village official, which reflect the unique social and cultural context of the area, or through more formal and public fora, such as town meetings, for conflict management. It will be necessary to identify key informants in the area of the MPA, such as elected community officials, senior fishers, respected village leaders, community organizations, and the MPA manager, to interview and ask an initial question about whether or not an MPA-related conflict exists. It will be important to separate conflicts associated with the MPA from other types of conflicts which may exist in the community.

The second step is to identify the issues at stake in the conflict and the stakeholders concerned. Class dimensions often put those who manage the resource against those who own nothing but whose livelihoods depend on the resource. Conflicts can take place at a variety of levels, from within the household to local, regional, societal, and global scales. Conflict may cut across these levels through multiple points of contact. The intensity of conflict may range from confusion and frustration among community members over poorly communicated management policies to violent clashes between groups and government.

To determine the characteristics of conflict, the following questions are asked in the conflict assessment:

- ❑ Who are the stakeholders concerned?
- ❑ What are the issues at stake in the conflict?
- ❑ What is the time period of the conflict (when did it begin, is it ongoing, date of resolution)?
- ❑ Who are the leaders/spokespeople?
- ❑ What is the intensity of conflict?
- ❑ What is the scale of conflict?
- ❑ Is the conflict ongoing?
- ❑ Has the conflict been managed or resolved?
- ❑ How and by whom was the conflict managed or resolved?

### *Requirements*

- Key informants.
- One interviewer.
- Paper/pencil.
- Records of conflict management meetings (if available).

❑ What agreement was reached?

If needed or desired, more detailed information about the conflict could be obtained by interviewing the leaders/spokespeople and, if appropriate, the individual or institution that negotiated/mediated/arbitrated the conflict.

Some MPAs or communities have established a conflict management forum or committee to address conflict. This forum or committee will hold with regular meetings or meetings on demand. They usually keep records or minutes of the meetings which could provide information to answer the questions above. Contact should be made with the MPA manager or community leader to determine if such a conflict management forum or committee exists.

## How to analyse and interpret results

The conflict assessment will provide detailed information on each conflict associated with the MPA. Write this information in a brief narrative report. Prepare as a matrix a table of conflicts associated with the MPA, showing each conflict: issue, stakeholders, time period, intensity, scale, ongoing/managed/resolved, and how managed/resolved.

## Strengths and limitations

When analysed over time, this information can provide the MPA management with information on the range of issues, the stakeholders, and the approaches to management/resolution. It can also provide information on whether or not conflicts associated with the MPA are increasing or decreasing.

### Outputs

- A narrative which reports the nature and characteristics of conflicts associated with the MPA.

It may be difficult to separate conflicts associated with the MPA from other types of conflicts which may exist in the community.

## Useful references and Internet links


Borrini-Feyerabend, G. (ed.) (1997). *Beyond Fences: Seeking Social Sustainability in Conservation*, 2 vols. IUCN, Gland, Switzerland.

Buckles, D. (ed.) (1999). *Cultivating Peace: Conflict and Collaboration in natural Resource Management*. International Development Research Centre, Ottawa, Canada and World Bank Institute, Washington, DC, USA.

Lewis, C. (1996). *Managing conflicts in protected areas*. IUCN, Gland, Switzerland and Cambridge, UK.


**▼ *A workshop with Imraguen fishermen in Banc d'Arguin National Park, Mauritania. Limiting resource use conflicts between stakeholder groups is of major concern to MPA managers due to the negative impacts that such conflicts can have on effective management efforts.***

Relates to goals and objectives

GOAL 1

1C

## *What is 'existence of a decision-making and management body'?*

Existence of an MPA decision-making and management body is a measure of the recognition of an institution that governs how the MPA is managed and used and a transparent process for management planning, establishing rules and regulations, and enforcing the rules and regulations.

## *Why measure it?*

The existence of a legally mandated MPA decision-making and management body will lead to more professional management of the MPA, that management will be more effective and accountable, and it will become easier to have a successful MPA. It should be noted that in some cases the management body (the group implementing the MPA management plan) may or may not be the same as the decision-making body and that this has implications for the likely effectiveness of the MPA (more effective when both bodies are the same).

## *How to collect the data*

First, the institution(s) that have some level of decision-making and management authority and responsibility for the MPA (international, national, regional, municipal) must be identified. This information is typically available in the MPA management plan. A typical MPA management plan will have an organization chart showing the lines of authority and responsibility for MPA management. If such an organization chart does not exist, one can be developed through interviews with MPA staff. The distance (both geographical and administrative) of the decision-making and management body from the MPA needs to be gauged as do the hierarchies of bodies and the relationships between them.

Second, the existence of each body should be confirmed by identifying a person responsible for its operation. The person should be interviewed to collect any documents explaining the function and powers of the body.

Third, the legal and formal or informal authority of the body should be recorded from papers of incorporation, plans or other documents.

Fourth, the frequency of meetings to determine the functionality of the decision-making body must be identified. The next stage is to observe the operation of the body at a meeting to witness the decision-making process and the roles and responsibilities of the different actors.

Optionally, key informants (resource users) in the community can be interviewed to identify and describe how and whom they believe has decision-making and management authority and responsibility for the MPA.

### *Requirements*

- MPA management plan.
- Papers of incorporation of an MPA decision-making and management body.
- Location of MPA decision-making and management body.
- Identification of MPA staff.
- Dates and location of meeting of body.
- One interviewer.
- Paper/pencil.

## *How to analyse and interpret results*

Develop an organization chart for the MPA listing all bodies with decision-making and management authority and responsibility. Prepare a narrative description of the authority and responsibility of each body as well as the mandate (formal/non-formal, legal) of the body.

## *Strengths and limitations*

While this indicator will list and describe each decision-making and management body associated with the MPA, it will not evaluate the effectiveness, credibility and accountability of the body. A more complete survey will need to be undertaken to collect this information.

### *Outputs*

- List and narrative description of the different MPA decision-making and management bodies, including a description of their mandate to make management decisions.

▲ ***Decision-making processes within the effective management of an MPA typically involve multiple parties and the input of stakeholders.***

## *Useful references and Internet links*

Berkes, F., Mahon, R., McConney, P., Pollnac, R. and Pomeroy, R. (2001). *Managing small-scale fisheries: alternative directions and methods.* International Development Research Centre, Ottawa, Canada. Available at www.idrc.ca/booktique

**Box G1**

### EXAMPLE FROM THE FIELD

At the Far Eastern Marine Reserve in Russia, in addition to the MPA administration (directors and his deputies), there is a Scientific Board including not only the scientists of the Institute for Marine Biology but also a group of reputable specialists from other scientific institutions. As a consultative body, a Council for Sustainable Development was established with participation of important local stakeholders, enforcement and environmental agencies.

## What is 'existence and adoption of a management plan'?

Existence and adoption of a management plan is a measure of the existence of a document which states the overall MPA goals and objectives to be achieved, the institutional structure of the management system, and a portfolio of management measures and whether the plan is enforceable.

## Why measure it?

The MPA management plan sets out the strategic directions for the MPA management programme. The effective management of the MPA is based on the achievement of goals and objectives through the use of appropriate management measures. The existence and adoption of a management plan means that there are strategic directions and actions for implementation of the MPA. An enforceable plan means that there is legislative support for the plan to be implemented.

## How to collect the data

First, the MPA manager should be sought out and asked to provide a copy of the MPA management plan and legislation in support of the MPA at the national and/or local level.

Second, a checklist should be prepared with the information listed on the right.

## How to analyse and interpret results

Using that list, prepare a narrative text describing the existence of the plan, its adoption, content/characteristics, and the enforceability (legal basis) of the plan.

The existence and adoption of an MPA management plan informs us that the MPA is guided by goals and objectives to achieve certain outcomes (for example, conservation, protection, research), that there is a basic strategy to achieve these goals and objectives, and that the overall plan has a legal mandate for implementation.

In some cases a formal management plan may not exist but there may be informal or goals and objectives that have been agreed upon by those associated with the MPA. This should be noted and described in narrative text.

### Requirements

- Name and address of the MPA manager or management body.
- Established time and place to meet with MPA manager.
- Management plan.
- Legislation in support of the MPA.
- Paper/pencil.

### Checklist of items on the existence and adoption of a management plan

1) The actual existence of the plan in printed form.
2) The management plan is reviewed to determine the:
   a) date of the current plan
   b) date of any updates
   c) adoption of plan
   d) date of adoption
   e) signatories of the plan adoption
   f) level of plan adoption (international, national, regional, municipal, local).
3) Completeness of the plan. Does it have sections addressing the following components:
   a) goals
   b) objectives
   c) management strategy
      i) advisory committees
      ii) interagency agreements
      iii) boundaries
      iv) zoning plan
      v) regulations
      vi) social, cultural, and resource studies plan
      vii) resource management plan
      viii) interpretive plan
   d) administration
      i) staffing
      ii) training
      iii) facilities and equipment
      iv) budget and business plans, finance sources
   e) surveillance and enforcement
   f) monitoring and evaluation of plan effectiveness.
4. Enforceability of the plan. Is there legislation at the national or local level to provide a legal basis for the plan and to be able to enforce the management measures?

**Relates to goals and objectives**

GOAL 1

1A

G3

### *Strengths and limitations*

While an MPA management plan may exist, that does not guarantee that it is good or that it is being followed or that its legitimacy is recognised by the local resource users. A bad or inappropriate plan that is implemented may be worse than no plan.

Note that in the case of a private MPA, the plan may not fit the level of completeness described above as this list is oriented toward recognition of the MPA by a national or locally defined authority. In the case of a private MPA, it is better to define completeness via the rights and rules given by the private MPA.

### *Outputs*

- Narrative text about the management plan.

### *Useful references and Internet links*

Hockings, M., Stolton, S., Dudley, N. and Parrish, J. (2002). *The Enhancing Our Heritage Toolkit, Book 2.* pp. 24-30.
Available at www.enhancingheritage.net

Salm, R.V., Clark, J.R. and Siirila, E. (2000). *Marine and Coastal Protected Areas: A Guide for Planners and Managers (3rd Edition).* Chapter 2. "Site Planning and Management". IUCN. Washington, DC, USA.

Box G2

## Example from the Field

At the Sian Ka'an Coastal Biosphere Reserve in Mexico, the current Management Plan (MP) is the result of a review done in 1996. The main purpose of this MP is to be a tool for the integration, follow-up and evaluation of the protection and sustainable use of natural resources' strategies. It is an instrument for planning and regulation, in which the activities, actions and basic regulations for the management and administration of the protected area are established. The MP contains a description of the physical, socio-cultural and natural resources' use characteristics of the MPA. After listing the major objectives of the Reserve, the MP states the strategy for the short-, medium- and long-terms, based on the following goals:

a) Guarantee the physical integrity of the area.

b) Promote reasonable use of the natural resources.

c) Foster social participation and representation in management and in the sustainable use of natural resources.

d) Spearhead research and education towards a better understanding and utilization of the natural resources of the areas and the environmental benefits that this would provide for the region.

e) Secure financing for the permanent and continuous operation of the area.

According to these goals, the MP is divided into five components with sub-components. Each of them has specific objectives and implementation strategies. The MP includes a section describing the basic legal framework and an annex in which are established Use Regulations and Zoning inside the limits of the PA – Core Zones, Buffer Zones and Critical Zones.

The MP is not a legal instrument because it has not been published in the Official Diary of the Federation. At the time of its creation, the Sian Ka'an Biosphere Reserve management was not aware of the importance of its official publication, and it was just published as a public policy to guide the management of the protected area. Despite the fact that the MP has no legal recognition, local resource users recognise, respect and observe its regulations. This means that they recognise the authority of the management body and, in some cases, collaborate with them in order to succeed in common management goals and objectives.

## What is 'local understanding of MPA rules and regulations'?

Local understanding of MPA rules and regulations by the community is a measure of whether stakeholders are aware of the rules and regulations and whether they understand the intent of the rules and regulations.

## Why measure it?

MPA rules and regulations define specifically what acts are required, permitted and forbidden by stakeholders and government agencies within the MPA. When stakeholders are aware of and have an understanding of the rules and regulations for management of the MPA, there is a greater chance for success of the MPA. Stakeholders may violate rules and regulations if they are not well understood or if they don't make sense to the stakeholders.

## How to collect the data

A sample of the stakeholders should be interviewed using a questionnaire to determine their awareness of and understanding of the MPA rules and regulations. In the case of a comprehensive plan for a large area, there may be a large number of rules and regulations with slight temporal or spatial variations. These variations should be considered when the questionnaire is designed.

### Requirements

- Copy of the MPA management plan.
- Copy of MPA rules and regulations.
- Questionnaire to be used to interview key informants.
- Data on rules and regulations violations.
- One interviewer.
- Paper/pencil.

**Relates to goals and objectives**

GOAL 1
1B

GOAL 4
4F

First, the relevant MPA rules and regulations and the institution(s) which declare each rule and regulation should be listed and briefly described.

Next, a series of questions should be asked to determine awareness and understanding. Any discussion that illustrates the thoughts of the respondents should be recorded. Questions to be asked include:

1. Are you aware of the existence of any rules and regulations for the management of the MPA? Yes____ No____
2. What are these rules and regulations? Please list as many as you know.
3. Which institution(s) have declared and developed each rule and regulation.

*For effective management to occur, the rules of the MPA must be accessible and clearly articulated and understood by all potential users.*

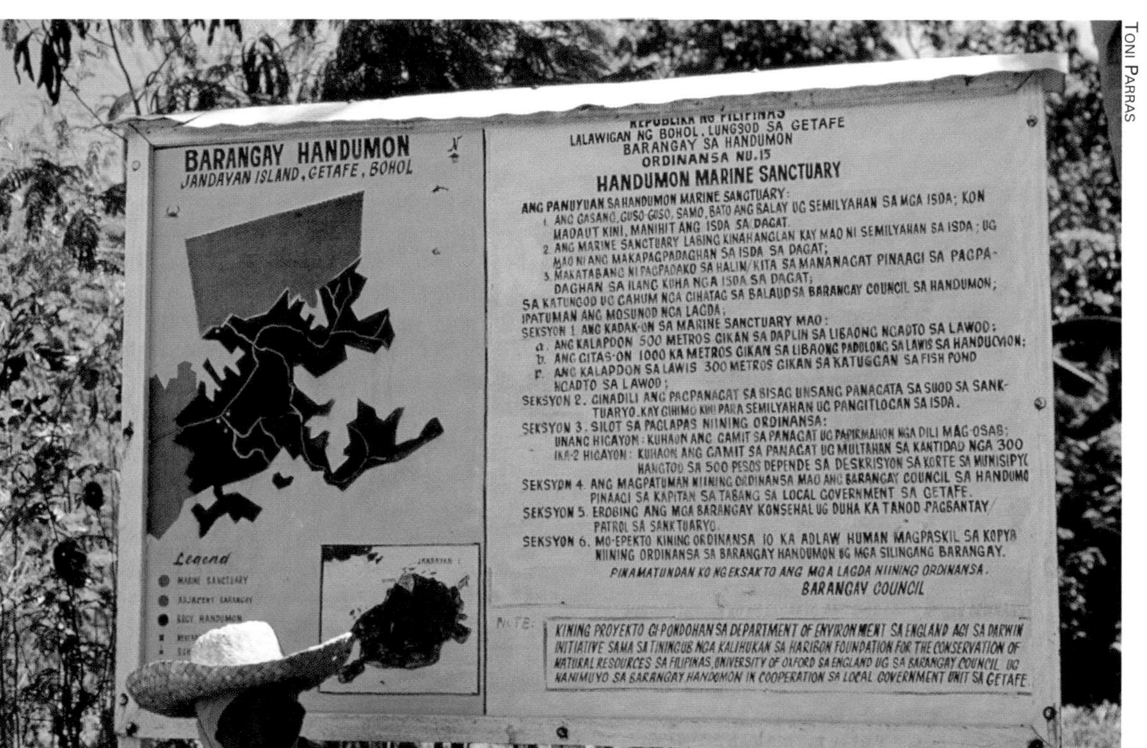


TONI PARRAS

4. For each informant, ask whether they regard the rules and regulations as being simple and clear:

   1 = rules and regulations are very complex and difficult to understand
   2 = rules are complex and difficult to understand
   3 = rules are of average complexity
   4 = rules are simple and easy to understand
   5 = rules are very simple and easy to understand

5. Do you feel that the rules and regulations design process was participatory?
6. Do you feel 'ownership' of the rules and regulations?
7. Do you feel that the rules and regulations are credible and appropriate?
8. Do you feel that the rules and regulations are socially acceptable to the stakeholders?
9. Which rules and regulations do you feel are acceptable or unacceptable?
10. Why?
11. Why were the rules and regulations designed the way they are?

These data can be collected at the start of the project and every year thereafter.

### How to analyse and interpret results

Tabulate the responses from all the questionnaires. Use simple statistical analysis (median, mode, standard deviation) on the data. Analyse the percentage of the MPA rules and regulations that individuals can name to measure understanding and awareness. Present in narrative format with tables. Record any interesting discussion about awareness and understanding of the rules and regulations that may be useful for supporting or revising the rules and regulations. The responses should be cross-checked against the rules and regulations in the plan.

#### Outputs

- Narrative description of the rules and regulations as understood by the stakeholders.

**Box G3**

## Example from the Field

Based on the number of signs, public outreach efforts, and media attention, it would be assumed that the public understand the rules and regulations for the Bird Island Marine Sanctuary of the Commonwealth of the Northern Mariana Islands. In contrast, recent events and violations suggest that the public does not have a clear understanding of the area's rules and regulations. A survey of users of the site, particularly non-English speaking users such as Japanese SCUBA divers, may shed additional light on community understanding (including dive operations). Since the known violations have all related to the taking of protected species, it could be reasoned that a more thorough understanding of the rules and regulations would enhance management effectiveness there.

### Strengths and limitations

A limitation of the indicator is that it does not measure level of participation of stakeholders in creating the rules and regulations and their perception of fairness of the rules and regulations. It should be noted that in some cases people who do not like the rules could pretend that they do not know about them or can provide other misleading responses making it difficult to obtain correct information.

### Useful references and Internet links


ICLARM/IFM (1996). *Analysis of fisheries co-management arrangements: a research framework. Fisheries Co-management Research Project WP 1.* ICLARM/.World Fish Center, Penang, Malaysia. www.co-management.org

Ostrom, E. (1990). *Governing the Commons: The Evolution of Institutions for Collective Action.* Cambridge University Press, Cambridge, UK.

## What is 'existence and adequacy of enabling legislation'?

Existence and adequacy of legislation to enable the MPA to accomplish its goals and objectives is a measure of formal legislation in place to provide the MPA with a sound legal foundation so that the goals and objectives of the MPA can be recognised, explained, respected, accomplished and enforced. In some areas, traditional law may also serve as a foundation for the MPA.

## Why measure it?

The establishment of an MPA more often than not requires the drafting and adoption of appropriate supportive legislation and in some cases the recognition of traditional laws. The purpose of this indicator is to ensure that the MPA management plan is supported by adequate legislation in order for its successful implementation.

## How to collect the data

The form and extent of legislation for MPAs will vary widely from country to country. The legal arrangements for MPAs may depend upon many elements, including the form of government, available finances, public administrative structures, level of government centralization/decentralization, lines of jurisdiction and decision-making, existence and legitimacy of traditional laws, and commonly accepted practice.

The first step is to collect all legal documents of pertinent laws relative to the MPA. These may exist at international, national, state/provincial and local levels. The laws may be identified in the MPA management plan. This will require talking to the MPA manager and reviewing the management plan and supporting documents. It may also require contacting various government agencies and offices to collect the documents. It should be noted that in addition to legislation related to the MPA, the achievement of the MPA goals and objectives may require that activities be undertaken outside of the MPA, such as water quality and integrated coastal zone management. Legislation related to these other associated activities should also be identified.

Second, a legal analysis should be conducted. It will involve three steps. First, to determine the existence of legislation to support the MPA. Second, to compare the MPA management plan (the goals and objectives, rules and regulations, management authority and responsibility, enforcement powers) with the existing legislation to determine compatibility. Third, to assess the appropriateness of the legislation.

To undertake the legal analysis, the questions to be asked include:

- ❑ What laws (formal and traditional) are in place (e.g. fisheries, tourism, water quality, integrated coastal zone management, forest)?
- ❑ What institutions are in place to implement the laws (governmental, non-governmental, traditional)?
- ❑ How current are the laws (when were they approved (year)?
- ❑ What is the form and extent of the legislation?
- ❑ Is the law at the appropriate level (local, state/province, national) to support the MPA?
- ❑ Does the legislation support the goals and objectives of the MPA?
- ❑ Are there sufficient laws to support the MPA?
- ❑ Are the laws appropriate to support the MPA?
- ❑ Are there legal provisions for sufficient penalties for violators of MPA rules and regulations?

### Requirements

- Legal documents of pertinent laws at different levels (international, national, state/provincial, local) for MPAs.
- MPA management plan.
- One interviewer.
- Paper/pencil.

## How to analyse and interpret results

Prepare a narrative report that focuses on answering the following three questions:

- ❑ Does a law exist to support the MPA? Yes/No
- ❑ Is it compatible with the MPA management plan? A little/mostly/very much
- ❑ Is it supportive of the MPA management activities and interventions? A little/mostly/ very much

**Relates to goals and objectives**

GOAL 2

2A 2C 2E

GOAL 4

4E

G5

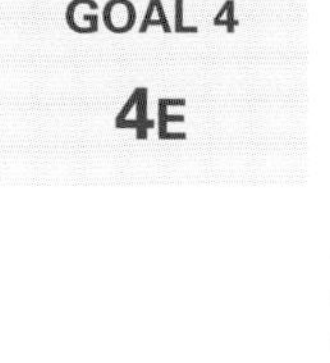

**Outputs**

- A report on the existence of laws for MPAs, the compatibility of the laws for MPAs, and recommendations (needs and types of legislation) for the MPA.

## Strengths and limitations

A subjective analysis can be biased by the opinion of the person doing the legal diagnosis. There is a need for a good understanding of the management goals and objectives and the legislative process.

G5

## Useful references and Internet links

Salm, R.V., Clark, J.R. and Siirila, E. (2000). *Marine and Coastal Protected Areas: A Guide for Planners and Managers (3rd Edition)*. Chapter 6. Institutional and Legal Framework. IUCN, Washington, DC, USA.

**Box G4**

### Example from the Field

The Bird Island Marine Sanctuary in the Commonwealth of the Northern Mariana Islands was established as a Class 1 No-Take Zone marine protected area in 2001 under Public Law 12-46. The Act explicitly states a number of permitted and prohibited activities relative to taking, hunting, fishing, harassment or destruction of fish, game, wildlife, plants, corals, reef, habitat, and marine life. Vessels are not allowed to enter the sanctuary and access to Bird Island proper, which contains a seabird colony, is prohibited. The Act promotes stewardship by having the site serve as a "living laboratory for educating students and teachers". The Act foresees criminal penalties (fines and imprisonment) for violations. Accordingly, any violation within the marine sanctuary related to a taking incurs a tripling effect in its prosecution (the Act, DFW protected area regulations, DFW takings regulations). However, the Act does not apply to the vast majority of the adjacent land areas (SUMBA, WCA) in the Bird Island Sanctuary.

Toni Parras

## What is 'availability and allocation of MPA administrative resources'?

Availability and allocation of MPA administrative resources is a measure of the capacity of the management team to administer and complete its various MPA activities through time, based on the degree of access to and level of enabling human, equipment and financial resources.

## Why measure it?

The operation of the MPA involves several activities such as surveillance and enforcement, staff training, budget and finances, monitoring and evaluation, environmental education, planning, and advisory committees. For example, surveillance and monitoring are critical parts of any MPA enforcement programme. The rationale is that some degree of illegal activities (for example, fishing, boating, pollution) can be anticipated as a response to a regulatory framework established for the MPA. An understanding of the availability of adequate budget, human resources and equipment to undertake surveillance and monitoring is important because these are the people and associated equipment which will be needed to undertake this activity. It is assumed that the more budget, human resources and equipment allocated to this activity, the greater will be the level of compliance with rules and regulations.

### Requirements

- Copy of the MPA management plan.
- List of MPA activities.
- List of MPA staff and associates involved with each activity.
- List of equipment available for each activity.
- List of minimum requirements or of ideal requirements to effectively undertake each activity from the management plan.
- MPA budget.
- One interviewer.
- Paper/pencil.

## How to collect the data

First, the various activities undertaken for MPA management such as the monitoring, control, surveillance and enforcement programme; environmental education; monitoring and evaluation; advisory committees; staff training etc., need to be identified.

The management plan should include sections which describe the activities. This will provide information on programme design for comparison with the current structure. The management plan should also provide information on the minimum requirements for or of ideal requirements for each activity. This can be used for a comparison with the existing resources available for these activities. If no such information exists, an interview should be conducted with the MPA manager to determine a list of activities undertaken by the MPA and minimum requirements or ideal requirements for the activities.

Next, an interview is conducted with the MPA manager and the designated staff member for each activity to obtain information about the current availability and allocation of resources to the activity. The focus of the questions asked should be:

- ❑ The access to and adequacy of resources to undertake the task.
- ❑ The appropriateness of operation of the activity to undertake the task.

It should be noted that some MPAs leave certain activities to other organizations, for example, surveillance may be conducted by national agencies, such as the Coast Guard or marine patrol. In this situation, the questions will need to be adapted to reflect this arrangement.

Questions to be asked of the MPA manager and the designated staff member include:

- ❑ What is the number of MPA staff assigned to the programme?
- ❑ What is the number of non-MPA staff (community members, fishers) assigned to the programme?
- ❑ What kind/level of training is provided to management and staff?
- ❑ What is the experience (type and years) and education (level) of each staff member?
- ❑ What is the budget for the activity?
- ❑ What equipment is available (boat, guard house, radio, GPS, binoculars, uniform, dive equipment, computers) for the activity?

**Relates to goals and objectives**

GOAL 1
**1D**

GOAL 4
**4A**

- ❑ What is the age and condition of equipment used?
- ❑ What is the level of equipment maintenance?
- ❑ What record keeping procedures are used?

Staff may be asked about the management arrangements (plans, senior staff, information feedback) to undertake the task.

## How to analyse and interpret results

Prepare a narrative report on the current availability and allocation of resources (budget, staff, equipment) for each activity. The report should address allocated resources as compared to needed resources and make recommendations for resources to undertake the programme. Record in the report feedback from the staff on the appropriateness of the resources, equipment and management to undertake the task.

The number of staff will give a measure of the importance given to this programme and is useful when planning the activity. The staff should have an adequate supply of resources and good quality equipment to undertake their assignment.

### Outputs

- Report on the current staffing and equipment for undertaking the surveillance and monitoring programme.

## Strengths and limitations

It may be difficult to separate out allocations for each individual activity.

## Useful references and Internet links


Salm, R.V., Clark, J.R. and Siirila, E. (2000). *Marine and Coastal Protected Areas: A Guide for Planners and Managers (3rd Edition).* IUCN, Washington, DC, USA.


***Adequate financial support and investment mechanisms are required for most long-term MPA operations, such as for the purchase of boats. Creative solutions, which may at first seem trivial, such as visitor souvenirs and gift shops, can sometimes end up providing significant sources of sustained revenues to assist management efforts.***

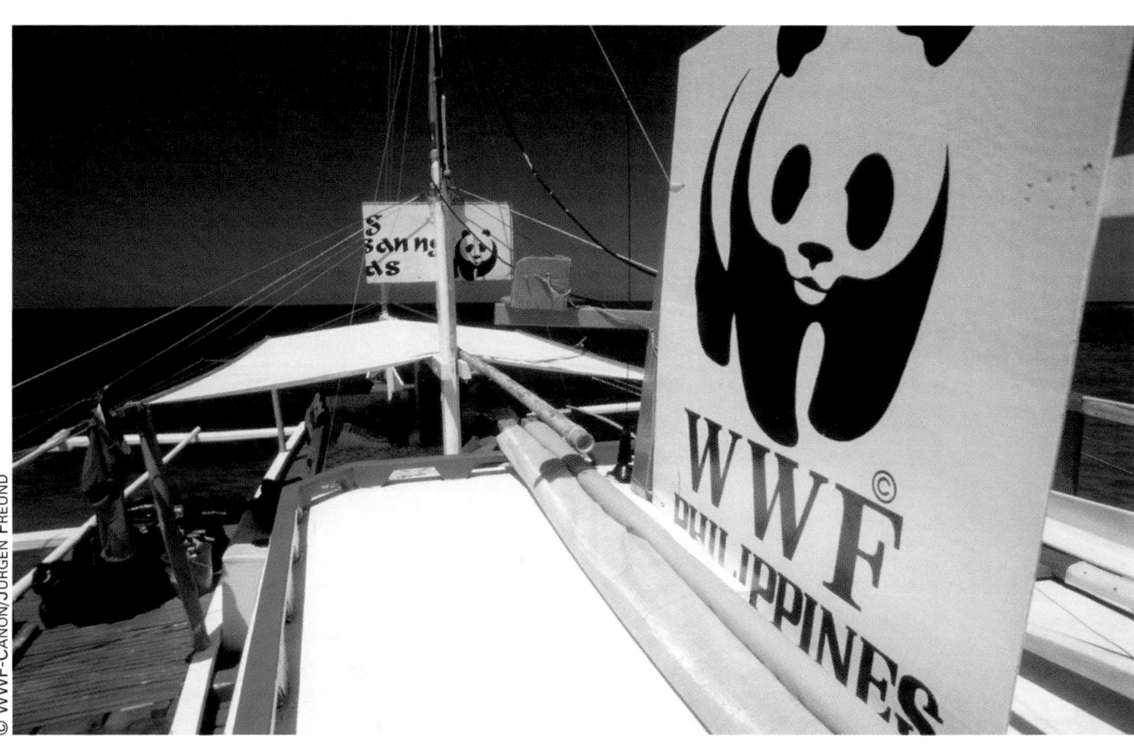

Box G5

## EXAMPLE FROM THE FIELD

In Biosphere Reserve Banco Chinchorro in Mexico, the following administrative resources were identified in the MPA:

### *Equipment*

- 1 Vessel of 33.3 feet. Belongs to the National Institute of Fisheries but is used in this MPA under an agreement between CONANP and INP.
- 3 Boats, 27 feet with two out-board motors (75 hp Yamaha) each.
- 4 Pick-ups of different characteristics (capacity).
- 1 Ultra light airplane – staff are still being trained to use it.
- 1 Office in Cancun City.
- 1 Biological Field Station (includes laboratory and facilities for communication, kitchen, library, and compressor for filling up SCUBA tanks). The building of this station has cost nearly US$500,000.

The equipment is rather new or has been renewed (GPS, radio, dive equipment, etc.). The equipment was ranked of medium to excellent condition.

### *Personnel*

There is a lack of personnel, especially for the monitoring of recreational service permits and fishing activities. Due to the lack of personnel, there are problems for controlling poaching and fishing management regulations. Four navy personnel are expected to be enrolled in surveillance activities. A comparison of the desired number of personnel mentioned in the management programme, shows that the programme ideally needs 22 people. The actual number is six (28% of the desired number of personnel in the MPA).

Only two staff personnel are assigned for surveillance activities. Personnel in charge of surveillance are trained. They belong to the Navy or SAGARPA (Ministry of Agriculture & Fisheries).

### *Staff experience*

| *Staff* | *Experience* |
|---|---|
| *Director* | 4.5 years |
| *Sub-director* | 4 years |
| *Secretary* | 8 months |
| *Technician* | 2 years |
| *Administrator* | 6 months |

### *Financing*

The total budget (including personnel wages) is 2.7 million Mexican pesos (approximately US$270,000) a year. This amount is only 37% of the amount requested by the management programme for the year 2003. Given that it is so short, it is easy to understood why there is a significant need for personnel in this MPA.

With support from the Summit Foundation, a fund (Fondo Patrimonial) has been established. One hundred and fifty thousand US dollars (US$150,000) have been incorporated and interest (approximately US$12,500) will now be used for different purposes and needs of the BRBCH. Fortunately this fund allows the hiring of personnel thereby solving one of the main constraints for this MPA.

Within the next nine years, this fund is expected to increase to a total amount of US$1,550,000.

Interest will provide approximately US$100,000 a year. This will double the annual available budget and have the advantage of allowing the hiring of new staff.

# Existence and application of scientific research and input

Relates to goals and objectives

GOAL 1

1A 1F

## What is 'existence and application of scientific research and input'?

Existence and application of scientific research and input is a measure of how research activities and scientific knowledge generated by studies at the MPA feed back into improved management; that is, the ability of the management team to access and use science to inform their management actions.

## Why measure it?

The management of complex ecosystems, such as those in which MPAs are established, is often subject to complex natural processes and significant human pressures. Because of this, effective management cannot occur in the absence of science. The natural sciences are vital to understanding ecosystem functions and change, and the social sciences are essential to identifying the sources of human-induced problems, and testing and applying appropriate solutions. Successful MPAs typically involve collaboration between managers and scientists at all stages, including: 1) in the formulation of MPA management policy and activity planning; 2) in the design and implementation of an MPA; and 3) in conducting, interpreting, and applying evaluative research to future management action.

To be useful, scientific information relevant to the marine environment and MPA practice must not merely exist. It must also be applicable to and actively used by MPA staff for management purposes. Scientists play a critical role in this process by bridging the information needs of managers, politicians, and the public as 'neutral' brokers.

### Common types of scientific study that can be useful to MPAs

There are many scientific techniques and procedures that can be useful to managers in their MPA planning and adaptation. In particular, these include:

- Environmental impact assessments.
- Marine and costal resource surveys.
- Focal species life history and reproductive biology studies.
- Ecological and population modelling.
- Economic assessment and valuation.
- Hazard and risk assessment.
- Legal and institutional analysis.
- Social and cultural profiling.
- Testing and review of management and control measures.
- Public education engagement.

## How to collect the data

There are four phases of data management for this indicator.

First, the presence and extent of scientific study will need to be determined. To do this, evaluators must determine whether scientific research is being conducted in or around the MPA. This can be done by checking relevant records and minutes of planning and management meetings for discussion and/or coordinating with scientific study. Subsequently, it will be necessary to interview those management staff who are in charge of supporting and/or coordinating with scientific researchers to learn about the needs, presence, and extent of current and completed scientific study, and how such work links to the management of the MPA. In some cases, there may be a designated group of scientists among MPA staff with whom to talk. There may also be a scientific advisory board with which to consult as to the type of research that is being undertaken or has been completed.

Second, scientific staff, coordinators, and/or external researchers need to be interviewed to obtain more detailed information and characterize the research designated activities. Questions to ask (for each study) include:

- ❑ What scientific study is being done? Have other similar studies already been completed?

### Requirements

- Access to MPA staff.
- Access to scientific study and results.
- Minutes of management meetings and processes.
- One interviewer.
- Paper/pencil.

CONSERVATION SOCIETY OF POHNPEI

**At Lenger Island MPA, scientific research is presented back to the local community who are involved in the management of the protected area.**

- ❑ Why is the study being done (what is the objective)? What is being measured and what methods are being used?
- ❑ Who is conducting the study? Who is the lead (principal investigator)? Which staff and external researchers are involved?
- ❑ Where is the study being done?
- ❑ What is the process of the study and what stage is it at?
- ❑ What is the study timeline? If the study has been completed, over what period was it completed?

In the case where a scientific study has already been completed, the following questions should be asked to determine to what degree the management team has had access to the results:

- ❑ What outputs were generated from the completed study?
- ❑ Who on the staff received the study findings? Which staff have ready access to scientific information?
- ❑ When were the results of the study formally presented to stakeholders, and precisely to whom? What forms of communication and results dissemination were used?
- ❑ Where are the outputs of the study currently located? How accessible are the results by the management team and public?

### Outputs

- Report on the current staffing and equipment for undertaking the surveillance and monitoring programme.

Finally, the extent to which scientific research and completed studies are being actively applied within the management and planning context of the MPA needs to be determined. To do this, MPA staff must be interviewed to determine if and how outputs from scientific studies and consultation are being applied. In this interview, the staff should be asked if there is a formal or informal mechanism for scientific information to enter into the MPA decision-making and/or management and planning processes. If so, has the scientific information actually been found to be useful after it has been brought into this process (i.e. is it applied and used?). Next, staff should be asked how scientific studies are identified and prioritized. It needs to be determined if there is an adequate budget for scientific studies and/or if outside funding is being sought. Lastly, the extent to which scientific results and expertise are being used for adaptive management and future decision-making should be determined.

## How to analyse and interpret results

The focus of the indicator is to determine whether or not scientific studies lead to changes in or outputs from management of the MPA.

Prepare a short narrative report which provides information on the characteristics of scientific research at the MPA and the uses of the outputs for management. Within this report, characterize the degree of presence, development, access, and application for each study or research need identified. Highlight any future research needs.

## Strengths and limitations

It may be difficult to identify the link between scientific research conducted at the MPA and its application in MPA management. All MPA staff and board of directors will need to be interviewed to identify if and how scientific studies are used.

## *Useful references and Internet links*


GESAMP(IMO/FAO/UNESCO-IOC/WMO/WHO/IAEA/UN/UNEP Joint Group of Experts on the Scientific Aspects of Marine Environmental Protection) (1996). "The contributions of science to coastal zone management". *Rep. Stud. GESAMP, (61)*. FAO, Rome.

Salm, R.V., Clark, J.R. and Siirila, E. (2000). *Marine and Coastal Protected Areas: A Guide for Planners and Managers (3rd Edition)*. IUCN Washington, DC, USA.




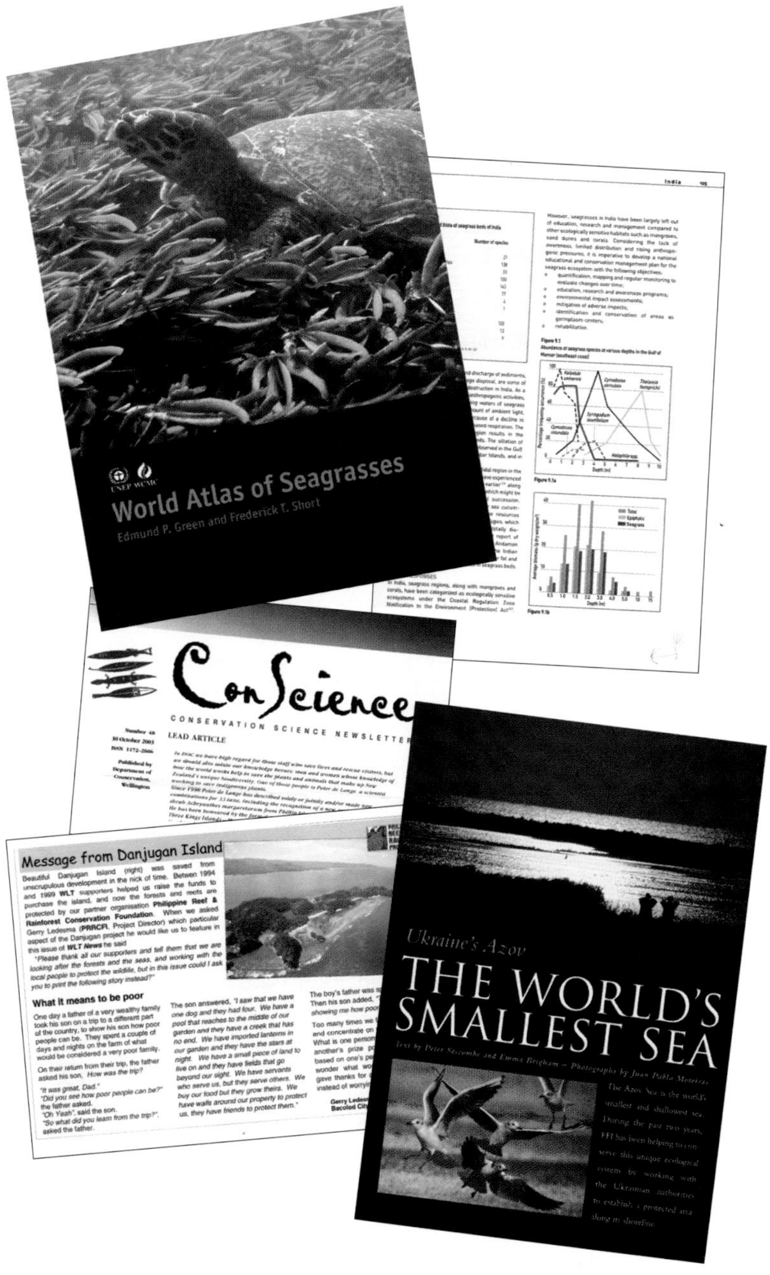


▲ ***Research and scientific knowledge generated by studies at the MPA can inform management.***

# Existence and activity level of community organization(s)

Relates to goals and objectives

GOAL 3

3C

Difficulty Rating 3 1–5



## What is 'existence and activity level of community organization(s)'?

Existence and activity level of community organization(s) measures whether a community organization exists, whether it is effectively organized to participate in management, and how active it is in MPA decision-making and management.

## Why measure it?

A community organization is a vital means for representing resource users and stakeholders and influencing the direction of MPA decision-making and management. The indicator provides useful information on community organizations associated with the MPA management. An understanding of these organizations can assist the MPA management in improving participation and representation of stakeholders in management and decision-making.

### Requirements

- List of community organizations.
- List of community organizations associated with the MPA.
- Minutes of previous meetings.
- One interviewer.
- Paper/pencil.

## How to collect the data

First, a list of community organization(s) associated with the MPA will need to be developed. A list may be available from the MPA management office. If no such list exists, the community organization(s) will need to be identified. This can be done through interviews of key informants. Key informants include, but are not limited to, government officials, community leaders, members of other organizations in the community, senior fishers, religious organizations, and non-governmental organizations.

Second, for each organization, the following information must be collected:

- ❑ Objectives/mission statement
- ❑ Functions/responsibilities
- ❑ Period of existence
- ❑ Number of different management bodies in which the organization participates

In addition, the following additional information may be collected on the organization:

- ❑ Spatial jurisdiction
- ❑ Legal authority
- ❑ Formal/informal administration

▼ ***Some individuals will choose to participate in the MPA management process through their membership within an organized community organization or other formal stakeholder group.***

JOHN PARKS/WWF

- ❑ Organizational chart
- ❑ Leadership structure
- ❑ Membership (number, requirements)
- ❑ Staff (number, expertise)
- ❑ Budget
- ❑ Meeting schedule
- ❑ Rules of operation
- ❑ Relationships/affiliations with other organizations

Third, to determine how active the organization is, it is useful to attend at least one of their meetings, and more if possible. At these meetings, the following should be observed:

- ❑ How many people attend the meeting
- ❑ The issues and level of discussion
- ❑ The procedures followed
- ❑ The decisions and consensus reached
- ❑ Whether rules of order are observed at the meeting
- ❑ Whether everyone is given a chance to talk
- ❑ Whether the meeting environment is organized or disorganized

Fourth, the leaders and members should be asked if they are satisfied with their ability to participate in management.

### *Outputs*

- A narrative report which identifies community organizations involved in MPA management and describes their characteristics and level of active involvement in MPA management.

If possible, an informal discussion should be held with the leaders and members to determine their feelings about the organization, how well it operates, and how well it represents their interests.

Finally, at meetings of the MPA, how many of the community organizations regularly participate in the meetings, and how active they are in terms of providing input and discussion at the meeting, should be observed. It is possible to evaluate how active the community organization is in the MPA management meetings by observing if:

- ❑ The input from the community organization represents the interests of one or two people or the whole group.
- ❑ Only representatives of the community organization attend the meetings or do members as well.
- ❑ The input provided by the community organization is relevant to the current issues being discussed.

NOAA Photo Library

Box G6

## EXAMPLE FROM THE FIELD

At Tubbataha Reef National Marine Park in the Philippines, four community organizations in Cagayancillo were assisted through training and facilitation of organizational processes. Of the four organizations involved in seaweed production, law enforcement, communication and training and livelihood fund management, only two remain active:

- Cagayancillo Core of Trainers (CATCO) – organized to provide training and communication services to the various activities of the Coastal Resource Management Team; and
- Cagayancillo Livelihood Committee – organized to manage a livelihood fund for sustainable resource management.

The seaweeds group and the law enforcement group had problems with leadership and are being assisted in possible re-structuring.

At the Banco Chinchorro Biosphere Reserve in Mexico, the MPA community is defined as a group of cooperatives and free fishers who conduct fishing activities within the limits of the reserve, living in palafitos, or huts (but with residences elsewhere). Other regular users who might increase in number are those people providing recreational services.

Community organizations involved in MPA management are the same as those on the Technical Advisory Committee (TAC) for the Biosphere Reserve.

### *How to analyse and interpret results*

Prepare a narrative report which lists the organization(s), mandate, organizational structure, period of existence, membership, resources, and relationship/affiliation with other organizations. The report should identify, for example, those organizations opposed and supportive of the MPA. The report should also include observations on the level of activity of each organization.

This indicator will provide information on the number of community organizations associated with the MPA, the objectives and structure of each organization, and how active the group is in terms of providing input to the MPA and in terms of other activities of its members. The results need to be interpreted against the background of the level of community or collective action in the country or location, which may be low in some cases.

### *Strengths and limitations*

It should be noted that not all MPAs have community organizations, for example, a high seas MPA or an isolated coral atoll with no one living on it or an MPA which is managed by a centralized authority. In these cases, this indicator is not relevant.

### *Useful references and Internet links*

Salm, R.V., Clark, J.R. and Siirila, E. (2000). *Marine and Coastal Protected Areas: A Guide for Planners and Managers (3rd Edition).* IUCN, Washington, DC, USA.

GOVERNANCE INDICATOR 9

# Degree of interaction between managers and stakeholders

**Relates to goals and objectives**

GOAL 4

4C

## What is 'degree of interaction between managers and stakeholders'?

Degree of interaction between managers and stakeholders is a measure of the number of regularly scheduled meetings between MPA managers and staff and stakeholders to discuss compliance with MPA management plans.

## Why measure it?

Discussion, input and participation from stakeholders with MPA staff about compliance with MPA management plans will lead to greater compliance and increased success of the MPA.

## How to collect the data

First, MPA staff are requested to provide records of regularly scheduled meetings between themselves and stakeholders. The number and location of meetings each year are recorded. Information is requested on the formal agenda, minutes of the meetings, topics of discussion, conflicts and solutions, and those in attendance. A review of these records will provide information on problems and issues related to compliance and enforcement.

### Requirements

- Records of regular meetings.
- Interview MPA staff and stakeholders.
- Meeting schedule between MPA staff and stakeholders.
- One interviewer.
- Paper/pencil.

Second, an interview should be conducted with stakeholders involved in these meetings to determine topics of discussion, conflicts and solutions. The stakeholders should be asked:

- ❑ Are there regularly scheduled meetings with MPA staff to discuss issues of compliance?
- ❑ Do you feel that your views are listened to and acted upon by MPA staff?
- ❑ Are these meetings open and transparent to all stakeholders?
- ❑ Are you allowed to participate in the making of rules and regulations?



▼ ***Regular interaction between MPA staff and relevant stakeholders allows for timely information exchange and an adequate period to gain community buy-in on management activities and changes.***

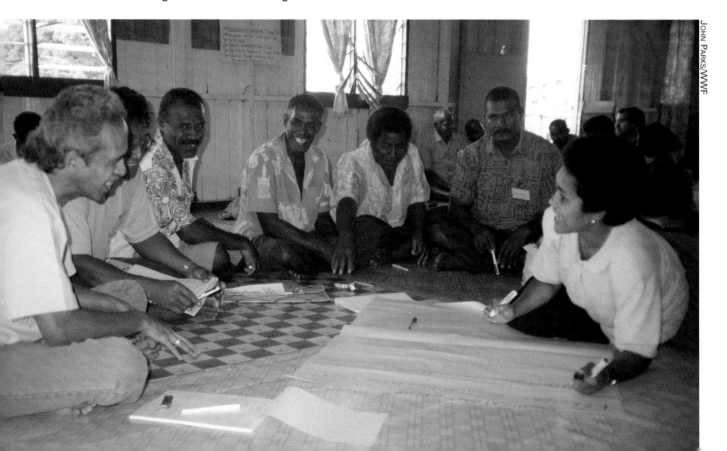

JOHN PARKS/WWF

Box G7

## Example from the Field

At the Banco Chinchorro Biosphere Reserve in Mexico, MPA managers and stakeholders were interviewed to assess the number of regularly scheduled meetings. We were told that there have been meetings of the Technical Advisory Committee to deal with tourist activities. Key stakeholders have always been present at these meetings. During these meetings different aspects of recreational activities have been discussed and clarified. Also, some decisions taken by the MPA staff have been taken during these meetings. For example, it was decided that none of the companies could bring tourists to Banco Chinchorro until agreements were established between the new tourist cooperatives agreed by fishers (co-ops) and experienced recreational operators.

Informal meetings have taken place to present different issues concerning tourism in BRBCH and fishing activities. There are no regular meetings to discuss problems or to clarify any aspect concerning this MPA. Records of meetings including agenda, minutes of the meetings, topics of discussion, conflicts and solutions and those in attendance were not provided.

According to managers of this MPA, not all the problems are solved. But if these are solved not all those attending fully agree. It was explained that this is very normal for any MPA. Not everyone has to agree to all aspects. Nevertheless consensus has to be reached as a part of the agreement procedure.

### Outputs

- A narrative report describing meetings between MPA staff and stakeholders.

### How to analyse and interpret results

Prepare a narrative report on the interviews and data collected. The report should include information from interviews with both MPA staff and stakeholders. It is important to identify any differences in information provided on number of meetings, discussion, and conflict and solutions. Tabulate the various topics discussed, resolutions made, and documentation of any consensus arrived at.

### Strengths and limitations

This indicator will provide useful information for improving surveillance, monitoring and enforcement arrangements through stakeholder input and participation; overall improvement in compliance behaviour of stakeholders; and reduction in enforcement costs.

### Useful references and Internet links

Salm, R.V., Clark, J.R. and Siirila, E. (2000). *Marine and Coastal Protected Areas: A Guide for Planners and Managers (3rd Edition).* IUCN, Washington, DC, USA.

**Relates to goals and objectives**

GOAL 4

4c

Difficulty Rating 3 (1–5)

## What is 'proportion of stakeholders trained in sustainable use'?

Proportion of stakeholders trained in sustainable resource use is a measure of the number of stakeholders who participated in training and with knowledge about sustainable resource use.

## Why measure it?

This indicator can be used to determine whether capacity-building efforts are resulting in a shift towards sustainable use of resources by stakeholders inside and outside the MPA. The linkage between training and education for stakeholders on sustainable resource use will be shown, as well as overall improvements in resource management and resource use. Information can be disaggregated for different types of training and broader awareness building. The results can be used to improve the effectiveness of the programme.

## How to collect the data

First, the total number of stakeholders and stakeholder organizations associated with the MPA must be identified.

Second, records should be sought from MPA staff on the number of stakeholders trained and the number and types of workshops and training and information dissemination on sustainable resource use provided to the stakeholders during planning and implementation of the MPA.

Third, MPA management staff must be interviewed and asked questions about capacity-building activities including:

- How large is the capacity-building budget compared to overall MPA budget?
- Were capacity-building activities provided during planning for the MPA to train stakeholders to use resources sustainably?
- Were capacity-building activities undertaken during implementation and are they still provided?
- Who makes decisions about the number and types of capacity-building activities – MPA management, resource users, both?

Next, the stakeholders must be interviewed to determine their level of knowledge and satisfaction with capacity-building activities and the quality of the activities. A short questionnaire should be used which would include questions such as:

- Were workshops and training courses provided to you during the planning of the MPA?
- How many and what types were provided?
- Were workshops and training courses provided to you during implementation of the MPA?
- How many and what types were provided?
- Were you satisfied with the workshops and training courses? Yes/No
- Why?
- Were you involved in the selection of the workshops and training courses?
- Have the workshops and training courses affected the way that you use resources? Yes/No
- Why?

JOHN PARKS

*Training of interested public in the sustainable use of their marine environment can not only change user behaviour and increase stakeholder knowledge of their natural surroundings, but can also help to secure community support for MPA efforts.*

### Requirements

- Records of training and workshops.
- Interviews with participants of training and workshops.
- Interviews with volunteer groups and community organizations.
- One interviewer.
- Paper/pencil.

- ❑ What types of information dissemination were most useful?
- ❑ What is sustainable resource use?
- ❑ Do you follow sustainable resource use practices?
- ❑ Have your resource use practices (for example, fishing, anchoring of boat) changed as a result of the training and workshops?
- ❑ If yes, in what way?
- ❑ If no, why not?

Many workshops and training sessions conduct evaluations after the activity to assess the effectiveness of the programme. These evaluations may be available from the trainers and can be reviewed to determine participant's level of satisfaction and knowledge gained from the activity and the skill level of the people trained.

### *How to analyse and interpret results*

Prepare a narrative report which provides an evaluation of the number of stakeholders who participated in training and with knowledge about sustainable resource use.

### *Strengths and limitations*

Those involved in capacity-building activities may not be able to answer all the questions.

### *Useful references and Internet links*

Salm, R.V., Clark, J.R. and Siirila, E. (2000). *Marine and Coastal Protected Areas: A Guide for Planners and Managers (3rd Edition).* IUCN, Washington, DC, USA.

**Box G8**

**Example from the Field**

At the Far East Marine Reserve in Russia, more than 25 persons have been trained or have had consultations with the MPA staff on the development of tourism business or aquaculture in the areas surrounding the reserve. This is clearly insufficient and a special programme is needed to facilitate the process.

### *Outputs*

- A narrative report.

John Parks/WWF

# Level of training provided to stakeholders in participation

Relates to goals and objectives

GOAL 3

3B

Difficulty Rating 2 1–5

## What is 'level of training provided to stakeholders in participation'?

Level of training provided to stakeholders in participation in MPA management is a measure of the amount and effectiveness of capacity-building efforts to empower stakeholders with knowledge, skills and attitudes to participate in MPA management.

## Why measure it?

To participate effectively in MPA management, stakeholders need to be empowered to have greater awareness about the needs for and functions of the MPA. Stakeholders need to be equipped with knowledge, skills and attitudes to prepare them to carry out new tasks and meet future challenges. Capacity-building must address not only technical and managerial dimensions but also attitudes and behavioural patterns. Capacity-building may be carried out by the MPA staff or by another organization, such as a non-governmental organization (NGO).

## How to collect the data

The first step is to identify if there is an operational training programme in place for stakeholders. This information should be available from MPA staff. Any documents describing the training programme should be obtained.

***Providing training opportunities for people to become involved in the management process not only secures public support for MPA efforts, but can also help to cut operating costs through the use of volunteers, such as this women's group in Fiji.***

JOHN PARKS/WWF

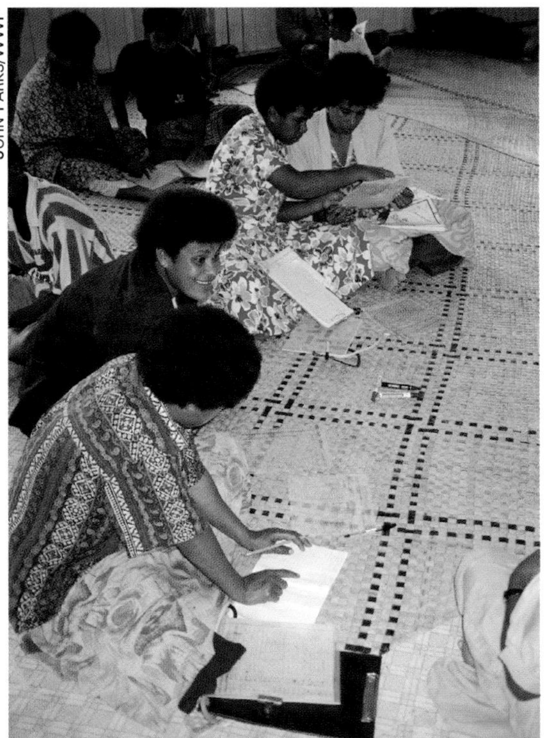

### Requirements

- Copy of MPA capacity-building programme.
- Access to workshop and training records provided to stakeholders by the MPA management or other organization.
- Interview of stakeholders to assess satisfaction with capacity-building activities.
- Interview of MPA management or other organization to assess level of attendance of stakeholders at capacity-building activities.
- One interviewer.
- Paper/pencil.

Second, the number and types of workshops and training courses provided to the stakeholders during planning and implementation of the MPA should be recorded. This information should be available from the MPA management office or other organization providing capacity-building.

Third, MPA management staff or other organizations providing training should be interviewed and asked questions about capacity-building activities including:

- ❑ How large is the capacity-building budget compared to overall MPA budget?
- ❑ Were capacity-building activities provided during planning for the MPA to empower stakeholders to actively participate in the planning?
- ❑ Were capacity-building activities undertaken during implementation and are they still provided?
- ❑ Who makes decisions about the number and types of capacity-building activities – MPA management, stakeholders, both?
- ❑ What are the skills of the staff who provide the training and do they need more training?
- ❑ Is the capacity-building budget sufficient to carry out the activities?
- ❑ Are there evaluation reports from the workshops/training or follow-up reports?

Fourth, the stakeholders should be interviewed to determine their satisfaction with capacity-building activities and the quality of the activities. A short questionnaire can be prepared; it should include questions such as:

- ❑ Were workshops and training courses provided to you during the planning of the MPA?
- ❑ How many and what types were provided?
- ❑ Were workshops and training courses provided to you during implementation of the MPA?
- ❑ How many and what types were provided?
- ❑ Were you satisfied with the workshops and training courses? Yes/No
- ❑ Why?
- ❑ Were you involved in the selection of the workshops and training courses?
- ❑ Have the workshops and training courses affected your support for the MPA? Yes/No
- ❑ Why?
- ❑ Were you satisfied with the training skills of the staff?
- ❑ Make a list of all the workshops and training and ask participants to rate their satisfaction on a scale of 1 (poor) to 5 (excellent).

Many workshops and training courses conduct evaluations after the activity to assess the effectiveness of the programme. These evaluations may be available from the trainers and can be reviewed to determine participants' level of satisfaction and knowledge gained from the activity.

As a follow-up activity to the workshops and training courses, the stakeholders' participation in MPA management meetings over time can be observed to determine if there are changes in participation and input as a result of the capacity-building activities. It will be possible through careful listening and observation, and using records of meetings, to determine if new ideas presented through the capacity-building activities are being presented and discussed at the meetings. For this data collection method to work, observations would be required prior to capacity-building activities and afterward.

Informal discussions with individual stakeholders can help to assess their level of satisfaction with their ability to participate in MPA management as a result of their participation in the workshops and training. Notes can be taken to record comments.

### *How to analyse and interpret results*

From the results prepare a narrative report which provides an evaluation of the achievements of capacity-building activities and makes recommendations for future activities.

**Box G9**

## Example from the Field

At the Sian Ka'an Biosphere Reserve in Mexico, one of the components of the annual operative programme is environmental education, which means that the federal government gives a particular amount of money for this component. Nevertheless, due to limited resources, it has been very hard to design and implement a formal education and training programme.

In response to these limitations, Sian Ka'an Biosphere Reserve has worked hard to find mechanisms, such as agreements with NGOs and exchanges empowered by financing organizations, to secure effective capacity-building actions in local communities. But even with limited funds, Sian Ka'an Biosphere Reserve has been offering environmental education to community members for many years. Since 1999, a training course for tour guides has been offered by the reserve to all those interested in conducting tourism activities in the community. This course provides the attendees with special accreditation to develop their activities. Other courses include using GPS, fly fishing, English, bird identification and co-management. Besides these courses, staff of the reserve have also worked with women and children in the community, offering courses in composting, and environmental education in elementary and secondary schools.

After all these years of work, 55% of community members (N=51) feel that one of the major things that SKBR has done well, as a management authority, is to provide environmental education to improve their quality of life, and to offer training courses that have contributed to the development of alternative and sustainable livelihoods in their community. Some 94% of respondents to the questionnaire have attended at least one of these courses, workshops or exchanges, and most of them – 80% – said that the information obtained from them has been indispensable/very useful in improving their economic activities.

▼ ***Level of utility of training courses offered by SKBR to members of the Punta Allen community***

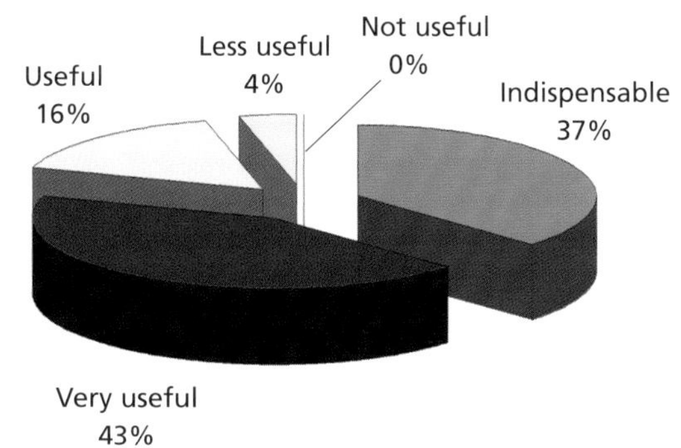

### Outputs

- Narrative report on the achievements of capacity-building activities.

## Strengths and limitations

Empowerment of stakeholders to participate in MPA management is important for its success. Information is provided for further capacity-building activities and evaluating how well past activities have done in terms of knowledge, skills and attitude development.

## Useful references and Internet links

Salm, R.V., Clark, J.R. and Siirila, E. (2000). *Marine and Coastal Protected Areas: A Guide for Planners and Managers (3rd Edition).* IUCN, Washington, DC, USA.

TONI PARRAS

# Level of stakeholder participation and satisfaction in management processes and activities

Relates to goals and objectives

GOAL 3

3A

## What is 'level of stakeholder participation and satisfaction in management process and activities'?

The level of stakeholder participation in the management of the MPA is a measure of the amount of active involvement of people in making MPA management decisions or involvement in management activities and of their satisfaction with their level of participation, including if their views and concerns are being heard and considered by MPA managers.

## Why measure it?

MPA managers have come to realize that the active participation of coastal resource stakeholders in the planning and management of an MPA can improve the success of the MPA. If stakeholders are involved in the MPA, feel that their views and concerns are being heard and considered, and feel ownership of it, they are more likely to support the MPA. If they are not satisfied, then they are more likely not to support the MPA. Stakeholders are important because they can support and sustain an MPA. They can be potential partners or threats in managing the MPA. An objective of many MPAs is to educate stakeholders that the MPA will lead to benefits. Measuring their level of satisfaction with participation in the MPA is therefore important and evidence of this.

## How to collect the data

Stakeholders are individuals, groups, or organizations of people who are interested, involved or affected (positively and negatively) by the MPA. They are motivated to take action on the basis of their interests or values. These stakeholders may or may not actually live within or adjacent to the site, but are people who have an interest in or influence on the MPA.

The process of identifying stakeholders and figuring out their respective importance about decisions in the MPA is called stakeholder analysis. A stakeholder analysis is an approach and procedure for gaining an understanding of a system by means of identifying the key actors or stakeholders in the system, and assessing their respective interests in that system. This method provides insights about the characteristics of individuals and/or groups and their respective relationships to the MPA. It also examines the stakeholders' interests in the MPA and the impact of the activity on the stakeholder. Such an analysis is usually conducted in a participatory way.

The stakeholders are first identified by looking at activities affecting the MPA either directly or indirectly. Primary and secondary stakeholders are identified for each activity. The fisher community or organization is considered a primary stakeholder of coastal resources. Some stakeholders may fall into several categories and should be identified separately. Other stakeholders include government agencies, private/business organizations, non-academic organizations, academic or research institutions, religious/cultural groups and donors.

### Requirements

- Identification of stakeholders.
- Questionnaire to identify stakeholder satisfaction.
- Key informants.
- Identification of formal and informal co-management arrangements in the MPA management plan.
- Identification of actual stakeholder participation in decision-making and management activities (when, how and how much).
- One interviewer/facilitator.
- Paper/pencil.

### Outputs

- Stakeholder analysis matrix.
- Stakeholder participation matrix.
- Table of overall score of the level of satisfaction of stakeholders with participation in MPA management.
- Narrative which reports the results of satisfaction score and which includes comments from the respondents and observations from the interviewer.
- An overall score of the degree of stakeholder participation in MPA management which can be measured over time to assess changes.

The different stakeholder groups may be listed in a table with information on name, activity, members, leaders/representatives, purpose, and degree of activity (very high, average, little). Stakeholder groups can be divided into smaller and smaller sub-groups depending on the particular purpose of stakeholder analysis. Ultimately, every individual is a stakeholder, but that level of detail is rarely required.

An approach to conducting a stakeholder analysis is to:

- Identify the main purpose of activity to be analysed.
- Develop an understanding of the MPA and decision-makers in the MPA.
- Identify and list stakeholders. Write their names on paper circles. Use larger circles for stakeholders with greater influence or power.
- Prepare a stakeholder analysis matrix:

| Proposed action: MPA | Positively affected (+) | Negatively affected (-) |
|---|---|---|
| Directly affected | | |
| Indirectly affected | | |

- Place stakeholder identification circles from point 3 (above) in the appropriate box of the stakeholder analysis matrix.
- Draw lines between the stakeholders to indicate the existence of some form of interaction or relationship.
- Identify stakeholder interests, characteristics and circumstances.
- Write the information from point 7 (above) for each stakeholder group.
- Discuss strategies or courses of action for addressing various stakeholder interests.

Once the stakeholders are identified, their degree of participation can be determined using one of two methods:

a) Observation of their participation in meetings of the MPA to see if the stakeholders and their representatives attend the meetings, express their opinion, and if their opinion is considered. Informal discussions can be held with individual stakeholders to assess their level of satisfaction with participation. Notes can be taken to record comments.

b) A survey is conducted to determine degree of participation. Respondents are asked about their level of participation. For example, respondents are shown a line with 10 marks on it, the first line indicating no participation and the tenth line indicating full and active participation. Respondents are asked to identify on the line their degree of participation in MPA management. The results are summed up by stakeholder group and by the total stakeholders. This method can be used over time to evaluate changes in participation. In addition, useful discussion about their participation in MPA management is recorded.

A survey is conducted to determine the stakeholder's level of satisfaction with participation in MPA management. Respondents are asked about their level of satisfaction with participation. For example, respondents are shown a line with five marks on it. The first line indicates dissatisfaction with the level of participation and the fifth line indicates full satisfaction with the level of participation. Respondents are asked to identify on the line their level of satisfaction with participation in MPA management. This method can be used over time to evaluate changes in level of satisfaction with participation. In addition, useful discussion about participation is recorded.

## How to analyse and interpret results

The stakeholder analysis provides a stakeholder analysis matrix and a participation matrix.

Sum up the results of the survey by stakeholder group and by the total number of stakeholders and present these in a table. An overall score of the level of satisfaction of stakeholders with participation in MPA management can be calculated and measured over time to assess changes. Write a narrative account which reports the results and includes comments from the respondents and observations from the interviewer.

The results will provide a quantitative measure of the degree of stakeholder participation and their level of satisfaction with their participation in MPA management which can be used to monitor and evaluate community involvement and to provide input for making necessary changes in the co-management arrangements. It should be noted that more participation is not necessarily better, so participation needs to be linked to the MPA plan which may specify low levels of participation.

## Strengths and limitations

It is often not easy to identify stakeholders and some may be missed, especially those who are poor, unorganized and powerless. Provides insights

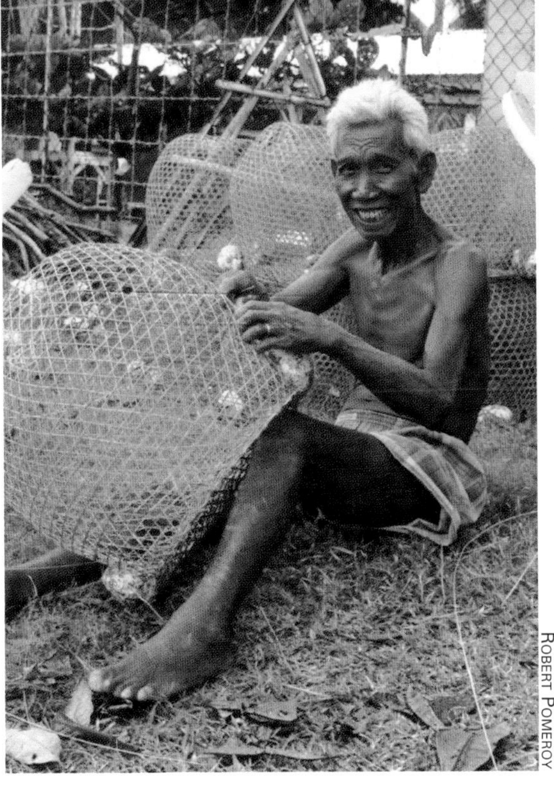


into the dynamics and relationships of different stakeholders with the MPA. It should also be noted that some stakeholders have unrealistic and unreasonable expectations of participation, and hence, low levels of satisfaction. Participation does not necessarily equate to satisfaction.

## Useful references and Internet links

Langill, S. (compiler) (1999). *Stakeholder Analysis. Volume 7. Supplement for Conflict and Collaboration Resource Book.* International Development Research Centre, Ottawa, Canada.

Box G10

## EXAMPLE FROM THE FIELD

At the Sian Ka'an Biosphere Reserve in Mexico, questionnaire responses revealed the following information about the perception of Punta Allen community members, on their level of participation in management decisions:

❑ Does SKBR consult with you about management decisions and strategies?

| *N=51* | % |
|---|---|
| Yes | 60% |
| No | 27% |
| Informs, not consults | 8% |
| Blank space | 5% |

❑ Level of participation:

| *N=51* | % |
|---|---|
| Very active | 2% |
| Active | 30% |
| Some | 34% |
| Few | 28% |
| Blank space | 6% |

At Mafia Island Marine Park in Tanzania, respondents were asked about their degree of satisfaction with their participation in management with the following results:

| | *Percent (N=404)* | |
|---|---|---|
| *Question:* | *1* | *2* |
| Highly involved | 11.6 | 11.6 |
| Moderately involved | 10.6 | 10.9 |
| Less involved | 10.6 | 9.4 |
| Not involved | 60.9 | 63.9 |
| Don't know | 6.2 | 4.2 |

| | *Percent (N=404)* |
|---|---|
| | *3* |
| Very satisfied | 23.0 |
| Moderately satisfied | 24.3 |
| Less satisfied | 6.2 |
| Not satisfied | 34.7 |
| Not satisfied at all | 7.4 |
| Don't know | 4.5 |

*Questions:*
1. *To what extent have you been involved in meetings and discussions with MIMP representatives from preparations to the present?*
2. *To what extent have you been involved in meetings and discussions with village leaders without MIMP?*
3. *Are you satisfied with the way you are involved in the management of MIMP?*

The results show that more than 60% of respondents feel they have not been involved in discussions about the marine park either with MIMP representatives or even with their own village leaders. Despite this, 47% of respondents are very satisfied or moderately satisfied with the level of participation and 42% are not satisfied or not satisfied at all. The results indicate quite a surprisingly high level of both participation and satisfaction considering the large size of the communities; nonetheless they also suggest that continued efforts are needed to improve participation mechanisms both within villages as well as between the villages and MIMP. For this reason a new initiative involving village-based natural resources management planning is being prepared by the MPA management together with district authorities. The results also hint that, not surprisingly, there is a certain proportion of the community that doesn't actually want to participate in management.

# Level of stakeholder involvement in surveillance, monitoring and enforcement

Relates to goals and objectives

GOAL 2

2E

GOAL 4

4A 4B 4D

## What is 'level of stakeholder involvement in surveillance, monitoring and enforcement'?

Level of stakeholder involvement in surveillance, monitoring and enforcement is a measure of the number of stakeholders who have participated in patrolling or other surveillance and monitoring activities.

## Why measure it?

Sharing surveillance, monitoring and enforcement activities with local stakeholders can be effective in controlling non-compliance behaviour through social and peer pressure. Increased participation of stakeholders provides them with more ownership over the MPA which should result in an overall improvement in enforcement and a decrease in violations. The point of this indicator is to document those tasks related to active stakeholder involvement in enforcement activities. These may range from simply stuffing envelopes, to attending enforcement hearings, to helping put up signposts.

## How to collect the data

As mentioned above, the type and level of stakeholder involvement in enforcement activities may range from stuffing envelopes containing announcements of new regulations, to attending enforcement hearings, to helping MPA staff put up signposts, to actively patrolling the MPA.

For the latter activity, ideally, all formal patrols are recorded on an ongoing basis so that this indicator should only require a synthesis of the existing patrol records. Patrol records are reviewed to determine who was involved in the patrols including:

- ❑ Number of non-MPA staff.
- ❑ Amount of time of non-MPA staff involved in the patrol.
- ❑ Stakeholder group affiliation of non-MPA staff.
- ❑ Type and number of activities that non-MPA staff were engaged in.

If patrols involving stakeholders are not recorded then this may require interviewing key stakeholders within the community who are involved in patrolling. The number of non-MPA staff involved in patrols can be compared to some ideal number of non-MPA staff established in the management plan to determine management effectiveness.

Stakeholders are interviewed to determine if they informally conduct surveillance and monitoring activities when they are in the area of the MPA. The stakeholders are asked:

- ❑ How they conduct the activity (e.g. causal or formal observation).
- ❑ How they report violations that they observe.
- ❑ Who they report violations to.
- ❑ What is done with reports of violations (is action taken)?
- ❑ Do you feel that compliance by stakeholders has improved as a result of your involvement?

For the other activities in which stakeholders may be involved, the MPA manager and staff are interviewed to identify what other enforcement activities stakeholders are involved in. As stated above, the number, amount of time and group affiliation of each stakeholder are identified. The names of the stakeholders are identified and they are interviewed to determine the reasons for their involvement, the amount of time involved and who they report to on the MPA staff. The stakeholders should be asked if they feel that their involvement has brought any improvement in overall community compliance and enforcement.

## How to analyse and interpret results

Prepare a narrative report which provides an evaluation of the number of stakeholders involved in surveillance, monitoring and enforcement.

## Strengths and limitations

This indicator reports on formal involvement in surveillance, monitoring and enforcement. It is much more difficult to obtain information on

### Requirements

- Patrol records.
- Interview stakeholders.
- One interviewer.
- Paper/pencil.

### Outputs

- Narrative report.

**Box G11**

## EXAMPLE FROM THE FIELD

At the Sapodilla Cayes Marine Reserve, five local fishers volunteer their time for monitoring and surveillance activities. These volunteers supplement the monitoring and surveillance activities of the regular MPA staff. The volunteers use their own boats and are provided with fuel. They are engaged in these activities for 6 hours a week. They are provided with VHF radios while on patrol and alert the rangers if they identify a violation. The volunteers were given 10 hours of training in rules, regulations and enforcement procedures by the MPA staff.

informal involvement, such as when fishing or when involved in tourism activity in the area.

### *Useful references and Internet links*

Salm, R.V., Clark, J.R. and Siirila, E. (2000). *Marine and Coastal Protected Areas: A Guide for Planners and Managers (3rd Edition)*. IUCN, Washington, DC, USA.

***When the public becomes actively engaged in surveillance and monitoring activities, such as these volunteers from the Banc d'Arguin, Mauritania, it can lead to win-win opportunities for both managers and the public with respect to the MPA.***

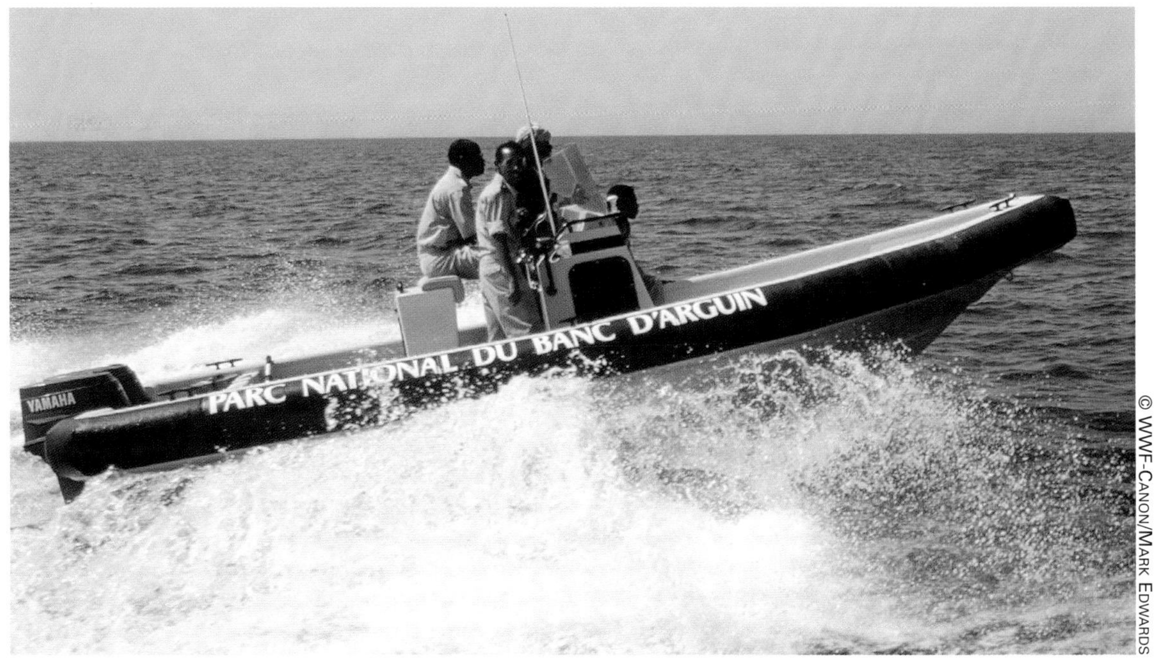

Relates to goals and objectives

GOAL 2

2E

GOAL 4

4A

## What are 'clearly defined enforcement procedures'?

Clearly defined enforcement procedures is a measure of the existence and description of guidelines and procedures developed for staff charged with enforcement responsibilities and how they are to act depending on the type of offence encountered.

## Why measure it?

Enforcement is a crucial step in the MPA management system. Clearly defined enforcement procedures allow MPA enforcement staff to more effectively undertake their duties and resource users to be aware of consequences of non-compliance.

## How to collect the data

First, in the management plan, the section which describes the monitoring, control, surveillance and enforcement programme for the MPA is identified. This will provide information on the enforcement programme and its structure. If no section on enforcement procedures exists, an interview is conducted with the MPA manager and the enforcement staff to identify the monitoring, control, surveillance and enforcement programme.

Second, an interview is conducted with the MPA manager and the designated enforcement staff member to obtain information about the enforcement guidelines. Questions to be asked include:

- ❑ Do formal enforcement guidelines and procedures exist?
- ❑ Do informal enforcement guidelines and procedures exist?
- ❑ Who prepared these guidelines and procedures?
- ❑ Describe the guidelines and procedures.
- ❑ Are they periodically reviewed and updated?
- ❑ Are staff trained in the guidelines and procedures?
- ❑ Is there coordination of the guidelines and procedures with other enforcement agencies?
- ❑ Are the enforcement guidelines and procedures appropriate to the task?
- ❑ Number of reported violations.
- ❑ Number of successful prosecutions due to clearly defined enforcement procedures.
- ❑ Number of attempted prosecutions that failed due to technicalities due to failure in procedure.
- ❑ Accessibility and availability of enforcement guidelines.

### Outputs

- Narrative report on the current MPA enforcement guidelines and procedures.

### Requirements

- Copy of the MPA monitoring, control, surveillance and enforcement section from the management plan.
- Copy of the enforcement guidelines.
- One interviewer.
- Paper/pencil.

## How to analyse and interpret results

Prepare a narrative report on the current enforcement guidelines and procedures, adequacy and availability of the guidelines, procedures to undertake enforcement actions, and recommendations for improvements.

## Strengths and limitations

Clearly defined enforcement guidelines and procedures will improve monitoring, surveillance and enforcement of the MPA thus benefiting the MPA management; will allow enforcement staff to act professionally; and will reduce the possibility of legal action against the MPA management by rule breakers. This measure will allow for a review of enforcement guidelines and procedures to ensure that they are implemented in a fair and equitable manner.

If no formal enforcement guidelines and procedures exist, information can still be obtained by interviewing MPA managers and staff and having them describe any informal procedures that they follow.

Box G12

## EXAMPLE FROM THE FIELD

In the Bird Island Marine Sanctuary in the Commonwealth of the Northern Mariana Islands there is confusion regarding which laws and regulations are to be enforced, and what penalties and/or prohibitions are applicable to the MPA in both the public's mind and the Division of Fish and Wildlife Enforcement Section. Recently, a number of violations have been overturned or had penalties substantially reduced because regulations conflicted with one another or were not suitably empowered by statute. In another incident, two non-English speaking non-resident workers were arrested for fishing in a marine sanctuary. The two were detained in jail for the majority of a day but the Department of Public Safety officers could not determine the appropriate bail to be set for the release of the alleged perpetrators. Eventually, the two individuals were released without any bail requirement.

This lack of clarity results from a historical lack of adequate focus on policy needs within the Division of Fish and Wildlife and because the agency's comments are frequently not incorporated into newly introduced legislation, amendments, and regulations. Furthermore, dedicated legal council for the agency has been lacking and legal council from the Attorney General's Office (AGO) is provided inconsistently. The limited enforcement activity that does occur tends to impact non-English speaking individuals disproportionately. This could be because they are least likely to be informed about Division of Fish and Wildlife rules and regulations, or because of perceptions relative to their resource use ethic. Overall, the lack of clearly defined procedures and the existence of conflicting laws and regulations reduce the effectiveness of the Division of Fish and Wildlife and create a poor public image.

### *Useful references and Internet links*

Salm, R.V., Clark, J.R. and Siirila, E. (2000). *Marine and Coastal Protected Areas: A Guide for Planners and Managers (3rd Edition).* IUCN, Washington, DC, USA.

# Enforcement coverage

Relates to goals and objectives

GOAL 4

4A

## What is 'enforcement coverage?

Enforcement coverage is a measure of the number of surveillance and monitoring patrols undertaken by MPA staff during a given time period and in a specified area.

## Why measure it?

This information is used to review the consistency of patrol activities. This information is a necessary prerequisite for assessing trends in violations or non-compliance since the latter is generally measured as the number of violations per patrol effort. It is also useful in determining how well the MPA management is meeting the goal of surveillance, monitoring and enforcement.

## How to collect the data

First, the management plan and the enforcement programme should have a section which describes the planned patrol schedule and procedures. This provides a base of information for comparison of actual patrols. If no such information exists, an interview is conducted with the MPA manager and staff involved in enforcement to describe the patrol schedule and procedures.

Second, patrol records are reviewed to calculate the patrol effort in terms of:

- Man-hours
- Total hours
- Number of patrols
- Variation in temporal and spatial patterns of patrols
- Patrol area ($km^2$)
- Number and type of infractions per patrol
- Number of unauthorized visitors caught and/or noticed

The above data can be disaggregated for different parts of the MPA and also different types of patrols (land, sea, MPA staff, community members). The actions undertaken during each patrol are reviewed to identify problems and needs to improve patrol activity. A map is prepared which shows patrol areas, number of patrols, and variation in temporal and spatial patterns of patrols.

Third, interviews are held with MPA staff to discuss patrol records and to learn about how patrols are undertaken and to identify problems and needs.

### Requirements

- Copy of patrol schedule and procedures.
- Patrol records.
- MPA quarterly/annual reports.
- Map of area.
- One interviewer.
- Paper/pencil.

### Outputs

- A narrative report
- A map showing distribution of patrols and types of activities occurring in and around the MPA

Fourth, interviews are conducted with resource users and stakeholders to learn about how patrols are undertaken, how the patrol officers act during a patrol, and problems and needs.

## How to analyse and interpret results

Prepare a narrative report which includes a discussion of the man-hours patrolling per month/year; hours patrolling per month/year; number of patrols/patrol days per month/year; number of patrols per area and type; and number and type of infractions. Map this information to show coverage of the MPA. Present in a table the types of action taken during each patrol, rank them and map them to identify trends, patterns and needs.

## Strengths and limitations

This indicator can lead to improvements in patrol and patrol coverage, in addition to improvements in overall enforcement of the MPA. Note that an increase in the number of illegal activities can not only result from increased patrols (positive trend) but also from increased poaching/violations (negative trend).

The usefulness of the indicator will depend on the accuracy of the patrol records.

## *Useful references and Internet links*

Salm, R.V., Clark, J.R. and Siirila, E. (2000). *Marine and Coastal Protected Areas: A Guide for Planners and Managers (3rd Edition).* IUCN, Washington, DC, USA.

Box G13

### EXAMPLE FROM THE FIELD

At Tubbataha Reef National Marine Park in the Philippines, rangers are required to conduct at least three random patrols every week. This is complemented by the operation of the radar at least every three hours. A logbook is maintained to monitor the number of intrusions detected through the radar and actual apprehensions. Apprehensions in the last three years have almost doubled. This may be attributable to the provision of the radar and more reliable patrol boats, enabling rangers' early detection of, and speedy response to, incursions.

NOAA PHOTO LIBRARY

# Degree of information dissemination to encourage stakeholder compliance

Relates to goals and objectives

GOAL 4

4B

## What is 'degree of information dissemination to encourage stakeholder compliance'?

Degree of information dissemination to encourage stakeholder compliance is a measure of the number and effectiveness of capacity-building efforts for stakeholders on the objectives and benefits, rules, regulations and enforcement arrangements of the MPA.

## Why measure it?

Training and education will increase stakeholder knowledge about rules, regulations and enforcement arrangements for the MPA in order to change behaviour and attitudes and increase compliance. Improvements in compliance with MPA rules and regulations by stakeholders should result from the training and education programme.

## How to collect the data

First, the number and types of workshops and training courses and information dissemination provided to the stakeholders during planning and implementation of the MPA are recorded. This information should be available from the MPA management office.

Second, MPA management staff are interviewed and asked questions about capacity-building and information dissemination activities including:

- ❑ How large is the capacity-building and information dissemination budget compared to the overall MPA budget?
- ❑ Were capacity-building activities provided during planning for the MPA on rules, regulations and enforcement arrangements?
- ❑ Were capacity-building activities undertaken during implementation and are they still provided?
- ❑ Who makes decisions about the number and types of capacity-building activities – MPA management, stakeholders, both?
- ❑ What types of information dissemination efforts were undertaken?

Third, the stakeholders are interviewed to determine their satisfaction with capacity-building and information dissemination activities and the quality of the activities. Stakeholders differ, they range from local fishers to foreign tourists. Several questionnaires may need to be developed for different stakeholder groups. A short questionnaire is prepared, including questions such as:

- ❑ Were workshops and training courses provided to you during the planning of the MPA?
- ❑ How many and what types were provided?
- ❑ Were workshops and training courses provided to you during implementation of the MPA?
- ❑ How many and what types were provided?
- ❑ Were you satisfied with the workshops and training courses? Yes/No
- ❑ Why?
- ❑ Were you involved in the selection of the workshops and training courses?
- ❑ What types of information dissemination were provided?
- ❑ Which were most effective for you?
- ❑ Why?
- ❑ Have the workshops and training courses affected your compliance behaviour? Yes/No
- ❑ Why?
- ❑ Do you have a better understanding of the rules, regulations and enforcement arrangements as a result of the workshops? Yes/No
- ❑ Do you have a better understanding of the purpose of the MPA as a result of the workshops? Yes/No
- ❑ Do you have a better understanding of coastal and marine ecosystems as a result of the information provided to you? Yes/No

### Requirements

- Copy of MPA capacity-building programme.
- Access to workshop and training records provided to stakeholders by the MPA management.
- Interview of stakeholders to assess satisfaction with capacity-building activities (education, training).
- Enforcement records.
- Records and output of information dissemination (mailings, media, publications, web, signs, etc.).
- One interviewer.
- Paper/pencil.

Many workshops and training courses conduct evaluations after the activity to assess the effectiveness of the programme. These evaluations may be available from the trainers and can be reviewed to determine participants' levels of satisfaction and knowledge gained from the training.

Enforcement records kept by the MPA are reviewed to assess changes in the number of violations by stakeholders who have attended the training. Names of stakeholders who have attended the training should be available from the participants list.

### How to analyse and interpret results

Prepare a narrative report describing the capacity-building efforts for stakeholders to enhance and support compliance with MPA rules and regulations. Develop a table showing correlation between capacity-building and information dissemination programmes and enforcement compliance records.

Measure effectiveness by comparing what activities have been undertaken with the different approaches to capacity-building and information dissemination presented in the management plan. The indicator will measure linkages between training and education and information dissemination for stakeholders on objectives and benefits, rules, regulations and enforcement arrangements and overall improvements in compliance. If the stakeholders were not involved in the development of the rules and regulations, compliance has been shown to be lower than if they did participate.

### Strengths and limitations

Interviewers need to be aware that stakeholder responses may be biased depending upon their individual or group agenda.

### Useful references and Internet links

Salm, R.V., Clark, J.R. and Siirila, E. (2000). *Marine and Coastal Protected Areas: A Guide for Planners and Managers (3rd Edition)*. IUCN, Washington, DC, USA.

#### Outputs

- A narrative report describing the capacity-building efforts for stakeholders to enhance and support compliance with MPA rules and regulations.
- A table showing correlation between capacity-building and information dissemination programmes and enforcement compliance records is developed.

Box G14

#### Example from the Field

The Hung Thac Marine Protected Area has provided fishers with four training courses on rules, regulations and enforcement arrangements for the MPA since it was established two years ago. In addition, comic books have been prepared and handed out to fishers to explain the rules, regulations and enforcement arrangements. Rangers meet informally with fishers on a regular basis and they have given a number of presentations at the local fisher organization meetings. Evaluations done at the four training sessions found that participants were well informed about the rules, regulations and enforcement arrangements for the MPA. In the second year of the MPA operation, violations were reduced by 80% from the first year. This is attributed to the training and education programme and to greater knowledge among the fishers.

Nelson Boisvert/Parks Canada

*Ecotourism such as sea-kayaking is often assumed to be a source of income, but several pilot sites indicated concern about the environmental impact of this activity.*

# APPENDIX *The MPA pilot sites*

To make this guidebook and the indicators accurate, flexible and applicable to your MPA and many other types of MPAs, a working draft of this guidebook was field-tested in diverse MPAs around the world. The MPA pilot projects were an integral part of the development of this guidebook. MPA sites were selected to represent a diversity of site characteristics, including; geographic locations, sizes, and type of management. In addition, sites had to meet several criteria, including; commitment of the site manager, capacity to conduct an evaluation and measure indicators, and available staff to participate. A training workshop was held for representatives from the pilot sites and technical assistance was provided to encourage participants to build on the project for future implementation at the site.

The training workshop was held in the autumn of 2002 and pilot site representatives selected relevant indicators to their sites, provided feedback on the indicator methods, and developed preliminary evaluation workplans. This workshop was followed by a 6-month field-testing period, although each site conducted the testing at various times and in differing amounts of time. At the end of the testing period, each site submitted a detailed report describing the test results and experiences in applying the guidebook at their MPA. These reports were used to revise and improve this guidebook and to provide you with examples on how to use many of the indicators.

There are a few summary points from those pilot sites that completed field-testing by the time this guidebook went to press:

- ❏ They were able to match their MPA goals and objectives with those in this guidebook.
- ❏ They were able to pick relevant indicators for their site.
- ❏ They were able to measure the indicators using the methods and with the participation and expertise of different professionals and other stakeholders at their sites.
- ❏ The most common constraints included the restriction of time to measure the indicators, interference of seasonal activities and weather, lack of experience to conduct evaluations, and unfamiliarity with certain indicators and methods.

This Appendix presents a summary information on each of the sites that have participated in the WCPA-Marine/WWF MPA Management Effectiveness Initiative.

*For more information on the MPA pilot sites go to http://effectiveMPA.noaa.gov/sites/pilotsites.html*

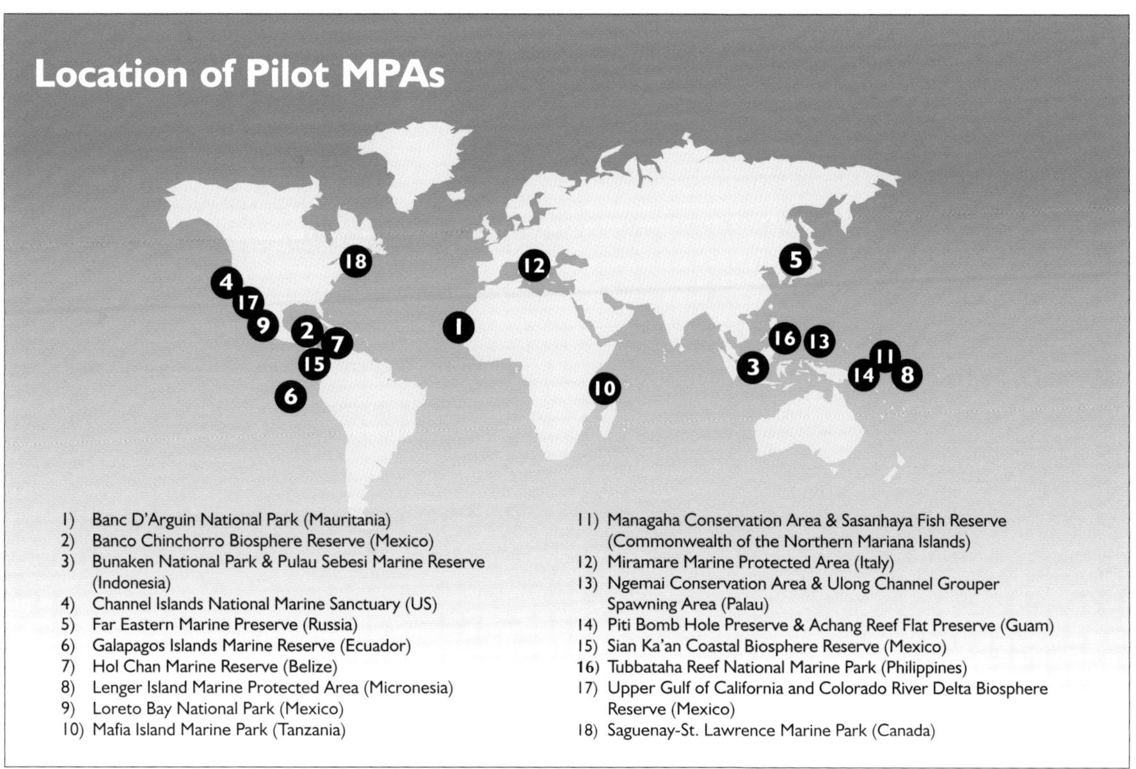

*LME = Large Marine Ecosystems. For more information: http://www.edc.uri.edu/lme/*

*RSP = Regional Seas Programme. For more information: http://www.unep.ch/seas/mappage1.html*

Areas (Small ≤ 20 km$^2$; Medium 21–1,999 km$^2$; Large ≥ 2,000 km$^2$)

## Aching Reef Flat Preserve (Guam)

- **LME**: n.a.
- **RSP**: South Pacific
- **Date of establishment**: Implemented on May 16, 1997 (Guam Public Law 24–21), but full enforcement began on 1 January 2001
- **Area (km$^2$)**: 4.85 (small)
- **Ecosystem type**:
  Coral reef
  Seagrass beds
  Mangroves
  Small estuarine lagoon and channel
- **Description of special resources; important ecological features; reason for establishing a protected area**: The mangroves and seagrass beds serve as a major nursery area for many juvenile marine animals including reef fishes in southern Guam.
- **Management objective**: No-take (but seasonal fishing is allowed for juvenile rabbitfish and scad mackerel).
- **Type of management structure**: Conventional
- **Geographic coordinates (approx.)**: 13°15′N, 144°40′E
- **World region**: Tropical
- **Nearest major city**: Hagatna (Agana)

## Banc D'Arguin National Park (Mauritania)

- **LME**: Canary Current
- **RSP**: West & Central Africa Programme
- **Date of establishment**: 1976
- **Area (km$^2$)**: 12,000 (large)
- **Ecosystem type**:
  Sand dunes
  Seagrass beds
  Mudflats
  Sand islands and islets
- **Description of special resources; important ecological features; reason for establishing a protected area**: Vast expanses of sea grass beds and mudflats (ca. 500 km$^2$), which offer ideal conditions for reproduction and growth of many species of birds, fish, shellfish, marine mammals and sea turtles.
- **Management objective**: Multiple
- **Type of management structure**: Conventional
- **Geographic coordinates**: 16°45′ W 19°21′ N–20°50′ N
- **World region**: Semi-arid
- **Nearest major city**: Nouakchott

## Banco Chinchorro Biosphere Reserve (Mexico)

- **LME**: Caribbean Sea
- **RSP**: Wider Caribbean
- **Date of establishment**: 19 July 1996
- **Area (km$^2$)**: 1,444 (Medium)
- **Ecosystem type**:
  Coral reefs
  Seagrass beds
  Mangroves
  Sandy ground
- **Description of special resources; important ecological features; reason for establishing a protected area**: The largest formation of the Mesoamerican Barrier Reef System, with a 52,494.83 hectares reef lagoon, four Cays (475.22 hectares), and interior lagoons (121.93 hectares).
- **Management objective**: Multiple
- **Type of management structure**: Conventional
- **Geographic coordinates**: 18°48′–18°21′N / 87°11′-87°28′ W
- **World region**: Mesoamerican Caribbean
- **Nearest major city**: Chetumal, located 130 km from Mahahual

## Bird Island (Commonwealth of the Northern Mariana Island – CNMI)

- **LME**: n.a.
- **RSP**: South Pacific Regional Environment Programme (SPREP)
- **Date of establishment**: April 2001
- **Area (km$^2$)**: 1.3 (Small)

- **Ecosystem type**:
  Native limestone
  Fringing coral reef
  Forest
- **Description of special resources; important ecological features; reason for establishing a protected area**: Fringing coral reef, blowhole used as popular swim hole and dive entrance to underwater tunnels, caves and fringing reefs, and rock island just off shore containing a seabird nesting colony.
- **Management objective**: No-take
- **Type of management structure**: Conventional
- **Geographic coordinates**: 145°48′ E & 15°15′ N. Boundaries: 1000ft seaward of low tide mark and 500ft inland
- **World region**: Tropical
- **Nearest major city**: San Roque, Saipan

### Bunaken National Park (Indonesia)

- **LME**: Indonesian Sea
- **RSP**: East Asian Seas
- **Date of establishment**: 1991
- **Area (km$^2$)**: 790 (Medium)
- **Ecosystem type**:
  Coral reef
  Mangrove
  Seagrass
  Deep coastal seawall & trenches
- **Description of special resources; important ecological features; reason for establishing a protected area**: Diverse corals and coral reef fish communities, diversity and abundance of mangroves extensive seagrass beds supporting dugong and sea turtle populations, and newly discovered group of resident coelacanths.
- **Management objective**: Multiple
- **Type of management structure**: Co-management
- **Geographic coordinates**: 1°35′N; 124°44′E
- **World region**: Tropical
- **Nearest major city**: Manado, North Sulawesi

### Channel Islands National Marine Sanctuary (USA)

- **LME**: California Current
- **RSP**: North-East Pacific
- **Date of establishment**: 1980
- **Area (km$^2$)**: 4,349 (Large)
- **Ecosystem type**:
  Kelp Forest
  Rocky Intertidal
- **Description of special resources; important ecological features; reason for establishing a protected area**: n.a.
- **Management objective**: n.a.
- **Type of management structure**: Co-management
- **Geographic coordinates**: 34°N, 120°W
- **World region**: Temperate Pacific
- **Nearest major city**: Santa Barbara, CA

### Far Eastern Federal Marine Preserve (Russian Federation)

- **LME**: Sea of Japan
- **RSP**: Northwest Pacific
- **Date of establishment**: 24 March 1978
- **Area (km$^2$)**: 0.64 (Small)
- **Ecosystem type**:
  Rocky Shore
- **Description of special resources; important ecological features; reason for establishing a protected area**: Coastal marine and island environment of Peter The Great Bay containing more than 2,700 marine species (many under international protection).
- **Management objective**: Multiple
- **Type of management structure**: Conventional
- **Geographic coordinates (approx.)**: 42.5°N, 131.5°E
- **World region**: Temperate and subtropical
- **Nearest major city**: Vladivostok

### Galapagos Islands Marine Reserve (Ecuador)

- **LME**: n.a.
- **RSP**: Southeast Pacific
- **Date of establishment**: 1998
- **Area (km$^2$)**: 135,000 (Large)
- **Ecosystem type**:
  Upwelling
  Volcanic Substrate

- **Description of special resources; important ecological features; reason for establishing a protected area**: The highly productive coastal waters support a rich food chain that extents not only from plankton to sharks and whales, but also to land plants, insects and birds. Galapagos sits on the equator but also lies in the path of cool nutrient rich currents, a combination that separates it apart from all other major island groups. Here corals, manta rays and other plants and animals typical of tropical seas share islands with penguins, fur seals and cool water species
- **Management objective**: Multiple
- **Type of management structure**: Co-management
- **Geographic coordinates**: 2°S/2°N, 89°/92°W
- **World region**: Tropical/arid
- **Nearest major city**: Guayaquil

## Hol Chan Marine Reserve (Belize)

- **LME**: Caribbean Sea
- **RSP**: Wider Caribbean
- **Date of establishment**: 2 May 1997
- **Area (km$^2$)**: 8 (Small)
- **Ecosystem type**:
  Coral Reef
  Seagrass
  Mangrove
- **Description of special resources; important ecological features; reason for establishing a protected area**: Reserve status was called by the community and by international organizations due to the unique formation of the channel, the abundant fishery resources (including conch and lobster) and the feasibility of including an interlinked system of coral reef, seagrass and mangrove habitats in this area.
- **Management objective**: Multiple
- **Type of management structure**: Co-management (semi-governmental)
- **Geographic coordinates (approx.)**: 17.7°N, 87.7°W
- **World region**: Mesoamerican Caribbean
- **Nearest major city**: San Pedro Town, Caye Caulker

## Lenger Island Marine Protected Area (Pohnpei Island, Federated States of Micronesia)

- **LME**: n.a.
- **RSP**: South Pacific Regional Environment Programme (SPREP)
- **Date of establishment**: February 2001
- **Area (km$^2$)**: 2 (Small)
- **Ecosystem type**: Coral Reef
- **Description of special resources; important ecological features; reason for establishing a protected area**: Siganidae spawning and aggregation site; Turtle hatchery; Diverse invertebrate species; and WWII Base.
- **Management objective**: No-take
- **Type of management structure**: Community-based
- **Geographic coordinates**: 7°N, 158°13′E
- **World region**: Tropical
- **Nearest major city**: Kolonia

## Loreto Bay National Park (Mexico)

- **LME**: Gulf of California
- **RSP**: Northeast Pacific
- **Date of establishment**: 19 July 1996
- **Area (km$^2$)**: 2,065 (Large)
- **Ecosystem type**:
  Dune vegetation
  Desert scrub
  Mangrove
  Rocky reef, sand and mud flats
  Rodolites
- **Description of special resources; important ecological features; reason for establishing a protected area**: Fish fauna of least 260 species. Five sea turtles in the Gulf of California are present in the park, all of them under protection. 90 terrestrial and 110 aquatic birds compose the bird fauna. 30 species of marine mammals out of 35 species reported in the Gulf of California (nine of them under protection).
- **Management objective**: Multiple
- **Type of management structure**: Conventional
- **Geographic coordinates**: 25°35′-26°07′N, 110°45′-111°21′W
- **World region**: Semi-arid

- **Nearest major city**: Loreto and La Paz, Baja California Sur

### Mafia Island Marine Park (Tanzania)

- **LME**: Agulhas Current
- **RSP**: Eastern Africa
- **Date of establishment**: 1995
- **Area (km²)**: 822 (Medium)
- **Ecosystem type**:
  - Mangroves
  - Seagrass beds
  - Coral reefs
  - Intertidal reef flats
  - Lagoon
  - Coastal forest
- **Description of special resources; important ecological features; reason for establishing a protected area**: The archipelago is formed of a number of very large islands and small-uninhabited coral atolls. Due to its position alongside the barrier, the island is the meeting place of large oceanic fish and the vast variety of fish common to the Indian Ocean coral reefs. There are over 400 species of fish in the park.
- **Management objective**: Multiple
- **Type of management structure**: Conventional with Co-management
- **Geographic coordinates**: 7°45′-8°9′S, 39°54′-39°30′E
- **World region**: Tropical
- **Nearest major city**: Dar es-Salaam

### Miramare Marine Protected Area (Italy)

- **LME**: Mediterranean
- **RSP**: Mediterranean
- **Date of establishment**: 1986
- **Area (km²)**: 1.2 (Small)
- **Ecosystem type**:
  - Tidal area
  - Rocky shore
  - Soft bottom
- **Description of special resources; important ecological features; reason for establishing a protected area**: Miramare focuses on issues related to education activities, scientific research, related to the reproductive biology of fish species and water quality.
- **Management objective**: No-take
- **Type of management structure**: Co-management
- **Geographic coordinates**: 45°42′N, 13°42′E
- **World region**: Mediterranean Sea
- **Nearest major city**: Trieste

### Ngemelis (Palau)

- **LME**: n.a.
- **RSP**: South Pacific
- **Date of establishment**: 1995
- **Area (km²)**: 30 (Medium)
- **Ecosystem type**:
  - Coral Reef
- **Description of special resources; important ecological features; reason for establishing a protected area**: Highly diverse reef wall.
- **Management objective**: No-take
- **Type of management structure**: Conventional
- **Geographic coordinates (approx.)**: 7.2°N, 134.6°E
- **World region**: Tropical Pacific
- **Nearest major city**: Koror

### Piti Bomb Holes Preserve (Guam)

- **LME**: n.a.
- **RSP**: South Pacific
- **Date of establishment**: 16 May 1997
- **Area (km²)**: 3.36 (Small)
- **Ecosystem type**:
  - Coral Reef
  - Sparse seagrass beds
- **Description of special resources; important ecological features; reason for establishing a protected area**: Extensive patch reefs in unique dissolution holes within Piti reef flat. Site includes various habitats needed for the life cycle of marine animals.
- **Management objective**: No-take
- **Type of management structure**: Conventional
- **Geographic coordinates (approx.)**: 13°27′N, 144°42′E
- **World region**: Tropical Pacific
- **Nearest major city**: Hagatna (Agana)

### Saguenay-St. Lawrence Marine Park (Canada)

- **LME**: Newfoundland-Labrador Shelf
- **RSP**: n.a.
- **Date of establishment**: 8 June 1998
- **Area (km$^2$)**: 1,138 (Medium)
- **Ecosystem type**:
  Cold-water estuary
  Tidal mud flats
  Underwater cliffs
  Nutrient rich cold-water upwellings
  Fjord
  Marshes
- **Description of special resources; important ecological features; reason for establishing a protected area**: Established for the protection of a severely depleted and endangered population of beluga whales. The area is a major summer feeding ground for a host of visiting whales species migrating from the Northern Atlantic. Fin, minke, blue, and humpback whales all converge on this area to feast on the high concentrations of krill found in the nutrient-rich waters.
- **Management objective**: Multiple use
- **Type of management structure**: Conventional (federal and provincial governments)
- **Geographic coordinates (approx.)**: 47°39′ - 48°23′ N, 69°17′ - 70°42′ W
- **World region**: Cold temperate
- **Nearest major city**: Saguenay and Rivière-du-Loup (within 15 km)

### Sasanhaya Fish Reserve (CNMI)

- **LME**: n.a
- **RSP**: South Pacific
- **Date of establishment**: October 1994
- **Area (km$^2$)**: 0.8 (Small)
- **Ecosystem type**:
  Fringing coral reef
  Fish reserves
- **Description of special resources; important ecological features; reason for establishing a protected area**: Unique coral features; popular dive site; fringing coral reef; historic WWII wrecks
- **Management objective**: No-take
- **Type of management structure**: Conventional
- **Geographic coordinates (approx.)**: 14°07′05″ N, 145°10′ E,
- **World region**: Tropical Pacific
- **Nearest major city**: Song Song, Rota

### Sian Ka'an Biosphere Reserve (Mexico)

- **LME**: Caribbean Sea
- **RSP**: Wider Caribbean
- **Date of establishment**: 20 January 1986
- **Area (km$^2$)**: 6,000 (Large)
- **Ecosystem type**:
  Coral Reef
  Coastal Lagoon
  Mangrove
  Tropical forest
- **Description of special resources; important ecological features; reason for establishing a protected area**: Coral reef and platform with a length of 120 km and depth of 60 m towards the Caribbean Sea, it is part of the second largest coral reef in the world.
- **Management objective**: Multiple
- **Type of management structure**: Conventional
- **Geographic coordinates (approx.)**: 19°05′ – 20°06′N, 87°30′ – 87°58′W
- **World region**: Mesoamerican Caribbean
- **Nearest major city**: Cancun and Carrillo Puerto

### Tubbataha Reef National Marine Park (Philippines)

- **LME**: Sulu-Celebes Sea
- **RSP**: East Asian Seas
- **Date of establishment**: 11 August 1998
- **Area (km$^2$)**: 332 (Medium)
- **Ecosystem type**:
  Atoll
  Coral Reef
- **Description of special resources; important ecological features; reason for establishing a protected area**: An atoll reef with a very high density of marine species; the North Islet serving as a nesting site for birds and marine turtles. A pristine coral reef with a 100 m perpendicular wall, extensive lagoons and two coral islands.

- **Management objective**: No-take
- **Type of management structure**: Co-management
- **Geographic coordinates**: 8°45′-9°00′N, 119°45′-120°04′E
- **World region**: Tropical
- **Nearest major city**: Puerto Princesa City, Palawan

## Upper Gulf of California and Colorado River Delta Biosphere Reserve (Mexico)

- **LME**: Gulf of California
- **RSP**: Northeast Pacific
- **Date of establishment**: 10 June 1993
- **Area (km$^2$)**: 9,340 (Large)
- **Ecosystem type**:
  Wetlands
  Shallow coastal marine
  Delta
  Estuary
- **Description of special resources; important ecological features; reason for establishing a protected area**: Marine/coastal habitats: Shallow marine-coastal semi-open waters, soft-bottom and sandy/muddy coastline, rocky areas (coquina formation), delta floodplain (intertidal and brackish wetlands, saltflats). Terrestrial habitats: Gran Desierto sand dunes, San Felipe desert (Sonora Desert)
- **Management objective**: Multiple
- **Type of management structure**: Conventional
- **Geographic coordinates**: 21°-22.5°N; 113°-116°W
- **World region**: Sub-tropical
- **Nearest major city**: San Diego, CA, and Mexicali, Mexico

# GLOSSARY

**Abiotic**: Factors that are non-biological but play an important role in an organism's environment (e.g. substrate, temperature, currents, pH).

**Abundance (of species)**: The number of individuals of a particular species occurring within a defined area.

**Accountability**: For this guidebook, this term implies the state of being accountable, subject to the obligation to report, explain or justify the establishment of an MPA, its achievements and failures, and the resources (material, financial, and human) spent for its functioning.

**Adaptive management:** The cyclical process of systematically testing assumptions, generating learning by evaluating the results of such testing, and further revising and improving management practices. The result of adaptive management in a protected area context is improved effectiveness and increased progress towards the achievement of goals and objectives.

**Allocation of resources**: The process of distributing resources among the various stakeholders or interested parties.

**Assessment**: See Evaluation. For the purpose of this guidebook, assessment and evaluation are used interchangeably, although we recognise that this term can be defined as the act of determining the importance, size or value of an object or process.

**Audience**: The participating, reading, viewing or listening public (the MPA stakeholders or group of interests).

**Basemap**: A map containing geographic features used for locational reference.

**Benthic (species)**: An organism that lives and/or reproduces in the Benthic Zone.

**Benthic (zone)**: A primary subdivision of the oceans that includes the entire sea bottom.

**Biomass**: The quantity of living matter (living organisms) expressed as unit of weight per unit area or unit volume.

**Biota**: The number of organisms that occupy an ecosystem.

**Broken stick**: A statistical model of random distribution of resources among species. It is as if a stick was broken into several pieces with no underlying relationships determining the size of each piece.

**Code sheet**: The translation of meaning of data collected and their codes.

**Co-management**: A partnership in which government and stakeholders share the authority and responsibility for making decisions about management of the resource. It may take many forms and involves a high degree of stakeholder participation.

**Community (biophysical definition)**: A collection of different and interacting populations of organisms (biota) found living together in a defined geographic area, including indigenous and exotic organisms.

**Community (human/social definition)**: A group of people with common interests (possibly living in a particular local area).

**Community composition**: The diversity and makeup of all species present within a community and their relative abundance (respective to one another). Species richness, dominance, diversity and relative abundance are all characteristics of community composition.

**Community-based management**: People-focused and community-focused management with a great deal of local stakeholder participation.

**Control groups**: A set of people used as a standard of comparison to the experimental group. The people in the control group have characteristics similar to those in the experimental group and are selected at random.

**Cryptic (species)**: Species that for their characteristics (life-cycle, environmental requirements, feeding patterns, etc.) are hard to find, or can be considered rare.

**Database**: The storage location of a data entry. A collection of data organized especially for rapid search and retrieval.

**Data cleaning**: Reviews of the data set in order to check for completeness and errors.

**Data coding**: The process of translating each datum point to prepare for analysis.

**Data entry**: The (often lengthy and tedious) process of moving cleaned, coded data into a permanent storage location from which to export the data so that it can be analysed.

**Data management**: The act, process or means by which data is managed. This may include the compilation, storage, safe-guarding, listing, organization, extraction, retrieval, manipulation and dissemination of data (Lake and Water Word Glossary – http://www.nalms.org/glossary/glossary.htm).

**Ecotone**: A transition area between two distinct habitats, where the ranges of the organisms in each bordering habitat overlap, and where there are organisms unique to the transition area.

**Environmental Impact Assessment**: The assessment of the environmental impacts likely to arise from a major action (i.e. legislation, a policy, a programme or project, etc.) significantly affecting the environment.

**Evaluation**: The judgement or assessment of achievement against some predetermined criteria; in this case the objectives for which the protected areas were established. Information on which such assessments can be based could come from many sources, but monitoring has a particularly important contribution to make in providing the basic data that should underpin the evaluation (Hockings *et al.*, 2000).

**Evaluation workplan**: A scheme of action, a method of proceeding planned in advance to perform an effectiveness evaluation (see Box 6).

**Focal species**: An organism of ecological and/or human value that is of priority interest for management through the MPA.

**Food web**: A representation of the energy flow through populations in a community.

**Food web integrity**: A measure of how supportive (for the members of the community) and reliable the trophic relationships are within the interconnected food chains of a community.

**Formal knowledge**: The degree of awareness of information generated by the scientific community and held by stakeholder and user groups about MPA use and ecosystem impacts.

**Geographic Information System (GIS)**: An organized collection of computer hardware, software, geographic data, and personnel designed to efficiently capture, store, update, manipulate, analyse and display all forms of geographically referenced information that can be drawn from different sources, both statistical and mapped (EPA Terminology Reference System).

**Goal**: A broad statement of what the MPA is ultimately trying to achieve.

**Habitat**: The living space of an organism, population, or community, as characterized by both its biotic and physical properties. Habitat types are distinguished from one another by their distinct biotic and abiotic composition and structure that forms living space.

**Habitat complexity**: The extent (area in $km^2$) and diversity (number) of habitat types and distinct zones found within a specified area.

**Habitat distribution**: The structure and spatial characterization of all habitat types represented.

**Habitat integrity**: The extent to which the distribution and complexity of living space in an area will persist over time.

**Indicator**: A unit of information measured over time that allows you to document changes in specific attributes of your MPA. It helps you to understand where you are, where you are going and how far you are from the goal (adapted from Hockings *et al.*, 2000).

**Intertidal (zone)**: Area located between the elevation of the lowest yearly tide and the elevation of the highest yearly tide.

**Key informant**: People with rank, experience or knowledge who can provide extensive insight information on a specific issue or situation (adapted from Bunce *et al.*, 2000).

**Log-normal**: A statistical model of distribution of resources among species determined by a number of interacting factors. This leads to a log-normal distribution in abundance classes, which means that the number of species falling within each class are plotted against the log value of the class category.

**Management body**: An institution (board of directors, executive committee, advisory board) that governs how the MPA is managed and used.

**Management effectiveness**: The degree to which management actions achieve the goals and objectives of a protected area.

**Marine Protected Area (MPA)**: Any area of intertidal or subtidal terrain, together with its overlying waters and associated flora, fauna, historical and cultural features, which has been reserved by law or other effective means to protect part or all of the enclosed environment (IUCN).

**Messaging**: A process for sharing evaluation results with a target audience. It should consider which messages and what formats will be used to communicate the results.

**Neritic (zone)**: The shallow regions of a lake or ocean that border the land. The term is also used to identify the biota that inhabits the water along the shore of a lake or ocean.

**Non-market value**: The economic value of activities that are not traded in any market, which includes direct uses, such as divers who have travelled to the MPA by private means; and indirect uses, such as biological support in the form of nutrients, fish habitat and coastline protection from storm surge.

**Non-use value**: Values that are not associated with any use and include existence value (the value of knowing that the resource exists in a certain condition), option value (the value of being able to use the resource in the future), and bequest value (the value of ensuring the resource will be available for future generations).

**No-take zone**: An area that is completely (or seasonally) free of all extractive or non-extractive human uses that contribute impact (some exceptions are permitted for scientific/research activities). Also called a "reserve" or "fully protected area".

**Objective**: A specific statement of what must be accomplished to attain a related goal.

**Ordinal scale**: A measurement that represents a ranking of a variable's values to observe overall trends. The ranking provides an indication of whether one value is "greater than" or "less than" other values.

**Outcomes**: The consequences, effects or real impacts of management actions. Outputs assess the extent to which the management objectives are being achieved.

**Outputs**: Resulting products and/or services, or achievements of a planned work programme that arise from a management activity.

**Participatory (Participation)**: A process involving/providing the opportunity for an individual person (every relevant stakeholder) to participate in management.

**Phenology**: Relations between environmental conditions (e.g. climate or temperature) and periodic biological events (e.g. reproduction).

**Practitioner**: Someone experienced in the technical skills and practice of conservation.

**Qualitative (data)**: Non-numerical data, often in the form of categorical data (e.g. preference, opinion, attitudes, etc.)

**Quantitative (data)**: Numerical data obtained by measuring objects or events.

**Recruitment success**: The degree of juvenile recruitment and survivorship experienced across populations of organisms that exist within a community.

**Results delivery strategy**: A method that outlines how to communicate the presentation formats identified and assigned to target audiences.

**Sedentary (species)**: An organism that lives in a fixed location, as with most plants, tunicates, sponges, etc.

**Semi-structured interviews**: An interview based on the use of a guide (e.g. notes or a questionnaire), but that has the freedom of an open conversation. It is recommended when there is only one chance to interview someone.

**Sessile (species)**: Describes an animal that is unable to move, or does not move very much. Examples include coral, sponges, barnacles and sea squirts.

**Stakeholder**: An individual, group or organization that influences or is otherwise interested, involved or affected by a particular MPA management strategy.

**Strategy**: The way you will move forward with your conservation and management efforts; what it is that you will actually do.

**Subtidal**: Area below the low-tide level.

**Survivorship**: The survival rate (probability) from a (recruitment) process or event.

**Telemetry**: The use of radio waves, telephone lines, etc., to transmit the readings of measuring instruments to a device on which the readings can be indicated or recorded.

**Threats**: Those factors that immediately impact biodiversity, food security, and livelihood.

**Trophic level**: The stage in a food chain or web leading from primary producers through herbivores to primary and secondary consumers.

**t-test**: A statistical parametric test assuming a normal distribution. The t-test is appropriate when you have a single interval dependent and a dichotomous independent, and want to test the difference of means of a criterion variable for two independent samples or for two dependent samples (for more information see, for example, A. Agresti and B. Finlay, *Statistical Methods for the Social Sciences*. 3rd edition, 1997).

TONY ECKERSLEY

# Other marine conservation books from IUCN

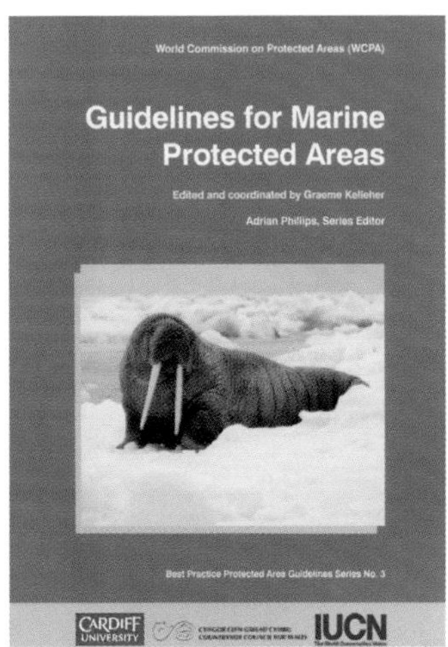


### *Guidelines for Marine Protected Areas*

Edited and coordinated by Graeme Kelleher
Series editor: Adrian Phillips

Creation and effective management of Marine Protected Areas (MPAs) have lagged behind those of protected areas on land, but they are just as important. The world urgently needs a comprehensive system of MPAs to conserve biodiversity and to help rebuild the productivity of the oceans. The aim of these Guidelines is to help countries establish systems of MPAs as a key component of integrated management of coastal and marine areas and as part of their sustainable development. The various actions to make an effective MPA are set out, from early planning stages to implementation. These Guidelines aim to help policy-makers, planners and field managers, whether working on conservation of nature or sustainable use of marine resources.

Best Practice Protected Area Guidelines Series No. 3
ISBN 2-8317-0505-3, 1999 | 295 x 210mm, xxiv + 107pp., colour maps
£16.50, US$24.75 | Order no. B542

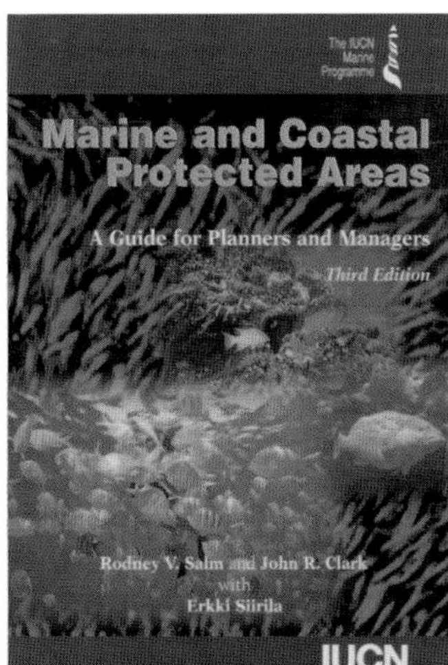


### *Marine and Coastal Protected Areas: A guide for planners and managers*

Rodney Salm, John Clark and Erkki Siirila, 3rd Edition

This is a new edition of the classic textbook on marine protected area (MPA) management in the tropics, originally produced as an output of the Bali World Parks Congress in 1982.

Approaches to planning and managing MPAs have evolved considerably. Major advances include innovative financing mechanisms, partnerships with the private sector and NGOs, and collaborative management between government and coastal communities. These advances have brought new approaches for MPA establishment and management that are more participatory, involving communities through interaction and collaboration rather than prescription. With new case studies and illustrations, the guide comes in a water-resistant cover for field use. It is intended for those who plan individual and/or national MPA systems and gives philosophical context for MPAs along with some basic principles and approaches.

ISBN 2-8317-0540-1, 2000 | 260 x 155mm, 387pp., b/w photos
£20.50, US$30.75 | Order no. B563

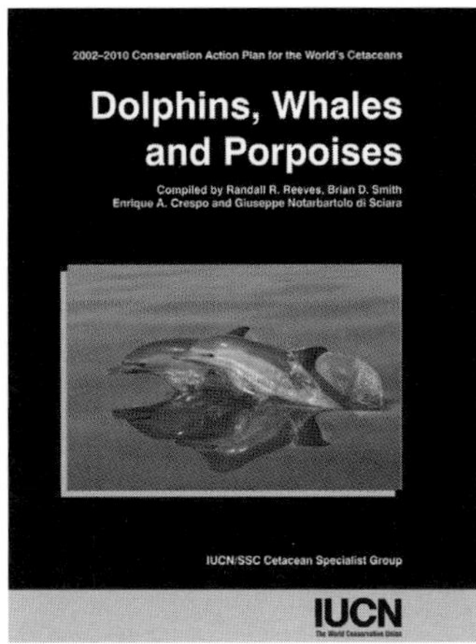

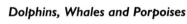

### *Dolphins, Whales and Porpoises*

2002–2010 Conservation Action Plan for the World's Cetaceans
Compiled by Randall Reeves, Brian D. Smith, Enrique A. Crespo and Giuseppe Notarbartolo di Sciara and the IUCN/SSC Cetacean Specialist Group

Consistent evaluation and new recommendations for action are required of protective measures to address threats that were unrecognised or non-existent until recently. Global warming, noise pollution and reduced availability of prey are now of great concern.
The all too familiar threats of accidental killing in fishing gear and exposure to toxic chemicals remain almost intractable. This Action Plan reviews threats and offers possible solutions. It also contains a thorough review of the status of species and a list of 57 recommended research projects and education initiatives.

ISBN 2-8317-0656-4, 2003 | 280 x 215mm, xi + 139pp., tables, b/w photos
£15.00, US$22.50 | Order no. B1157